CW00422026

Migrant Health and Resilience

In an era of escalating conflict-induced and climate-induced migration and cross-border interactions, transnational-competence (TC) preparation for displaced persons, members of their host communities, humanitarian responders, and health-care professionals is increasingly critical. Building on insights from those engaged with a range of humanitarian crises and global justice contexts along with multidisciplinary research findings, this cutting-edge volume provides practical guidelines for preparing stakeholders for effective short-term and long-term responses to challenges arising in the wake of population dislocation generated by armed conflict, persecution, and climate change.

Addressing the need to equip humanitarian care-givers and care-receivers with valuable skills for working together across barriers and boundaries, the guidance presented in the book enables educators, trainers, and field-based multinational and local responders to enhance and evaluate the quality and sustainability of humanitarian efforts that promote and bolster resilience and belonging and augment well-being, justice, and sustainable development. It features comprehensive TC teaching and learning strategies coupled with tailored on-site and remote approaches and methods.

Authoritative and insightful, *Migrant Health and Resilience* will be essential reading for the staff of NGOs, international organizations, national and local governments, and professional bodies working in development and humanitarian crisis contexts, as well as for students, higher-education instructors, scholars, and evaluators.

Peter H. Koehn is University of Montana Professor Emeritus in Political Science. He established UMT's Migration Studies, Global Public Health, International Development Studies programs and co-founded its Climate Change Studies program. He is a Fulbright New Century Scholar and recipient of the Association of Public and Land Grant Universities' (APLU) 2011 Michael P. Malone Award for international leadership. He has taught at universities and/or conducted research in Ethiopia, Eritrea, Nigeria, Namibia, China, Hong Kong, Belize, and Finland. He recently authored *Transnational Mobility and Global Health: Traversing Borders and*

Boundaries in the Routledge Studies in Development, Mobilities and Migration series.

Phyllis Bo-yuen Ngai is Director of the International Development Studies and Migration Studies programs, Clinical Associate Professor in the School of Social Work, and Associate Professor NTT in the Department of Communication Studies at the University of Montana. Dr. Ngai's research interests lie at the crossroads of development studies, Indigenous studies, intercultural studies, and communication for social change. Her recent research explores culturally sensitive health communication for enhancing American Indian health, Indigenous organization approaches to sustainable development, global discourses and local interpretations of Indigenous Peoples' Rights, and NGO approaches to women's issues in Southeast Asia. She is the author and co-author of numerous professional journal articles, book chapters, and monographs on intercultural communication training, social justice education, partnerships with Indigenous communities, and rural development. Dr. Ngai has taught in the United States and Asia and conducted research and delivered guest lectures/workshops at universities in Norway, Finland, China, Cambodia, Myanmar, Vietnam, Ethiopia, and Canada.

Juha I. Uitto is Director of the Independent Evaluation Office (IEO) of the Global Environment Facility (GEF), the oldest public financial mechanism for multilateral environmental agreements, including conventions on biodiversity, climate change, desertification, and harmful chemicals. He specializes in evaluating the nexus between the environment and development. Since 1999, he has worked as evaluator with the GEF and the United Nations Development Programme (UNDP), where he served as Deputy Director of the UNDP-IEO and, prior to that, Evaluation Advisor. Throughout the 1990s, he was environment and sustainable development research and training program coordinator at the United Nations University. He has published widely on topics related to evaluation, sustainable development, and environmental hazards. A native of Finland, Juha Uitto was educated at the Universities of Helsinki and Lund. He holds a PhD in Social and Economic Geography from the latter.

Diana M. Diaków is a Polish multilingual psychologist specializing in trauma-informed and culturally responsive child and family mental health treatment and assessment. She has supported migrant and marginalized communities in refugee camps, outpatient clinics, schools, and non-profit organizations in Poland, Ukraine, Ireland, Slovakia, Croatia, Greece, Indonesia, Kurdistan, the USA, and Colombia. Diana launched Mental Health and Psychosocial Support (MHPSS) programs in the Ritsona refugee camp in Greece. She has conducted research and published internationally on topics related to resilience, trauma, school-based mental health treatment, social justice, and cultural diversity. After graduating from Kazimierz Wielki University in Poland, Diana gained academic and clinical training at Harvard Medical School, Utah School of Medicine, and the University of Montana, where she earned her PhD in Psychology. She is a recipient of the Art Nezu Dissertation Diversity Award and the P.E.O. International Peace Scholarship. Dr. Diaków also is a linguist, specialized in Arabic.

Susan Martin is the Donald G. Herzberg Professor Emerita of International Migration at Georgetown University. She is also an Adjunct Professor at the University of Montana. She was the founder and Director of Georgetown's Institute for the Study of International Migration and the Certificate Program on Refugees and Humanitarian Emergencies. Prior to joining Georgetown's faculty, Dr. Martin was the Executive Director of the U.S. Commission on Immigration Reform, which was mandated by statute to advise the President and Congress on US immigration and refugee policy. She received her PhD in the History of American Civilization from the University of Pennsylvania. Dr. Martin has authored or edited more than a dozen books and numerous articles and book chapters. She serves on the boards of Rutgers University, the Center for Migration Studies, and the Jesuit Refugee Service USA.

Routledge Global Health Series

Series Editors: Nana K. Poku and Jane Freedman

This timely series provides robust and multi-disciplinary assessments of the actors and dynamics shaping the health of humanity under globalized and still globalizing conditions. Books in the series come from a range of disciplinary perspectives in order to address the complex interactions of human and natural systems and the roles of governments and international organizations in protecting the health of their citizens.

The series welcomes full proposals, outlines and general queries on all themes and issues pertinent to global health. This includes medical, political, sociological, and economic perspectives on health, health governance and health finance; poverty and insecurity; the prevention and treatment of important but under-researched diseases; gender and health; the implications of global pandemics; and the varieties and challenges posed by the growing, worldwide expectation of some form/degree of Universal Health Coverage.

Living with HIV and Dying with Aids
Diversity, Inequality and Human Rights in the Global Pandemic
Lesley Doyal with Len Doyal

Civil Society Organizations and the Global Response to HIV/AIDS
Julia Smith

Illicit Medicines in the Global South
Public Health Access and Pharmaceutical Regulation
Mathieu Quet

Migrant Health and Resilience
Transnational Competence in Conflict and Climate Displacement Situations
Peter H. Koehn, Phyllis Bo-yuen Ngai, Juha I. Uitto and Diana M. Diaków. With a foreword by Susan Martin

For more information about this series, please visit: www.routledge.com/Global-Health/book-series/ASHSER-1232

Migrant Health and Resilience

Transnational Competence in Conflict and Climate Displacement Situations

Peter H. Koehn, Phyllis Bo-yuen Ngai, Juha I. Uitto and Diana M. Diaków

With a Foreword by Susan Martin

Routledge
Taylor & Francis Group

LONDON AND NEW YORK

First published 2024
by Routledge
4 Park Square, Milton Park, Abingdon, Oxon OX14 4RN

and by Routledge
605 Third Avenue, New York, NY 10158

Routledge is an imprint of the Taylor & Francis Group, an informa business

© 2024 Peter H. Koehn, Phyllis Bo-yuen Ngai, Juha I. Uitto, and Diana M.
Diaków

The right of Peter H. Koehn, Phyllis Bo-yuen Ngai, Juha I. Uitto, and Diana
M. Diaków to be identified as authors of this work has been asserted in
accordance with sections 77 and 78 of the Copyright, Designs and Patents
Act 1988.

British Library Cataloguing-in-Publication Data
A catalogue record for this book is available from the British Library

Library of Congress Cataloging-in-Publication Data
Names: Koehn, Peter H., author.
Title: Migrant health and resilience : transnational competence in conflict
and climate displacement situations / Peter H. Koehn, Phyllis Bo-yuen
Hgai, Juha I. Uitto, Diana M. Diaków ; with a foreword by Susan Martin.
Description: Abingdon, Oxon ; New York, NY : Routledge, 2023. |
Series: Routledge global health series | Includes bibliographical references
and index.
Identifiers: LCCN 2023004755 | ISBN 9781032214931 (hardback) |
ISBN 9781032361574 (paperback) | ISBN 9781003330493 (ebook)
Subjects: LCSH: Refugees--Health and hygiene. | Refugees--Mental health. |
Emigration and immigration--Health aspects. | Emigration and immigration--
Psychological aspects.
Classification: LCC RA564.9.R43 K64 2023 | DDC 362.1086/914--dc23/eng/
20230527
LC record available at https://lccn.loc.gov/2023004755

ISBN: 978-1-032-21493-1 (hbk)
ISBN: 978-1-032-36157-4 (pbk)
ISBN: 978-1-003-33049-3 (ebk)

DOI: 10.4324/9781003330493

Typeset in Goudy
by Taylor & Francis Books

Contents

Boxes

Foreword

Susan Martin

Mass displacement, climate change, and public health are three of the defining issues of the twenty-first century. *Migrant Health and Resilience: Transnational Competence in Conflict and Climate Displacement Situations* brings them together with a series of recommendations to improve the capacity to respond effectively to the needs of the millions of people displaced by conflict and environmental change. This book could not be timelier, given the large and growing number of people around the globe who have been displaced by conflicts—such as those seen in Syria and, more recently, Afghanistan and Ukraine—as well as disasters made more frequent and dangerous by the effects of climate change.

As of mid-2022, there were more than 100 million individuals displaced globally from conflict and human rights abuses alone. Internally displaced persons constituted the largest proportion, at 60 million; another 32 million are refugees and others living outside of their country of origin who are in need of international protection; 4.6 million are asylum seekers, who are applying for recognition as refugees (UNHCR, 2022). There were also almost 6 million Palestinian refugees under the mandate of the UN Relief and Works Administration (UNRWA, 2022). In addition, 30.7 million people were displaced by disasters in 2020 alone. Although most people displaced by disaster are able to return home relatively quickly, almost 6 million of them were in a more protracted situation as of the end of 2021 (Internal Displacement Monitoring Center, 2022).

The current situation is likely to worsen in the years ahead, especially as concerns disaster displacement. As the Fifth Assessment report of the Intergovernmental Panel on Climate Change (IPCC) concludes, climate change poses profound consequences for human mobility (IPCC, 2014). In the short term, extreme weather events are the most direct pathway from climate change to migration but in the longer term, significant movements will result from slow-onset processes such as sea-level rise, coastal erosion, warming, water stress, and loss of agricultural productivity (ibid.; Rigaud et al., 2018; Zickgraf, 2021). Most experts believe that mobility in the context of climate change will be primarily internal (except for low-lying small island states without higher elevations) or immediate cross-border into neighboring countries (McLeman and Gemenne, 2018; Boas et al., 2022, pp. 3366–3371). Such migration could be particularly challenging for receiving communities and countries with few resources, legal structures, or institutional capacity to respond to the needs of the displaced and host populations. Geographical proximity might also mean that destination areas face some of the same environmental challenges as areas of migration origin (e.g., drought, desertification) and could offer little respite in this regard. Some long-distance movements are also inevitable, given the scope of migration today; the countries of North America, Europe, and Oceania, as well as regional economic powers within the Global South, will no doubt experience increased migration due at least in part due to environmental drivers, amplified by a changing climate.

The public health implications of these trends are immense, as discussed in this book. COVID-19 has shown the world that the nexus between infectious disease and human mobility has multiple aspects. People who move bring diseases with them; at the same time, the presence of infectious disease has a profound effect on the ability of people to migrate and the extent to which migrant health needs are addressed. My own research demonstrates that the response to COVID-19—particularly the almost universal restrictions on travel early in the pandemic—led to several changing patterns of mobility (Martin and Bergmann, 2021). First, travel bans resulted in involuntary immobility for many people, including asylum seekers who would otherwise have been admitted to pursue their claims to refugee status (ibid., pp. 664–669). Perhaps the most publicized such policy was Title 42 of the US public health code that was used to refuse entry of asylum seekers into the United States.[1] Second, the pandemic was accompanied by a shift from rural to urban to urban to rural movements in many countries. As the pandemic's immediate effects were seen in overcrowded hospitals in mostly urban areas, many people who had migrated to these centers returned home, often precipitously. In India, for example, thousands of people who had been working in urban areas returned on foot to the villages in which they were born because of an absence of other transport options (Mukhra, Krishan, and Kanchan, 2020, pp. 736–738; Bhowmick, 2020). With no employment in India's cities and the rapid spread of the virus, return to even poorer rural areas would at least provide shelter and sustenance.

The pandemic highlighted two further intersections of public health with migration and displacement—the crucial role played by migrants in providing health services in destination areas and, conversely, weaknesses in health systems that made it difficult to address the needs of refugees, displaced persons, and other migrants. In many countries, non-nationals do not qualify for public benefits, including health services, because of their immigration status or lack thereof (Caulford and Vali, 2006, pp. 1253–1254; Guadagno, 2020, pp. 5–6). Migrants were explicitly left out of initiatives to combat the pandemic in some countries. In Singapore, for example, migrant workers were not eligible at the start of the pandemic for the free masks and hand sanitizers provided to citizens (Chia and Poh, 2020). In other cases, migrants were but one population living in poverty who did not have access to vaccines and other medical interventions.

These examples highlight the necessity of increasing transnational competence in the context of growing displacement from conflict and climate change. Despite significant progress in responding to the health-care needs of refugees and displaced persons during the past 40 years, much more needs to be done. To understand just how bad the situation was previously, take the situation in refugee camps in Thailand, Somalia, and Sudan in the early 1980s where infectious disease was rampant and the basic tools of public health were missing. According to Michael Toole and Ronald Waldman (1988, p. 237), "a review of mortality data from these camps indicates that crude mortality rates (CMRs) were up to 40 times higher than those for the non-refugee populations in the host countries." The principal causes of excess mortality were acute respiratory infections, diarrheal diseases, malaria, measles, and undernutrition. As the authors concluded, most deaths "could have been prevented by adequate food rations, clean water, measles immunization, and an oral rehydration programme" (ibid., p. 237). Moreover, few camps had functioning reproductive health programs for women of child-bearing ages. Women and adolescent girls had little if any access to family planning, pre- or post-natal care, trained midwives or physicians, treatment for sexually transmitted diseases, or rape counseling despite the high frequency of sexual and gender-based violence to which they were subjected (Martin, 1992, pp. 38–45).

During the 1990s, health care for refugees and displaced persons began to professionalize. The Centers for Disease Control issued a report in 1992 emphasizing that:

> Preparing for the health problems experienced by large populations displaced by natural or man-made disasters is among the greatest challenges facing public health officials in the world today. The diversity of problems experienced in long- and short-term refugee situations demands a diversity of approaches in disease surveillance, control, and prevention.

Notable were new provisions to battle infectious diseases before they became life-threatening. In particular, UNHCR ramped up its efforts to immunize children under the age of 5 for measles as quickly as possible (UNHCR, 1998). It also emphasized the need to address diarrheal diseases, acute respiratory infections, and malaria, when prevalent (ibid.). UNHCR, the World Health Organization, and the UN Fund for Population Activities developed a set of guidelines on reproductive health care (UNHCR, WHO, and UNFPA, 1999). It was followed by a minimum initial service package to guide the implementation of reproductive health programs at each stage of the refugee cycle from onset to solutions.

During the past decade, attention has shifted toward the health needs of refugees and displaced persons in urban areas, where the majority now live. A key challenge is integration of refugees and displaced persons into local health-care systems while still addressing specific needs of those who have been uprooted from their homes. This has been particularly difficult in locations that do not have sufficient facilities and programs for local populations, let alone newcomers. The absence of psycho-social programs for those who have experienced the type of trauma seen by refugees and displaced persons is especially problematic.

Lagging behind, but recognized as essential, is the involvement of refugees and displaced persons in decision-making regarding all things affecting their lives and well-being. The slogan "nothing about us without us"[2] is finally taking hold after decades of failed promises of greater refugee participation (Milner, et al., 2022, p. 581). Refugee-led organizations—such as the Refugee Congress in the United States and the Global Refugee-Led Network, internationally—participate actively in UNHCR meetings. In October 2022, Basma Alawee, a member of the U.S. Refugee Advisory Board, joined the U.S. delegation to UNHCR's Executive Committee, where she spoke about the importance of refugee participation:

> We believe that engaging and empowering those with lived experience in displacement will lead to better and more effective humanitarian protection programs and solutions. Being a former refugee from Iraq, it is critically important for me personally, that no other refugee endures the same challenges that my family faced over the course of our displacement journey. I hope my participation today inspires the collective will of this body, to create similar opportunities for meaningful engagement and partnership for refugee leaders across the world.
>
> (cited in U.S. State Department, 2022)

Her call for action is the essence of this book. Koehn, Ngai, Uitto, and Diaków provide a framework for teaching transnational-competence skills to equip humanitarian responders with greater ability to help displaced persons from different ethnic backgrounds. They also intend to equip dislocated persons with skills to integrate more readily into new communities and live healthier and more sustainable lives. With these skills, those who have been uprooted from their homes will be able to enhance their resiliency and health outcomes. At the same time, the new transnational competencies learned by humanitarian workers will help them advocate more successfully for policy changes that address the drivers of conflict and climate displacement as well as the effects of displacement on vulnerable populations. With even more displacement likely in the years to come, these skills will be essential to the well-being of millions of people.

Notes

1 Under Title 42 of the Public Health Service Act of 1944, the Director of the Centers for Disease Control has the power, when faced with the potential spread of an infectious disease, "to prohibit, in whole or in part, the introduction of persons

and property from such countries or places as he [sic] shall designate in order to avert such danger" [that is the spread of a communicable disease] "for such period of time as he [sic] may deem necessary for such purpose."

2 This term has a long history, dating back to the Latin phrase *Nihil de nobis, sine nobis*. Its more recent usage came to prominence in the work of disability advocates who argued that disabled persons should be at the table when any decisions were made about them.

References

Bhowmick, Nilanjana. 2020. "'They Treat Us Like Stray Dogs': Migrant Workers Flee India's Cities." *National Geographic* 27. Available at: https://www.nationalgeographic.com/history/article/they-treat-us-like-stray-dogs-migrant-workers-flee-india-cities.

Boas, Ingrid; Wiegel, Hanne; Farbotko, Carol; Warner, Jeroen; and Sheller, Mimi. 2022. "Climate Mobilities: Migration, Im/mobilities and Mobility Regimes in a Changing Climate." *Journal of Ethnic and Migration Studies* 48 (14): 3365–3379.

Caulford, Paul; and Vali, Yasmin. 2006. "Providing Health Care to Medically Uninsured Immigrants and Refugees." *Canadian Medical Association Journal* 174 (9): 1253–1254.

Centers for Disease Control. 1992. "Famine-Affected, Refugee, and Displaced Populations: Recommendations for Public Health Issues." *Morbidity and Mortality Weekly Report* 41 (RR-13). Available at: https://www.cdc.gov/mmwr/preview/mmwrhtml/00019261.htm.

Chia, Jasmine; and Poh, Yong Han. 2020. "Amid COVID-19 Crisis, Southeast Asia's Migrant Workers Fall Through the Cracks." *The Diplomat* 31. Available at: https://thediplomat.com/2020/03/amid-covid-19-crisis-southeast-asias-migrant-workers-fall-through-the-cracks/.

Guadagno, Lorenzo. 2020. *Migrants and the COVID-19 Pandemic: An Initial Analysis*. Geneva: Institute of Migration.

Internal Displacement Monitoring Centre. 2022. *Global Report on Internal Displacement 2022*. Available at: https://www.internal-displacement.org/global-report/grid2022/.

IPCC (Intergovernmental Panel on Climate Change). 2014. *Climate Change 2014: Impacts, Adaptation, and Vulnerability. Part A: Global and Sectoral Aspects. Contribution of Working Group II to the Fifth Assessment Report of the Intergovernmental Panel on Climate Change*, edited by C.B. Field; V.R. Barros; D.J. Dokken; K.J. Mach; M. D. Mastrandrea; T.E. Bilir; M. Chatterjee, … and L.L. White. Cambridge: Cambridge University Press.

Martin, Susan Forbes. 1992. *Refugee Women*. London: Zed Press.

Martin, Susan; and Bergmann, Jonas. 2021. "(Im)Mobility in the Age of COVID-19." *International Migration Review* 55 (3): 660–687.

McLeman, Robert; and Gemenne, François. 2018. "Environmental Migration Research: Evolution and Current State of the Science." In *Routledge Handbook of Environmental Displacement and Migration*, edited by Robert McLeman and François Gemenne. London: Routledge, pp. 3–16.

Milner, James; Mustafa, Alio; and Rez, Gardi. 2022. "Meaningful Refugee Participation: An Emerging Norm in the Global Refugee Regime." *Refugee Survey Quarterly* 41 (4): 565–593.

Mukhra, Richa; Krishan, Kewal; and Kanchan, Tanuj. 2020. "COVID-19 Sets Off Mass Migration in India." *Archives of Medical Research* 51 (7): 736–738.

Rigaud, Kanta Kumari; de Sherbinin, Alex; Jones, Bryan; Bergmann, Jonas; Clement, Viviane; Ober, Kayly; Schewe, Jacob; ... Midgley, Amelia. 2018. *Groundswell : Preparing for Internal Climate Migration.* Washington, D.C.: World Bank.

Toole, Michael J.; and Waldman, Ronald J. 1988. "An Analysis of Mortality Trends among Refugee Populations in Somalia, Sudan, and Thailand." *Bulletin of the World Health Organization* 66 (2): 237.

UNHCR. 1998. *Handbook for Emergencies.* Geneva: UNHCR.

UNHCR. 2022. *Mid-Year Trends.* Geneva: UNHCR.

UNHCR; WHO; and UNFPA. 1999. *Inter-Agency Field Manual on Reproductive Health in Refugee Situations.* Geneva: UNHCR.

UNRWA. 2021. "UNRWA in Figures." Available at: https://www.unrwa.org/sites/default/files/content/resources/unrwa_in_figures_2021_eng.pdf.

U.S. State Department. 2022. "U.S. Plenary Statement – UNHCR Executive Committee. U.S. Mission to International Organizations in Geneva." Available at; https://geneva.usmission.gov/2022/10/11/u-s-plenary-statement-unhcr-executive-committee/.

Zickgraf, Caroline. 2021. "Climate Change, Slow Onset Events and Human Mobility: Reviewing the Evidence." *Current Opinion in Environmental Sustainability* 50: 21–30.

Abbreviations

ALNAP	Active Learning Network for Accountability and Performance
CC	cultural competence
CDP	critical digital pedagogy
CHEs	complex humanitarian emergencies
CoP	community of practice
COP21	Conference of Parties to the United Nations Framework Convention on Climate Change
DMIS	developmental model of intercultural sensitivity
EU	European Union
FDPs	forcibly displaced persons
FRAME	Framework for Assessing, Monitoring, and Evaluating the Environment in Refugee-related Operations
GDP	gross domestic product
GFMD	Global Forum on Migration and Development
GHG	greenhouse gas
GMG	Global Migration Group
IBL	inquiry-based learning
ICT	information and communication technology
IDP	internally displaced person
IFRC	International Federation of Red Cross and Red Crescent Societies
IIE	Institute of International Education
ILO	International Labour Organization
IOM	International Organization for Migration
IPCC	Intergovernmental Panel on Climate Change
ISIS	Islamic State in Iraq and Syria
KNOMAD	Global Knowledge Partnership on Migration and Development
LGBTI	Lesbian Gay Bisexual Transgender Intersex
M&E	monitoring and evaluation
MDGs	Millennium Development Goals
MHPSS	mental health and psychosocial support

MOOCs	massive open online courses
MSF	Médecins Sans Frontières
MT	metric tons
NASA	National Aeronautics and Space Administration
NGO	non-governmental organization
OECD	Organization for Economic Cooperation and Development
PDD	Platform on Disaster Displacement
PTSD	post-traumatic stress disorder
SBL	simulation-based learning
SDGs	Sustainable Development Goals
SIDS	small island developing states
TC	transnational competence
ToC	theory of change
UK	United Kingdom
UNDP	United Nations Development Programme
UNEP	United Nations Environmental Programme
UNESCO	United Nations Educational, Scientific and Cultural Organization
UNHCR	United Nations High Commission for Refugees
UNHSP	United Nations Human Settlements Programme
USA	United States of America
USB	Universal Serial Bus stick
WHO	World Health Organization

Introduction

The Role of Transnational-Competence Preparation in Enhancing the Health and Resilience of Displaced Persons and Their Hosts

Scholarship that treats population displacement and migrant health merits front-and-center inclusion on the dynamic issue slate of contemporary global health politics (McInnes, Lee, and Youde, 2020, p. 2). Coincident with the arrival of the pandemic era, "social networks, globalization, climate change, economic opportunity, demographics and war are throwing more people together with more 'other' people in more remote places than ever before" (Friedman, 2019). In 2018 alone, conflicts displaced (both internally and across borders) nearly 71 million people – the highest level recorded since World War II (Cumming-Bruce, 2019). At the end of 2020, 82.4 million forcibly displaced persons (FDPs), including 26.4 million official refugees[1] – people who fled their countries of origin because of persecution, armed conflict, or grave human-rights violations – were scattered around the globe.[2] Spurred by the Russian invasion of Ukraine,[3] more than 100 million men, women, and children had been displaced by mid-2022 (Hassan and Westfall, 2022).[4] Extreme weather events, some triggered or exacerbated by climate change, uprooted another 23 million or more other people around the world (Cole, 2020, p. 205; Sengupta, 2021; Kaplan and Dennis, 2021; Butros, Gyberg, and Kaijser, 2021, p. 842; Aleinikoff and Martin, 2022, p. 5). With massive climate-induced migration looming on the horizon, we face a future with even more people on the move in desperate pursuit of security and opportunity.

In short, "we are facing one of the biggest challenges of the 21st century: an unprecedented wave of human displacement that shows no sign of stopping even when confronted by a pandemic of global proportions ..." (Arias and Araluce, 2021, p. 568). Coincidentally, although funding for humanitarian relief responses has surged in recent decades, the existing apparatus for responding to displaced populations is deficient and frequently disconnected from development (Hoffman, 2021, pp. 121, 127),[5] resulting all too often in "chronic, insecure containment" (Eckenwiler and Wild, 2021, pp. 234–235). Whereas humanitarian responses have addressed emergencies, "development builds resilience to emergencies" (Hoffman, 2021, p. 123; also Lovey, O'Keeffe, and Petignat, 2021, p. 2). The reinforcing continuum of short-term emergency assistance and long-term efforts to build socio-economic capabilities is explicitly

DOI: 10.4324/9781003330493-1

recognized in the U.N.'s 2016 *Agenda for Humanity* (see Hoffman, 2021, pp. 123–124; also see Aleinikoff and Martin, 2022, p. 47).

In the face of surging migration and vulnerable emplacements, protecting and promoting the health of people on the move and their hosts are growing priorities and moral responsibilities (Hoffman, 2021, pp. 123–124). *Migrant Health and Resilience: Transnational Competence in Conflict and Climate Displacement Situations* addresses the pressing need to build durable responses in the wake of wrenching human dislocation, compounding health challenges, migrant resilience and resourcefulness, inadequate training approaches, and a rethinking of approaches to humanitarian action. Specifically, we aim to support the development of innovative approaches that ensure long-term impact by focusing attention on the commonly overlooked promise of transboundary training and education in protracted life-disrupted contexts (Ramsay and Baker, 2019, p. 76). The migration-development nexus connects critical experiential dimensions of transnational migration studies (Ozkazanc-Pan, 2019, p. 478), health, and resilience with objectives embodied in the United Nations' Sustainable Development Goals (SDGs),[6] the New York Declaration for Refugees and Migrants,[7] the Global Compact for Safe, Orderly and Regular Migration, the Global Compact for Migration,[8] the Global Compact on Refugees,[9] and the United Nations' Framework Convention on Climate Change (see Martin, Bergmann, Rigaud, and Yameogo, 2021, p. 147; Micinski, 2021, pp. 135, 140–145). Further, since 2017, the World Bank's International Development Association has provided substantial financial support on "favorable terms" to refugees and host communities (Milner, 2021, p. 423).

Throughout the world, children and adults spatially displaced by persecution, armed conflict, and environmental disasters who often find themselves in a protracted "holding pattern" (Walker, Hein, Russ, Bertleff, and Caspersz, 2010, p. 2223) encounter challenging living conditions in unfamiliar and insecure surroundings. Individuals who successfully "navigate the perils of migration, and perhaps detention and encampment, are often exemplars of self-determination … Yet many are also fragile" (Eckenwiler and Wild, 2021, p. 243). The daunting stressors that many individual and family migrants encounter include:

> loss of close relationships, uncertainty about decision to immigrate, uncertainty about being assigned refugee status, changes in financial status, loss of lifestyle, country and roots, change in cultural norms … [and] employment, and ability to communicate in language other than one's own …
>
> (Pickren, 2014, p. 20)

The COVID-19 pandemic exacerbated the health and survival dangers of uprooting, being on the move (Eckenwiler and Wild, 2021, p. 238; Allahi, 2021), and being forced to interact in close proximity with strangers. For persons in camps and other similarly vulnerable conditions, "it is often impossible to follow practices such as social distancing, hand-washing and isolating those who are sick and most at risk" (Berger, 2020).

To help forcibly displaced persons survive, adjust, integrate, and prosper, concerned individuals and collectivities that encompass multiple nationality and professional backgrounds and funding sources arrive on the scene. We refer to such crisis responders as "humanitarian-care providers"; their numbers likely exceed 300,000 today and the challenges they encounter increasingly are complex and long-term (Walker, Hein, Russ, Bertleff, and Caspersz, 2010, p. 2223).[10] Increasingly, non-governmental organizations (NGOs) and other responders recognize the need to provide competency-based training for their workforce either directly or through specialized service agencies (Teitelbaum, 2019).

When displaced persons encounter humanitarian-care providers of diverse backgrounds, the nature of interpersonal interactions becomes critical because all parties confront daily challenges that require collaboration across multiple transnational social fields (Ozkazanc-Pan, 2019, pp. 21–23, 40, 52–53, 89, 116; Pincock, Betts, and Easton-Calabria, 2020, p. 9).[11] In both camps and spontaneous settlements, migrants themselves constitute critical, but often underutilized, resources who provide essential "bottom-up" sources of informal assistance (Jones, 2020; Pincock, Betts, and Easton-Calabria, 2020, p. 15). In the absence of adequate and responsible skill development for all responding participants, key avenues for migrant health care and well-being are foreclosed. In such demanding and multi-faceted encounters, therefore, transnational competence (TC) is at a premium. It is telling in this connection that today's professionals find flexible skills embedded in TC (e.g., "leadership, communication and collaboration") in short supply and value training in these domains more highly than specific technical-skill training (cited in Brooks, 2018). Our intention is to demonstrate how TC enhances the work and lives of both care-providers and care-receivers.

Although transnational competence can be enriched by informed experience, its foundational components require advance preparation. This operationally focused book is designed to facilitate TC learning and mastery on the part of both current and future humanitarian-care providers and the displaced persons they assist. Refining and further developing the transnational-competence (TC) framework developed by Peter Koehn and the late James Rosenau (2010) enable the authors to elaborate a detailed compass for TC development with utility for persons dislocated by persecution, armed conflict, and/or climate disasters along with humanitarian responders dedicated to providing for their short-term and sustainable health, livelihood, and dreams. In this way, *Migrant Health and Resilience: Transnational Competence in Conflict and Climate Displacement Situations* envisions filling the need for a useful practical work grounded in transdisciplinary insight and informed by best practices in training and sustainable evaluation. At the same time, our discussion aims to offer applicable guides of value for university educators, learners, and researchers preparing for contemporary migration challenges of various complexion that require transnational collaboration (see, for instance, Pilkington, et al., 2016, p. 5; Edwards, 1996, pp. 20–24).[12]

Constructing an appropriate process and curriculum for TC development in the face of conflict- and climate-induced migration that will facilitate sustainable impacts on the ground (Teitelbaum, 2019) is informed in this work by three novel approaches. First, we utilize theory of change and backward mapping from desired outcomes and impacts (see, for instance, Ssosse, Wagner, and Hopper, 2021, p. 7) to identify generic TC development needs along with evaluation indicators. This approach, which is inclusively conducted for humanitarian-care trainers drawn from international and local organizations, unaffiliated responders, displaced community members, and hosts, constitutes an innovative application of a methodology that has proven valuable in the context of developing and evaluating environmental *programs* launched by international development agencies (Todd and Craig, 2021). Where deemed useful, the step-by-step process detailed here can be also employed to identify additional TC training needs that are tailored to fit site-specific circumstances.

Second, we devote equal attention to the competency needs of persons who move and of those who aim to help in arrival sites and contexts. This perspective operates within the fundamental reality that uprooting has broad effects; that is, the lived experiences of those displaced also impact persons who stay behind and persons on the receiving and assisting end (Martin, Bergmann, Rigaud, and Yameogo, 2021, p. 143). The arising challenges and opportunities involve time, timing, and capacity. In most humanitarian-response situations, the immediate and pressing demands of dislocation preclude systematic and sustained attention to competence development. We intend for this book to be available as a best-practice guide for reference during that window of opportunity when humanitarian-care providers are seeking professional development, preparing for field assignments, and/or participating in training workshops.[13] At the same time, we appreciate that migrants "collectively organize to help themselves and their communities" (Pincock, Betts, and Easton-Calabria, 2020, p. 1) and, therefore, directly incorporate their agency (Hoffman, 2021, pp. 121–122) in the envisioned field-based competency development. Furthermore, we provide guides for fast-track TC development adjusted to the educational backgrounds, competency gaps, and career-path needs of the often-neglected humanitarian workers who are recruited from displaced and host communities.

Our third innovative approach involves the introduction of e-learning in TC preparation and on-going competency maintenance/expansion. An e-learning approach requires bold new thinking about how to bring useful and sustained distance education to challenged humanitarian-care trainers. At the same time, e-learning for all involved parties carries the promise of repeated contact and long-term, even life-long, learning.

To provide context for the discussion in the chapters to follow, we begin by documenting and unraveling the current and likely future dimensions of the global dislocation crisis. This analysis leads to identification of the structurally displaced people of immediate and future concern in this work: refugees and political asylum seekers, other conflict-displaced persons, and climate-generated migrants.

The Global Dislocation Crisis

In this time of transnational migration,[14] people, including particularly vulnerable children and persons of all genders, increasingly are compelled to move.[15] Migration involves "a stay of some substantial duration" (Lindley, 2014, p. 8). The stay of a migrant can "involve return; back-and-forth, circular movements between places; step-wise, onward movement from place to place over time; and the construction of simultaneous translocal/transnational worlds" (ibid.). Each phase of the migration experience involves new and interconnected societal and individual impacts (Gushulak and Mac-Pherson, 2006) as well as "on-going" encounters and exchanges "between/among people across relations of difference that are themselves constantly shifting" (Ozkazanc-Pan, 2019, p. 20; also pp. 29, 51–55, 102).

Our applied analysis primarily is concerned with *transnational* mobility under conditions of extended exile. Most transnational migration flows in South-South directions (Hossain, Khan, and Short, 2017, pp. 1–2; Ionesco, Mokhnacheva, and Gemenne, 2017, pp. 8–9; Betts, 2021); roughly 37 percent follow South to North routes and "only 3% from developed to developing countries" (WHO, 2010, pp. 8–9).[16] In mid-2022, Turkey hosted the largest numerical refugee population (3.8 million) and Lebanon the highest on a per-capita basis (1 in 8) (Hassan and Westfall, 2022).

People are displaced and cross borders based on a specific but complex combination "and quite often also a culmination" of multiple factors (Lindley and Hammond, 2014, p. 66) that include political, economic, sociocultural, environmental, aspirational, and health-related considerations (Hamlin, 2021, pp. 3–4, 9–10, 155).[17] The interconnectors of agency and structure are multiple and multiplying, and their determinant, preventive, and impact implications often are complex and underexplored. Typically shaped by interacting elements of multiple and even offsetting considerations and conditioned by the capacity to relocate, migration can be predominantly reactive or proactive. Although all migrations are the outcome of contextual "interactions between human agency and structural forces beyond the immediate control of ordinary people … it is also apparent that some migrations … are motivated more obviously by the immediate threat of violence and conflict than by economic interests" (Mavroudi and Nagel, 2016, p. 119; also Koehn, 1991).[18]

Refugees and Conflict-Displaced Persons

Refugees and other conflict-induced migrants constitute one of the human "scourges" of complex humanitarian emergencies (CHEs). CHEs refer to socio-political crises "in which large numbers of people die from war, displacement, disease and hunger, owing to man-made disasters ..." (Klugman, 1999, pp. 1–2; also see pp. 8–16). By the end of 2020, countries around the world hosted more than 26 million officially recognized refugees and other "persons of concern" to the United Nations High Commissioner for Refugees (UNHCR) who had fled life-threatening violence. Women and their dependents account for the vast majority of refugees (Penttinen and Kynsilehto, 2017, p. 35). Another 41 million people had been internally displaced by armed conflict, generalized violence, and/or violations of human rights (ibid.; also see Price, 2019, pp. 38–39).[19] The 2022 Russian invasion of Ukraine resulted in additional displacements, including more than 5 million people who crossed into Poland, Moldova, Hungary, and other countries.[20] The common denominator in this massive uprooting is the frequently deliberate "force factor" (Mandic, 2021).[21] Notwithstanding the 1949 Geneva Conventions' non-combatant protections, exposed and unprotected civilians bear the brunt of most casualties resulting from contemporary armed conflicts (see Koehn, 2019, pp. 61–63).

In light of structural neglect and lack of access to education and healthcare services prior to displacement, compounded by physical and emotional trauma and other dislocation effects, persons fleeing persecution and armed conflict "often have special and distinct healthcare needs with a higher burden of infectious diseases" (Rashid, Cervantes, and Goez, 2020, p. 476). Maintaining health remains a particularly challenging proposition for persons who escape active-conflict theatres and join the internally displaced or flee across national borders (Koehn, 2019). Following persistent discrimination in access to medical care, arbitrary killings, and village destruction in Myanmar, for instance, members of the persecuted Rohingya ethnic group encounter life-threatening health conditions in Rakhine State, in camps for internally displaced persons, and in refugee camps in Bangladesh (Ives, 2016). All people on the move have been "disproportionately exposed" to COVID-19 (Finell, Tiilikainen, Jasinskaja-Lahti, Hasan, and Muthana, 2021, pp. 1–2) and refugees have experienced elevated rates of infection, related mortality, and trauma in its wake.

The externalization, "outsourcing," or "offshoring" of South-North migrants is now commonplace (Hyndman and Giles, 2017, pp. 8–9; Arias and Araluce, 2021, pp. 570–572; Hamlin, 2021, p. 17). Australia, the European Union, Japan, and the United States seek to deter arrivals by enlisting poor countries to contain migrants in their regions of origin and by exacerbating the perils involved in pushing further (Fisher and Taub, 2019; also see Solomon, 2016; Eckenwiler and Wild, 2021, p. 236; Milner, 2021, p. 424; Stephens, 2019). Border controls and immigration restrictions "increase the costs and risks of migrating to wealthy countries" (Flahaux and De Haas, 2016, p. 4; also pp. 18–21; Arias and Araluce, 2021, p. 571). Thousands of Central Americans have perished at the Mexico-United States border (Pottie, Hui, and Schneider, 2016, p. 292) and roughly 1 in 20 who attempt to cross the Mediterranean Sea fail to survive the journey (Fisher and Taub, 2019). In combination, externalization and exclusionary practices "contribute to long-term displacement in sites within the global South ..." and at the periphery of the wealthy North (Hyndman and Giles, 2017, pp. 8, 32; Arias and Araluce, 2021, p. 572).[22]

Unsurprisingly, then, the majority of refugees and conflict-displaced persons are hosted in the Global South (see, for instance, Kamara and Renzaho, 2016, p. 81). Most of those who have fled Syria, for instance, remain in the Middle East.[23] Turkey, Lebanon, Jordan, Iran, and Pakistan all host more than half a million persons forced to flee their home country by armed violence (Matlin, et al., 2018, p. 35; Pottie, Hui, and Schneider, 2016, p. 293). In contrast to the "dominance of perspectives of teaching [those with a refugee background] in the context of the global North" (Ramsay and Baker, 2019, p. 76), our focus is on training and learning in Southern humanitarian-emergency contexts.

Resettlement Conditions

Camps, sorting centers (Agier, 2011, pp. 39, 52), spontaneous border-crossing places of shelter (Eckenwiler and Wild, 2021, p. 235), and settlements feature in the locational distribution of conflict-provoked migrants. Camps refer to living places where inhabitants are dependent on external assistance. In contrast, the term "settlement" indicates that residents are primarily "responsible for their own subsistence" although in some cases aid agencies still provide for education and health care (Mavroudi and Nagel, 2016, p. 137). In terms of living conditions,

> refugee camp residents appear most often in the international media ... [although] the even larger numbers of people who are internally displaced and the people who 'self-settle' in regional towns and cities constitute a hugely important, if less visible and accessible component of displacement.
> (Lindley and Hammond, 2014, p. 67; also Matlin, et al., 2018, p. 35)

Due to human rights violations and the discriminatory policies encountered in many countries,[24] displaced persons and families also face a dire risk of homelessness, which compounds distress.[25]

Camps

Today, millions of externally and internally displaced people (IDPs) are forced to live, often for long periods and even for multiple generations (Lindley and Hammond, 2014, p. 67; Silove, Ventevogel, and Rees, 2017, p. 130), in camps. Some camps approach the population size of cities (Koser and Martin, 2011, p. 3). Although the refugee camps set up by the UNHCR can range from fewer than 2,000 persons to as many as 200,000 residents, they commonly "shelter between 5,000 and 10,000 people" (Agier, 2011, pp. 53–55). Furthermore, "protracted refugee situations" of five years or longer in exile are the norm (La Rocca, 2018).

For the vast majority of refugees and conflict-displaced migrants, what matters most are conditions in poor hosting countries and treatment received from local and international humanitarian responders. While camps offer shelter, food, and initial reductions in mortality, crowding and poor sanitary conditions compound the risks of illness and death from communicable diseases (see Koehn, 2019, pp. 67–68; Kitsantonis, 2019a, 2019b). At the height of COVID-19 infections, several camps in Greece lacked soap and clean water, space for social distancing; additional mobility restrictions "deepened human suffering and increased existing tensions" (Meer, Hill, Peace, and Villegas, 2021, pp. 867). Ensuring adequate security within refugee camps can be also challenging (Koser and Martin, 2011, p. 3). The highly valued relief items distributed by NGOs can make camp recipients targets for attack (Duggan, 2008, p. 290) and camp managers typically are neither authorized nor positioned to provide protection for vulnerable refugee populations (see Jones, 2020; Davies, 2010, pp. 97–98).

Viet Thanh Nguyen (2019, p. 18), refugee, writer, university professor, and scholar, unmasks the horrors of refugee camps in this compelling passage:

> Keeping people in a refugee camp is punishing people who have committed no crime except trying to save their own lives and the lives of their loved ones. The refugee camp belongs to the same inhuman family as the internment camp, the concentration camp, the death camp. The camp is the place where we keep those who we do not see as fully being human, and if we do not actively seek their death in most cases, we also often do not actively seek to restore many of them to the life that they had before, the life we have ourselves.

We can, and must, do a better job of enhancing opportunities and restoring life prospects to camp populations in the pandemic era (also see Kertes, 2018, p. 120).

Sorting Centers

Sorting centers encompass "transit centres, waiting zones, holding and detention centres … under the direct control of national administrations … police institutions, U.N. agencies and/or humanitarian NGOs" (Agier, 2011, pp. 46–47, 50–51; also see Turner, 2015, p. 139). The Trump Administration favored the use of immigrant-incarceration centers operated by private prison companies (Dickerson, 2019). Conditions vary for people residing in sorting centers and the length of stay can be of short or long duration. Since asylum seekers awaiting decisions can subsist in holding centers for years

(Agier, 2011, pp. 47–49), their situation lends itself to educational interventions that are similar to those envisioned in this book for camp populations.

Spontaneous Settlements

Millions of refugees and IDPs spontaneously settle in urban areas (see, for instance, ibid., pp. 42–45; Wells, Lawsin, Hunt, Youssef, Abujado, and Steel, 2018, p. 1; Eckenwiler and Wild, 2021, p. 235); they arrive with diverse migration backgrounds, vulnerabilities, assets, expectations, and aspirations (Haysom, Pantuliano, and Davey, 2012, pp. 113–114, 117, 130–132). In many places, sprawling and densely populated self-settled and self-organized areas precariously support massive numbers of transnationally displaced persons. In Southern host countries, conflict-generated transmigrants who live outside official camps usually are "among the poorest and most vulnerable" residents who must share services that previously "were inadequate even when used by a smaller population" (Martin, et al., 2017, p. 111; also Matlin, et al., 2018, p. 35).[26] In Bangladesh, a massive unofficial camp (a dense collection of bamboo and tarp huts) populated by several hundred thousand Rohingya who fled uprooting in Myanmar exists alongside the official UNHCR camp. There are no toilets and "every medical treatment post … has a line that snakes nearly around the camp" (Solomon, 2017). For the 30 percent of the Rohingya refugee population under age 5, exposure to horrific trauma, hyperstressed conditions, and developmental setbacks due to malnutrition in such settlements portend a "massive mental health crisis for children," according to Lalou Holdt, Save the Children's mental health adviser (Beech, 2017). Here, soccer provides a "joyful escape" from unhealthy living conditions. A 24-year-old Rohingya refugee, Mohammed Ismail, explained to a *New York Times* reporter that "When I play football, the sadness and anger is far away. But after I finish, it always comes back" (Thompson, 2017; also see Koehn and Koehn, 2016).

In short, "the refugee experience confronts us with humanity at its most challenged – forcibly uprooted and in flight from violence, caught between countries, facing an uncertain future – but it also provides some of the most striking examples of human resilience" (Kirmayer, 2014, p. vii). In light of practical barriers to migrant/care-provider match and the absence of adequately prepared staff, interactions become particularly daunting in settlement centers and host community contexts. TC development for those in limbo and dedicated responders offers a humane and promising way forward for engaging resilience in the interest of individual well-being and sustainable development.

Climate-Induced Migrants

The relationship between climatic change and conflict is not direct, but there is evidence of complex links among climate, conflict, and migration (von

Uexkull and Buhaug, 2021; Aleinikoff and Martin, 2022, p. 23). Climatic variations and events have long triggered human migrations. In the contemporary period, human-induced climate change exacerbates pre-existing vulnerabilities (McMichael, Barnett, and McMichael, 2012, pp. 646–647; Koehn, 2016; Sengupta, 2020) and threatens human health both directly and indirectly. For instance, climate change is responsible for increases in unliveable hot zones and associated heat-related stress and mortality (Schwartz, 2021) and is indirectly linked to a host of health conditions, including cholera, the spread of insect-borne diseases, and malnutrition (Bell, 2010, p. 2). There is broad scientific agreement that global warming and ocean warming are altering storms in at least five ways that generate increased population dislocation: (1) more powerful hurricane winds; (2) unleashing of higher precipitation amounts; (3) slower wetter patterns that worsen flooding; (4) enlarging the zone of hurricanes – that is, more storms are making landfalls in higher latitudes; and (5) greater intensity and volatility – for instance, less warning when tropical storms develop into category-4 hurricanes (Penney, 2020; also Aleinikoff and Martin, 2022, p. 8).

Examples of climate-induced displacement abound. The Government of China has resettled more than one million environmental migrants in Ningxia Hui Autonomous Region along the ancient Silk Road in the wake of climate change and other land and water stressors (Wong, 2016, p. A1). In the face of long-term drought with no end in sight, millions of Iranians are on the move to provincial towns and cities (Sengupta, 2018). In rapid permafrost-warping Siberia due to extraordinary local warming of greater than 3 degrees Celsius since preindustrial times, the homes and livelihoods of 5.4 million people have been disrupted by forest and peatland fires, forcing thousands to move to the regional capital (Troianovski and Mooney, 2019; Pierre-Louis, 2019; Troianovski, 2021). An estimated 6 million persons in Bangladesh have been displaced or negatively affected by climate-induced disasters in recent years and others live in an extremely vulnerable situation (Ahmed, 2018, pp. 7, 10–11). Forced historically onto marginal lands, many Native Americans living on reservations in the USA are threatened by climate-induced perils (Flavelle and Goodluck, 2021). When subsisting off the land becomes unimaginable, climate-displaced youth from Niger, Mali, and Chad are joining their conflict-displaced contemporaries on the arduous and dangerous journey north to Libya and places beyond. In the wake of two devastating hurricanes that struck four million people living in impoverished areas of Honduras in rapid succession in late 2020, a surge of displaced families fled north (Kitroeff, 2021).

Future Outlook

In short, migration induced by climatic disturbances, often in combination with other stressors, has arrived with a vengeance. And, much more is on the way. In 2019, the Intergovernmental Panel on Climate Change (IPCC) warned that climate change, combined with land and water exploitation, threatens to produce severe food shortages that will lead to increases in cross-border migration (Flavelle, 2019a). The Pentagon considers the potential of "mass migration events" due to climatic change a major threat to U.S. security (Klare, 2019, pp. 112–117). The extent of climate-induced migration could easily dwarf the numbers of armed conflict-generated migrants the world has witnessed (Obama, cited in Davis, Landler, and Davenport, 2016). The number of people vulnerable to sea-level rise alone will continue to grow in the face of population growth, in-migration to coastal cities, land subsidence, storm surges, and small island encroachments. In recognition of the devastating connections, the Paris Agreement adopted at the Conference of Parties to the United Nations Framework Convention on Climate Change (COP21) specifically references links between climate change, displacement, and migration (Ionesco, Mokhnacheva, and Gemenne, 2017, pp. 95, 112–113).

Employing the advanced digital-elevation model CoastalDEM, Scott Kulp and Benjamin Strauss (2019) estimate that 310 million people will occupy land below projected high-tide lines by 2050.[27] As risk perceptions and awareness of the likely threats posed by climate change grow,[28] those who are most vulnerable will "choose to move to places perceived as offering a better life" (McMichael, Barnett, and McMichael, 2012, pp. 646–647, 650; Bardsley and Hugo, 2010, pp. 241, 246). Members of vulnerable populations, especially persons living in coastal megacities and densely settled delta areas,[29] both will resort to migration as a "proactive diversification strategy" in anticipation of climate-change impacts and move abruptly in the wake of climate-influenced disasters (ibid., pp. 239, 242, 244–245, 248; Box 7.1; Aleinikoff and Martin, 2022, p. 5). Most of these movers are likely to join the ranks of the internally displaced. Like other population movements, migrants fleeing climate-change disasters and risks will be prone to suffer health maladies, malnutrition, injuries, mental anguish, and loss of life (Matlin, et al., 2018, p. 12; McMichael, Barnett, and McMichael, 2012, pp. 649, 651; Carballo, Smith, and Pettersson, 2008, p. 33).

Proactive, Facilitated, and Sustainable Relocation

Given the costs and vulnerability of massive flood-control engineering projects and the increase in superstorms enhanced by climate change, *evacuation* is the more effective wave of the future (see Dooley, Inoue, and Yamamitsu, 2019).[30] It is time to plan for prospects that massive resettlement of ecological migrants will be required in the face of environmental impacts precipitated by climate change (e.g., sea-level rise and firestorms) as well the likelihood that substantial proactive population flows will occur in anticipation of such developments (see Koehn, 2019, pp. 190–196). Stephen Parodi (2019), who oversaw physicians and care teams during northern California's massive Tubbs fire in 2017, alerts us that "medical evacuees are the new refugees of climate change."

In the face of the new threats involving frequent hazard encounters, the spread of infectious disease, food insecurity, and unavailability of clean water, associated with climate change, facilitated migration to protected areas can diminish health risks and facilitate access to health services (Ionesco, Mokhnacheva, and Gemenne, 2017, p. 87). When properly planned and executed as an adaptive response to climate change, "the move to a new location can alleviate health deficits from undernutrition or freshwater shortages, avoid the physical dangers of extreme weather events and degraded physical environments, and enhance access to medical facilities" (McMichael, Barnett, and McMichael, 2012, p. 648). The most promising approaches to climate adaptation incorporate community-centered methods, strengthening local government capacity, and multi-sectoral/multi-stakeholder partnerships (Uitto and Shaw, 2006, pp. 97–101; Heine and Petersen, 2008, pp. 48–49; Aleinikoff and Martin, 2022). The vulnerability of climate migrants is reduced and the health and social costs of traumatized relocation minimized

> by allowing adequate time for community consultations and planning, paying compensation at a level equal to the standard of housing and materials in the host community, ensuring that the money and resources made available to assist communities to relocate is spent on those communities … employing the people being moved wherever labor is required, and providing support for housing, health services, mental health services, employment, and education.
>
> (McMichael, Barnett, and McMichael, 2012, p. 651)

Relocations, evacuations, and resettlements are not cheap (Bardsley and Hugo, 2010, p. 256) or without incurred costs (Treaster and Harmon, 2019). The livelihood and sustainable-development needs of climate-displaced populations and their hosting communities "far outstrip" currently available funding from multilateral, bilateral, and NGO sources (Aleinikoff and Martin, 2022, p. 33). Adequate funding needs to be secured to ensure that sustainable relocation and other climate-change adaptation measures will be addressed in an ethically responsible and healthy manner. Transnational-competence training for movers, responders, and hosts is an oft-overlooked, but essential, component of successful and humane climate-resettlement efforts.

TC-Training Contexts

In *Migrant Health and Resilience: Transnational Competence in Conflict and Climate Displacement Situations*, we are concerned with sustainable capability enhancements for persons displaced by conflict or climatic disruption. Camps, holding centers, planned and self-organized settlements all fall within the scope of attention.

Basic assistance to dislocated persons, even after the crisis situation has passed, is vital for survival. However, "humanitarian aid to refugees [and others] stuck in extended exile is only a palliative; it relieves the short-term hunger and suffering, but does nothing to address the long-term insecurity and protection of persons" (Hyndman and Giles, 2017, pp. 6–7). To address this development shortfall, the acquisition of transnational competence opens new and enhanced resilience-reinforcing and skill-rebuilding opportunities for conflict-driven and climate-induced migrants.

Regrettably, existing training courses in the fields of development, health, and migration typically are simply "not effective" in light of frequent confrontations with multiple boundary-crossing demands. Peter Taylor (2003, p. 1) reports that:

> [they] do not enable participants to gain useful new knowledge and the skills and attitudes to apply it. This means that the behaviour of the learners is unlikely to change, so the outcome of the training is not useful or sustainable.

Trainers and Trainees

Our contribution specifically addresses the compelling need to equip humanitarian-care providers with relevant skills for assisting dislocated persons who possess different and diverse nationality, ethnic, experiential, and qualification backgrounds. Systematic transnational-competence training is essential in preparing today's multinational responders for the diverse camp, self-settled, and host populations they will encounter.

We also recognize a parallel need to equip dislocated persons with skills relevant for advancing personal/family integration and belonging in a new location and for contributing to sustainable development. When both migrants and care-responders possess TC, positive outcomes and impacts can be maximized. Transnational competence in health care is particularly valuable because "addressing migrant health is a necessary precondition to full realization of the benefits of migration for those who migrate and for both countries of origin and destination" (WHO, 2010, p. 55).

Historically, these challenges remain largely unaddressed in medical and public-health education (Rashid, Cervantes, and Goez, 2020, p. 476; Koehn and Swick, 2006) as well as in preparation for humanitarian emergencies. However, a recent scoping review identified "increasing interest among educators in developing educational opportunities for medical students to gain more training" in refugee health (Rashid, Cervantes, and Goez, 2020, p. 476). While medical schools and public-health programs move slowly forward, *Migrant Health and Resilience: Transnational Competence in Conflict and Climate Displacement Situations* aims to fill the urgent field-training gap.

Applications of Theory of Change

In our suggested approach to bringing about transformative change, formative research is linked to competency gaps, training approaches, and outcome and impact evaluation. Theory of change involves a conceptualization or design of an intervention that "specifies a chain of causal assumptions that link inputs, processes, outputs and ultimate results, account for preconditioning factors and unforeseen events that … very often have determining effects on the ultimate outcomes and impacts" (Nilsson, 2012, p. 51). The initial application of the theory-of-change method identifies key elements and assumed chains of causality that lead directly or indirectly to attaining overall objectives (Zint, 2011, p. 336) and to the enhanced and sustained benefits intended for all participants.

Backward Mapping

The backward-design method required for developing a theory of change is where TC development needs and context-specific training/learning approaches are first identified. This leads us to integrate the theory-of-change method elaborated in Chapter 4 with TC development applications that simultaneously are linked to evaluation planning.

Richard Hummelbrunner (2012, pp. 262–263; also pp. 254–255) suggests that quickly elaborated impact diagrams offer a useful tool for clarifying "impact-creating processes" and understanding of "expected effects and the ways to achieve them." In addition, there are theory-based approaches that enable participants to evaluate in a prospective manner what would need to happen in the broader landscape for an intervention to contribute to a tangible impact after it has been completed and the immediate outcomes have been evaluated (Vaessen and Todd, 2008).

Outcome and Impact Evaluations

Evaluators recognize that outcomes and impacts will be contextual rather than uniform. Fragility and conflict affect intervention performance in distinct and concrete ways (GEF IEO, 2021). At the summative stage, evaluators look for evidence of indirect and direct impacts. How plausible is it that specific interventions contributed to observed TC outcomes and sustainable development impacts? How likely is it that the impact would have occurred or would have occurred in a slower way without the intervention (Zazueta and Negi, 2014)? Ultimately, the vital evaluation question becomes: did anticipated links among intervention drivers and outcomes and impacts remain valid and in effect during implementation (Hummelbrunner, 2012, pp. 254, 263)? It also is important to account for any unintended consequences of the intervention (Nanthikesan and Uitto, 2012).

While individual capability outcomes constitute the critical consideration in TC evaluations, the big picture also is factored in. Formative and summative evaluations of stakeholder assets and deficiencies, the prevailing distribution of power and authority, along with outcomes and impacts, are essential. TC evaluators remain aware of the need to address both individual and policy-level changes.

The Structure of the Book

As action sites where "different ways of doing things meet" (Migdal, 2004, pp. 6, 23), boundary interfaces often involve uncertainty, tension, and creative opportunity. Solidarity across boundaries emerges as a potent potential force for change (Upshur, Benatar, and Pinto, 2013, pp. 30–32). Chapter 1 ("Transnational Competence: Vision and Value") affirms the potential role of TC in rectifying the personal losses that accompany spatial displacement and advancing prospects that "the 'native' and the 'alien' may come to balance relations of hospitality and hostility and recognize a political solidarity in shared experiences, interest and goals" (Fisher, 2016). This analysis highlights the importance of TC preparation for *all* players involved in humanitarian relocation processes. In addition to elaborating the basic TC framework, the aim of this chapter is to establish its visionary value for training persons dislocated by armed conflict, persecution, and climate-change impacts as well as their care contributors.

Chapter 2 ("Conflict-Displaced Migration: Drivers, Context, Stakeholders, and Needs") focuses on the conditions that refugees and other conflict-induced transnational migrants encounter in camps and informal settlements in the Global South. Health conditions feature in our analysis. In the context of conflict-displaced migration, we identify key care-providers, including international organizations, local and transnational NGOs, spontaneous responders, national and subnational governments, hosts, and migrant community members.

Chapter 3 ("Climate-Displaced Migration: Drivers, Context, Stakeholders, and Needs") provides key contextual details regarding climate-induced transnational and internal displacements. Here, we identify unfolding drivers and distinguish climate-migration conditions, with a focus on health challenges. We also identify key responders, including international organizations, local and transnational NGOs, national and subnational governments, and host community members along with climate-displaced persons and those particularly vulnerable to climate displacement.

Chapter 4 ("TC Development for Population Displacement Needs") applies needs assessment with specific reference to the diverse stakeholders affected by or responding to population displacement. Specifically, we distinguish conflict-displacement and climate-displacement stakeholders by existing skill deficiencies and relevant training-background characteristics. Our treatment establishes the link between formative research, needs assessment (with specific reference to the diverse stakeholders affected by or responding to population displacement), and elaboration of a theory of change at individual TC and grassroots levels. Identifying assets[31] and deficiencies along with intended training outcomes and impacts by applying theory-of-change methods opens up pathways to promising skill development interventions. Intended TC development *outcomes* are:

1   to equip humanitarian responders with TC skill sets relevant for assisting dislocated persons who possess diverse nationality and ethnic backgrounds;
2   to equip dislocated persons with TC skill sets relevant for advancing personal/family integration and health promotion in a new location and for contributing to local adaptation and sustainable development;
3   to ensure that initiated TC training programs incorporate lessons learned and become self-sustaining.

Intended TC development *impacts* are:

1   dislocated individuals/families use their new transnational competencies to enhance resilience/health and achieve integration and belonging in a new location;
2   dislocated individuals/families use their new transnational competencies to contribute to health promotion, adaptation, and sustainable development;
3   humanitarian responders use their new transnational competencies to advocate successfully for policy changes that mitigate persecution, conflict-induced migration, or climate-generated dislocations.

The core of the book's contribution centers on specific, adaptable, and feasible TC development approaches. Chapters 5 and 6 provide detailed practical suggestions for on-site and remote skill development for providers caring for migrants and for those displaced by armed conflict, persecution, or climatic disruptions. Incorporating insights drawn from field experience, Chapter 5 ("Guidelines for TC Training: Humanitarian Responders") presents designs for adaptable site-based and e-learning TC training programs for conflict- and climate-dislocation responders and Chapter 6 ("Guidelines for TC Training: Displaced Persons and Host Communities") sets forth training guides aimed at equipping persons dislocated by armed conflict, persecution, or climatic events with TC skill sets relevant for advancing personal/family integration and belonging in a new location and for contributing to resilience, adaptation, and sustainable development. In both situations, the pathway to enhanced equity and inclusion for those displaced must incorporate strategic advocacy, and a functional transnational competence (see, for instance, Pottie and Gruner, 2016, pp. 337–339).

In these training efforts, transnational learning networks, local communities of practice, and "learning organisations with a global outlook in low- and middle-income countries can be effective boundary-spanners, and need to be supported" (Sheikh, Schneider, Agyepong, Lehmann, and Gilson, 2016). Thus, both chapters identify evidence-based digital resources that are useful and available for remote support and continuous TC learning. Free and secure, WhatsApp initially became "the lingua franca among people who, whether by choice or force, have left their homes for the unknown" (Manjoo, 2016, p. B1). By 2021, however, WhatsApp became a disputable source of communication due to changes in encryption. Many NGOs opted to use alternative tools (e.g., Signal) instead.

An adaptable TC assessment scheme centered on outcomes and impacts at individual and grassroots levels, along with recommendations on the process of evaluation for conducting tailored TC development and TC e-learning outcome and impact evaluations (also see Galleli, Hourneaux, and Munck, 2019), constitutes the core contribution of Chapter 7 ("Framework for Evaluating Conflict- and Climate-Displaced TC Development and Impacts"). The initially developed theory of change forms the basis for final evaluation. At this point, theory-of-change assumptions (e.g., how risk and opportunity perceptions changed; how available resources changed approaches, outcomes, and impacts) are tested. Did project leaders make decisions informed by theory of change all along the way?[32]

With regard to conflict- and climate-induced migration, young, emerging, and Indigenous evaluators are needed to inspire and complement the approaches of internationally recognized evaluation specialists (see Rishko-Porcescu, 2018, pp. 307–309). Developing climatic-transformative evaluation capabilities will require concerted effort on the part of institutions of higher learning along with face-to-face, on-line, and blended training modules, webinars, blogs, and conferences (ibid., p. 309).

The concluding chapter, Chapter 8 ("Ways TC Development Can Improve Resettlement Outcomes and Impacts") anticipates continued internal and transnational displacement and health crises generated by armed conflicts, climate disruptions, and pandemics. Here, we focus on envisioning the future, with particular attention to outcomes and impacts. The health, resilience, and welfare of dislocated people will depend on carefully planned and properly supported approaches to resettlement (Cyril and Renzaho, 2016, pp. 231–232) that feature TC preparation. The concluding contribution emphasizes the need to "integrate migration policies and the role of migrants, their communities and diasporas, into development strategies" (Ionesco, Mokhnacheva, and Gemenne, 2017, p. 95). Proactive policy and partnering initiatives need to engage the drivers of transnational human mobility and the resulting conditions. Coordinated, adaptive approaches, informed by TC and suited for humanitarian responders, for physical and mental health-care providers, for hosts, and for migrants themselves are required. For maximum effectiveness in terms of desired outcomes and impacts, TC development will need to incorporate certain essential core elements and, at the same time, "recognize [and reflect] the complexity and heterogeneity of migration – in terms of motivating factors and diversity in duration and destinations and in the demographic and socio-economic characteristics of migrants" (McMichael, Barnett, and McMichael, 2012, p. 650).

Notes

1 https://www.unhcr.org/60b638e37/unhcr-global-trends-2020
2 Phillip Cole (2020, pp. 214–215) presents a strong argument that "the word 'forced' is unnecessary as the idea of 'displacement' already contains it." Not mandating 'forced' in the definition allows for recognition of degrees of migrant agency over mobility (why, when, where, and how) and for anticipatory movements.
3 Within four months of Russia's invasion, "5.2 million refugees from Ukraine were recorded across Europe, one of the biggest mass displacements since World War II … Central and Eastern Europe … [hosted] a disproportionate share of newcomers compared with relatively wealthy Western Europe" (Rauhala, Ledur, and Aries, 2022). According to the International Organization for Migration, the conflict had internally displaced at least another 6 million Ukrainians by mid-2022 (Stern, 2022).
4 Two-thirds came from five countries: Syria, Venezuela, Afghanistan, South Sudan, and Myanmar (Hassan and Westfall, 2022).
5 The international community, T. Alexander Aleinikoff and Susan Martin (2022, pp. 6, 47; also pp. 5–6, 25, 40) conclude, have "constructed a landscape of silos" and "no coherent structure for global governance … currently exists" that would "identify gaps and overlaps," explore "synergies and efficiencies," and coordinate

> [the] six policy and operational sectors that are engaged in work related to environmental mobility: (1) climate change and environmental degradation; (2) disaster risk reduction; (3) migration and displacement; (4) development; (5) human rights; and (6) conflict resolution, peace-building and security.

> To fill this vacuum, they advocate creation of a non-operational, policy-focused "multi-stakeholder platform, accompanied by a multi-donor trust fund to carry out platform functions," encompassing the continuum of "prevention, response, and solution" (ibid., p. 3; also see pp. 43, 46–47 for details). At the national level, increased U.S. interagency coordination in the interests of advancing a "holistic view" also is a principal recommendation of the White House's *Report on the Impact of Climate Change on Migration* (2021, pp. 6, 30).

6 Peter Hoffman (2021, pp. 121, 131) maintains, however, that "the SDGs did not address deficiencies in humanitarianism" and that "humanitarianism and development have differed over the client; for development, it has been governments, but for humanitarianism, it has been the people."
7 The non-binding New York Declaration, endorsed unanimously by the U.N. General Assembly in 2016, engages member states in "a new approach to respond to the needs of refugees and host communities, primarily by reinforcing the connections between humanitarian and development approaches" (Milner, 2021, p. 422). Through the Declaration, U.N. member states agreed to provide "humanitarian financing that is adequate, flexible, predictable and consistent, to enable host countries and communities to respond both to the immediate humanitarian needs and to their longer-term development needs" (ibid.). It further calls for "mainstreaming migration in national plans for development … [and] humanitarian assistance" (Micinski, 2021, p. 142).
8 Including "'recognition of foreign qualifications'" and "integrating migration into development planning at local, national, regional, and global levels," (ibid., pp. 143–144), climate-change-disaster preparedness, and "strengthening collaboration between humanitarian and development actors to address longer-term resilience and coping capacities" (Aleinikoff and Martin, 2022, p. 13).

9　The Global Compact on Refugees, affirmed by the U.N. General Assembly in December 2018, centers on "a close and complementary relationship between humanitarian and development actors ... along with a greater role for refugees themselves in the planning and implementation of new programming" (Milner, 2021, p. 424). On the status and impact of the "soft" (i.e., non-binding) international law embodied in the Global Compacts, see Hilpold (2020).

10　Civil-military cooperation in health and humanitarian responses in the wake of natural disasters, including climate-induced situations, is widely accepted. However, even "last resort" and independent military assistance in conflict-provoked displacements is "complicated" and "controversial" and carries heightened risks for humanitarian aid workers. In both cases, military providers are not positioned to undertake sustainable-development initiatives and are unlikely to be prepared with TC without additional training (see Kamradt-Scott and Smith, 2020).

11　Today's transnationals, including those who stay behind, operate "within a social field spanning multiple and interrelated scales including the local, national, regional, and the global in contrast to existing only in bounded nation-states" (Ozkazanc-Pan, 2019, p. 21).

12　This charge includes co-training by NGOs and universities (Walker, Hein, Russ, Bertleff, and Caspersz, 2010, p. 2225). On the value of integrating emergency management training into university public-administration education in ways that would develop the competencies of future humanitarian responders, see Hu and Zhang (2020). A June 16, 2021 webinar sponsored by the Refugee Studies Center at Oxford University featured practice guidance for *co*-producing research among academics, non-governmental responders, and community members.

13　We recognize that, given the proliferation of specific-purpose training, the case for generic competence must be compelling in order to overcome "reluctance within the humanitarian sector" to embrace "standards or overarching requirements" (Walker, Hein, Russ, Bertleff, and Caspersz, 2010, p. 2225).

14　While interchangeable, we prefer the term "transnational" to "international" in the context of migration in recognition of the fluidity of population movements and the "connectivity between migrants and non-migrants across national borders" (Faist, Fauser, and Reisenauer, 2013, p. 2).

15　Susan Martin, et al. (2021, p. 144) remind humanitarian care-providers, policy-makers, and researchers not to ignore "forced immobility": "the most vulnerable groups too often have the fewest opportunities to adapt locally or move away from risk." Fortunately, in health and other behavioral arenas, maintaining transnational connection with migrants, particularly those who gain insights and develop new skills, can benefit "non-mobile" family members and friends (Villa-Torres, et al., 2017, p. 71).

16　In 2018, countries in Sub-Saharan Africa accounted for "eight of the ten fastest growing international migrant populations" (Connor, 2018).

17　On tourism-induced displacement, see Hashimoto, Harkonen, and Nkyi (2021, pp. 160–164).

18　The situation of captured ISIS followers, including tens of thousands of affiliated women and children, presents special challenges. Imprisoned former ISIS fighters are apt to radicalize other prisoners. Once "violent zealots" have been separated from "reluctant accessories" and nonparticipants, preparation for societal reintegration along with tailored de-radicalization can proceed. In this context, training programs should emphasize children (see Yee, 2019).

19　Beginning in April 2020, state-imposed COVID-related travel restrictions and border closures restricted transnational migration (Meer, Hill, Peace, and Villegas, 2021, pp. 864–865).

20　Ukraine Emergency: Aid, Statistics and News | USA for UNHCR (www.unrefu gees.org) (accessed May 24, 2022).

21 Danilo Mandic (2021, pp. 4, 27) maintains that migration theory has neglected "the particular state and non-state actors – especially foreign – … that engage in battles, massacres, expulsions, bombings and the like." He adds that refugees "matter because they are manifestations of dynamics of modern warfare, nationalism, revolution and state formation."

22 The challenges arising from mass displacement include caring for nearly 23,000 vulnerable unaccompanied minors from multiple countries in Africa who arrived in Europe in 2016 (Sorensen, 2016) and for children initially separated from their parents on arrival in the USA in 2018 (Shear, Sullivan, and Kanno-Youngs, 2019).

23 https://pewresearch.us1.list-manage.com/track/click?u=434f5d1199912232d416897e4&id=2b05c4bdc0&e=e3bfd228a0 (accessed February 14, 2018).

24 See, for instance, Kitsantonis (2019a).

25 https://refugee-rights.eu/wp-content/uploads/2021/06/RRE_pushbacks-homelessness-and-human-rights-abuses.pdf

26 In northern Uganda, villages have shared communal land with refugees (mainly from South Sudan) and absorbed refugee children into the host school system (Goldstein, 2018; also see Agier, 2011, p. 41).

27 Another study concludes that, at current rates of GHG emissions, coastal flooding will place 204 million people at risk of dislocation by 2050 (Plumer, 2020).

28 The North Carolina coast is subject to some of the most rapid sea-level rise in the world (see Velasquez-Manoff, 2019).

29 Among the most threatened areas, according to a 2019 study, are Shanghai, Ho Chi Minh City, Bangkok, Mumbai, and Basra (Lu and Flavelle, 2019).

30 The Government of Quebec prohibited the rebuilding of homes damaged by 50 percent or more of their value in any area that was inundated by floods in 2017 or 2019 (Flavelle, 2019b).

31 Too often, for instance, the intercultural communication assets of refugees tend to be ignored (Ngai and Koehn, 2002).

32 Interview with J. Douglas Storey, Director, Communication Science & Research, Center for Communication Programs, Bloomberg School of Public Health, Johns Hopkins University, November 22, 2019.

References

Agier, Michel. 2011. *Managing the Undesirables: Refugee Camps and Humanitarian Government*. Cambridge: Polity.

Ahmed, Bayes. 2018. "Who Takes Responsibility for the Climate Refugees?" *International Journal of Climate Change Strategies and Management* 10 (1): 5–26.

Aleinikoff, T. Alexander; and Martin, Susan. 2022. *The Responsibility of the International Community in Situations of Mobility Due to Environmental Events*. Zolberg Institute Working Paper Series 2022–2021. New York: Zolberg Institute on Migration and Mobility, The New School. Published online July 25.

Allahi, Fahimeh. 2021. "The COVID-19 Epidemic and Evaluating the Corresponding Responses to Crisis Management in Refugees: A System Dynamic Approach." *Journal of Humanitarian Logistics and Supply Chain Management* 11 (2): 347–366.

Arias, Adriana G.; and Araluce, Olga A. 2021. "The Impact of the COVID-19 Pandemic on Human Mobility among Vulnerable Groups: Global and Regional Trends." *Journal of Poverty* 25 (7): 567–581.

Bardsley, Douglas K.; and Hugo, Graeme J. 2010. "Migration and Climate Change: Examining Thresholds of Change to Guide Effective Adaptation Decision-Making." *Population and Environment* 32: 238–262.

Beech, Hannah. 2017. "Hands Tied by Old Hope, Diplomats in Myanmar Stay Silent." *New York Times*, October 13, p. A14.

Bell, Erica J. 2010. "Climate Change: What Competencies and Which Medical Education and Training Approaches?" *BMC Medical Education* 10 (31): 1–9.

Berger, Miriam. 2020. "From Kenya to Gaza to Bangladesh, Threat Grows for High-Risk Populations." *Washington Post*, September 3.

Betts, Alexander. 2021. "Refugees: Overcoming Prejudices." *UNESCO Courier*, 4.

Brooks, David. 2018. "It's Not the Economy, Stupid." *New York Times*, November 30, p. A29.

Butros, Deniz; Gyberg, Veronica B.; and Kaijser, Anna. 2021. "Solidarity Versus Security: Exploring Perspectives on Climate Induced Migration in UN and EU Policy." *Environmental Communication* 15 (6): 842–856.

Carballo, Manuel; Smith, Chelsea B.; and Pettersson, Karen. 2008. "Health Challenges." *Forced Migration Review* 31 (October): 32–33.

Cole, Phillip. 2020. "Global Displacement in the 21st Century: Towards an Ethical Framework." *Journal of Global Ethics* 16 (2): 203–219.

Connor, Phillip. 2018. "International Migration from Sub-Saharan Africa Has Grown Dramatically Since 2010." *Pew Research Center Fact Tank*, February 28.

Crisp, Nigel. 2010. *Turning the World Upside Down: The Search for Global Health in the 21st Century*. London: Royal Society of Medicine Press. Cumming-Bruce, Nick. 2019. "Number of Refugees Is Soaring to Records." *New York Times*, June 20, p. A6.

Cyril, Sheila; and Renzaho, Andre M.N. 2016. "Invisible and Suffering: Prolonged and Systematic Detention of Asylum Seekers Living in Substandard Conditions in Greece." In *Globalisation, Migration and Health: Challenges and Opportunities*, edited by Andre M.N. Renzaho. London: Imperial College Press, pp. 207–254.

Davies, Sara. 2010. *Global Politics of Health*. Cambridge: Polity.

Davis, Julie H.; Landler, Mark; and Davenport, Coral. 2016. "Obama on Climate Change: The Trends Are 'Terrifying.'" *New York Times*, September 8.

Dickerson, Caitlin. 2019. "Migrant Children Pay Price as Trump Seeks to Extend Detention: Health Professionals Warn of Trauma." *New York Times*, December 9, p. A12.

Dooley, Ben; Inoue, Makiko; and Yamamitsu, Eimi. 2019. "In Japan, a Grim Reappraisal of Nature's Threat." *New York Times*, October 17, p. A4.

Duggan, Ann. 2008. "A Role for Emergency Humanitarian Aid Organizations in Peace?" In *Peace through Health: How Health Professionals Can Work for a Less Violent World*, edited by Neil Arya and Joanna Santa Barbara. Sterling, VA: Kumarian Press, pp. 287–292.

Eckenwiler, Lisa; and Wild, Verina. 2021. "Refugees and Others Enduring Displacement: Structural Injustice, Health, and Ethical Placemaking." *Journal of Social Philosophy* 52: 234–250.

Edwards, Michael. 1996. "The Getting of Wisdom: Educating the Reflective Practitioner." In *Educating for Real: The Training of Professionals for Development Practice*, edited by Nabeel Hamdi and Amr El-Sherif. London: Intermediate Technology Publications.

Faist, Thomas; Fauser, Margit; and Reisenauer, Eveline. 2013. *Transnational Migration*. Cambridge: Polity.

Finell, Eerika; Tiilikainen, Marja; Jasinskaja-Lahti, Inga; Hasan, Nasteho; and Muthana, Fairuz. 2021. "Lived Experiences Related to the COVID-19 Pandemic among Arabic-, Russian- and Somali-speaking Migrants in Finland." *International Journal of Environmental Research and Public Health* 18 (5): 2601. doi:10.31234/osf.io/o2v7r (accessed March 3, 2021).

Fisher, Jean. 2016. "Migration's Silent Witnesses: Maria Thereza Alves' Seeds of Change." Available at: http://www.jeanfisher.com/migrations-silence-witnesses-maria-thereza-alves-seeds-change/ (accessed December 3, 2016).

Fisher, Max; and Taub, Amanda. 2019. "Trump's Immigration Measures Follow European Example." *New York Times*, July 19, p. A6.

Flahaux, Marie-Laurence; and De Haas, Hein. 2016. "African Migration: Trends, Patterns, Drivers." *Comparative Migration Studies* 4: 1–25.

Flavelle, Christopher. 2019a. "The Food Supply Is at Dire Risk, U.N. Experts Say." *New York Times*, August 8, pp. A1,A7.

Flavelle, Christopher. 2019b. "In U.S., a Struggle to Rebuild: In Canada, an Order to Move." *New York Times*, September 11, pp. A1,A14.

Flavelle, Christopher; and Goodluck, Kalen. 2021. "Native Americans Feel Brunt of Climate Change." *New York Times*, June 28, pp. A1, A14–A15.

Friedman, Thomas L. 2019. "President Trump, Come to Willmar." *New York Times*, May 15, p. A23.

Galleli, Barbara; Hourneaux, Flavio Jr.; and Munck, Luciano. 2019. "Sustainability and Human Competences: A Systematic Literature Review." *Benchmarking: An International Journal* (January): n.p.

GEF IEO. 2021. *Evaluation of GEF Support in Fragile and Conflict-Affected Situations*. Washington, D.C.: Global Environment Facility, Independent Evaluation Office.

Goldstein, Joseph. 2018. "As the Rich Shun Refugees, Uganda Offers Solace." *New York Times*, October 29, p. A4.

Griggs, Troy. 2018. "Sea Is Rising, and the Land Is Sinking." *New York Times*, March 8, p. A20.

Gushulak, Brian; and MacPherson, Douglas W. 2006. "The Basic Principles of Migration Health: Population Mobility and Gaps in Disease Prevalence." *Emerging Themes in Epidemiology* 3 (3). doi:10.1186/1742-7622-3-3.

Hamlin, Rebecca. 2021. *Crossing: How We Label and React to People on the Move*. Stanford, CA: Stanford University Press.

Hashimoto, Atsuko; Harkonen, Elif; and Nkyi, Edward. 2021. *Human Rights Issues in Tourism*. London: Routledge.

Hassan, Jennifer; and Westfall, Sammy. 2022. "Fleeing: Global Displacement at Record High, U.N. Says." *Washington Post*, June 19, p. A21.

Haysom, Simone; Pantuliano, Sara; and Davey, Eleanor. 2012. "Forced Migration in an Urban Context: Relocating the Humanitarian Agenda." In *World Disasters Report 2012*, edited by Roger Zetter. Geneva: International Federation of Red Cross and Red Crescent Societies (IFRC), pp. 113–143.

Heine, Britta; and Petersen, Lorenz. 2008. "Adaptation and Cooperation." *Forced Migration Review* 31 (October): 48–50.

Hilpold, Peter. 2020. "Opening Up a New Chapter of Law-Making in International Law: The Global Compacts on Migration and for Refugees of 2018." *European Law Journal* 26: 226–244.

Hoffman, Peter J. 2021. "What Does 'Leave No One Behind' Mean for Humanitarians?" In *Routledge Handbook on the UN and Development*, edited by Stephen Browne and Thomas G. Weiss. London: Routledge, pp. 121–134.

Hossain, Moazzem; Khan, M. Adil; and Short, Patricia. 2017. "An Overview of South-South Migration: Opportunities, Risks and Policies." In *South-South Migration: Emerging Patterns, Opportunities and Risks*, edited by Patricia Short; Moazzem Hossain' and M. Adil Khan, London: Routledge, pp. 1–10.

Hu, Qian; and Zhang, Haibo. 2020. "Incorporating Emergency Management into Public Administration Education: The Case of China." *Journal of Public Affairs Education* 26 (2): 228–249.

Hummelbrunner, Richard. 2012. "Process Monitoring of Impacts and Its Application in Structural Fund Programmes." In *Governance by Evaluation for Sustainable Development: Institutional Capacities and Learning*, edited by Michal Sedlacko and Andre Martinuzzi. Cheltenham: Edward Elgar, pp. 253–266.

Hyndman, Jennifer; and Giles, Wenona. 2017. *Refugees in Extended Exile: Living on the Edge*. London: Routledge.

Ionesco, Dina; Mokhnacheva, Daria; and Gemenne, François. 2017. *The Atlas of Environmental Migration*. London: Routledge.

Ives, Mike. 2016. "Study Finds Medical Bias Against a Muslim Group." *New York Times*, December 6, p. A6.

Jones, Lynne. 2020. *The Migrant Diaries*. New York: Refuge Press.

Kamara, Joseph; and Renzaho, Andre M.N. 2016. "The Social and Health Dimensions of Refugees and Complex Humanitarian Emergencies." In *Globalisation, Migration and Health: Challenges and Opportunities*, edited by Andre M.N. Renzaho. London: Imperial College Press, pp. 73–122.

Kamradt-Scott, Adam; and Smith, Frank. 2020. "Military Assistance During Health Emergencies." In *The Oxford Handbook of Global Health Politics*, edited by Colin McInnes; Kelley Lee; and Jeremy Youde. Oxford: Oxford University Press, pp. 197–216.

Kaplan, Sarah; and Dennis, Brady. 2021. "In Disastrous Summer, Climate Inaction Lurks." *Washington Post*, July 25, pp. A1,A10.

Kertes, Joseph. 2018. "Second Country." In *The Displaced: Refugee Writers on Refugee Lives*, edited by Viet Thanh Nguyen. New York: Abrams Press, pp. 113–120.

Kirmayer, Laurence J. 2014. "Foreword." In *Refuge and Resilience: Promoting Resilience and Mental Health among Resettled Refugees and Forced Migrants*, edited by Laura Simich and Lisa Andermann. New York: Springer, pp. vii–ix.

Kitroeff, Natalie. 2021. "Stay or Go? Storms Were a Tipping Point for Many Hondurans." *New York Times*, April 7, pp. A1,A11.

Kitsantonis, Niki. 2019a. "Greece Aims to Shutter Notorious Refugee Camps." *New York Times*, November 21, p. A7.

Kitsantonis, Niki. 2019b. "'A Struggle for Survival' in Greek Migrant Camps." *New York Times*, November 1, p. A8.

Klare, Michael T. 2019. *All Hell Breaking Loose: The Pentagon's Perspective on Climate Change*. New York: Metropolitan Books.

Klugman, Jeni. 1999. *Social and Economic Policies to Prevent Complex Humanitarian Emergencies: Lessons from Experience*. Helsinki: UNU World Institute for Development Economic Research.

Koehn, Justin; and Koehn, Jason. 2016. "Beach Volleyball with Refugees: A Testimonial." *Jeanette Rankin Peace Center Newsletter* (Winter/Spring):4.

Koehn, Peter H. 1991. *Refugees from Revolution: U.S. Policy and Third-World Migration*. Boulder, CO: Westview Press.

Koehn, Peter H. 2016. *China Confronts Climate Change: A Bottom-up Perspective.* London: Routledge.

Koehn, Peter H. 2019. *Transnational Mobility and Global Health: Traversing Borders and Boundaries.* London: Routledge.

Koehn, Peter H.; and Rosenau, James N. 2010. *Transnational Competence: Empowering Professional Curricula for Horizon-Rising Challenges.* Boulder, CO: Paradigm Publishers.

Koehn, Peter H.; and Swick, Herbert. 2006. "Medical Education for a Changing World: Moving Beyond Cultural Competence into Transnational Competence." *Academic Medicine* 81, (6): 548–556.Koser, Khalid; and Martin, Susan. 2011. "The Migration-Displacement Nexus." In *The Migration-Displacement Nexus: Patterns, Processes, and Policies,* edited by Khalid Koser and Susan Martin. New York: Berghahn Books, pp. 1–13.

Kulp, Scott A.; and Strauss, Benjamin H. 2019. "New Elevation Data Triple Estimates of Global Vulnerability to Sea-level Rise and Coastal Flooding." *Nature Communications* 10, 4844. doi:10.1038/s41467-019-12808-z.

Larocca, Rachel. 2018. "Montana to Africa: Refugee Health in Missoula." Presentation at The University of Montana, March 7.

Lindley, Anna. 2014. "Exploring Crisis and Migration: Concepts and Issues." In *Crisis and Migration: Critical Perspectives,* edited by Anna Lindley. London: Routledge, pp. 1–23.

Lindley, Anna; and Hammond, Laura. 2014. "Histories and Contemporary Challenges of Crisis and Mobility in Somalia." In *Crisis and Migration: Critical Perspectives,* edited by Anna Lindley. London: Routledge, pp. 46–72.

Lovey, Thibault; O'Keeffe, Paul; and Petignat, Ianis. 2021. "Basic Medical Training for Refugees via Collaborative Blended Learning: Quasi-Experimental Design." *Journal of Medicine Internet Research* 23 (3): 1–14.

Lu, Denise; and Flavelle, Christopher. 2019. "Erased by Rising Seas by 2015." *New York Times,* October 30, p. A6.

Mandic, Danilo. 2021. "What Is the Force of Forced Migration? Diagnosis and Critique of a Conceptual Relativization." *Theory and Society*April: 1–30. doi:10.1007/s11186-021-09446-0.

Manjoo, Farhad. 2016. "A Shared Lifeline for Millions of Migrants." *New York Times,* December 22, pp.B1,B7.

Martin, Susan F.; Bergmann, Jonas; Rigaud, Kanta; and Yameogo, Nadege D. 2021. "Climate Change, Human Mobility, and Development." *Migration Studies* 9 (1): 142–149.

Martin, Susan F.; Davis, Rochelle; Benton, Grace; and Waliany, Zoya. 2017. *Responsibility Sharing for Refugees in the Middle East and North Africa: Perspectives from Policymakers, Stakeholders, Refugees and Internally Displaced Persons.* Report 2017: 8. Stockholm: Delmi, The Migration Studies Delegation.

Matlin, Stephen A.; Depoux, Anneliese; Schutte, Stefanie; Flahault, Antoine; and Saso, Luciano. 2018. "Migrants' and Refugees' Health: Towards an Agenda of Solutions." *Public Health Reviews* 39 (27): 1–50.

Mavroudi, Elizabeth; and Nagel, Caroline. 2016. *Global Migration: Patterns, Processes, and Politics.* London: Routledge.

McInnes, Colin; Lee, Kelley; and Youde, Jeremy. 2020. "Global Health Politics: An Introduction." In *The Oxford Handbook of Global Health Politics,* edited by Colin McInnes; Kelley Lee; and Jeremy Youde. Oxford: Oxford University Press, pp. 1–5.

McMichael, Celia; Barnett, Jon; and McMichael, Anthony J. 2012. "An Ill Wind? Climate Change, Migration, and Health." *Environmental Health Perspectives* 120 (5): 646–654.

Meer, Nasar; Hill, Emma; Peace, Timothy; and Villegas, Leslie. 2021. "Rethinking Refuge in the Time of COVID-19." *Ethnic and Racial Studies* 44 (5): 864–876.

Micinski, Nicholas R. 2021. "Migration and Development in the UN Global Compacts." In *Routledge Handbook on the UN and Development*, edited by Stephen Browne and Thomas G. Weiss. London: Routledge, pp. 135–147.

Migdal, Joel S. 2004. "Mental Maps and Virtual Checkpoints: Struggles to Construct and Maintain State and Social Boundaries." In *Boundaries and Belonging: States and Societies in the Struggle to Shape Identities and Local Practices*, edited by Joel S. Migdal. Cambridge: Cambridge University Press, pp. 3–23.

Milner, James. 2021. "Refugees and International Development Policy and Practice." In *Introduction to International Development: Approaches, Actors, Issues, and Practice*, edited by Paul Haslam; Jessica Shafer; and Pierre Beaudet. Oxford: Oxford University Press, pp. 408–425.

Nanthikesan, Suppiramaniam; and Uitto, Juha I. 2012. "Evaluating Post-Conflict Assistance." In *Assessing and Restoring Natural Resources in Post-Conflict Peacebuilding*, edited by David Jensen and Stephen Lonergan. London: Routledge, pp. 389–408.

Ngai, Phyllis B.; and Koehn, Peter H. 2002. *Organizational Communication in Refugee-Camp Situations*. New Issues in Refugee Research Working Paper No. 71. Geneva: United Nations High Commission for Refugees.

Nguyen, Viet Thanh. 2019. "Introduction." In *The Displaced: Refugee Writers on Refugee Lives*, edited by Viet Thanh Nguyen. New York: Abrams Press, pp. 11–22.

Nilsson, Måns. 2012. "Tools for Learning-Oriented Environmental Appraisal." In *Governance by Evaluation for Sustainable Development: Institutional Capacities and Learning*, edited by Michal Sedlacko and Andre Martinuzzi. Cheltenham: Edward Elgar, pp. 45–60.

Ozkazanc-Pan, Banu. 2019. *Transnational Migration and the New Subjects of Work: Transmigrants, Hybrids and Cosmopolitans*. Bristol: Bristol University Press.

Parodi, Stephen. 2019. "Can Hospitals Survive the Flames?" *New York Times*, November 2, p. A27.

Penney, Veronica. 2020. "5 Ways Climate Is Changing Hurricanes." *New York Times*, November 11, p. A19.

Penttinen, Elina; and Kynsilehto, Anita. 2017. *Gender and Mobility: A Critical Introduction*. London: Rowman & Littlefield.

Pickren, Wade E. 2014. "What Is Resilience and How Does It Relate to the Refugee Experience? Historical and Theoretical Perspectives." In *Refuge and Resilience: Promoting Resilience and Mental Health among Resettled Refugees and Forced Migrants*, edited by Laura Simich and Lisa Andermann. New York: Springer, pp. 1–26.

Pierre-Louis, Kendra. 2019. "Complex Fires Gain Ferocity as Earth Heats: A Look at Hot Spots around the World." *New York Times*, August 29, pp. A1,A8,A9.

Pilkington, F. Beryl; Mbai, Isabella; Mangeni, Judith; and Abuelaish, Izzeldin. 2016. "*An Education Model for Building Health Care Capacity in Protracted Refugee Contexts*." IDRC Policy Brief. Available at: Bher.org/2016/11/04/idrc-policy-brief/ (accessed November 16, 2019).

Pincock, Kate; Betts, Alexander; and Easton-Calabria, Evan. 2020. *The Global Governed? Refugees as Providers of Protection and Assistance*. Cambridge: Cambridge University Press.

Plumer, Brad. 2020. "Storm Surges Amplify Peril of Rising Seas, Study Finds." *New York Times*, July 31, p. B3.

Pottie, Kevin; and Gruner, Doug. 2016. "Health Equity: Evidence-based Guidelines, e-learning and Physician Advocacy for Migrant Populations in Canada." In *Globalisation, Migration and Health: Challenges and Opportunities*, edited by Andre M.N. Renzaho. London: Imperial College Press, pp. 329–343.

Pottie, Kevin; Hui, Chuck; and Schneider, Fabien. 2016. "Women, Children and Men Trapped in Unsafe Corridors." In *Globalisation, Migration and Health: Challenges and Opportunities*, edited by Andre M.N. Renzaho. London: Imperial College Press, pp. 291–303.

Price, Susanna. 2019. "Introduction." In *Country Frameworks for Development Displacement and Resettlement: Reducing Risk, Building Resilience*, edited by Susanna Price and Jane Singer. London: Routledge, pp. 1–24.

Ramsay, Georgina; and Baker, Sally. 2019. "Higher Education and Students from Refugee Backgrounds: A Meta-Scoping Study." *Refugee Survey Quarterly* 38: 55–82.

Rashid, Marghalara; Cervantes, Andrea D.; and Goez, Helly. 2020. "Refugee Health Curriculum in Undergraduate Medical Education (UME): A Scoping Review." *Teaching and Learning in Medicine* 32 (5): 476–485.

Rauhala, Emily; Ledur, Julia; and Aries, Quentin, 2022. "Where Have Ukrainian Refugees Gone?" *Washington Post*, July 3, p. A17.

Rishko-Porcescu, Antonina. 2018. "Building Evaluation Capacities for Evaluation of the SDGs: The Role of Young and Emerging Evaluators." In *People, Planet and Progress in the SDG Era: Proceedings from the National Evaluation Capacities Conference 2017*. New York: Independent Evaluation Office, United Nations Development Programme, pp. 307–312.

Schwartz, John. 2021. "Study Ties 1/3 of Heat Deaths to Climate Change." *New York Times*, June 1.

Sengupta, Somini. 2016. "Record 65 Million People Displaced, U.N. Says." *New York Times*, June 20, p. A3.

Sengupta, Somini. 2018. "Warming, Water Crisis, then Unrest: Iran Fits a Pattern." *New York Times*, January 19, p. A4.

Sengupta, Somini. 2020. "Hotter Planet Already Poses Fatal Threats, Report Finds." *New York Times*, December 3, p. A15.

Sengupta, Somini. 2021. "Crises Forced 40.5 Million from Homes Amid COVID." *New York Times*, May 21, p. A9.

Shear, Michael D.; Sullivan, Eileen; and Kanno-Youngs, Zolan. 2019. "What Will Trump's Tough New Asylum Policy Mean for Migrants on the Border?" *New York Times*, April 17.

Sheikh, Kabir; Schneider, Helen; Agyepong, Irene A.; Lehmann, Uta; and Gilson, Lucy. 2016. "Boundary-Spanning: Reflections on the Practices and Principles of Global Health." *BMJ Global Health* 1. doi:10.1136/bmjgh-2016-000058.

Silove, Derrick; Ventevogel, Peter; and Rees, Susan. 2017. "The Contemporary Refugee Crisis: An Overview of Mental Health Challenges." *World Psychiatry* 16 (2): 130–138.

Solomon, Ben C. 2017. "In Grim Camps, Desperate Scene for Rohingya." *New York Times*, September 30, pp. A1,A11.

Solomon, Gofie. 2016. "*Emigration and Transnational Involvement in the Horn of Africa*." Paper presented at the Annual Meeting of the American Political Science Association, Philadelphia, PA,September 1–4.

Sorensen, Martin S. 2016. "Abuses of Young Refugees in Denmark Mirror Perils across Europe." *New York Times*, December 20, p. A4.

Ssosse, Quentin; Wagner, Johanna; and Hopper, Carina. 2021. "Assessing the Impact of ESD: Methods, Challenges, Results." *Sustainability* 13 (2854): 1–26. doi:10.3390/su13052854.

Stephens, Bret. 2019. "Immigration Policies Worse Than Trump's." *New York Times*, July 6, p. A19.

Stern, David L. 2022. "A Divide Fades." *Washington Post*, July 23, p. A9.Taylor, Peter. 2003. *How to Design a Training Course: A Guide to Participatory Curriculum Development*. London: Continuum.

Teitelbaum, Pamela. 2019. *Pilot Evaluation to Assess the Impact of eLearning on Humanitarian Aid Work: Final Report*. Geneva: Medair, Humanitarian Leadership Academy.

Thompson, Nathan A. 2017. "For Rohingya Refugees in Bangladesh, Soccer is a Joyful Escape." *New York Times*, July 31, p. A9.

Todd, David; and Craig, Rob. 2021. "Assessing Progress towards Impacts in Environmental Programmes Using the Field Review of Outcomes to Impacts Methodology." In *Evaluating Environment in International Development*, 2nd edn, edited by Juha I. Uitto. London: Routledge, pp. 111–136.

Treaster, Joseph B.; and Harmon, Amy. 2019. "'Iffy' Forecasts Add to Anxiousness over Whether to Stay Put or Go." *New York Times*, August 31, p. A12.

Troianovski, Anton. 2021. "As Frozen Land Burns, Siberia Trembles." *New York Times*, July 19, pp. A6–A7.

Troianovski, Anton; and Mooney, Chris. 2019. "Radical Warming in Siberia Leaves Millions on Unstable Ground." *Washington Post*, October 3.

Turner, Simon. 2015. "What Is a Refugee Camp? Explorations of the Limits and Effects of the Camp." *Journal of Refugee Studies* 29 (2): 139–147.

Uitto, Juha I.; and Shaw, Rajib. 2006. "Adaptation to Changing Climate: Promoting Community-based Approaches in the Developing Countries." *SANSAI: An Environmental Journal for the Global Community* 1: 93–107.

Upshur, Ross E.G.; Benatar, Solomon; and Pinto, Andrew D. 2013. "Ethics and Global Health." In *An Introduction to Global Health Ethics*, edited by Andrew D. Pinto and Ross E.G. Upshur. London: Routledge, pp. 16–35.

Vaessen, Jos; and Todd, David. 2008. "Methodological Challenges of Evaluating the Impact of the Global Environment Facility's Biodiversity Program." *Evaluation and Program Planning* 31: 231–240.

Velasquez-Manoff, Moises. 2019. "Stands of Lonely Trees Trace the Insidious Rise of the Sea." *New York Times*, October 9, pp. A14–A15.

Villa-Torres, Laura; Gonzalez-Vazquez, Tonatiuh; Fleming, Paul J.; Gonzalez-Gonzalez, Edgar L.; Infante-Xibille, Cesar; Chavez, Rebecca; and Barrington, Clare. 2017. "Transnationalism and Health: A Systematic Literature Review on the Use of Transnationalism in the Study of the Health Practices and Behaviors of Migrants." *Social Science & Medicine* 183: 70–79.

Von Uexkull, Nina; and Buhaug, Halvard. 2021. "Security Implications of Climate Change: A Decade of Scientific Progress." *Journal of Peace Research* 58 (1): 3–17.

Walker, Peter; Hein, Karen; Russ, Catherine; Bertleff, Greg; and Caspersz, Dan. 2010. "A Blueprint for Professionalizing Humanitarian Assistance." *Health Affairs* 29 (December): 2223–2230.

Wells, Ruth; Lawsin, Catalina; Hunt, Caroline; Youssef, Omar Said; Abujado, Fayzeh; and Steel, Zachary. 2018. "An Ecological Model of Adaptation to

Displacement: Individual, Cultural and Community Factors Affecting Psychological Adjustment among Syrian Refugees in Jordan." *Global Mental Health* 5: 1–13. doi:10.1017/gmh.2018.30.

White House. 2021. *Report on the Impact of Climate Change on Migration.* Washington, D.C.: The White House.

Wong, Edward. 2016. "Wrenching Resettlement in China, with More Likely to Come." *New York Times*, October 25, pp. A1,A10.

WHO (World Health Organization). 2010. "*Health of Migrants: The Way Forward.*" Report of a Global Consultation, Madrid, Spain, March 3–5. Geneva: WHO.

Yee, Vivian. 2019. "To Some, Children of ISIS Are Victims, to Others, They're Risks." *New York Times*, May 9, p. A4.

Zazueta, Aaron; and Negi, Neeraj. 2014. "*Measuring Climate Change and Development Benefits of Project Interventions: Challenges and Prospects.*" Paper presented at the 2nd International Conference on Evaluating Climate Change and Development,GEF Independent Evaluation Office, Washington, D.C., November 4–6.

Zint, Michaela. 2011. "Evaluating Education for Sustainable Development Programs." In *World Trends in Education for Sustainable Development*, edited by Walter L. Filho. Frankfurt: Peter Lang, pp. 329–347.

1 Transnational Competence

Vision and Value

Extending beyond basic intelligence, competence embodies "the individual potential for cognitive and affective response to a specific request or situation; in this sense, the term is close to what is expected in 'real life'" (Ssosse, Wagner, and Hopper, 2021, p. 13). In the disturbed and unsettled migration contexts we are concerned with in this book, competence involves the skills and dispositions to engage effectively and responsibly with arising challenges. When preparing stakeholders for escalating population displacements, why should we privilege "transnational" competence (TC) over its closest conceptual competitors – "global" and "cultural or intercultural" competence?

Terminological Conceptualization

First, we need a term that captures the porous nature of nation-state borders in a time of unparalleled human mobility and interconnectedness. Transnational migration dynamics "cross, alter, transcend, and even transform" today's fluid jurisdictions and boundaries (Khagram and Alvord, 2006, pp. 65–66). In this chapter, we will show why the TC framework best enables the development of skill sets of value to both displaced persons and humanitarian responders.

Limitations of Global Competence

When attached to competence in human interactions, *transnational* is less universalistic than "global;" yet it encompasses more than cultures and states (see Rizvi and Lingard, 2010, p. 31). Since few, if any, individuals interact on a world-wide scale, global competence is neither practicable nor necessary. Although the central aspects of global-competence education overlap with several dimensions of TC, its approach is far less comprehensive. Moreover, global-competence education emphasizes broad global issues and worldviews (Colvin and Edwards, 2018, pp. 5, 8, 10) while TC training and education aim to prepare people for specific, immediate interactions.

Increasingly, human interactions traverse interconnected boundaries, many of which are not primarily culturally defined or globally integrated

DOI: 10.4324/9781003330493-2

(Rizvi and Lingard, 2010, pp. 24–25). Banu Ozkazanc-Pan (2019a, p. 479) adds that such "meaning-making" actions can occur by way of "networks and communications, enabled by technology and multimedia, that are maintained through different stages of migration." Ann Florini and P.J. Simmons (2000, p. 7) also opt for "transnational" rather than "global" in their discussion of border-crossing civil society in recognition of "the fact that rarely are these ties truly global, in the sense of involving groups and individuals from every part of the world."

We need a construct that does not sacrifice attention to the capacity to cross and pivot back and forth along multiple and fluid frontiers in the process of addressing interdependent migration challenges. "Transnational" captures the multiplicity and "super-diversity" (Vertovec, 2010b, pp. 66, 90) of contemporary domestic-foreign boundary exchanges, without requiring global reach.

Limitations of Cultural and Intercultural Competence

The versatility and theoretical power of TC in comparison with CC (cultural competence) are starkly revealed when considered in the context of the medical consultation.[1] In an era of migration, transmigration, and global-local connectivity, many health outcomes are shaped by transnational inter-actions among care providers and recipients who meet in settings where nationality/ethnic match (see Kirmayer, 2012, pp. 151–153) is a foreclosed option (Murdoch-Eaton, Redmond, and Bax, 2011, p. 564). In many huma-nitarian-emergency contexts, responders encounter uprooted persons who are in transition from a multitude of unique nation-state contexts. The journey itself, including the resettlement process (Almoshmosh, Bahloul, Barkil-Oteo, Hassan, and Kirmayer, 2020, p. 22) and beyond, constitutes a "profoundly formative and transformative experience" (Benezer and Zetter, 2015, p. 297; also pp. 302, 307; Ozkazanc-Pan, 2019b, p. 89). Culture-compe-tence education, initially intended for mastery of specific domestic two-culture interactions (Zweifler and Gonzalez, 1998, p. 1058; Taylor, 2003, p. 555; Wear, 2006, pp. 92–93), is of limited utility in the diverse, hybrid, shifting, and trans-nationally demanding emergency-care environment populated by refugees, other forced migrants, and climate-displaced persons who maintain and pivot among a multiplicity and simultaneity of distant and proximate ties (see Villa-Torres, et al., 2017, p. 71; Vertovec, 2010a, p. 6).

In this fluid environment, Robin Cohen and Nicholas Van Hear (2020, p. 20; also see Vertovec, 2010b, pp. 88–89; Rizvi and Lingard, 2010, p. 30), report that:

> Through habituation or conscious choice, migrants are able to combine traces of a diasporic past with contemporary interactions involving host and other migrant communities. The result is a continuous process of hybridization and creolization, the melding, making, and remaking of new [plural] identities.

Ozkazanc-Pan (2019a, p. 483) adds that identities constantly are "nego-tiated during encounters with different places, people and ideas in a trans-national fashion." In Ozkazanc-Pan's (2019b, p. 51; also pp. 52–53) elaboration: "hybrid signifies a new kind of self that arises as a result of the distinct context, experiences, and set of social and material practices that a person engages in to understand themselves and those around them." Since influential interactions for migrants can be virtual as well as proximate, hybridity often is "forged across space and place" through one's unique "transnationally informed" connections and networks. Consequently, "hybrid selves form differently even if facing the same set of ['locally groun-ded'] circumstances and conditions" (ibid., pp. 51–52; also p. 116). In most cases, nevertheless, context remains "an important and differentiating factor in how hybrid selves come to form" (ibid., p. 53). Further, "identity con-struction is never complete" and "addition is the overwhelmingly popular choice" (Cohen and Van Hear, 2020, p. 21).

Income, education, occupation, and wealth differences, along with the multidimensional nature of human experience, also generate considerable intragroup variation and "multiple and overlapping belongings" (Rizvi and Beech, 2020, p. 131). Consequently, in individual emergency care encoun-ters, responders are confronted by the dynamic interplay with culture of gender, chosen lifestyles, and engagements (Cohen and Van Hear, 2020, pp. 20–21), socio-economic status, past and present living and environmental conditions, education, political position and events, discrimination/persecu-tion, and transborder connections. Thus, "targeting social determinants of health" offers "a more persuasive and evidence-based strategy for eliminating health disparities than cultural competence or cultural congruence" (Powell, 2016, p. 6; also pp. 7, 9).[2]

Migrant variability means that the single-dimension and standardized-list approach to diagnosis and treatment associated with CC approaches is pro-blematic (Kirmayer, 2012, pp. 150, 153, 155; Sears, 2012, pp. 546, 550). By focusing on a lengthy and elaborate list of presumably internally homo-geneous, static, and timeless culture-specific characteristics (Hirsch, 2003, p. 239; Ozkazanc-Pan, 2019b, p. 53), "groups of people are often essentialized, lumped together, all of their members possessing traits unilaterally" (Wear, 2003, pp. 550–551; also Duffy, 2001, pp. 487–491; Kirmayer, 2012, p. 160).[3] Among other gaps, recipes of cultural characteristics miss the complexity and diversity of perspectives and behaviors that exist *within* ethnic groups due to mixed origins and migration experiences, class differences, unique backgrounds, the extent of sustained transnational association and partici-pation (Rosenau, 1992, p. 28; Warriner, 2021, p. 53),[4] and hybrid-identity formation (Kirmayer, 2012, pp. 154–155). Indeed, "for many people, fixed ascribed identities (ethnic, racial, gendered, religious, or national) are increasingly seen as irritating, irrelevant, or even oppressive" (Cohen and Van Hear, 2020, p. 20).

In today's interconnected and interactive world, interpersonal diversity only can be fully appreciated in the context of the transnational spaces, social fields, and mobile subjectivities (Ozkazanc-Pan, 2019b, pp. 20, 39–40) that shape, sustain, elaborate, modify, and transform identities. Transnational migration, in particular, involves traversing "the boundaries of 'us' versus 'them'" as well as crossing jurisdictional boundaries (Chee and Jakubiak, 2020, p. 119; also Warriner, 2021, p. 53). Rather than referencing cultural lists and centering on static descriptions of ethnic identity, then, the most promising emergency-care approaches focus on ethnographic inquiry regarding experiential influences (Anghel and Grierson, 2020, p. 489),[5] intersections with power relations (Ozkazanc-Pan, 2019b, p. 39; Pon, 2009, pp. 60–61), opportunities to access resources, and socio-economic status. Jennifer Hirsch (2003, p. 242) ascertains that "the most problematic aspect of the cultural competence paradigm is that it reifies racial and ethnic differences as the key explanatory variables to which we must attend and reduces the salience of social class factors" (also see Fuller, 2002, p. 200; Merryfield and Wilson, 2005, p. 61).

Attention needs to focus on the vagaries of individual cultural/subcultural/blended-culture orientations, on unrecognized commonalities as well as subtle differences, and on building cross-border interpersonal alliances that are sufficiently powerful to transform the conditions that underlie poor health and suffering (Hirsch, 2003, p. 238; Wear, 2006, p. 95). These demands for versatile skills require an approach to diversity competence that moves beyond cultural, or intercultural, training (Fohrer, Erne, and Finlay, 2019, p. 7; Frenk, et al., 2010, p. 1954; Hanesova and Theodoulides, 2022, p. 36; Matlin, Depoux, Schutte, Flahault, and Saso, 2018, pp. 23, 43) – no less "mastery" (Pon, 2009, pp. 65, 69). A more holistic framework of skill development and application that is multidimensional, multifunctional, and interdisciplinary is needed for complex humanitarian and sustainable development circumstances (Trad, 2019, p. 295; Hanesova and Theodoulides, 2022, p. 21) as well as for medical education (see Koehn and Rosenau, 2010, p. 7).[6]

The TC Framework

The earliest published resource highlighting the term "transnational competence" appeared in a 1997 volume issued as an Institute of International Education (IIE) Research Report. The report, titled *Towards Transnational Competence: Rethinking International Education (A U.S.-Japan Case Study)*, was prepared by the Task Force for Transnational Competence with support from the U.S.-Japan Foundation. The narrow focus of the IIE report, and the edited book published three years later (Hawkins and Cummings, 2000), is on ways to improve "international education" in the United States and Japan (Task Force for Transnational Competence, 1997, p. 9). Task Force members recognized that "education in the future will need to place greater emphasis" on TC.[7] The Task Force's capsule description of TC's "core elements" touched on analytic, creative, and communicative abilities as well as on technical skills (ibid., pp. 5–6; Cummings, 2000, p. 8). However, this interesting initiative was short-lived.[8]

In 2002, Peter Koehn and the late James Rosenau published an independently constructed comprehensive TC framework based on cross-disciplinary meta-analysis (Koehn and Rosenau, 2002). Their inclusive vision of transnational competence, which provides the foundation for the TC applications encountered in this book, is fundamentally a transactional one. Individual competence enables the development and application of collective competence on an organizational basis (Galleli, Hourneaux, and Munck, 2019) in both local and distant contexts. Transnational capability, then, is expressed (or not expressed) in human encounters; specifically, in face-to-face and virtual interpersonal interactions and collaborations. Importantly, moreover, acquiring TC is "open to all people no matter what ethnic, political, or social backgrounds they have" (Fohrer, Erne, and Finlay, 2019, p.7; also p. 15 regarding any age).

Transnational competence places priority on *skill* acquisition and application; that is, "what you do" (Trompenaars and Wooliams, 2009, p. 440), for what ends, and with what consequences (Rizvi and Lingard, 2010, p. 176). In the holistic TC conceptualization that guides the skill development approach set forth in *Migrant Health and Resilience: Transnational Competence in Conflict and Climate Displacement Situations*, transnational competence involves the design of education and training initiatives aimed at developing sets of five clearly differentiated capabilities: analytic, emotional, creative/imaginative, communicative, and functional.[9] These skill sets are presented in outline form in Box 1.1. The sections of this chapter that follow elaborate on the explicitly transboundary dimensions of each skill domain that enable application in the contexts of displacement and migration (Matlin, et al., 2018, p. 45).

Box 1.1 Dimensions of Transnational Competence

Analytic Competence

- Ability to achieve a reasonably complete understanding of the central beliefs, values, practices, and paradoxes of counterpart culture(s) and society(societies) – including political and ethnic awareness
- Ability to link needs and conditions in new settings to one's own circumstances and vice versa
- Ability to discern risks and benefits and to assess complex alternative socio-technical paths
- Ability to discern effective transboundary interaction strategies and to learn from past successes and failures

Emotional Competence

- Motivation and ability to open oneself up continuously to divergent cultural influences and experiences
- Ability to assume genuine interest in, and to maintain respect for, different values, traditions, experiences, feelings, and challenges
- Ability to comprehend emotional messages conveyed by people with vastly different backgrounds
- Ability to manage multiple identities
- Sense of transboundary efficacy

Creative/Imaginative Competence

- Ability to foresee and exploit the synergistic potential of diverse group perspectives in collective problem solving
- Collaborative ability to articulate novel and shared transboundary syntheses
- Ability to envision viable mutually acceptable alternatives
- Ability to tap into diverse cultural sources for inspiration

Communicative Competence

- Proficiency in and use of counterparts' spoken/written language
- Skill in interpretation and in using an interpreter
- Proficiency in and relaxed use of interculturally appropriate nonverbal cues and codes
- Ability to listen to and discern different and unfamiliar messages
- Ability to engage in meaningful transboundary dialogues; to facilitate mutual self-disclosure
- Contextual ability to avoid and resolve communication misunderstandings across diverse communication styles

Functional (Project/Task) Competence

- Ability to relate to counterpart(s) and to develop and maintain positive and trusting interpersonal relationships
- Ability to apply/adapt procedural insights, empathy, and imagination in transboundary interactions
- Flexible ability to employ extensive and complex range of accommodative organizational strategies and interaction paths
- Ability to overcome problems/conflicts and accomplish immediate and transformative goals when dealing with transnational and transboundary challenges and globalization/localization pressures
- Ability to build and activate professional and societal resources that mitigate socio-economic inequities, power differentials, exclusionary policies, and other institutionalized constraints

Analytic Competence

Skill in processing multi-source information (Keraly and Gering, 2021) is a prerequisite for analytic competence. In this connection, "mere 'declarative' knowledge (that relating to facts and data) is not sufficient to promote change" (Ssosse, Wagner, and Hopper, 2021, p. 13). Also central to analytic TC are probing, reflecting, and converting information into usable social understanding,[10] reasoning, and action. In the context of massive displacements, effective humanitarian responders are T-shaped professionals who bring depth of disciplinary insight crossed with breadth of transdisciplinary analytic skills (Enders and de Weert, 2009, p. 262).

The skills-first nature of TC is particularly important in understanding the facilitative promise of analytic competence. Among professionals, including emergency responders, analytic competence primarily involves developing the *ability to search for, locate, select, assemble, organize, process, interpret, synthesize, critically assess, and apply relevant and reliable generic and context-specific knowledge, data, ethical expectations, and rules* (see Ping, 2003; Frenk, et al., 2010, p. 1952; Hanesova and Theodoulides, 2022, pp. 31, 40). The paramount objective of transnational analytic preparation is mastering the procedural knowledge (Ssosse, Wagner, and Hopper, 2021, p. 13) and tools that provide access to a reliable repository of concepts and useful procedural insights that illuminate previously unfamiliar circumstances.

Transnational analytic competence includes the process of *acquiring a reasonably complete understanding of the complex beliefs, values, practices, and paradoxes of interface individuals, groups, networks, and communities along with the ability to render individually accurate attributions of interpersonal behavior.* Analytic TC moves beyond exclusive reliance on cultural analysis (Gregg and Saha, 2006, p. 546) to include awareness of additional interests/concerns and "areas for potential cross-identity cooperation" (Maynard, 1999, pp. 164–165). As Merry Merryfield (2001, p. 266; 2002, p. 19) has shown, developing the habit of identifying, discriminating amongst, consulting, comparing, linking, and evaluating diverse perspectives and indigenous sources of information is crucial in these analytic processes.

Transnational analytic skills are further enhanced by systematic capacity to *comprehend the interacting economic, political, historical, scientific, and cultural forces behind global and local dynamics and benefits and costs at subnational, national, supranational, and transnational levels.* The transnationally competent graduate also possesses the ability to analyze how the intersection of local, national, and international opportunities and constraints influences his/her role in contributing to and shaping the challenges of migrant well-being and sustainable development (also see Hanesova and Theodoulides, 2022, pp. 29, 37, 39).

In transnational humanitarian-care interactions involving migrants, accurate needs assessments are crucial (Walker, Hein, Russ, Bertleff, and Caspersz, 2010, p. 2227). The ability to *grasp unfamiliar, ambiguous, and unstable resettlement settings, operations, and underlying dynamics* is essential in this connection (Anghel and Grierson, 2020, p. 489). In such situations, "successful players benefit from knowing who the key people are ... knowing the local rules that apply to their activities, and having an understanding of local negotiating practices" (Cummings, 2000, p. 8).[11] Valuable analytic abilities include critical thinking (Ssosse, Wagner, and Hopper, 2021, p. 14), "alertness to the political consequences of behavior in everyday work and social settings," and skill in analyzing the institutional structure that frames decision-making processes in specific transboundary contexts (Dinges, 1983, p. 178). Analytic skill in developing accurate and reasonably comprehensive understandings of power relationships/imbalances (Kirmayer, 2012, pp. 157–158) and other key contextual determinants of behavior facilitates the transnational competence of emergency responders by reducing prospects for costly and dangerous mistakes due to false assumptions and/or insufficient information, by revealing ignored needs and uncovering opportunities, and by minimizing unrealistic expectations (Maynard, 1999, p. 164; Goleman, 1998, p. 162).

The ability to link unfolding economic, social, technical, environmental, health, and political conditions in the stakeholder's context to one's own circumstances and outcomes (and vice versa) constitutes another analytic skill promoting transnational competence. Migration challenges inherently involve an extraordinary interconnectivity of settings, events (Salzman, 1999, p. 10), processes, and variables. Skillful transnational actors are able to *define, trace, and anticipate the multiple, complex, circuitous, and rapidly evolving connections and reactions among distant developments and proximate conditions and to connect their own actions to transboundary objectives and consequences* (see Ssosse, Wagner, and Hopper, 2021, p. 14).[12]

Transnational analytic competence further involves assessments of alternative technical, political, and cultural paths. The transnational path assessment process begins with the selection and sequential arrangement of relevant features from the transboundary context "for elaborating a course of action" (Connolly and Bruner, 1974, p. 3). Skillful migration-responding actors are able to *identify numerous, detailed, and complex strategic action paths and assess their appropriateness for particular problem-addressing situations.*[13] This skill requires simultaneity of consciousness (that is, being able to sustain and mine multiple complex world-views without collapsing them into simple dichotomies) and simultaneity of place (that is, being simultaneously engaged in knowledge-building and comprehension at virtual sites alongside one's physical location).

Finally, transnational analytic competence involves discerning where, when, and how transboundary collective action can be effective and identifying viable interaction and transaction strategies. In this connection, the skillful humanitarian-emergency responder seeks to *identify and understand the underlying rules, processes, and ethical standards at work in specific collaborative situations and to determine how diverse individuals and organizations are likely to confront new situations and manage long-standing ones.*[14]

Emotional Competence

Emotional competence is a valuable professional resource that draws upon six principal skill dimensions. The first is centered on motivation. Nation-state "transcenders" are distinguished by "their curiosity and willingness to explore the complexities [and benefits] of diversity" (Cortes and Wilkinson, 2009, p. 21). Specifically, the emotionally skillful person possesses the *motivation (even eagerness) continuously to open up and adapt to unfamiliar and ambiguous cultural influences and transboundary experiences.* In the context of displacement, the daily challenge is to hone empathy by actively seeking to hear "people whose voices have been silenced" (Garrett, 2018). This skill also requires "resolve not to run away" that stems from persistence in managing anxiety and frustration (Anderson, 1994, p. 313; Lustig and Koester, 1996, p. 63; Cherniss, 2002, p. 5; Goleman, 1995, pp. xii, 34).

Passion to serve, coupled with humility (i.e., willingness to seek advice, engage in self-reflection, and acknowledge and learn from one's limitations and mistakes), enriches transnational emotional competence. Furthermore, the committed and passionately motivated care provider often is found inspirational by colleagues and laypersons. The capacity to address challenges with passion can contribute "the spice that enhances all other ingredients with greatness" (Seidman, 2007, p. 295; also p. 287).

The ability to assume a *genuine interest in new patterns of language, family life, cuisine, customs, etc., and to maintain respect for a multiplicity of different (including non-mainstream) values, beliefs, traditions, experiences, challenges, and preferred communication styles* comprises a third TC-enhancing emotional skill (Kirmayer, 2012, pp. 158; Walker, et al., 2010, p. 2227Dorgan, Lang, Floyd, and Kemp, 2009, p. 1574; Ssosse, Wagner, and Hopper, 2021, p. 14). The complexity and richness of diversity and hybridity are explored in depth and celebrated (Held, 2002, p. 58; Cortes and Wilkinson, 2009, p. 23). This skill requires recognition that there are many values worth living by (Appiah, 2006. p. 144) and withholding judgmental attributions (biases) based on perceived socio-economic, ethnic, gendered, religious, and/or political differences (Hanesova and Theodoulides, 2022, p. 39). In short, emotionally competent actors are "aware of the limits of their own perspectives and thus value opportunities to see the world through others' eyes" (Landler-Pardo, Elyashiv, Levi-Keren, and Weinberger, 2022, pp. 393–394).

Another dimension of transnational emotional competence involves the ability to *discern unspoken emotional messages conveyed by people with vastly different backgrounds* (Goleman, 1998, pp. 18, 24, 27, 135). One way to conceptualize this talent is as "attunement," or "the ability to enter other minds and learn what they have to offer" (Brooks, 2011). For humanitarian-care providers, this skill centers on empathizing and emotionally connecting with the unique feelings, needs, experiences, motivations, and/or work styles of a diverse set of associates and migrants; that is, "to construct the world as they do and to experience the action tendencies and emotions that they do" (Taft,

1981, p. 82; also Pattee, 2020; Meyer, Johnson, and McCandless, 2022, pp. 353, 356) while "maintaining the essential distinction between self and other" (Landler-Pardo, et al., 2022, p. 391).[15] Even though value change might be an outcome of empathetic understanding, empathy does not require agreement on values or beliefs (Appiah, 2006. p. 78). Moreover, although compassion might (or might not) result from empathetic understanding, empathy "is not an emotional state of feeling sympathetic or sorry for someone" (Coulehan and Block, 1997, p. 27; also Pattee, 2020).[16]

Transnational empathy includes learning to *understand how others with different backgrounds view one's own decision-making process* (Cortes and Wilkinson, 2009, p. 23). Relatedly, forging empathic bridges and connectedness with other people involves recognition that one's "individual as well as collective fate is inextricably linked to that of others" (Cushner, 1998, p. 369; also see Homer-Dixon, 2000, pp. 395–396). Further, persons "who can 'reason from the point of view of others' are better equipped to resolve, and resolve fairly, the challenging transboundary issues that create overlapping communities of fate" (Held, 2002, p. 58)[17] – including stress reduction and enhanced life satisfaction (Salovey, Woolery, and Mayer, 2001, p. 283).

Transnational emotional competence also requires the ability to *manage one's own and others' multiple and fluid identities* (e.g., ethnicity or nationality, religious affiliation, gender, organizational, relational) in particular situations. It is rare for people to present themselves in constant, fixed ways in transboundary relationships, and increasingly easy to move from one identification to another without fear of losing any. The salience and intensity of enacted identities vary across situations, collaborators, and/or time. Boundary-transcending individuals must be skilled at identifying, activating, enriching, and guiding multiple identities in transnational problem-solving situations.

Self-confidence, or a *sense of personal transnational efficacy tempered with humility* (Fohrer, Erne, and Finlay, 2019, pp. 17, 20), constitutes the culminating emotional skill. Transnational self-confidence, which often is developed through perseverance, "involves learning that one can do things with a certain likelihood of success and, moreover, with a fair likelihood of being able to run the course again should one fail" (Connolly and Bruner, 1974, p. 5; also Landler-Pardo, et al., 2022, p. 394). Transnational self-efficacy strengthens the emergency responder's willingness to "take risks and seek out more demanding challenges" (Goleman, 1995, pp. 89–90). To be effective in addressing the many challenges and uncertainties associated with dislocation, threats to physical and mental health, integration, and sustainable development, participants need to be confident that they can bring about change and make a difference in their own socio-cultural context, their counterparts, and/or a mutually understood inter-place, based on shared meanings and procedural understandings that are adapted to, but different from, the other contexts (Weber, 2003, p. 200; Taylor, 2008, p. 91).

Creative/Imaginative Capacity

While imagination is recognized as an important part of everyday life (Appadurai, 1996, pp. 5, 7), its potential transnational implications and applications require special attention. Imagination provides essential fuel for transnational action. The freeing-up of transboundary imaginative capacities is one of the most powerful forces available for responding strategically to the challenging immediate and prolonged conditions associated with forced migration.

Four closely related skill dimensions promote transnational creative/imaginative competence. The first involves the *catalytic ability to foresee and mobilize the synergistic relevance of diverse perspectives* in collective transboundary-problem-solving (Goleman, 1998, p. 27). In a deterritorialized world, "the new power of the imagination ... is inescapably tied up with images, ideas, and opportunities that come from elsewhere" (Appadurai, 1996, p. 54). Diversity provides a "proven way to increase the randomness of concept combinations" (Johansson, 2004, p. 79). After playing Brazilian music and exploring instruments such as the Mongolian *morin khuur*, Yo-Yo Ma's musical performances have become broader and richer, demonstrating the inventive "edge effect" attributable to transboundary encounters (Keller, 2007, pp. B7–B13).[18] David Brooks (2019) refers to this creative process as "harvesting the wisdom embedded in other people's lifeways."

Because variegated perspectives create novel connections, the participation of diverse stakeholders in a common project "often triggers a new way to look at and contend with" problems (Bammer, 2005, p. 6). By expanding the pool of available alternatives, diffusion and diversity enable teams to move beyond blockages or "sticking points" (Page, 2007, pp. 9–10, 16; also Dreifus, 2008, p. D2; He and Berry, 2022, p. 141). Transnationally co-creative actors *learn to reframe problems, to envision alternative resolutions, to advance the envisioning process* (Cortes and Wilkinson, 2009, p. 29), to adapt (Spitzberg and Changnon, 2009, pp. 24, 28–29; Walker, et al., 2010, p. 2224), *to reconcile* (Trompenaars and Wooliams, 2009, pp. 443, 447, 450), and *to leverage the rich potential inherent in multiple-perspective endeavors* (Cummings, 2000, p. 8). The successful mixing and merging of the dissimilar backgrounds and viewpoints of multiple actors is likely to produce collective accomplishments that exceed the sum total of the separate contributions (Moran, Harris, and Moran, 2007, p. 229; He and Berry, 2022, p. 141).

A third creative/imaginative skill dimension is the ability to *articulate novel transnational syntheses and resyntheses of multisource knowledge and aspirations* (Cortes and Wilkinson, 2009, pp. 18, 23) in ways that can be that can be shared. Creative nation-state transcenders are able to inspire and collaborate with counterparts of diverse identities, trainings, and locations in the design and nurturing of previously unimagined and contextually appropriate approaches to new and ambiguous migration challenges (Anghel and Grierson, 2020, p. 488; Hanesova and Theodoulides, 2022, p. 31). They are skilled in envisioning "creative adaptation[s] of global resources to address local priorities" (Frenk, et al., 2010, p. 1952; also Galleli, Hourneaux, and Munck, 2019).

A closely related creative capability is the *continuous ability to (co-)envision new paradigms, unmet needs, viable alternative futures* (Kirmayer, 2014, p. viii; He and Berry, 2022, p. 135), *processes, and roles* that are mutually acceptable among collaborators who possess diverse identities. TC-envisioning skills include maintaining a future orientation, recreating and enriching personal and organizational visions (Cortes and Wilkinson, 2009, p. 18), creative accommodation, resilience through adaptation of "new, hybrid identities" (Kirmayer, 2014, p. vii), and perceiving opportunities for transboundary resource mobilization. What has already been imagined also must be translated into contextually viable action plans. The special challenge facing the transnationally located and engaged individual is to create one's own transformative role when existing role definitions are loosely defined and/or unstable. Creating new role definitions "demands both imagination and an orientation toward the future" (Werdell, 1974, p. 290).

Responders and migrants with the ability to tap into diverse socio-cultural, technical, artistic, and spiritual (Fohrer, Erne, and Finlay, 2019, p. 15; Taylor, 2008, p. 91) sources for inspiration— the fourth creative/imaginative skill – will strengthen and/or reinforce other dimensions of transboundary imagination. By frequenting boundaries where concepts from different fields clash, combine, and intersect with diverse human perspectives and experiences, care providers will be more likely to *perceive synergistic potentials, to envision transnationally acceptable alternatives, and to identify innovative and shared syntheses.* Frans Johansson (2004, pp. 2, 16–17, 20, 22–23, 46–47) calls this place the "Intersection" and refers to the resulting "explosion of remarkable innovations" as "the Medici Effect."[19]

Communicative Facility

Among persons from different ways of life who hold diverse perspectives and value preferences, individual capacities for understanding, empathy, synergy, and collaboration are influenced by the ability to engage in meaningful conversations. As the world shrinks and the stakes expand, the philosopher Kwame Appiah (2006, p. xxi) foresees, "conversations across boundaries can be delightful, or just vexing; what they mainly are, though, is inevitable."

Based primarily on the extensive literature dealing with intercultural communication, five skill dimensions are identified in the transnational-communicative-competence domain. First is *facility in the spoken and written language used by one's counterparts.* This skill, which opens otherwise closed doors along the road to achieving analytic, emotional, imaginative, and functional competency, is most completely actualized by verbal fluency in the others' first language – coupled with "willingness to use it" (Brislin, 1993, p. 215) with emotional power (Goleman, 1998, p. 24).

Beyond English (see Guilherme, 2007), academic researchers and global leaders differ over the necessity of language competence in contemporary transnational interactions. Out of 19 skills rated important for professional success in an international organization, the 135 high-level respondents in the 2003 RAND study ranked "written and oral English language skills" eighth and "foreign language fluency" nineteenth (Bikson, et al., 2003, p. 25).[20] While personal linguistic fluency in another language can be a behavioral asset, achieving it is impractical in transnational situations involving multiple and revolving first languages. Such interactions call for *skill in interpretation and in using an interpreter*. The TC interpreter, moreover, "not only translates but also acts a mediator" who explains underlying perspectives (Adams, Gardiner, and Assefi, 2004, p. 1548). In humanitarian work, it is especially important that interpreters are supported by employers and trained on how to work with traumatized populations as well as how to navigate their own (often ongoing) mental health problems and stresses emerging from serving high-need populations.

Transnationally skillful actors also develop *proficiency in nonverbal-communicative behavior* as well as in interpreting facial expressions, gestures, posturing, use of space, body movement, pace, and other cues (Ngai, 2001). For instance, nonverbally conveying empathic awareness is one particularly useful transnational communicative skill in dislocated contexts (Landler-Pardo, et al., 2022, pp. 394, 400; Alred, 2003, pp. 20–21). This vital skill in dealing with different communication styles often is overlooked in transboundary training and education (Hannigan, 1990, p. 103; Landler-Pardo, et al., 2022, p. 394) and in defusing potential conflict situations (Ting-Toomey, 2009, pp. 100–102; Landler-Pardo, et al., 2022, p. 394). Actors proficient in transnational nonverbal communication typically responds in a calm, confident, and spontaneous manner that is situationally appropriate to the cues and codes embedded in counterpart behavior. When mistakes are made, they are able to recognize signals indicating inappropriate behavior and adjust accordingly (Taft, 1981, pp. 76–77).

Effective transnational communication further requires proficiency in *deep, "open-heart" listening and understanding* (Kirmayer, 2012, pp. 158–159; Landler-Pardo, et al., 2022, pp. 396, 400; Rosen, Digh, Singer, and Phillips, 2000, pp. 98–99). Among migrant-health-care providers, transnational communicative competence includes "the ability to explore patients' perspectives, ideas, concerns, and expectations" (Dorgan, et al., 2009, p. 1574). In the challenging multi-professional environment encountered in humanitarian emergencies, mindful responders need to "listen carefully for team members' feelings and ideas about the three main aspects of team life: the individual members' needs, the group's cohesion, and the task to be accomplished" (Crosby, 1999, p. 65; also Walker, et al., 2010, p. 2227; Ting-Toomey, 2009, p. 104). The level of inter-professional and transnational communicative capability achieved depends, in part, on the extent to which particular individuals discover common "points of entry to cross-cultural conversations" (Appiah, 2006, p. 97) and situationally specific transboundary rules and messages are discerned (Hammick and Anderson, 2009, pp. 210–211).

A final transnational communication skill bears directly on collaborative interactions across influence arenas. The public conversations initiated by transnationally competent actors consist of ongoing reflective dialogues rather than "frozen snapshots" (Wang, 2008, p. 59). The *contextual ability to engage in appropriate and meaningful dialogue, to facilitate mutual self-disclosure, deftly to balance directness and indirectness, and to resolve communication misunderstandings across diverse communication styles* promotes the initiation and sustenance of positive interpersonal relations (see Hecht, Collier, and Ribeau, 1993, pp. 25–28; Spitzberg and Changnon, 2009, p. 20). Among emergency responders, authentic and revealing transnational communication is advanced by *welcoming feedback* from migrants and communities "regardless of its validity or the eloquence with which it is phrased" (Sarkissian, 2009, pp. 172, 207).

Functional (Project/Task) Adroitness

Possession of the above four skill sets does not ensure transnational competence. One "can have the necessary information, be motivated by the appropriate feelings and intentions, and still lack the behavioral skills necessary to achieve competence" (Lustig and Koester, 1996, p. 63). Successful interactions in today's interconnected world also require transnational functional, or operational, expertise (Goodman, 1998, p. vii). As Fohrer, Erne, and Finlay (2019, pp. 18–19) observe, "functional competence is the fundament where all competencies come together, and it is, thus, the root of application/psycho-motoric action."

Transnationally competent individuals are active agents who contribute to and shape operations and outcomes across multiple boundaries and contexts. In general, their actions must be perceived by counterparts with diverse identities as appropriate and valuable for "achieving mutual goals or satisfying the requirements of particular tasks" in specific situations (Dinges, 1983, p. 193). In the migration context, this behavioral challenge requires a final set of six transferable operational skills that underlie effective social and technical problem solving and project/task performance in transboundary situations.

The *ability to relate to stakeholders and to develop and maintain positive interpersonal relationships* grounded in the mutual discovery of common aspirations and shared humanity underlies functional TC.[21] A foundational key to success in building rapport and common ground is the capacity to behave in ways that demonstrate interest in how different people experience the world and interpret events (Lustig and Koester, 1996, pp. 330–331). It is important to recognize that rapport-building does not require common value perspectives or preclude the expression of divergent opinions, behavioral differences, and even critical assessment of aspects of the counterpart's lifeworld.

However, the value of "caring" remains front and center. Caring for stake-holders, place, the environment, and ourselves is a powerful driver underlying united efforts to address migration and health challenges (Hunter, 2021).

Other valuable expressions of the transnational relationship-building skill are:

> a willingness to treat local counterparts as equals and to share work with them, a willingness to spend time on the job and off with local counterparts and to make an effort to get to know the locals and their families, an interest in the local culture, a willingness to learn the local language, an interest in more than just doing the job they came to do, and a lack of concern about differences in race and status.
>
> (Schneider, 1997, p. 11; see also Goleman (1998, pp. 209–210); Holm and Malete (2010, p. A29); Colvin and Edwards (2018, p. 10); Hanesova and Theodoulides (2022, p. 39))

These skill expressions are consistent with the attributes discovered to generate "swift trust" and "deeper trust" by the Emergency Capacity Building project (Ojelay-Surtees, 2007, pp. 7–105; also Fancher, Ton, Meyer, Ho, and Paterniti, 2010, p. 266). The deep trust dimension of functional competence also involves willingness to divulge truths about oneself and/or one's professional life as well as the ability to build trust in ways that diverse others value (Rosen, et al., 2000, p. 98). Interpersonal trust and caring for others stand out as factors accounting for individual behavioral adjustments that reduced the spread of COVID-19 in Australia and elsewhere in the world (Cave, 2022). It is important to bear in mind that "trust is not given once and for all; its continued extension depends on ongoing signs of good will, and any indication of ill will destroys trust irreparably" (Blumczynski and Wilson, 2023, p. 5).

The establishment of positive interpersonal relations is particularly valuable for transnational-functional performance because "in intercultural encounters, overall goodwill, respect, and enthusiasm allow people to generate 'credit,' and their credit allows mistakes to be ignored and forgiven" (Brislin, 1993, p. 215; Goleman, 1998, p. 209). Contrariwise, lack of interpersonal rapport erodes other TC skills – including emotional self-confidence and the ability to comprehend contextual constraints and opportunities. In responder-migrant situations, the ability to engage in personal disclosure (Rosen, et al., 2000, p. 98; Landler-Pardo, et al., 2022, p. 393) facilitates interpersonal and interprofessional rapport.

In addition, successful transnational actors are adept at *nurturing instrumental transboundary relationships, teams, networks, alliances, and partnerships* (Rosen, et al., 2000, p. 281). They are "connectors" who fashion and maintain an exceptionally large number of interpersonal links across diverse systems (Barabasi, 2002, pp. 43, 55–56). They are skilled in initiating and managing positive collaborative undertakings both interprofessionally and "with individuals of highly diverse backgrounds and perhaps even across former conflict lines" (Taylor, 2008, p. 98; also Hanesova and Theodoulides, 2022, p. 33).

Functional adroitness also involves the ability to *apply analytic insights, empathy, imagination, and communicative proficiency* in transboundary collective actions. Skill in attaining desired network outcomes builds on employing high levels of transnational analytic, emotional, creative, and communicative competence for integrated problem-solving (Ssosse, Wagner, and Hopper, 2021, p. 14). For instance, effective "milieu-moving" (Vertovec and Rogers, 1998, p. 8) actors must accurately identify stakeholders, assess sources and levels of power, read multiple and shifting identities, select actions compatible with other participants' context and perspectives (Landler-Pardo, et al., 2022, p. 393), ascertain common objectives, empower trainees, apply effective communication strategies, and appropriately respond to multidimensional and changing situations. The capacity to "leverage diversity" (Goleman, 1998, p. 27) greatly enhances these functional skill sets.

Skillful humanitarian responders possess the ability to *employ an extensive array of transnationally accommodative organizational strategies* – including diverse and satisfying interaction paths and the management of differences between headquarters and project field sites (Dadfar and Gustavsson, 1992, pp. 90–91). Skill in navigating complex local and globally networked channels builds on a high level of transnational analytic competence and is most effective when linked with the capacity to demonstrate flexibility and to improvise when interacting with team and project collaborators through selective application from an expansive repertoire of situationally appropriate actions.

In addition, operational competence requires skill in overcoming technical and social problems, conflicts, and uncertainties along with ability to *ensure the participation of key stakeholders and to achieve collective transformative goals when dealing with transnational challenges* and tensions among globalization and localization pressures (Morrison, 2000, p. 125). Skill in attaining desired project outcomes encompasses the ability to *manage conflict and forge compromises* through cross-boundary negotiation and skill in inter-organizational coordination and cross-functional operations (Marquardt and Berger, 2000, p. 19). At the same time, functionally collaborative responders recognize where the limits of their own professional expertise and TC are reached and those of others kick in (Hammick and Anderson, 2009, p. 213). Functionally TC inter-professional responders recognize when the daunting migrant challenges faced call for multidisciplinary, interdisciplinary, and transdisciplinary collaborations (Gordon, 2009, p. 63).

Finally, in the interest of advancing equity of opportunity and social justice for migrants, transnational functional competence necessitates rigor and vigor in ethics, engagement, and advocacy (also see Meyer, Johnson, and McCandless, 2022, pp. 356, 359; Reimers, 2009, p. A29; Kirmayer, Kronick, and Rousseau, 2018). Foremost within the advocacy skill subset is the *ability to act in ways that advance transformative changes in those domestic and international economic, social, institutional, and legal/policy conditions that produce systematic disparities* that constrain migrant justice and well-being (Fohrer, Erne, and Finlay, 2019, pp. 16–17, 20, 25; Taylor, 2008, p. 91). Practicing the emotional competence of empathy reveals avenues for directing specific actions aimed at sources of suffering (Kramer, 2017, p. B9). Along with skill in issue bundling and policy framing (see, for instance, Koehn, 2008, pp. 62–72), TC trainees learn to build and activate coalitions and collective professional and societal resources that mitigate socio-economic inequities, ecological damage, power differentials, exclusionary policies, and other structural and institutionalized constraints on migrant well-being, integration, belonging, and sustainable development (see Kirmayer, Kronick, and Rousseau, 2018, p. 119; Fohrer, Erne, and Finlay, 2019, p. 14; Hanesova and Theodoulides, 2022, p. 39). Skill in connecting previously unconnected innovators and advocates across sectors and borders is emphasized in TC functional development.

Limitations and Relative Strengths of the TC Framework

Competency – particularly the extensive portfolio of demanding skill sets required for TC – is *relative*, never completely realized, and *contextual* in that successful application is contingent on "both a specific relational context and a particular situational context" (Lustig and Koester, 1996, pp. 57–58). Although the components of transnational-competence preparation aim to facilitate effective functioning in a wide variety of transboundary situations, participating responders and migrants will possess different combinations of analytic, emotional, creative/imaginative, communicative, and functional skills. Like emotional intelligence (Goleman, 1998, p. 25), no one will master all of the skill domains that comprise TC. In Robert Hanvey's terms "any given individual may be rich in certain elements and relatively lacking in others" (2001, p. 217). Many different paths and TC combinations lead to excellence in role performance (Hollenbeck, McCall, and Silzer, 2006, p. 399) and the types and degree of transnational competence required in migration situations will "vary by the nature of the task" (Lambert, 1994, p. 288; also Warriner, 2021, p. 56). To maximize opportunities for beneficial outcomes in each transboundary interaction, however, the training participant's profile of strengths should be spread across all five TC domains and typically include at least two specific skill sets in each domain.

Humanitarian-emergency responders are likely to serve in different and often unanticipated foreign settings over the course of their careers; they cannot assume that their skill strengths are universally transferable from one transboundary context and displacement challenge to another (also see Spitzberg and Changnon, 2009, p. 6). One can be minimally TC in an initial set of transboundary interactions and highly competent in the next (and vice versa). Moreover, each TC skill set is always subject to change, and one's competence profile can expand through learning and adaptation or implode over time due to lack of use and/or faulty direction. Thus, aspirations to become transnationally competent require commitment to a life-long and life-wide learning process sprinkled with a heavy dose of humility (Tervalon and Murray-Garcia, 1998, pp. 117–125) that includes "identification of learning opportunities, overcoming obstacles to successful learning, [and] … reflective thinking about one's own learning processes" (Hanesova and Theodoulides, 2022, p. 40). In short, "the *journey* toward improving personal performance in cross-border situations is the destination" (Fohrer, Erne, and Finlay, 2019, p. 6; emphasis added). Like cosmopolitanism, TC is a dynamic and "performative" disposition; an "ongoing project" that is "always in process of changing as people interact across different contexts" that are both immediate and distant (Rizvi and Beech, 2020, p. 131).

TC in the Pandemic Era

The following chapters specifically address two linked and vital global-health and sustainable-development challenges in the context of forced migration: "how to professionalize a core humanitarian assistance workforce … and how to transcend cultural competence to develop 'transnational' competence" (Greysen, Richards, Coupet, Desai, and Padela, 2013, p. 8). Because TC preparation addresses the multiple skills required by humanitarian-care providers, migrants, and hosts to succeed in forced-migration contexts, we expect that trainees will find transnational competence applications more powerful and rewarding than intercultural-competence applications are when challenged by practical, multidimensional, transboundary interfaces. The TC framework is particularly relevant and inclusive in that it addresses conditions brought about by population movement, multiple identities, porous boundaries, socio-economic divides, and health crises. Adaptable TC preparation also resolves the culture-centered conundrum that has entangled intercultural and CC education by emphasizing diverse and flexible approaches that are transferable to multi-place interactions involving both care providers and migrants, who possess a multiplicity of ethno-cultural, political, economic, and social identities. And, TC development is distinguished by its emphasis on advocacy in addressing institutional and policy inequities rooted in local, national, and international conditions.

One of our challenges in this book is to show how specific transnational competencies can be applied in responding to humanitarian emergencies under pandemic conditions. The world-wide COVID-19 event amplified humanitarian crises and challenged responders who suddenly had to become literate in public health, epidemiology, and online learning (Allahi, 2021, p. 348) in addition to their multiple other responsibilities. Going forward, these circumstances will require the ability to access and process accurate current information and knowledge, sustained service commitment and resilience, on-site and immediate creativity, persuasive communication, rapid decision making, and transnational collaboration among providers, migrants, and host communities. Development of critical TC skill sets for application in the pandemic era will be elaborated in the chapters to follow in the specific contexts of conflict- and climate-induced displacement.

Notes

1 This discussion draws upon Koehn and Swick (2006).
2 Indeed, "the literature on cultural competency has, by and large, not linked cultural competency activities with the outcomes that could be expected to follow from them" (Brach and Fraser, 2000, p. 184; also p. 203).
3 In short, "essentialism is a technique of oversimplification leading to false conclusions" (Fuller, 2002, p. 199).
4 On the latter point, see, for instance, Koehn and Tiilikainen (2007), pp. 2–9.
5 Including inclusion and exclusion (Chee and Jakubiak, 2020, p. 119) and exposure to trauma (Adams, Gardiner, and Assefi, 2004, p. 1548).
6 Lynne Healy (2008, p. 362) cites the same insufficiency of the cultural-competence approach in social work education. A TC framework is needed that incorporates preparing graduates and trainees to serve a diverse set of care receivers *and* to engage the action agenda that is integral to the social justice mission of the social work profession (also see McRell and Grace, 2022).
7 In their 1997 book, the authors refer to transnational competence with the acronym TNC. We prefer TC to avoid confusion with the already widely used TNC in reference to "transnational corporations."
8 The Task Force Coordinator, Education Professor William Cummings at The George Washington University, explained that he moved on to other projects (personal interview with Peter Koehn, November 29, 2007).
9 Bianca Fohrer, Roland Erne, and Graham Finlay (2019, pp. 3, 8, 14, 16, 19) find the TC framework "inclusive," but would add a sixth "transformative" competence. In our view, their important contributions regarding transformative competence fit under the advocacy dimension of TC's functional domain (see below). Also see the largely parallel set of human competencies for sustainability management identified through literature review by Barbara Galleli, et al. (2019, Tables IV and V).
10 That is, "about the aims and intentions of others" (Ssosse, Wagner, and Hopper, 2021, p. 13).
11 Confirmed by J. Douglas Storey, Director, Communication Science and Research, Department of Health, Behavior & Society, Bloomberg School of Public Health, Johns Hopkins University. Interview with Phyllis Ngai and Peter Koehn, November 22, 2019.
12 The ability to prepare for the future in order to navigate in the "Metaverse" environment of automated-information exchanges and avatars (Hanesova and Theodoulides, 2022, p. 31) will be a valuable asset in this connection.
13 Less skillful individuals will evaluate fewer paths in constructing their scenarios and will rely more on "either-or" or "mine-yours" choices (Rosenau and Fagen, 1997, p. 662).
14 Out of 19 skills rated important for professional success in an international organization, the 135 high-level respondents in the 2003 RAND study ranked "general cognitive skills (e.g., problem solving, analytic ability)" first overall, "ability to think in policy and strategy terms" seventh, "substantive knowledge in a technical or professional field" twelfth, "multidisciplinary orientation" thirteenth, and "knowledge of international affairs, geographic area studies" fourteenth (Bikson, et al., 2003, p. 25).

15 Richard Mollica (2006, pp. 223–224) advises that care providers who enter into empathic relationships, "which transfer the pain experienced by the patient into the mind and body of the clinician," need to find ways to practice "self-healing within themselves."

16 Nevertheless, since "compassionless capability can be dangerous," Matthew Hirshberg (2006, pp. 165, 173, 175) persuasively argues, emotional "capability must be balanced with a strong dose of compassion to yield citizens [one could readily include 'professional care providers'] who will make the world a better place."

17 Out of 19 skills rated important for professional success in an international organization, the 135 high-level respondents in the 2003 RAND study ranked "ambiguity tolerance, adaptivity" third, "minority sensitivity" ninth, and "empathy, nonjudgmental perspective" eleventh (Bikson, et al., 2003, p. 25).

18 For examples of other South-to-North innovation diffusions, see Khagram and Levitt (2008, p. 33).

19 Out of 19 skills rated important for professional success in an international organization, the 135 high-level respondents in the 2003 RAND study ranked "innovative, able to take risks" tenth (Bikson, et al., 2003, p. 25).

20 On the relative lack of importance of second-language facility as a reported intercultural competence, see Spitzberg and Changnon (2009, p. 15).

21 Out of 19 skills rated important for professional success in an international organization, the 135 high-level respondents in the 2003 RAND study ranked "interpersonal and relationship skills" second, "the ability to work well in different cultures and with people of different origins" fifth, and "ability to work in teams" sixth (Bikson, et al., 2003, p. 25).

References

Adams, Kristina M.; Gardiner, Lorin D.; and Assefi, Nassim. 2004. "Healthcare Challenges from the Developing World: Post-Immigration Refugee Medicine." *British Medical Journal* 328: 1548–1552.

Allahi, Fahimeh. 2021. "The COVID-19 Epidemic and Evaluating the Corresponding Responses to Crisis Management in Refugees: A System Dynamic Approach." *Journal of Humanitarian Logistics and Supply Chain Management* 11 (2): 347–366.

Almoshmosh, Nadim; Bahloul, Hussam J.; Barkil-Oteo, Andres; Hassan, Ghayda; and Kirmayer, Laurence J. 2020. "Mental Health of Resettled Syrian Refugees: A Practical Cross-cultural Guide for Practitioners." *Journal of Mental Health Training, Education and Practice* 15 (1): 20–32.

Alred, Geof. 2003. "Becoming a 'Better Stranger': A Therapeutic Perspective on Intercultural Experience and/as Education." In *Intercultural Experience and Education*, edited by Geof Alred; Michael Bynam; and Mike Fleming. Clevedon: Multilingual Matters, pp. 14–30.

Anderson, Linda E. 1994. "A New Look at an Old Construct: Cross-cultural Adaptation." *International Journal of Intercultural Relations* 18 (3): 293–328.

Anghel, Roxana; and Grierson, J. 2020. "Addressing Needs in Liminal Space: The Citizen Volunteer Experience and Decision-making in the Unofficial Calais Migrant Camp – Insights for Social Work." *European Journal of Social Work* 23 (3): 486–499.

Appadurai, Arjun. (1996) *Modernity at Large: Cultural Dimensions of Globalization.* Minneapolis, MN: University of Minnesota Press.

Appiah, Kwame A. 2006. *Cosmopolitanism: Ethics in a World of Strangers.* New York: W.W. Norton.

Bammer, Gabriele. 2005. "Integration and Implementation Sciences: Building a New Specialization." *Ecology and Society* 10 (2): 6.

Barabasi, Albert-Laszlo. 2002. *Linked: The New Science of Networks*. Cambridge, MA: Perseus Publishing.

Benezer, Gadi; and Zetter, Roger. 2015. "Searching for Directions: Conceptual and Methodological Challenges in Researching Refugee Journeys." *Journal of Refugee Studies* 28 (1): 297–318.

Bikson, Tora K.; Treverton, Gregory F.; Moini, Joy; and Lindstrom, Gustav. 2003. *New Challenges for International Leadership: Lessons from Organizations with Global Missions*. Santa Monica, CA: RAND.

Blumczynski, Piotr; and Wilson, Steven. 2023. "Are We All in This Together?" In *The Languages of COVID-19: Translational and Multilingual Perspectives on Global Healthcare*, edited by Piotr Blumczynski and Steven Wilson. New York: Routledge, pp. 1–11.

Brach, Cindy; and Fraser, Irene. 2000. "Can Cultural Competency Reduce Racial and Ethnic Health Disparities? A Review and Conceptual Model." *Medical Care Research and Review* 57 (Suppl. 1): 181–217.

Brislin, Richard. 1993. *Understanding Culture's Influence on Behavior*. Fort Worth, TX: Harcourt Brace Jovanovich.

Brooks, David. 2011. "The New Humanism." *New York Times*, March 3, p. A23.

Brooks, David. 2019. "How to Beat Trump on Immigration." *New York Times*, November 8, p. A27.

Cave, Damien. 2022. "Why Australia's Covid Death Rate Is Only One-tenth of U.S. Level." *New York Times*, May 16, pp. A1,A6.

Chee, Wai-Chi; and Jakubiak, Cori. 2020. "The National as Global, the Global as National: Citizenship Education in the Context of Migration and Globalization." *Anthropology and Education* 51 (2): 119–122.

Cherniss, Cary. 2002. "Emotional Intelligence and the Good Community." *American Journal of Community Psychology* 30 (1): 1–10.Cohen, Robin; and Van Hear, Nicholas. 2020. *Refugia: Radical Solutions to Mass Displacement*. London: Routledge.

Colvin, Richard L.; and Edwards, Virginia. 2018. *Teaching for Global Competence in a Rapidly Changing World*. Paris: OECD/New York: Asia Society.

Connolly, Kevin; and Bruner, Jerome. 1974. "Competence: Its Nature and Nurture." In *The Growth of Competence*, edited by Kevin Connolly and Jerome Bruner. London: Academic Press, pp. 3–7.

Cortes, Carlos E.; and Wilkinson, Louise C. 2009. "Developing and Implementing a Multicultural Vision." In *Contemporary Leadership and Intercultural Competence: Exploring the Cross-Cultural Dynamics Within Organizations*, edited by Michael A. Moodian. Los Angeles. CA: Sage, pp. 17–31.

Coulehan, John J.; and Block, Marian R. 1997. *The Medical Interview: Mastering Skills for Clinical Practice*, 3rd edn. Philadelphia, PA: F.A. Davis.

Crosby, Barbara C. 1999. *Leadership for Global Citizenship: Building Transnational Community*. Thousand Oaks, CA: Sage.

Cummings, William K. 2000. "Transnationalism and Transnational Competence." In *Transnational Competence: Rethinking the U.S.-Japan Educational Relationship*, edited by John N. Hawkins and William K. Cummings. Albany, NY: State University of New York Press, pp. 7–24.

Cushner, Kenneth. 1998. "Intercultural Education from an International Perspective: Commonalities and Future Prospects." In *International Perspectives on Intercultural*

Education, edited by Kenneth Cushner. Mahwah, NJ: Lawrence Erlbaum Associates, pp. 353–370.

Dadfar, Hossein; and Gustavsson, Peter. 1992. "Competition by Effective Management of Cultural Diversity: The Case of International Construction Projects." *International Studies of Management and Organization* 22 (4): 81–92.

Dinges, Norman. 1983. "Intercultural Competence." In *Handbook of Intercultural Training*, vol. II, edited by Dan Landis and Richard W. Brislin. New York: Pergamon, pp. 176–202.

Dorgan, Kelly A.; Lang, Forrest; Floyd, Michael; and Kemp, Evelyn. 2009. "International Medical Graduate-Patient Communication: A Qualitative Analysis of Perceived Barriers." *Academic Medicine* 84 (11): 1567–1575.

Dreifus, Claudia. 2008. "In Professor's Model, Diversity = Productivity: A Conversation with Scott E. Page." *New York Times*, January 8, p. D2.

Duffy, Mary E. 2001. "A Critique of Cultural Education in Nursing." *Journal of Advanced Nursing* 36 (4): 487–495.

Enders, Jürgen; and de Weert, Egbert. 2009. "Towards a T-shaped Profession: Academic Work and Career in the Knowledge Society." In *The Changing Face of Academic Life: Analytical and Comparative Perspectives*, edited by Jürgen Enders and Egbert de Weert. Basingstoke: Palgrave Macmillan, pp. 251–272.

Fancher, Tonya L.; Ton, Hendry; Meyer, Oanh Le; Ho, Thuan; and Paterniti, Debora A. 2010. "Discussing Depression with Vietnamese American Patients." *Journal of Immigrant and Minority Health* 12: 263–266.

Florini, Ann M.; and Simmons, P.J. 2000. "What the World Needs Now?" In *The Third Force: The Rise of Transnational Civil Society*, edited by Ann M. Florini. Washington, DC: Carnegie Endowment for International Peace, pp. 1–15.

Fohrer, Bianca; Erne, Roland; and Finlay, Graham. 2019. "Transnational Competence: A Transformative Tool?" *Labor Studies Journal* 46 (1): 1–31.

Frenk, Julio; et al. 2010. "Health Professionals for a New Century: Transforming Education to Strengthen Health Systems in an Interdependent World." *Lancet* 376: 1923–1958.

Fuller, Kathleen. 2002. "Eradicating Essentialism from Cultural Competency Education." *Academic Medicine* 77 (3): 198–201.

Galleli, Barbara; Hourneaux, Flavio Jr.; and Munck, Luciano. 2019. "Sustainability and Human Competences: A Systematic Literature Review." *Benchmarking: An International Journal* January. doi:10.108/BIJ-12-2018-0433.

Garrett, Henry J. 2018. "The Kernel of Human (or Rodent) Kindness." *New York Times*, December 29, p. A21.

Goleman, Daniel. 1995. *Emotional Intelligence*. New York: Bantam Books.

Goleman, Daniel. 1998. *Working with Emotional Intelligence*. New York: Bantam Books.

Goodman, Louis W. 1998. "Foreword." In *Preparing Global Professionals for the New Century: Issues, Curricula and Strategies for International Affairs Education*, edited by Michele C. Titi. Washington, DC: Association of Professional Schools of International Affairs, p. vii.

Gordon, Frances. 2009. "Interprofessional Capability as an Aim of Student Learning ." In *Interprofessional Education: Making It Happen*, edited by Patricia Bluteau and Ann Jackson. New York: Palgrave Macmillan, pp. 59–79.

Gregg, Jessica; and Saha, Somnath. 2006. "Losing Culture on the Way to Competence: The Use and Misuse of Culture in Medical Education ." *Academic Medicine* 81 (6): 542–547.

Greysen, S. Ryan; Richards, Adam K.; Coupet, Sidney; Desai, Mayur M.; and Padela, Aasim I. 2013. "Global Health Experiences of U.S. Physicians: A Mixed Methods Survey of Clinician-Researchers and Health Policy Leaders." *Globalization and Health* 9 (19): 1–10.

Guilherme, Manuela. 2007. "English as a Global Language and Education for Cosmopolitan Citizenship." *Language and Intercultural Communication* 7 (1): 72–90.

Hammick, Marilyn; and Anderson, Elizabeth. 2009. "Sustaining Interprofessional Education in Professional Award Programmes." In *Interprofessional Education: Making It Happen*, edited by Patricia Bluteau and Ann Jackson. New York: Palgrave Macmillan, pp. 202–226.

Hanesova, Dana; and Theodoulides, Lenka. 2022. *Mastering Transversal Competences in a Higher Education Environment: Through Processes of Critical Thinking and Reflection*. Banska Bystrica, Slovakia: Belianum. doi:10.24040/2022.9788055720159.

Hannigan, Terence P. 1990. "Traits, Attitudes, and Skills that Are Related to Intercultural Effectiveness and Their Implications for Cross-Cultural Training: A Review of the Literature." *International Journal of Intercultural Effectiveness* 14 (1): 89–111.

Hanvey, Robert G. 2001. "An Attainable Global Perspective." In *Changing Perspectives on International Education*, edited by Patrick O'Meara; Howard D. Mehlinger; and Roxanna Ma Newman. Bloomington, IN: Indiana University Press, pp. 217–225.

Hawkins, John N.; and Cummings, William K. (Eds.). 2000. *Transnational Competence: Rethinking the U.S.-Japan Educational Relationship*. Albany, NY: State University of New York Press.

He, Jing; and Berry, Frances. 2022. "Crossing the Boundaries: Reimagining Innovation and Diffusion." *Global Public Policy and Governance* 2: 129–153.

Healy, Lynne M. 2008. *International Social Work: Professional Action in an Interdependent World*, 2nd edn. Oxford: Oxford University Press.

Hecht, Michael L.; Collier, Mary Jane; and Ribeau, Sidney A. 1993. *African American Communication: Ethnic Identity and Cultural Interpretation*. Newbury Park, CA: Sage Publications.

Held, David. 2002. "Culture and Political Community: National, Global, and Cosmopolitan." In *Conceiving Cosmopolitanism: Theory, Context, and Practice*, edited by Steven Vertovec and Robin Cohen. Oxford: Oxford University Press, pp. 48–58.

Hirsch, Jennifer S. 2003. "Anthropologists, Migrants, and Health Research: Confronting Cultural Appropriateness." In *American Arrivals: Anthropology Engages the New Immigration*, edited by Nancy Foner. Oxford: James Currey, pp. 229–257.

Hirshberg, Matthew. 2006. "Teaching Compassionate Social Studies." In *Values Education for Citizens in the New Century*, edited by Roger H. M. Cheng; John C. K. Lee; and Leslie N. K. Lo. Hong Kong: Chinese University Press, pp. 165–196.

Hollenbeck, George P.; McCall, Morgan W. Jr.; and Silzer, Robert F. 2006. "Leadership Competency Models." *Leadership Quarterly* 17: 398–413.

Holm, John D.; and Malete, Leapetsewe. 2010. "Nine Problems that Hinder Partnerships in Africa." *Chronicle of Higher Education*, June 18, pp. A28–A29.

Homer-Dixon, Thomas. 2000. *The Ingenuity Gap*. New York: Alfred A. Knopf.

Hunter, Arnagretta. 2021. *Toward Our Human Future: Catastrophic Risk, the Public Good, and the Importance of Humanity*. Sydney: Commission for the Human Future, June 10.

Johansson, Frans. 2004. *The Medici Effect*. Cambridge. MA: Harvard Business School Press.

Keller, Johanna. 2007. "Yo-Yo Ma's Edge Effect." *Chronicle of Higher Education*, March 23, pp. B10–B13.

Keraly, Gabor; and Gering, Zsuzsanaa. 2021. "Having Nothing but Questions? The Social Discourse of Higher Education Institutions' Legitimation Crises." *Journal of Future Studies* 25 (4): 57–70.

Khagram, Sanjeev; and Alvord, Sarah. 2006. "The Rise of Civic Transnationalism." In *Transnational Civil Society: An Introduction*, edited by Srilatha Batliwala and L. David Brown. Bloomfield, CT: Kumarian, pp. 65–81.

Khagram, Sanjeev; and Levitt, Peggy. 2008. "Constructing Transnational Studies." In *Rethinking Transnationalism: The Meso-Link of Organisations*, edited by Ludger Pries. London: Routledge, pp. 21–39.

Kirmayer, Laurence J. 2012. "Rethinking Cultural Competence." *Transcultural Psychiatry* 49 (2): 149–164.

Kirmayer, Laurence J. 2014. "Foreword." In *Refuge and Resilience: Promoting Resilience and Mental Health among Resettled Refugees and Forced Migrants*, edited by Laura Simich and Lisa Andermann. New York: Springer, pp. vii–ix.

Kirmayer, Laurence J.; Kronick, Rachel; and Rousseau, Cecile. 2018. "Advocacy as Key to Structural Competency in Psychiatry." *JAMA Psychiatry* 75 (2): 119–120.

Koehn, Peter H. 2008. "Underneath Kyoto: Emerging Subnational Government Initiatives and Incipient Issue-Bundling Opportunities in China and the United States." *Global Environmental Politics* 8 (1): 53–77.

Koehn, Peter H.; and Rosenau, James N. 2002. "Transnational Competence in an Emergent Epoch." *International Studies Perspectives* 3 (May): 105–127.

Koehn, Peter H.; and Rosenau, James N. 2010. *Transnational Competence: Empowering Professional Curricula for Horizon-Rising Challenges*. Boulder, CO: Paradigm Press.

Koehn, Peter H.; and Swick, Herbert. 2006. "Medical Education for a Changing World: Moving Beyond Cultural Competence into Transnational Competence." *Academic Medicine* 81 (6): 548–556.

Koehn, Peter H.; and Tiilikainen, Marja. 2007. "Migration and Transnational Health Care: Connecting Finland and Somaliland." *Siirtolaisuus – Migration* 34 (1): 2–9.

Kramer, Paul A. 2017. "History in a Time of Crisis." *Chronicle of Higher Education*, February 24, pp. B6–B9.

Lambert, Richard D. 1994. "Summary and Prospectus." In *Educational Exchange and Global Competence*, edited by Richard D. Lambert. Portland, ME: Council on International Educational Exchange, pp. 281–293.

Landler-Pardo, Gabriella; Elyashiv, Rinat A.; Levi-Keren, Machal; and Weinberger, Yehudith. 2022. "Being Empathic in Complex Situations in Intercultural Education: A Practical Tool." *Intercultural Education* 33 (4): 391–405.

Lustig, M. W.; and Koester, J. 1996. *Intercultural Competence: Interpersonal Communication across Cultures*, 2nd edn. New York: HarperCollins.

Marquardt, Michael J.; and Berger, Nancy O. 2000. *Global Leaders for the Twenty-first Century*. Albany, NY: State University of New York Press.

Matlin, Stephen A.; Depoux, Anneliese; Schutte, Stefanie; Flahault, Antoine; and Saso, Luciano. 2018. "Migrants' and Refugees' Health: Towards an Agenda of Solutions." *Public Health Reviews* 39 (27): 1–50.

Maynard, Kimberly A. 1999. *Healing Communities in Conflict: International Assistance in Complex Emergencies*. New York: Columbia University Press.

McRell, Amanda S.; and Grace, Breanne L. 2022. "Social Work, Social Justice and Americentrism by Design: Transnationalism in United States Social Work

Education." *Higher Education Research & Development.* http://doi.org/10.1080/07294360.2022.2052816.

Merryfield, Merry M. 2001. "Pedagogy for Global Perspectives in Education: Studies of Teachers' Thinking and Practice." In *Changing Perspectives on International Education,* edited by Patrick O'Meara; Howard D. Mehlinger; and Roxanna Ma Newman. Bloomington. IN: Indiana University Press, pp. 244–279.

Merryfield, Merry M. 2002. "The Difference a Global Educator Can Make." *Educational Leadership* 90 (2): 119–121.

Merryfield, Merry M.; and Wilson, Angene. 2005. *Social Studies and the World: Teaching Global Perspectives.* Silver Spring, MD: National Council for the Social Studies.

Meyer, Seth J.; Johnson, Richard G. III; and McCandless, Sean. 2022. "Meet the New Es: Empathy, Engagement, Equity, and Ethics in Public Administration." *Public Integrity* 24 (4–5):353–363.

Mollica, Richard. 2006. *Healing Invisible Wounds: Paths to Hope and Recovery in a Violent World.* Orlando, FL: Harcourt, Inc.

Moran, Robert T.; Harris, Philip R.; and Moran, Sarah V. 2007. *Managing Cultural Differences: Global Leadership Strategies for the 21st Century.* Amsterdam: Elsevier.

Morrison, Allen J. 2000. "Developing a Global Leadership Model." *Human Resource Management* 39 (2 and 3): 117–131.

Murdoch-Eaton, Deborah; Redmond, Anthony; and Bax, Nigel. 2011. "Training Healthcare Professionals for the Future: Internationalism and Effective Inclusion of Global Health Training." *Medical Teacher* 33: 562–569.

Ngai, Phyllis B. 2001. "Nonverbal Communication Behavior in Intercultural Negotiations: Insights and Applications Based on Findings from Ethiopia, Tanzania, Hong Kong, and the China Mainland." *World Communication* 29 (4): 3–35.

Ojelay-Surtees, Bimla. 2007. *Building Trust in Diverse Teams: The Toolkit for Emergency Response.* Dorset: Oxfam GB.

Ozkazanc-Pan, Banu. 2019a. "'Superdiversity': A New Paradigm for Inclusion in a Transnational World." *Equality, Diversity and Inclusion* 38 (4): 477–490.

Ozkazanc-Pan, Banu. 2019b. *Transnational Migration and the New Subjects of Work: Transmigrants, Hybrids and Cosmopolitans.* Bristol: Bristol University Press.

Page, Scott E. 2007. *The Difference: How the Power of Diversity Creates Better Groups, Firms, Schools, and Societies.* Princeton, NJ: Princeton University Press.

Pattee, Emma. 2020. "How to Improve Your Ability to Empathize with Others." *New York Times,* October 5, p. B6.

Ping, Charles. 2003. "Educational Imperatives for a New Era: The University Must Actively Encourage Mobility." Paris: UNESCO. Available at: http://portal.unesco.org/education/en/ev.php-URL_ID=7687%26URL_DO=.

Pon, Gordon. 2009. "Cultural Competency as New Racism: An Ontology of Forgetting." *Journal of Progressive Human Services* 20 (1): 59–71.

Powell, Dorothy L. 2016. "Social Determinants of Health: Cultural Competence Is Not Enough." *Creative Nursing* 22 (1): 5–10.

Reimers, Fernando. 2009. "'Global Competency' Is Imperative for Global Success." *Chronicle of Higher Education,* January 30, p. A29.

Rizvi, Fazal; and Beech, Jason. 2020. "Global Mobilities and the Possibility of a Cosmopolitan Curriculum." In *Curriculum of Global Migration and Transnationalism,* edited by Elena Toukan; Ruben Gaztambide-Fernandez; and Sardar Anwaruddin. London: Routledge, pp. 125–133.

Rizvi, Fazal; and Lingard, Bob. 2010. *Globalizing Education Policy*. London: Routledge.

Rosen, Robert; Digh, Patricia; Singer, Marshall; and Phillips, Carl. 2000. *Global Literacies: Lessons on Business Leadership and National Cultures*. New York: Simon & Schuster.

Rosenau, James N. 1992. *The United Nations in a Turbulent World*. Boulder, CO: Lynne Rienner Publishers.

Rosenau, James N.; and Fagen, W. Michael. 1997. "A New Dynamism in World Politics: Increasingly Skillful Individuals?" *International Studies Quarterly* 41 (4): 655–686.

Salovey, Peter; Woolery, Alison; and Mayer, Joehn D. 2001. "Emotional Intelligence: Conceptualization and Measurement." In *Blackwell Handbook of Social Psychology: Interpersonal Processes*, edited by Garth J.O. Fletcher and Margaret S. Clark. Oxford: Blackwell Publishers, pp. 278–307.

Salzman, Philip C. 1999. *The Anthropology of Real Life: Events in Human Experience*. Prospect Heights, IL: Waveland Press.

Sarkissian, Wendy. 2009. *Kitchen Table Sustainability: Practical Recipes for Community Engagement with Sustainability*. London: Earthscan.

Schneider, Karen. 1997. "Transpatriate Success Factors: A Concurrent Validation Study in China." Unpublished PhD dissertation, University of Houston.

Sears, Karen P. 2012. "Improving Cultural Competence Education: The Utility of an Intersectional Framework." *Medical Education* 46: 545–551.

Seidman, Dov. 2007. *How: Why HOW We Do Anything Means Everything … in Business (and in Life)*. New York: John Wiley & Sons.

Spitzberg, Brian H.; and Changnon, Gabrielle. 2009. "Conceptualizing Intercultural Competence." In *The SAGE Handbook of Intercultural Competence*, edited by Darla K. Deardorff. Los Angeles, CA: Sage, pp. 2–52.

Ssosse, Quentin; Wagner, Johanna; and Hopper, Carina. 2021. "Assessing the Impact of ESD: Methods, Challenges, Results." *Sustainability* 13 (2854): 1–26. doi:10.3390/su13052854.

Taft, Ronald. 1981. "The Role and Personality of the Mediator." In *The Mediating Person: Bridges between Cultures*, edited by Stephen Bochner. Boston: G.K. Hall, pp. 53–88.

Task Force for Transnational Competence. 1997. *Towards Transnational Competence: Rethinking International Education (A U.S.-Japan Case Study)*, IIE Research Report No. 28. New York: Institute of International Education.

Taylor, Janelle S. 2003. "Confronting 'Culture' in Medicine's 'Culture of No Culture.'" *Academic Medicine* 78 (6): 555–559.

Taylor, Peter. 2008. "Higher Education Curricula for Human and Social Development ." In *Higher Education in the World 3: New Challenges and Emerging Roles for Human and Social Development*. London: Palgrave Macmillan, pp. 89–101.

Tervalon, Melanie, and Murray-Garcia, Jann. 1998. "Cultural Humility versus Cultural Competence: A Critical Distinction in Defining Physician Training Outcomes in Multicultural Education." *Journal of Health Care for the Poor and Underserved* 9 (2): 117–125.

Ting-Toomey, Stella. 2009. "Intercultural Conflict Competence as a Facet of Intercultural Competence Development: Multiple Conceptual Approaches." In *The SAGE Handbook of Intercultural Competence*, edited by Darla K. Deardorff. Los Angeles, CA: Sage, pp. 100–120.

Trad, Sloan P. 2019. "A Framework for Mapping Sustainability Within Tertiary Curriculum." *International Journal of Sustainability in Higher Education* 20 (2): 288–308.

Trompenaars, Fons; and Wooliams, Peter. 2009. "Toward a General Framework of Competence for Today's Global Village." In *The SAGE Handbook of Intercultural Competence*, edited by Darla K. Deardorff. Los Angeles, CA: Sage, pp. 438–455.

Vertovec, Steven. 2010a. "Introduction: New Directions in the Anthropology of Migration and Multiculturalism." In *Anthropology of Migration and Multiculturalism: New Directions*, edited by Steven Vertovec. London: Routledge, pp. 1–17.

Vertovec, Steven. 2010b. "Super-Diversity and Its Implications." In *Anthropology of Migration and Multiculturalism: New Directions*, edited by Steven Vertovec. London: Routledge, pp. 65–95.

Vertovec, Steven and Rogers, Alisdair. 1998. "Introduction." In *Muslim European Youth: Reproducing Ethnicity, Religion, Culture*. Aldershot: Ashgate, pp. 1–24.

Villa-Torres, Laura; Gonzalez-Vazquez, Tonatiuh; Fleming, Paul J.; Gonzalez-Gonzalez, Edgar L.; Infante-Xibille, Cesar; Chavez, Rebecca; and Barrington, Clare. 2017. "Transnationalism and Health: A Systematic Literature Review on the Use of Transnationalism in the Study of the Health Practices and Behaviors of Migrants." *Social Science & Medicine* 183: 70–79.

Walker, Peter; Hein, Karen; Russ, Catherine; Bertleff, Greg; and Caspersz, Dan. 2010. "A Blueprint for Professionalizing Humanitarian Assistance." *Health Affairs* 29 (12): 2223–2230.

Wang, Tina. 2008. "Intercultural Dialogue and Understanding: Implications for Teachers." In *Teaching in Transnational Higher Education: Enhancing Learning for Offshore International Students*, edited by Lee Dunn and Michelle Wallace. New York: Routledge, pp. 57–66.

Warriner, Doris. 2021. "Theorizing the Spatial Dimensions and Pedagogical Implications of Transnationalism." In *Curriculum of Global Migration and Transnationalism*, edited by Elena Toukan; Ruben Gaztambide-Fernandez; and Sardar Anwaruddin. London: Routledge, pp. 52–61.

Wear, Delese. 2003. "Insurgent Multiculturalism: Rethinking How and Why We Teach Culture in Medical Education." *Academic Medicine* 78 (6): 549–554.

Wear, Delese. 2006. "Respect for Patients: A Case Study of the Formal and Hidden Curriculum." In *Professionalism in Medicine: Critical Perspectives*, edited by Delese Wear and Julie M. Aultman. New York: Springer, pp. 87–101.

Weber, Susanne. 2003. "A Framework for Teaching and Learning 'Intercultural Competence.'" In *Intercultural Experience and Education*, edited by Geof Alred; Michael Bynam; and Mike Fleming. Clevedon: Multilingual Matters, pp. 196–212.

Werdell, Philip. 1974. "Futurism and the Reform of Higher Education." In *Learning for Tomorrow: The Role of the Future in Education*, edited by Alvin Toffler. New York: Vintage Books, pp. 272–311.

Zweifler, J., and Gonzalez, A. M. 1998. "Teaching Residents to Care for Culturally Diverse Populations." *Academic Medicine* 73 (10): 1056–1061.

2 Conflict-Displaced Migration
Drivers, Context, Stakeholders, and Needs

This chapter focuses on the conditions that refugees and other conflict-induced transnational migrants encounter in displaced circumstances in the Global South. In the context of conflict-displaced migration, we identify the major challenges that face care responders and stakeholders and emphasize the value of transnational competence. Special attention is devoted to the emotional distress and mental health as well as the resilience of conflict-displaced migrants. This chapter's discussion draws, in part, on Diana Diaków's first-hand experience as a Mental Health and Psychosocial Support (MHPSS) humanitarian-aid worker in refugee camps and informal migrant settlements in Greece.

Drivers of Conflict-Displaced Migration

Although rooted in the interaction of wider external and internal forces, "localized, micro-level" engagements govern the decision to move among most conflict-displaced migrants (Mandic, 2021, p. 4; see also Koehn, 1991, pp. 38–46). Coupled with direct threats to physical health and economic sustainability, the indirect health consequences of armed conflict include damage to infrastructure (e.g., power supplies), to hospitals and health centers, and to water treatment and sewage treatment facilities along with overwhelmed and diminished service providers (Ostergard and Griffin, 2020, pp. 151–152). Coercive acts, catalytic precipitating events, and the capacity and opportunity to escape all play driving roles in conflict-displaced migration (Koehn, 1991, pp. 47–48; Mandic, 2021, p. 6). Camps, detention centers,[1] and informal settlements (see Jordan, 2021; Mwangu, 2022)[2] constitute the generic spatial contexts that encompass migrants "displaced by selective (e.g., persecution, ethnic cleansing) or generalized (e.g., war, anarchy) violence and coercion" fostered by political/military/social actors (Mandic, 2021, pp. 2–3; Anghel and Grierson, 2020, p. 490).[3]

Vulnerability in the wake of globally snowballing displacement (Hoffman, 2021, p. 126) forms the contemporary backdrop for the settlement discussion highlighted in this chapter. Typically, conflict-generated displacement involves "a sudden and often massive loss of resources, the pattern of deprivation potentially compounding over time" (Silove, Ventevogel, and

DOI: 10.4324/9781003330493-3

Rees, 2017, p. 133; also White House, 2021, p. 17). Simultaneously, the impetus of displacement initiates a "homing" process that allows refugees to reclaim their sense of agency and self-efficacy by creating spaces inspired by their nostalgia and dreams of future homes (Zibar et al., 2022, pp. 83–116).

Displacement Contexts

Informal Settlements

Millions of FDPs (forcibly displaced persons) and IDPs (internally displaced persons)[4] spontaneously settle in urban areas; they arrive with diverse migration backgrounds, vulnerabilities, assets, expectations, and aspirations (Haysom, Pantuliano, and Davey, 2012, pp. 113–114, 117, 130–132). With the exception of Sub-Saharan Africa, a majority of refugees now reside in cities (Betts, 2021, p. 2; Dryden-Peterson, 2016, p. 138; Toole, 2019, p. 56).[5] Urban refugees in the Global South are "largely a 'hidden' population, living anonymously, usually solely responsible for their own subsistence" (Mavroudi and Nagel, 2016, p. 137), and reluctant to register "for fear of being deported or returned to refugee camps" (Mutiso, et al., 2019, p. 205). Migrants "who 'self-settle' in regional towns and cities constitute a hugely important, if less visible and accessible component of displacement" (Lindley and Hammond, 2014, p. 67). For instance, nearly two-thirds of the Syrian refugees who arrived in Lebanon live outside camps – "scattered over 1,000 municipalities, most of which are in impoverished urban areas" (Kamara and Renzaho, 2016, p. 89; also Toole, 2019, p. 56). In Uganda, financially constrained local governments that are short of staff are primarily responsible for providing multitudes of arriving refugees with shelter and basic social services and managing land-allocation issues (Kamei, 2022, pp. 64–66).

Conflict-generated transmigrants who live outside official camps usually are "among the poorest and most vulnerable" residents who must share services that previously "were inadequate even when used by a smaller population" (Martin, Davis, Benton, and Waliany, 2017, p. 111). For instance, Moria camp, located on the Greek island of Lesvos, had the capacity to host around 3,000 people. In 2018, however, it was home to almost 9,000 FDPs (International Rescue Committee, 2018). Even those numbers are likely underestimated given that many displaced individuals and families sheltered outside of the gates of Moria due to the lack of resources and ethnic tensions within the camp. This overcrowded camp employed only four licensed psychologists in 2018 (ibid.). Such understaffing is particularly problematic given the severity of ever-present mental health crises among the camp community, such as suicidality and self-harm among minors. Given that first responders typically are not equipped with clinical training that would allow them to deliver sustainable and targeted MHPSS services, these mental health needs ideally should be referred to specialists (Diaków, 2021, pp. 114–121).

At the same time, host communities, along with local hospitals and other health infrastructure, often are overwhelmed by the numbers of arriving conflict-induced transborder migrants (Haysom, Pantuliano, and Davey, 2012, pp. 116–118, 123; Toole, 2019, p. 75; Kamei, 2022, p. 64). Unfamiliar with their new, typically economically disadvantaged and insecure living conditions, urban FDPs are not likely to gain meaningful employment[6] and suffer "comparable mental health problems to their counterparts living in refugee camps or rural areas" (Mutiso, et al., 2019, p. 205). Their hidden status, coupled with the absence of designated refugee services, results in unaddressed physical health and mental health needs (ibid., pp. 205–206).[7]

Camps

Today, millions of externally and internally displaced people are forced to live, often for long periods and even for multiple generations, in camps. In Africa, most conflict-displaced persons, particularly women and children, find themselves in domestic or foreign camps (Betts, 2021, p. 2).[8] Cindy Horst (2006, p. 21) notes that "it is common for refugee populations to be concentrated in camps that are located in remote, ecologically and politically marginal areas." Frequently, "camps are simultaneously [forced] depoliticized and [in response to the resulting gap] hyper-politicized" (Turner, 2015, p. 145).

Informal camps can arise from self-settlement activity. Consider, for instance, the dynamic situation that prevailed in the 2001 self-settlement of about 4,000 Liberian refugees on unused land in Buedu District of Sierra Leone until the UNHCR forcibly closed it in 2002. According to Michel Agier (2011, p. 41), "the refugees in the Buedu encampment had a rigorous organization, with a 'chairman' and secretary who kept a precise count of the arrivals and departures of Liberians." Exceptionally, Uganda favors established development-supported rural settlements in close proximity to local populations rather than camps "in order to give the refugees an opportunity to re-establish their livelihoods and become self-sustaining" (Mwangu, 2022, pp. 435–437). In Nakivale, a settlement inhabited by over 100,000 refugees from seven countries of origin, a majority of households engage in income-generating activities that provide food to local markets, generate innovative, mutually beneficial, business practices adapted by refugees and hosts, and contribute to cultural diversity (ibid., pp. 438, 441–444; also see Kamei, 2022, p. 62).

Over time, quintessentially among inter-generational displaced Palestinian sites, occupants have formed "camp-cities or large [and often cosmopolitan] urban districts" (Agier, 2011, p. 53; also Perouse de Montclos and Kagwanja, 2000, p. 211; Hyndman and Giles, 2017, p. 2; Berger, 2020; Giles, 2018, pp. 165, 167). Commonly, refugee camps transform for those who have been "born and marry there, have buried their dead and established a range of relationships with the local population" into "spaces of identification"

(Agier, 2011, p. 56). Such temporary, albeit indeterminant,[9] and highly constricted spaces become "eternal" (ibid.; also see Farhat, et al., 2018, p. 2; Mbai, Mangeni, Abuelaish, and Pilkington, 2017, p. 164).[10]Agier (2011, p. 84; emphasis added) concludes that "neither repatriation, nor integration, nor resettlement; ... 'encampment' really is the UNHCR's 'fourth solution' – not admitted, but systematically preferred" (also see Hyndman and Giles, 2017, pp. xiii–xiv, 2, 4, 10, 72–73, 77, 127–128). This description coincides with Viet Thanh Nguyen's (2018, p. 17) reflection that "displaced persons are mostly unwanted where they fled from; unwanted where they are, in refugee camps; and unwanted where they want to go."[11]

Still, camp boundaries frequently are transgressed (Turner, 2015, p. 146; Betts, 2021, p. 2),[12] both physically and virtually – thanks to homeland and global diasporic connections (Dryden-Peterson, Dahya, and Adelman, 2017, p. 1018; also see Pincock, Betts, and Easton-Calabria, 2020, p. 45; Cohen and Van Hear, 2020, pp. 58–59; Horst, 2006, pp. 29, 207),[13] the widespread availability of mobile phones, and improved internet access (Hyndman and Giles, 2017, p. 55). Inspired by transnational kin networks and aided by breakthrough technologies, today's displaced populations are "simultaneously anchored" in receiving places and "pivoting back and forth" with homeland and diasporic places (Ozkazanc-Pan, 2019, p. 23).[14] Robin Cohen and Nicholas Van Hear (2020, p. 59; emphasis added) conclude that "*transnationalism* is what displaced and dispersed people do, or have to do, to make a life worth living." The presence of individual agency to transcend even constrained physical locations (ibid., p. 28) offers fertile ground for the distance-training opportunities discussed in Chapters 5 and 6.

Commonly, "social life, power relations, hierarchies and sociality are remolded in the camp" (Turner, 2015, p. 144). Camps become a microcosm of refugees' recollections of childhood homes recreated meticulously despite the scarcity of resources (Zibar et al., 2022, pp. 83–116). In Greece, refugee families created home decorations and equipment using recycled materials to furnish small gardens or guest rooms attached to their ISO Boxes, painted country flags on the walls, cooked meals that smelled like home, danced and played music, and enjoyed traditional games with neighbors. These practices are an element of *refugeehood* and an important resilience factor that anchors displaced persons in a sense of familiarity and nurturing memories (see Gupta, 2022).

In some camp circumstances, "'sector leaders' appear from among the initial tent heads; churches or video shops are built out of mud brick and covered with plastic sheets from the UNHCR or NGOs; market places and football pitches are improvised, etc." (Agier, 2011, p. 55; also see Anghel and Grierson, 2020, p. 490). In Nepal, refugees from Bhutan exercised responsibility for daily camp functioning through a Camp Management Committee, a Camp Secretary, sector heads, and a Counselling Board.[15] In many displacement situations, refugees form self-help organizations that "engage in collective action ... across economic, political and social contexts" and "a smattering of NGOs," including the Finnish Refugee Council in Kampala, Uganda, provide "capacity-building programmes" for refugee-community organizations (Pincock, Betts, and Easton-Calabria, 2020, pp. 1–3, 13, 25, 28, 91, 112).[16] One breakthrough key to successful engagement for refugee community organizations is linkage with a transnational network that can supply funding and training (ibid., p. 29).[17] Displaced youth in the camps often manifest remarkable resilience. For instance, youth leaders in the Ritsona refugee camp created and delivered educational programs for their peers and self-advocated and established collaboration with international and national agencies to access resources for educational capacity-building (e.g., preparing language-lesson plans).

The COVID pandemic unexpectedly facilitated a surge of online and remote support systems and networks that became available to refugee leaders. Nevertheless, camp residents continue to confront technological inequities such as unstable Wi-Fi connection, limited signal coverage, etc. Technological shortfalls can present serious hazards given that camp sites often include unsafe environments for youth, especially girls, due to a plethora of factors, including the absence of supervised community spaces, a shortage of culturally responsive programs, and lack of infrastructure such as appropriate lighting that would ensure safe passages to activities operated by on-site groups.

Detention Facilities

Physical health and mental health conditions in detention centers and the health impact of prolonged detention under substandard living conditions merit serious attention (see Cyril and Renzaho, 2016, p. 247).[18] In their case study of the impacts of detention policy and practice on migrant health in Greece, Sheila Cyril and Andre Renzaho (ibid., pp. 216–217, 220–224; also Garcia-Zamora, 2017, p. 590) found that authorities confined asylum seekers and other detainees in "inhumane conditions … including overcrowded cells without proper ventilation or sunlight, poor sanitation and low hygiene." Detained migrants were at high risk of acquiring infectious diseases; substandard conditions, along with physical and emotional abuse, contributed to a majority of the health problems they confronted – including the aggravation of chronic and mental health conditions. In Greece and elsewhere, however, "NGOs have played a powerful role in improving the conditions in detention facilities" (Cyril and Renzaho, 2016, pp. 246, 239–242).[19] MSF (Doctors Without Borders), in particular, has provided primary-health care, personal hygiene kits, treatment of infectious diseases, interpretative and psychological assistance, and other health-related services (ibid., pp. 237–238).

Extremely vulnerable lesbian, gay, bisexual, transgender, and intersex individuals are especially prone to experience abuse and lack of access to appropriate medical care during immigration detention (Frew, Fausch, and Cox, 2016, p. 4). LGBTI persons face heightened levels of harassment, discrimination, psychological abuse, physical and sexual violence by detention staff as well as other detainees. They are frequently segregated in conditions falling below those of the general detainee population and well-established international standards, or are subjected to policies of solitary confinement, which have been shown to have severe mental and physical health consequences.

(ibid., p. 4)

Many sexual minorities are "traumatized by experiences in detention" (Tabak and Levitan, 2013).

Detention facilities also are sites where children are subjected to sexual abuse and trafficking. Moreover, "even very short periods of detention can undermine a child's psychological and physical wellbeing and compromise their cognitive development" (Sampson, et al., 2015, p. 22). UNHCR advocates an end to the detention of children and the immediate release of any children still confined (UNHCR, 2014, p. 17).

Responders and Stakeholders

Various U.N. agencies share responsibility in medium- to large-scale disaster recoveries under the "cluster system" policy introduced in 2005 (Agier, 2011, pp. 57, 59, 203–204; Vadivelu, 2014, pp. 181–182).[20] "Humanitarian government," a collaborative organizational infrastructure composed of staff and leadership drawn from U.N. agencies along with different international and domestic humanitarian and development NGOs,[21] "constructs, manages and controls" camps for IDPs[22] and refugees (Agier, 2011, pp. 201–202),[23] attends to inter-agency coordination,[24] and initiates joint programming of benefit both to displaced persons and their host communities (Milner, 2021, p. 423; also see Toole, 2019, p. 75; Anderson and Woodrow, 1998, p. 73). UNHCR exercises its overall responsibility for coordinating refugee camp interventions by subcontracting to multiple agencies and NGOs (Horst, 2006, p. 80).[25]

The interventions sponsored by U.N. agencies tend to "privilege formal 'implementing partners' and 'operational partners', and these are usually international or national NGOs, not refugee-led organizations" (Pincock, Betts, and Easton-Calabria, 2020, p. 2). For instance, UNHCR's limited "community-mobilization" initiatives "rarely provide refugees with the freedom to address the needs they themselves identify or to pursue their own scope of work" (ibid., p. 2; also Jones, 2020, pp. 133, 136–137). The prevailing outcome is a bifurcation of roles and identities among the privileged "voluntary migrant" professional "supracitizens" and the constrained involuntary refugee "subcitizens" (Hyndman, 2000, p. 111).

In most camps, NGOs such as CARE, the Red Cross, and MSF and international organizations, including UNHCR, employ thousands of refugees as community intermediaries (Agier, 2011, pp. 139–140, 203). Temporary expatriate humanitarian-care providers, assisted by rudimentally trained community health workers, endeavor to provide basic health services (Pilkington and Mbai, 2016, p. 5; Pilkington, Mbai, Mangeni, and Abuelaish, 2016, pp. 4–5). Silove, Ventevogel, and Rees (2017, p. 132) recognize the necessity of task shifting; "i.e., the transfer of skills to primary care and lay workers in order to undertake specific mental health interventions of various types under supervision." In Chapters 5 and 6, such community-resource persons will feature as subjects and agents of transformative transnational-competence training.

The middle level of the typical camp hierarchy is filled by merchants and traders and the lowest level by the most numerous groups of destitute recipients of humanitarian assistance (Agier, 2011, p. 140; Perouse de Montclos and Kagwanja, 2000, pp. 212–213). In most camp situations, the latter (especially girls) possess "limited access to primary education, let alone secondary and higher education" (Dahya and Dryden-Peterson, 2017, pp. 286, 288–289; also Dryden-Peterson, Dahya, and Adelman, 2017, pp. 1012, 1020; Dickerson, 2020). A majority of refugees and conflict-displaced people are under age 18 and about 4 million lack access to school education (Ramsey and Baker, 2019, pp. 56, 68). As Sarah Dryden-Peterson et al. point out, "global commitments to Education for All and the Sustainable Development Goals will not be realized unless the educational needs of refugee children are met" (2017, p. 1012; also Lovey, O'Keeffe, and Petignat, 2021, p. 2).

At the same time, and consistent with the objectives of the "Leave No One Behind" concept embodied in the 2016 *Agenda for Humanity* and the *Charter for Change* (Hoffman, 2021, p. 124) as well as in the U.N. Sustainable Development Goals 2030,[26] the capability-training needs of affected host community members and altruistic citizen volunteers intent on offering emergency assistance must be addressed (Pilkington and Mbai, 2016, p. 5; Perouse de Montclos and Kagwanja, 2000, p. 218; Anghel and Grierson, 2020, pp. 489–490; Teissen and Lough, 2019, pp. 305–306; Jones, 2020, p. 15). It is within the shared challenging and insufficiently resourced displacement context (Hoffman, 2021, pp. 129–131; Marume, January, and Maradzika, 2018, p. 383;), then, that the sustainable health promotion (Pilkington and Mbai, 2016, p. 11; Pilkington, et al., 2016, p. 5) and personal-development and community-development initiatives for sustaining well-being envisioned here require TC training.

Views from the Field: Health Challenges and Therapeutic Needs

It is understandable that many people opt to flee from armed conflicts and repressive governments that threaten their health and mortality status. For survivors, the road ahead is paved with peril. An African war-zone study carried out by Physicians for Human Rights concluded that the "first killer is flight" for desperately poor persons driven by conflict from a fragile existence into a hostile and personally threatening environment where health services are nonexistent or not functioning (Lacey, 2005). Health risks encountered by dislocated persons "arise at every stage along their journeys, from before the migration process starts, during travel and at transit and destination points" as well as for repatriates (Matlin, et al., 2018, pp. 7–9). The most severe health consequences for dislocated migrants "occur in the acute emergency phase, during the early stage of relief efforts" and involve "high mortality rates" (Toole, 2019, p. 57).

Both those who move and those who stay are equally entitled to the right to health as specified in Article 25 of the *Universal Declaration of Human Rights* along with access to humanitarian medicine (see Gunn, 2010, pp. 164–165). This section identifies critical health-care challenges faced by conflict-dislocated persons and introduces promising approaches for responding to the needs of displaced populations. Contributors to emotional distress, severe mental health disorders, physical health conditions, and resilience opportunities all receive attention.

Emotional Distress

The "emotional distress" concept captures the multiple migration stressors encountered in settlement contexts by refugees "who do not meet diagnostic criteria for mental illness" (Ballard-Kang, 2020, p. 26). Post-departure stressors include worries about economic survival and persons left behind, living in unhealthy and insecure conditions, inadequate access to water, food, shelter, and health care, isolation and loneliness, loss of meaningful roles and social support, discrimination, social exclusion, and stigmatization experiences, inequitable access to medical, psychological and educational services, and fear of being sent or deported to an unsafe place compounded by delays in resolving uncertain immigration status (Koehn, 2013; Ballard-Kang, 2020, p. 35; Almosh-mosh, Bahloul, Barkil-Oteo, Hassan, and Kirmayer, 2020, pp. 21–23; Marume, January, and Maradzika, 2018, p. 378; Sleijpen, Boeije, Kleber, and Mooren, 2016, p. 173; Halsey, Alarood, Nawaiseh, and Mir, 2022; Silove, Ventevogel, and Rees, 2017, pp. 133–134; Jones, 2020, pp. 137, 157; Matlin, et al., 2018, pp. 9, 19). The absence of, or extremely limited access to, employment opportunities and host-country rights typically leads refugees inhabiting camps "to inactivity, apathy and dependence on humanitarian care and assistance" or to informal and often illegal activity (Agier, 2011, p. 55). In such circumstances, "moral suffering, or even psychological disturbance bound up with lack of occupational activity, play an important part in individual daily life … In a repetitive way, the refugees express, above all, feelings of impotence and uselessness" (ibid., p. 137; also Eckenwiler and Wild, 2021, p. 239).

As expected,

> the greater number of post-migration [post-departure] stressors reported
> by an individual, the higher their level of emotional distress due to a

decreased belief that they can function effectively in both cultures. Conversely, the higher the level of emotional distress, the more vulnerable the individual is to further post-migration stressors due to a reduction in bicultural self-efficacy.

(Ballard-Kang, 2020, p. 35)

Stressful resettlement conditions, exclusions, and potential re-traumatization prospects are particularly pronounced for LGBTI persons (D'souza, Blatman, Wier, and Patel, 2022, pp. 357–358, 360). A prerequisite intervention for addressing mental health problems and promoting resilience, therefore, involves advancing supportive environments that enable displaced populations and other affected persons "to restore their resource base (personal, familial, social, material)" and strengths, reduce daily stresses (Silove, Ventevogel, and Rees, 2017, pp. 133–134; also D'souza, et al., 2022, pp. 359–360), and find empowerment through competency development.[27]

Given that humanitarian aid workers play a crucial role in refugees' socio-ecology of resilience (i.e., they provide frontline psychosocial support), field workers' poor mental health outcomes themselves constitute an additional risk factor for the well-being of FDPs. Diaków (2021, pp. 114–116) qualitatively investigated humanitarian-aid workers' experiences and reported that the most common psychosocial concerns included signs of burnout, anxiety, depression, stress-related disorders, and adjustment problems. Therefore, TC training for humanitarian workers should include stress management and trauma stewardship in connection with the development of emotional competence.

Severe Mental Health Disorders and Care Needs

Derrick Silove and colleagues report that mental health professionals working with refugees in Africa find that "a large proportion of the patients they consult manifest one or more ... forms of severe mental disorder." Applying a comprehensive perspective regarding the refugee experience, mental disorder associated with prolonged emotional distress, grieving, and/or adjustment difficulties constitutes "the endpoint of an imbalance in the multiplicity of countervailing environmental factors that impact on refugees rather than an expression of innate or intrapsychic problems at an individual level" (Silove, Ventevogel, and Rees, 2017, pp. 133–134). Specifically,

the refugee experience, which involves a sequence of adversity that traverses epochs of conflict, dislocation, flight, transition and resettlement, erodes the integrity of all five psychosocial systems [safety and security, interpersonal bonds and networks, justice, roles and identities, and existential meaning and coherence], thereby weakening social structures and institutions and exerting deleterious effects on the mental health of individuals.

(ibid., p. 134; also Almoshmosh, et al., 2020, p. 21)

"Precarious entitlements and conditional rights" coupled with prolonged detention and uncertainty about one's future (Hyndman and Giles, 2017, pp. xiv, 2) and multiple daily stressors – including internal tensions generated by unsafe, unhealthy, and economically vulnerable living environments (Silove, Ventevogel, and Rees, 2017, pp. 133–134; Arias and Araluce, 2021, pp. 571–572), crowding (Pilkington and Mbai, 2016, p. 5; Kitsantonis, 2021; Marume, January, and Maradzika, 2018, p. 378), "enforced proximity" (Sigona, 2015, pp. 8, 12), separation from family and other traditional support networks (Silove, Ventevogel, and Rees, 2017, p. 134), and hostile "host society attitudes of racism and xenophobia" (ibid., p. 135), compound the adverse (and sometimes initially suppressed and invisible) mental health wounds of past traumas. These conditions are associated with high levels of anxiety and depression among both Convention and *prima facie* refugees[28] (Farhat, et al., 2018, p. 8; Silove, Ventevogel, and Rees, 2017, p. 132; Matlin, et al., 2018, p. 19; Hyndman and Giles, 2017, pp. 10, 47; Wells, et al., 2018, p. 3; Mutiso, et al., 2019, pp. 204–205; Sualp, Okumus, and Molina, 2022, p. 320) and among undocumented migrants detained in removal centers (Kellezi, Wakefield, Bowe, Stevenson, and McNamara, 2021, p. 579). In the face of COVID-19, moreover, camp authorities further restricted movement in and out of camps and "suspended activities considered nonessential, including school and sports" (Berger, 2020). According to Doctors Without Borders COVID-19 Coordinator Caroline Willemen with specific reference to the Moria camp on the Greek island of Lesvos, "opportunities to get yourself out of this hell for a few hours have been vastly reduced," which "has had a very negative impact on people's mental health" (cited in ibid.; also see Allahi, 2021, p. 348). At the height of the pandemic, the Moria camp authorities congested FDPs in unsafe shelters eventually burnt to the ground, leaving at least 11,500 asylum seekers, including 4,000 young children, in despair for days (UNHCR, 2020).

Although UNHCR, WHO, governments, NGOs, and specialist agencies share responsibility for mental health support for refugees, the "reality is that most refugees with mental health problems will never receive appropriate services" due to scarcity and inequity in service provision (Silove, Ventevogel, and Rees, 2017, pp. 130, 132, 134, 137). Among care-seeking self-settled urban refugees, primary health-care providers typically lack training in identifying mental health needs and differ in ethnic and cultural backgrounds (Mutiso, et al., 2019, p. 211). The failure of humanitarian-aid workers to become versed in refugees' backgrounds and lack of language proficiency contribute to misinterpretation of mental health needs and hinder the delivery of MHPSS services (Diaków and Goforth, 2020, pp. 247–249; also see O'Brien and Federici, 2020, p. 130). Lacking transnational competence, moreover, primary-care providers often fail to discern migrant mental health challenges and migration-connected stressors, to provide culturally responsive and useful mental health treatment,[29] and to engage in effective referrals (Sainola-Rodriguez and Koehn, 2006; Diaków, 2021, p. 134).

Nevertheless, inequities "develop, diffuse, and reassemble" across contexts (Ozkazanc-Pan, 2019, p. 96). Thus, camps also provide a "place of new beginnings where sociality is remolded in new ways" (Turner, 2015, p. 139; also Sigona, 2015, p. 12) and transformative therapeutic landscapes can be established by supportive care providers (Sampson and Gifford, 2010, pp. 116–117; Eckenwiler and Wild, 2021, pp. 242–243). For instance, while non-Muslim and Western humanitarian aid workers tend to stigmatize gender-based cultural norms observed among Muslim refugee communities (e.g., families' protectiveness of female refugee youth) and view sibling support and supervision as a lack of parental care, among many Middle Eastern refugee communities, the aforementioned sociocultural phenomena are a manifestation of hidden resilience (Diaków and Goforth, 2020, p. 241). Hidden resilience is an underrepresented concept in the field of MHPSS studies that encapsulates socioculturally unconventional, or even stigmatized, coping strategies that can be seen as protective factors under adverse circumstances (e.g., displacement). Although limited or lack of parental supervision can be a risk factor in non-displacement settings, sibling supervision often offers a strong source of support for unaccompanied minors in camps.

For the *displaced*, building ties to one's place of resettlement has "particular saliency ... when it comes to restoring health and promoting well-being" (Sampson and Gifford, 2010, p. 117). From interactions with refugees at his Harvard clinic, Richard Mollica (2006, pp. 14–15, 100, 177) discovered that migrants possess an underappreciated capacity to recover from traumatic events and engage in self-healing through natural and imaginative wellness-promoting strategies, including work, altruistic, and spiritual practices. The journey to psychosocial well-being can be further enhanced by focusing on activities that introduce joy, laughter, and hope in the lives of migrants, including entertainment and sports programs, ethno-specific culinary adventures, storytelling and artistic projects, and exposure to outdoor (sun-splashed) physical exercise (Reitmanova and Gustafson, 2009, p. 51; Mollica, 2006, pp. 196–197, 204–206; Jones, 2020, pp. 15, 136–137; Moore, 2017; Matlin, et al., 2018, p. 21). By linking their spatially disconnected lifeworlds, migrants are transforming the boundaries of mental health care by introducing outlooks, possibilities, and helpful practices in origin as well as arrival places (Tiilikainen and Koehn, 2011).

Physical Health Challenges and Responses

As soon as persons fleeing conflict or persecution reach a place of safety outside their country of origin, physical ills associated with extreme danger and hardships become manifest (Jones, 2020, p. 86) and they often "require urgent medical attention in order to avoid further mortality and morbidity" (Pottie, Hui, and Schneider, 2016, p. 299). Among children who have been exposed to violence, moreover, the risk "for long-term health problems [including 'smoking, obesity, high-risk sexual behavior'] increases" (Ostergard and Griffin, 2020, p. 153).

Along with the immediate multinational response, the nature of the host country's reception of border crossers will constitute "a major determinant of their health, well-being and social integration" (Kirmayer, 2014, p. viii). The health condition of refugee children and their mothers often is affected negatively by insufficient antenatal care available to women during pregnancy (Benage, et al., 2015, pp. 3–16). Cultural and linguistic responsiveness plays a crucial role. Torun et al. (2018, p. 604) found that Syrian refugees displaced in Turkey encountered challenges using the health-care system due to the language barrier and limited assistance navigating a foreign health-care system.

In the late 1990s, the Sphere Project and the minimum standards set forth in its Humanitarian Charter articulated "technical measures for increasing the effectiveness of humanitarian aid, including areas such as minimum daily nutrient intake, the size of tents and access to water" (Davies, 2010, p. 111). Nevertheless, residents of camps and shelters often endure poor sanitary conditions (Pilkington and Mbai, 2016, p. 5), confront insufficient space for social distancing and isolation (Allahi, 2021, p. 362), are negatively impacted by environmental degradation (Karl and Karl, 2022, pp. 389–390; Mwangu, 2022, p. 445), are susceptible to debilitating cholera epidemics (Toole, 2019, p. 63), and are chronically plagued by viruses that "wend endlessly through the tents" (Dickerson, 2020; also see Toole and Waldman, 1997; Adams, Gardiner, and Assefi, 2004, p. 1548). Health care typically is limited to acute medical interventions and is not equipped to deal with determinants of health, chronic conditions, long-term care, and the needs of people with disabilities (Eckenwiler and Wild, 2021, p. 242). Without informed multisectoral (Allahi, 2021, pp. 348, 352, 358) interventions, including environmental mainstreaming (Karl and Karl, 2022, pp. 390, 392, 398),[30] camp life itself diminishes prospects for maintaining health, the "meta-capability necessary for all other capabilities" (Eckenwiler and Wild, 2021, p. 238).

Most "refugees and internally displaced persons in camps and camp-like settings are subject to cramped and poor living conditions that are not conducive to physical distancing and other COVID infection-control measures" (McAuliffe, Freier, Skeldon, and Blower, 2021, p. 11; also p. 33). In short, "with their mobility, malnourishment, lack of adequate shelter, and limited access to sufficient medical care, refugees are highly vulnerable to pathogenic colonization" (Price-Smith, 2009, p. 162; also p. 185). NGO-operated clinics inside camps tend to be "understaffed and overwhelmed" (Jones, 2020, pp. 83, 346).

COVID-19 further diminished the limited on-site presence of qualified and transnationally competent humanitarian-care providers in urban, camp, and detention contexts. Outbreaks of infections forced care providers to pause the delivery of aid, sometimes for several weeks, leaving camp residents without support. Refugee camps and reception points in Greece provide a dreadful illustration of the conundrum of pandemic-related negative outcomes hamstrung by austerity policies. Specifically, Greece closed its borders in March–April 2020, which almost entirely disabled the reception of forcibly displaced youth in South-eastern Europe (UNICEF, 2020). National restrictions on movement trapped refugees living in camps (e.g., Ritsona) and disabled them from accessing specialized health care or legal services in nearby cities (e.g., Chalkida, Athens) due to quarantines, the shrinking presence of on-site NGO humanitarian responders, and shortages in transportation.

At the same time, people living in receptor areas become vulnerable to negative health effects due to the influx of infectious diseases and additional burdens placed on local health facilities (Whitaker, 1999; McMichael, Barnett, and McMichael, 2012, p. 650; Kamara and Renzaho, 2016, p. 81). The promise of COVID-response initiatives like those launched by dislocated persons on Lesvos is instructive in this connection. There, in collaboration with local women,

> migrants from different countries set up an awareness team to provide information in their communities about the virus. They also set up wash stations, gave out hygiene products and created a mask making factory [that] ... distributed masks throughout the camp and to nurses at a local hospital.
>
> (Jones, 2020, p. 397)

It is important, therefore, that additional (often long-term) health resources be made available, preferably through community-based organizations, to both newcomers and existing inhabitants in recipient places (McCracken and Phillips, 2017, p. 311; Martin, et al., 2017, pp. 111–112; Davies, 2010, pp. 98, 110; Whitaker, 1999).

The Promise of Transnational-Competence Training and Education

A TC approach emphasizes an asset perspective (resilience enhancement, potential nurturing, and community-facilitated support) instead of focusing on deficits (Mawani, 2014, p. 29; Sleijpen, et al., 2016, p. 175). Taking into consideration the specific settlement context within which individuals are embedded, the challenge is to generate humanitarian aid processes and supportive community-based and peer-based interactions that reinforce resilience and survival skills developed during the migration process, enable the adoption of coherent and efficacious hybrid and fluid identities (Kirmayer, 2014, p. vii), and build and restore confidence in one's ability to maintain physical and mental well-being along with capacity to function successfully and contribute to sustainable development both locally and transnationally. Durable migration outcomes include local integration leading to belonging and security, relocation abroad leading to viable opportunities for personal and professional development and well-being, or repatriation to the country of origin leading to lasting safety and re-connection to nourishing roots and networks. Encounters with transnationally competent medical personnel, humanitarian responders, and social and mental health and psychosocial support workers constitute critical responses required for reaching durable migration outcomes. Chapters 5 and 6 elaborate on pathways to stakeholder TC.

Notes

1 For undocumented migrants in the UK, "time in detention can range from one day to a few years, and 30%–35% are detained for longer than 29 days" (Kellezi, Wakefield, Bowe, Stevenson, and McNamara, 2021, p. 579). On the perils faced by children in U.S. detention centers reported by physicians in a letter to the U.S. Senate's Whistleblower Protection Caucus, see Jordan (2018a); also see Jordan (2018b).
2 Informal settlements are "home" to a majority of young refugees in Greece.
3 Between 2011 and 2016, armed conflicts and related abuses displaced nearly half the entire population of Syria (Almoshmosh, Bahloul, Barkil-Oteo, Hassan, and Kirmayer, 2020, pp. 20–21).
4 Toole (2019, p. 57) notes that:

> the health status of IDPs may be worse than that of refugees because access to these populations by international relief agencies is often difficult and dangerous. Also, IDPs may suffer more injuries because they are usually located closer to zones of conflict than are refugees.

5 Jennifer Hyndman (2000, p. 159) found that "socio-economic status, gender, and class are factors determining who remains in the camps and who sets up independent households in urban areas."
6 Alexander Betts (2021, p. 3) reports partially contrary East African research findings that "refugees earn more, own more, and work more in the city, but are not necessarily happier, healthier, or better fed that those who live in camp-like settings."
7 UNHCR's ideal aim "in urban settings is for refugees to access quality health services at a level similar to that of nationals" (cited in Toole, 2019, p. 75).
8 For an in-depth treatment of life in the Dadaab Refugee Complex, see Rawlence (2016).
9 That is a context of "limbo with no promise of an ending" (Turner, 2015, p. 142).
10 Eckenwiler and Wild (2021, p. 237) maintain that most camp dwellers experience such confined living conditions as "living in an open-air prison."
11 Nguyen further maintains (2018, p. 18) that

> keeping people in a refugee camp is punishing people who have committed no crime except trying to save their own lives and the lives of their loved ones … The camp is the place where we keep those who we do not see as fully being human, and if we do not actively seek their death in most cases, we also often do not actively seek to restore many of them to the life they had before, the life we have ourselves.

12 Hyndman (2000, p. 159) provides the example of the young Somali man who "commuted daily from Marafa camp to work in the shop owned by his brother [in Malindi]."

13 Cindy Horst (2006, p. 211) points out that these connections can be strained as well as mutually rewarding.

14 Robin Cohen and Nicholas Van Hear (2020, p. 59) suggest that "the centre of gravity of many of the world's ethno-national groups that have become diasporized – including the Tamils, Palestinians, Kurds, Nepalis, Somalis, Afghans, and Armenians, to give just a few examples – lie outside the country of origin."

15 http://bhutaneserefugees.com (accessed January 28, 2019).

16 Pincock, Betts, and Easton-Calabria (2020, p. 119) note that refugee-led organizations are "almost entirely neglected in … the Global Compact on Refugees" and found that those "that succeed do so largely by bypassing formal delegation structures."

17 For details regarding the activities of five outstanding East African examples, see ibid., pp. 29–30.

18 Conditions experienced in Syria's detention centers often are lethal; from 2011 through 2015, conservative estimates indicate that more than 17,000 detainees died in custody across Syria (Amnesty International, 2016, p. 7).

19 Monitoring detention places also is "an essential activity and part of UNHCR's supervisory responsibility" (UNHCR, 2014, p. 12).

20 The cluster approach aims to improve operational coordination in humanitarian-relief situations by assigning leading agencies to 11 specific sectors that report to the United Nations Emergency Relief Coordinator (Chan, 2017, pp. 184–185). According to Alexander Aleinikoff and Susan Martin (2022, p. 38), the cluster system has led to "stronger partnerships between U.N. and other humanitarian organizations, and … higher quality proposals for raising funds for humanitarian operations." In some cases, however, the cluster approach has resulted in "the exclusion of national governments and local civil society from decision-making and implementation of humanitarian programs." On Lesvos and Samos, volunteer groups invented their own humanitarian cluster system "on the run, from the ground up" that involved a daily overall coordination meeting and avoided activity duplication (Jones, 2020, pp. 104, 352).

21 Agier (2011, p. 203) reports that "a dozen or so international NGOs mobilize 90 per cent of the total funds of humanitarian NGOs, and a small number of these have budgets larger than that of the UNHCR itself."

22 NGOs are the principal managers of particularly precarious camps for the internally displaced.

23 In 2006, UNHCR assumed responsibility for handling IDPs in camps (Agier, 2011, p. 203).

24 The Global Migration Group (GMG) of 22 U.N. agencies or entities meets to share information related to migration and to coordinate their related programs (Micinski, 2021, p. 139).

25 See, for instance, http://bhutaneserefugees.com (accessed January 28, 2019).

26 https://sdgs.un.org/

27 In addition to education and acculturation strategies, common sources of resilience among young refugees include social support, religion, avoidance, and hope for a better future (Sleijpen, et al., 2016, pp. 158, 169–171).

28 Although they are not official "Convention" refugees, UNHCR accepts field responsibility for civilians displaced by conflict (Agier, 2011, p. 57).

29 For a multi-layer approach to addressing diverse mental health and psychosocial support needs in post-disaster situations, see Chan (2017, pp. 160–162). Silove, Ventevogel, and Rees (2017, p. 134) report that "evidence suggests that various forms of psychotherapy are relatively effective in ameliorating symptoms of PTSD, depression and anxiety."

30 For instance, "through sustainable initiatives on energy generation, alternative cooking options, proper solid waste management and a safe water system, it is possible to save forests and improve women's safety and security in humanitarian crises and post-conflict situations" (Karl and Karl, 2022, p. 398).

References

Adams, Kristina M.; Gardiner, Lorin D.; and Assefi, Nassim. 2004. "Healthcare Challenges from the Developing World: Post-Immigration Refugee Medicine." *British Medical Journal* 328: 1548–1552.

Agier, Michel. 2011. *Managing the Undesirables: Refugee Camps and Humanitarian Government*. Cambridge: Polity.

Aleinikoff, T. Alexander; and Martin, Susan. 2022. *The Responsibility of the International Community in Situations of Mobility Due to Environmental Events*. Zolberg Institute Working Paper Series 2022–2021. New York: Zolberg Institute on Migration and Mobility, The New School.

Allahi, Fahimeh. 2021. "The COVID-19 Epidemic and Evaluating the Corresponding Responses to Crisis Management in Refugees: A System Dynamic Approach." *Journal of Humanitarian Logistics and Supply Chain Management* 11 (2): 347–366.

Almoshmosh, Nadim; Bahloul, Hussam J.; Barkil-Oteo, Andres; Hassan, Ghayda; and Kirmayer, Laurence J. 2020. "Mental Health of Resettled Syrian Refugees: A Practical Cross-Cultural Guide for Practitioners." *Journal of Mental Health Training, Education and Practice* 15 (1): 20–32.

Amnesty International (AI). 2016. "'It Breaks the Human': Torture, Disease and Death in Syria's Prisons." London: AI. Available at: https://www.amnesty.org/en/documents/mde24/4508/2016/en/ (accessed August 7, 2017).

Anderson, Mary B.; and Woodrow, Peter J. 1998. *Rising from the Ashes: Development Strategies in Times of Disaster*. Boulder, CO: Lynne Rienner.

Anghel, Roxana; and Grierson, J. 2020. "Addressing Needs in Liminal Space: The Citizen Volunteer Experience and Decision-Making in the Unofficial Calais Migrant Camp – Insights for Social Work." *European Journal of Social Work* 23 (3): 486–499.

Arias, Adriana G.; and Araluce, Olga A. 2021. "The Impact of the COVID-19 Pandemic on Human Mobility among Vulnerable Groups: Global and Regional Trends." *Journal of Poverty* 25 (7): 567–581.

Ballard-Kang, Jennifer L. 2020. "Using Culturally Appropriate, Trauma-Informed Support to Promote Bicultural Self-Efficacy among Resettled Refugees: A Conceptual Model." *Journal of Ethnic and Cultural Diversity in Social Work* 29 (1–3): 23–42.

Benage, Matthew; Greenough, Greg P.; Vinck, Patrick.; Omeira, Nada; and Pham, Phuong. 2015. "An Assessment of Antenatal Care among Syrian Refugees in Lebanon." *Conflict and Health* 9 (8): 1–11. https://doi.org/10.1186/s13031-015-0035-8.

Berger, Miriam. 2020. "From Kenya to Gaza to Bangladesh, Threat Grows for High-Risk Populations." *Washington Post*, September 3.

Betts, Alexander. 2021. "Refugees: Overcoming Prejudices." *UNESCO Courier*, 4.

Chan, Emily Ying Yang. 2017. *Public Health Humanitarian Responses to Natural Disasters*. London: Routledge.

Cohen, Robin; and Van Hear, Nicholas. 2020. *Refugia: Radical Solutions to Mass Displacement*. London: Routledge.

Cyril, Sheila; and Renzaho, Andre M.N. 2016. "Invisible and Suffering: Prolonged and Systematic Detention of Asylum Seekers Living in Substandard Conditions in Greece." In *Globalisation, Migration and Health: Challenges and Opportunities*, edited by Andre M.N. Renzaho. London: Imperial College Press, pp. 207–254.

Dahya, Negin; and Dryden-Peterson, Sarah. 2017. "Tracing Pathways to Higher Education for Refugees: The Role of Virtual Support Networks and Mobile Phones for Women in Refugee Camps." *Comparative Education* 51 (2): 284–301.

Davies, Sara. 2010. *Global Politics of Health*. Cambridge: Polity.

Diaków, Diana M. 2021. "Humanitarian Workers' Perspectives on Mental Health and Resilience of Refugee Youth: Implications for School Psychology." PhD dissertation, University of Montana.

Diaków, Diana M.; and Goforth, Anisa N. 2020. "Supporting Muslim Refugee Youth during Displacement: Implications for International School Psychologists." *School Psychology International* 42 (3): 238–258. https://doi.org/10.1177/0143034320987280.

Dickerson, Caitlin. 2020. "Trading Fear at Home for Misery on America's Doorstep." *New York Times*, October 24, p. A12.

Dryden-Peterson, Sarah. 2016. "Refugee Education in Countries of First Asylum: Breaking Open the Black Box of Pre-Resettlement Experiences." *Theory and Research in Education* 14 (2): 131–148.

Dryden-Peterson, Sarah; Dahya, Negin; and Adelman, Elizabeth. 2017. "Pathways to Educational Success among Refugees: Connecting Locally and Globally Situated Resources." *American Educational Research Journal* 54 (6): 1011–1047.

D'souza, Finola; Blatman, Zachary; Wier, Samuel; and Patel, Mitesh. 2022. "The Mental Health Needs of Lesbian, Gay, Bisexual, and Transgender (LGBT) Refugees: A Scoping Review." *Journal of Gay & Lesbian Mental Health* 26 (4): 341–366.

Eckenwiler, Lisa; and Wild, Verina. 2021. "Refugees and Others Enduring Displacement: Structural Injustice, Health, and Ethical Placemaking." *Journal of Social Philosophy* 52: 234–250.

Farhat, Jihane B.; Blanchet, Karl; Bjertrup, Pia J.; Veizis, Apoltolos; Perrin, Clement; Coulborn, Rebecca M.; Mayaud, Philippe; and Cohuet, Sandra. 2018. "Syrian Refugees in Greece: Experience with Violence, Mental Health Status, and Access to Information During the Journey and While in Greece." *BMC Medicine* 16 (40): 1–12.

Frew, Amy; Fausch, Aline; and Cox, Kaleb. 2016. *LGBTI Persons in Immigration Detention*. Victoria, Australia: International Detention Coalition.

Garcia-Zamora, Jean-Claude. 2017. "The Global Wave of Refugees and Migrants: Complex Challenges for European Policy Makers." *Public Organization Review* 17: 581–594.

Giles, Wenona. 2018. "The Borderless Higher Education for Refugees Project: Enabling Refugee and Local Kenyan Students in Dadaab to Transition to University Education." *Journal on Education in Emergencies* 4 (1): 164–184.

Gunn, S. William A. 2010. "The Humanitarian Imperative in Major Health Crises and Disasters." In *Understanding the Global Dimensions of Health*, edited by S.W.A. Gunn. New York: Springer, pp. 159–168.

Gupta, Alisha H. 2022. "Uprooted from Home, Migrants Often Pine for the Little Things." *New York Times*, October 24, p. A13.

Halsey, Kayla; Alarood, Salameh; Nawaiseh, Mohammed; and Mir, Ghazala. 2022. "An Exploration of Politicized Healthcare Access for Syrian and Palestinian Refugees in Jordan: A Question of Equity." *International Journal of Migration, Health and Social Care* 18 (1): 51–65.

Haysom, Simone; Pantuliano, Sara; and Davey, Eleanor. 2012. "Forced Migration in an Urban Context: Relocating the Humanitarian Agenda." In *World Disasters Report 2012*, edited by Roger Zetter. Geneva: International Federation of Red Cross and Red Crescent Societies (IFRC), pp. 113–143.

Hoffman, Peter J. 2021. "What Does 'Leave No One Behind' Mean for Humanitarians?" In *Routledge Handbook on the UN and Development*, edited by Stephen Browne and Thomas G. Weiss. London: Routledge, pp. 121–134.

Horst, Cindy. 2006. *Transnational Nomads: How Somalis Cope with Refugee Life in the Dadaab Camps of Kenya*. New York: Berghahn Books.

Hyndman, Jennifer. 2000. *Managing Displacement: Refugees and the Politics of Humanitarianism*. Minneapolis, MN: University of Minnesota Press.

Hyndman, Jennifer; and Giles, Wenona. 2017. *Refugees in Extended Exile: Living on the Edge*. London: Routledge.

International Rescue Committee. 2018. "Unprotected, Unsupported, Uncertain. Recommendations to Improve the Mental Health of Asylum Seekers on Lesvos." Available at: https://www.rescue.org/sites/default/files/document/3153/unprotecte dunsupporteduncerta.in.pdf

Jones, Lynne. 2020. *The Migrant Diaries*. New York: Refuge Press.

Jordan, Miriam. 2018a. "Doctors Blow Whistle on Dangers Migrant Children Face in Detention." *New York Times*, July 19, p. A14.

Jordan, Miriam. 2018b. "Federal Report Cites Disregard for Safety at Immigrant Detention Facility." *New York Times*, October 4, p. A15.

Jordan, Miriam. 2021. "Squalid Border Camp Closed: A New One Is Worse." *New York Times*, August 30, p. A13.

Kamara, Joseph; and Renzaho, Andre M.N. 2016. "The Social and Health Dimensions of Refugees and Complex Humanitarian Emergencies." In *Globalisation, Migration and Health: Challenges and Opportunities*, edited by Andre M.N. Renzaho. London: Imperial College Press, pp. 73–122.

Kamei, Satomi. 2022. "Cross-Border Refugee Crisis and Local Governments in the West Nile Region, Uganda." In *Perspectives on the State Borders in Globalized Africa*, edited by Yuichi Sasaoka; Aime Raoul; Sumo Tayo; and Sayoko Uesu. London: Routledge, pp. 54–70.

Karl, Alexandre A.; and Karl, Julia S. 2022. "Human Rights for Refugees: Enhancing Sustainable Supply Chain to Guarantee a Health Environment in Refugee Settlements." *Journal of Humanitarian Logistics and Supply Chain Management* 12 (3): 382–403.

Kellezi, Blerina; Wakefield, Juliet; Bowe, Mhairi; Stevenson, Clifford; and McNamara, Niamh. 2021. "Healthcare Provision Inside Immigration Removal Centres: A Social Identity Analysis of Trust, Legitimacy and Disengagement." *Applied Psychology Health and Well-Being* 13: 578–601.

Kirmayer, Laurence J. 2014. "Foreword." In *Refuge and Resilience: Promoting Resilience and Mental Health among Resettled Refugees and Forced Migrants*, edited by Laura Simich and Lisa Andermann. New York: Springer, pp. vii–ix.

Kitsantonis, Niki. 2021. "Arson Charges for Refugee in Greek Camp." *New York Times*, February 26, p. A10.

Koehn, Peter H. 1991. *Refugees from Revolution: U.S. Policy and Third-World Migration*. Boulder, CO: Westview Press.

Koehn, Peter H. 2013. "Mental Health and Migration." In *The Encyclopaedia of Global Human Migration*, edited by Immanuel Ness, vol. 4. Oxford: Blackwell Publishing, pp. 2164–2168. doi:10.1002/9781444351071.wbeghm362.

Lacey, Marc. 2005. "In Africa, Guns Aren't the Only Killers." *New York Times*, April 25.

Lindley, Anna; and Hammond, Laura. 2014. "Histories and Contemporary Challenges of Crisis and Mobility in Somalia." In *Crisis and Migration: Critical Perspectives*, edited by Anna Lindley. London: Routledge, pp. 46–72.

Lovey, Thibault; O'Keeffe, Paul; and Petignat, Ianis. 2021. "Basic Medical Training for Refugees via Collaborative Blended Learning: Quasi-Experimental Design." *Journal of Medicine Internet Research* 23 (3): 1–14.

Mandic, Danilo. 2021. "What Is the Force of Forced Migration? Diagnosis and Critique of a Conceptual Relativization." *Theory and Society* (April): 1–30. doi:10.1007/s11186-021-09446-0.

Martin, Susan F.; Davis, Rochelle; Benton, Grace; and Waliany, Zoya. 2017. *Responsibility Sharing for Refugees in the Middle East and North Africa: Perspectives from Policymakers, Stakeholders, Refugees and Internally Displaced Persons.* Report 2017:8. Stockholm: Delmi, The Migration Studies Delegation.

Marume, Anesu; January, James; and Maradzika, Julita. 2018. "Social Capital, Health-Seeking Behavior and Quality of Life among Refugees in Zimbabwe: A Cross-Sectional Study." *International Journal of Migration, Health and Social Care* 14 (4): 377–386.

Matlin, Stephen A.; Depoux, Anneliese; Schutte, Stefanie; Flahault, Antoine; and Saso, Luciano. 2018. "Migrants' and Refugees' Health: Towards an Agenda of Solutions." *Public Health Reviews* 39 (27): 1–55.

Mavroudi, Elizabeth; and Nagel, Caroline. 2016. *Global Migration: Patterns, Processes, and Politics.* London: Routledge.

Mawani, Farah N. 2014. "Social Determinants of Refugee Mental Health." In *Refuge and Resilience: Promoting Resilience and Mental Health among Resettled Refugees and Forced Migrants*, edited by Laura Simich and Lisa Andermann. New York: Springer, pp. 27–50.

Mbai, Isabella I.; Mangeni, Judith N.; Abuelaish, Izzeldin; and Pilkington, F. Beryl. 2017. "Community Health Worker Training and Education in a Refugee." In *Science Research and Education in Africa: Proceedings of a Conference on Science Advancement*, edited by Alain L. Fymat and Joachim Kapalanga. Newcastle Upon Tyne: Cambridge Scholars Publishing, pp. 163–186.

McAuliffe, Marie; Freier, Luisa F.; Skeldon, Ronald; and Blower, Jenna. 2021. "The Great Disrupter: COVID-19's Impact on Migration, Mobility and Migrants Globally." In *World Migration Report 2022*, edited by Marie McAuliffe and A. Triandafyllidou. Geneva: International Organization for Migration, pp. 151–172.

McCracken, Kevin; and Phillips, David R. 2017. *Global Health: An Introduction to Current and Future Trends.* London: Routledge.

McMichael, Celia; Barnett, Jon; and McMichael, Anthony J. 2012. "An Ill Wind? Climate Change, Migration, and Health." *Environmental Health Perspectives* 120 (5): 646–654.

Micinski, Nicholas R. 2021. "Migration and Development in the UN Global Compacts." In *Routledge Handbook on the UN and Development*, edited by Stephen Browne and Thomas G. Weiss. London: Routledge, pp. 135–147.

Milner, James. 2021. "Refugees and International Development Policy and Practice." In *Introduction to International Development: Approaches, Actors, Issues, and Practice*, edited by Paul Haslam; Jessica Shafer; and Pierre Beaudet. Oxford: Oxford University Press, pp. 408–425.

Mollica, Richard F. 2006. *Healing Invisible Wounds: Paths to Hope and Recovery in a Violent World.* Orlando, FL: Harcourt.

Moore, Temple. 2017. "Strengths-Based Narrative Storytelling as Therapeutic Intervention for Refugees in Greece." *World Federation of Occupational Therapists Bulletin* 73 (1): 45–51.

Mutiso, Victoria; Warsame, Abdulkadir H.; Bosire, Edna; Musyimi, Christine; Musau, Abednego; Isse, Maimuna M.; and Ndetei, David M. 2019. "Intrigues of Accessing Mental Health Services among Urban Refugees Living in Kenya: The

Case of Somali Refugees Living in Eastleigh, Nairobi." *Journal of Immigrant and Refugee Studies* 17 (2): 204–221.

Mwangu, Alex R. 2022. "An Assessment of Economic and Environmental Impacts of Refugees in Nakivale, Uganda." *Migration and Development* 11 (3): 433–449.

Nguyen, Viet Thanh. 2018. "Introduction." In *The Displaced: Refugee Writers on Refugee Lives*, edited by Viet Thanh Nguyen. New York: Abrams Press, pp. 11–22.

O'Brien, Sharon; and Federici, Frederico M. 2020. "Crisis Translation: Considering Language Needs in Multilingual Disaster Settings." *Disaster Prevention and Management* 29 (3): 129–143.

Ostergard, Robert L. Jr.; and Griffin, Jeffrey A. 2020. "Global Health and Human Security." In *The Oxford Handbook of Global Health Politics*, edited by Colin McInnes; Kelley Lee; and Jeremy Youde. Oxford: Oxford University Press, pp. 143–160.

Ozkazanc-Pan, Banu. 2019. *Transnational Migration and the New Subjects of Work: Transmigrants, Hybrids and Cosmopolitans*. Bristol: Bristol University Press.

Perouse de Montclos, Marc-Antoine; and Kagwanja, Peter M. 2000. "Refugee Camps or Cities: The Socio-Economic Dynamics of the Dadaab and Kakuma Camps in Northern Kenya." *Journal of Refugee Studies* 13 (2): 205–222.

Pilkington, F. Beryl; and Mbai, Isabella. 2016. "Researching the Gap between the Existing and Potential Community Health Worker Education and Training in the Refugee Context: An Intersectoral Approach." Final Interim Report to IDRC. July 31. Toronto: York University.

Pilkington, F. Beryl; Mbai, Isabella; Mangeni, Judith; and Abuelaish, Izzeldin. 2016. "An Educational Model for Building Health Care Capacity in Protracted Refugee Contexts." IDRC Policy Brief. August. Toronto: York University.

Pincock, Kate; Betts, Alexander; and Easton-Calabria, Evan. 2020. *The Global Governed? Refugees as Providers of Protection and Assistance*. Cambridge: Cambridge University Press.

Pottie, Kevin; Hui, Chuck; and Schneider, Fabien. 2016. "Women, Children and Men Trapped in Unsafe Corridors ." In *Globalisation, Migration and Health: Challenges and Opportunities*, edited by Andre M.N. Renzaho. London: Imperial College Press, pp. 291–303.

Price-Smith, Andrew T. 2009. *Contagion and Chaos: Disease, Ecology, and National Security in the Era of Globalization*. Cambridge, MA: MIT Press.

Ramsay, Georgina; and Baker, Sally. 2019. "Higher Education and Students from Refugee Backgrounds: A Meta-Scoping Study." *Refugee Survey Quarterly* 38: 55–82.

Rawlence, Be. 2016. *City of Thorns: Nine Lives in the World's Largest Refugee Camp.* New York: Picador.

Reitmanova, S., and Gustafson, D.L. 2009. "Mental Health Needs of Visible Minority Immigrants in a Small Urban Center: Recommendations for Policy Makers and Service Providers." *Journal of Immigrant and Minority Health* 11: 46–56.

Sainola-Rodriguez, Kirsti; and Koehn, Peter H. 2006. "The Mental-Health Needs of Political-Asylum Seekers and Resident Foreign Nationals in Finland: Patient Perspectives and Practitioner Recognition." *Sosiaalilaaketieteellinen Aikakausilehti* [*Journal of Social Medicine*] 43: 47–59.

Sampson, Robyn; Chew, Vivienne; Mitchell, Grant; and Bowring, Lucy. 2015. *There are Alternatives: A Handbook for Preventing Unnecessary Immigration Retention*, rev. edn. Victoria, Australia: International Detention Coalition.

Sampson, Robyn; and Gifford, Sandra M. 2010. "Place-Making, Settlement and Well-Being: The Therapeutic Landscapes of Recently Arrived Youth with Refugee Backgrounds." *Health & Place* 16: 116–131.

Sigona, Nando. 2015. "Campzenship: Reimagining the Camp as a Social and Political Space." *Citizenship Studies* 19 (1): 1–15.

Silove, Derrick; Ventevogel, Peter; and Rees, Susan. 2017. "The Contemporary Refugee Crisis: An Overview of Mental Health Challenges." *World Psychiatry* 16 (2): 130–138.

Sleijpen, Marieke; Boeije, Hennie R.; Kleber, Rolf J.; and Mooren, Trudy. 2016. "Between Power and Powerlessness: A Meta-Ethnography of Sources of Resilience in Young Refugees." *Ethnicity & Health* 21 (2): 158–180.

Sualp, Kenan; Okumus, F. Elif E.; and Molina, Olga. 2022. "Group Work Training for Mental Health Professionals Working with Syrian Refugee Children in Turkey: A Needs Assessment Study." *Social Work with Groups* 45 (3–4):319–335.

Tabak, Shana; and Levitan, Rachel. 2013. "LGBTI Migrants in Immigration Detention." *Forced Migration Review* 42: 47–49.

Teissen, Rebecca; and Lough, Benjamin J. 2019. "International Volunteering Capacity Development: Volunteer Partner Organization Experiences of Mitigating Factors for Effective Practice." *Forum for Development Studies* 46 (2): 299–320.

Tiilikainen, Marja; and Koehn, Peter H. 2011. "Transforming the Boundaries of Healthcare: Insights from the Transnational Outlooks and Practices of Somali Migrants." *Medical Anthropology* 30 (5): 1–27.

Toole, Mike. 2019. "Health in Humanitarian Crises." In *The Health of Refugees: Public Health Perspectives from Crisis to Settlement*, 2nd edn, edited by Pascale Allotey and Daniel D. Reidpath. Oxford: Oxford University Press, pp. 54–84.

Toole, M.J.; and Waldman, R.J. 1997. "The Public Health Aspects of Complex Emergencies and Refugee Situations." *Annual Review of Public Health* 18: 283–312.

Torun, Perihan; Karaaslan Mücaz, Maltem; Sendikli, Büşra; Acar, Ceyda; Shurtleff, Ellyn; Dhrolia, Sophia; and Herek, Bülent. 2018. "Health and Health Care Access for Syrian Refugees Living in Istanbul." *International Journal of Public Health* 63 (5): 601–608. https://doi.org/10.1007/s00038-018-1096-4.

Turner, Simon. 2015. "What Is a Refugee Camp? Explorations of the Limits and Effects of the Camp." *Journal of Refugee Studies* 29 (2): 139–147.

UNHCR (United Nations High Commission for Refugees). 2014. *Beyond Detention: A Global Strategy to Support Governments to End the Detention of Asylum-Seekers and Refugees, 2014–2019*. Geneva: UNHCR.

UNHCR (United Nations High Commission for Refugees). 2020. Official Press Release, September 11. Available at: https://www.unhcr.org/news/briefing/2020/9/5f5b3a774/unhcr-shocked-fires-moria-asylum-center-ramping-support-affected-asylum.html

UNICEF (United Nations International Child's Emergency Fund). 2020. *Refugee and Migrant. Children in Greece*. Available at: https://www.unicef.org/eca/media/10861/file.

Vadivelu, Vijayalakshmi. 2014. "Evaluating Disaster Risk Management in the Face of Climate Change." In *Evaluating Environment in International Development*, edited by Juha I. Uitto. London: Routledge, pp. 172–193.

Wells, Ruth; Lawsin, Catalina; Hunt, Caroline; Youssef, Omar Said; Abujado, Fayzeh; and Steel, Zachary. 2018. "An Ecological Model of Adaptation to Displacement: Individual, Cultural and Community Factors Affecting Psychological

Adjustment among Syrian Refugees in Jordan." *Global Mental Health* 5: 1–13. doi:10.1017/gmh.2018.30

Whitaker, Beth E. 1999. "Changing Opportunities: Refugees and Host Communities in Western Tanzania." New Issues in Refugee Research Working Paper No. 71. Geneva: United Nations High Commission for Refugees (UNHCR).

White House. 2021. *Report on the Impact of Climate Change on Migration*. Washington, D.C.: White House.

Zibar, Layla; Abujidi, Nurhan; and de Meulder Brandenburg, Bruno. 2022. "Who/ What Is Doing What? Dwelling and Homing Practices in Syrian Camps – The Kurdistan Region of Iraq." In *Making Home(s) in Displacement: Critical Reflections on a Spatial Practice*, edited by Luce Beeckmans; Alessandra Gola; Ashika Singh; and Hilde Heynen. Leuven: Leuven University Press, pp. 83–116.

3 Climate-Displaced Migration
Drivers, Context, Stakeholders, and Needs

The Sixth Assessment Report of the Intergovernmental Panel on Climate Change (IPCC), released in 2022, recognizes that "through displacement and involuntary migration from extreme weather and climate events, climate change has generated and perpetuated vulnerability" (IPCC, 2022, p. 11). The Report goes on to state that "in rural areas vulnerability will be heightened by compounding processes including high emigration, reduced habitability and high reliance on climate-sensitive livelihoods" and that "future exposure to climatic hazards is also increasing globally due to socioeconomic development trends including migration, growing inequality and urbanization" (ibid., p. 13). In 2021, a group of international scientists summarized predictions that Earth is headed for "a ghastly future of mass extinction, declining health, and climate-disruption upheavals." They added that climate-induced mass migration and more pandemics are inevitable without urgent action and that "the gravity of the situation requires fundamental changes to global capitalism, *education*, and equality" (Bradshaw, et al., 2021; emphasis added). From Abrahm Lustgarten's vantage point (2020a), "of all the devastating consequences of a warming planet — changing landscapes, pandemics, mass extinctions — the potential movement of hundreds of millions of climate refugees across the planet stands to be among the most important." This chapter is devoted to exploring the upstream and downstream drivers of climate-induced migration, arising stakeholder TC training needs in displacement contexts, and promising responses that promote health and resilience.

Climate, Climate Change, and Migration: Looming Outlooks

According to the National Aeronautics and Space Administration, climate "refers to the long-term (usually at least 30 years) regional or even global average of temperature, humidity, and rainfall patterns over seasons, years, or decades." Climate change involves "long-term change in the average weather patterns that have come to define Earth's local, regional and global climates"[1] – specifically, alterations in "temperature, precipitation patterns, the frequency and severity of certain weather events, and other features of the climate system" (White House, 2021, p. 4). Widespread climate change-

DOI: 10.4324/9781003330493-4

induced dangers to human health of extreme heat and weather events, wild-fires, air pollution, and the spread of water-borne and insect-borne diseases are now commonplace (see Filho, et al., 2022, p. 376). An "extreme event" involves "a time and place in which weather, climate, or environmental conditions – such as temperature, precipitation, drought, or flooding – rank above a threshold value near the upper or lower end of the range of historical measurement" (White House, 2021, p. 7). Between 2008 and 2016, sudden onset weather hazards displaced an average of 21.5 million people annually (ibid., p. 4).

In one model, unliveable hot zones are likely to expand from 1 percent of current planetary land area to 19 percent by 2070 (Lustgarten, 2020b). With future temperature increases expected to reach or exceed 1.5°C of warming (IPCC, 2021), climatic change is particularly likely to generate persistent and drastic impacts on health and migration tendencies in lower-latitude countries like India (Ives, 2017; Plumer and Popovich, 2017; McMichael, Barnett, and McMichael, 2012, p. 647).

The World Bank estimates that unchecked climate change will push up to 130 million people into poverty in the next decade (Nishio, 2021).[2] This outcome is particularly unfair, as poor people contribute the least to climate change. In addition, the socio-economic resilience and well-being of poor people are disproportionately at risk from natural disasters (Hellegatte, Vogt-Schilb, Bangalore, and Rozenberg, 2017, pp. 4, 7–8). People living on the edge in countries least responsible for greenhouse gas (GHG) emissions also face particular psychological vulnerability to climate-change stressors (Baker, 2021). Migration decisions, however, involve complex considerations and must be analyzed in context (Kelman, 2015).

Relocation is "often a forced, or even brutal, decision when a disaster leaves no other alternative or where adaptation efforts in the face of environmental degradation have not proved successful" (Ionesco, Mokhnacheva, and Gemenne, 2017, p. 70). When living off the land becomes unimaginable in the Sahel, climate-displaced youth from Niger, Mali, and Chad are joining their conflict-displaced contemporaries on the perilous journey north to Libya and places beyond. For high-latitude people especially reliant on the natural environment, such as the Inuit, climate change disrupts traditional diets and sustenance (McMichael, 2013, p. 1336), and generates harmful health consequences. In middle (particularly coastal) latitudes, the severity of storms and flooding exacerbated by climate change results in elevated levels of long-term destruction, dislocation, and risk (Leonhardt, 2017).[3] Small island developing states (SIDS) are particularly vulnerable to the devastating effects of climate change due to the limited size of their resource base and economies, remoteness, and exposure to sea-level rise and weather events (Batra and Norheim, 2022).

One study of slow-onset changes in the West and East Antarctica ice sheets warns that "the sea level could rise as much as six feet [about 1.8 meters] by the end of this century," with catastrophic consequences for sea-proximate dwellings, property, and buildings (cited in Gillis, 2017, p. A12; also see Pierre-Louis, 2018). The inevitable melting of the Greenland ice sheet will trigger nearly another "foot [30 cm] of global sea-level rise ... [by] the year 2100" (Mooney, 2022). At current rates of GHG emissions, a different study anticipates that coastal flooding will place 204 million people at risk of dislocation as early as 2050 (Plumer, 2020). While all coastal areas are subject to climatic impacts, sea-level rise will not be uniform across the globe, but will be influenced by factors such as topography, thermal expansion, ocean currents, and resources available for protective measures. For people inhabiting coastal areas, the rate at which seas rise will matter more than the height (Goodell, 2017, pp. 10–14). In a worst-case scenario, "a rapid deterioration of Antarctica might ... cause the sea to rise so fast that tens of millions of coastal refugees would have to flee inland, potentially straining societies to the breaking point" (Gillis, 2017, p. A11; also see Goodell, 2017, pp. 52–55, 69, 182).

Vulnerability to flooding is exacerbated by other changes in weather patterns. There is broad scientific agreement that global warming and ocean warming are changing storms in at least five ways: (1) generating more powerful hurricane winds; (2) unleashing higher amounts of rainfall; (3) producing slower, wetter patterns that worsen flooding; (4) enlarging the zone of hurricanes, i.e., more storms are making landfalls in higher latitudes; and (5) increasing intensity and volatility, resulting in less warning when tropical storms develop into category 4 hurricanes (Penney, 2020).

While risks and vulnerabilities to climate change have been widely recognized in science, coastal cities are growing faster than inland places and effective response strategies have been slow to emerge (Fuchs, Conran and Louis, 2011). Guangzhou, Shanghai, and Tianjin rank among the world's most exposed megacities in terms of infrastructure assets (UNHSP, 2011, p. 71). Shanghai is particularly vulnerable to the layering of coastal hazards, including land subsidence (Blackburn and Marques, 2013, pp. 4, 12–13). In these three densely populated and economically dynamic centers alone, a sizeable proportion of China's annual GDP, and up to 130 million people, are at risk (Adger, et al., 2001, p. 577). According to former U.S. Energy Secretary Stephen Chu, sea-level rise would displace greater numbers of people in China than in any other country, including Bangladesh (cited in Bradsher, 2009, p. A10).[4] Unplanned migration of such magnitude "has significant public health implications at its origins, along the migration routes and in the receptor areas" (Samet and Zhang, 2014, p. 292).

The number of people vulnerable to sea-level rise continues to increase in the face of population growth, in-migration to coastal cities, land sinking, storm surges, and small island encroachments (see Lustgarten, 2020a; 2020b). Clearly, and likely inevitably, sea-level rise accompanied by coastal erosion, storm surges, and saltwater intrusions will generate millions of climate migrants – especially in low-income countries where infrastructure is of poor quality and resources are not available to build seawalls and restore and raise buildings/roads (Goodell, 2017, pp. 220–221, 231; Sengupta and Lee, 2020).

In short, migration triggered by climate stressors and accompanying health threats, often in combination with other contributors, including poor people's inability to rebuild, has arrived with a vengeance. And, more is on the way. Consequently, migration becomes an increasingly imperative form of climate adaptation (Butros, Gyberg, and Kaijser, 2021, p. 851).

Drivers of Climate-Displaced Migration

In light of the devastating connections, the Paris Agreement adopted at the Conference of Parties to the United Nations Framework Convention on Climate Change (COP21) specifically referenced links between climate change, displacement, and unintended migration (Ionesco, Mokhnacheva, and Gemenne, 2017, pp. 95, 112–113)[5] and established a task force charged with providing "recommendations on integrated approaches to avert, minimize, and address displacement related to the adverse impacts of climate change" (White House, 2021, p. 25). The threats associated with climatic change, particularly uninhabitable renderings associated with sea-level rise, have prodded the "'rediscovery' of the environment as determining factor in migration" (Ionesco, Mokhnacheva, and Gemenne, 2017, p. 2; also see Skeldon, 2021, p. 107; Aleinikoff and Martin, 2022, p. 5).[6] Coincidentally, the connection of habitat destruction with the Ebola outbreak and the COVID pandemic dramatically demonstrated "how closely related environmental health and human health are" (Uitto, 2021, pp. 437–438).

Scientists expect that climate change in conjunction with other contributors will result in growing population displacement and migration (Nansen Initiative, 2015, p. 8). Typhoons (hurricanes), exacerbated monsoons (Fountain, 2022b), floods (Chan, 2017, p. 97), wildfires (Zhong, 2022a), and droughts (Chan, 2017, pp. 102–103, 105–106; McMichael, Barnett, and McMichael, 2012, pp. 648–649), along with immediate or anticipated sea-level rise feature as phenomena inducing climate migration. Prolonged and recurrent drought "undermines livelihoods and is a principal cause of displacement for millions who rely on subsistence agriculture and pastoralism in substantial parts of East and West Africa" (Martin and Zetter, 2012, p. 24; also Chan, 2017, p. 103). When drought conditions reinforce "conflict or other political factors, food insecurity may be the factor that forces populations that have exhausted all their coping strategies to migrate or starve" (Martin and Zetter, 2012, p. 24). According to the United Nations, by 2025, there will be 1.8 billion people in countries and regions with absolute water scarcity and two-thirds of the world's population are likely to be living under water-stressed conditions.[7] In Syria, the African Sahel region, and Somalia, "water scarcity and conflict" already have contributed to the migration of millions of desperate persons (Sullivan and Townsend, 2022, p. 915; Walsh, 2022).

As noted above, sea-level rise alone threatens to generate millions of transnational climate migrants. In large measure, rising ocean levels can be attributed to GHG emissions from China, the USA, the European Union (EU), Russia, and India (see Butros, Gyberg, and Kaijser, 2021, p. 852). Although China has overtaken the USA as the world's largest emitter of GHGs (see Bradsher and Krauss, 2022), and other newly industrialized middle-income countries (MICs) are quickly following suit, it is the countries in North America and Europe that account for the overwhelming amount of emissions in historical terms (Bearak and Popovich, 2022). And still today, their per-capita emissions clearly outstrip those from other parts of the world. According to World Bank data, annual per-capita GHG emissions in 2019 were: Australia 15.2 MT; the USA 14.7 MT; Japan 8.5 MT; Germany 7.9 MT; China 7.6 MT; India 1.8 MT; and Benin 0.6 MT.[8]

Although the Pacific region is responsible only for a tiny fraction of global GHG emissions, small island states face some of the most severe migration pressures associated with climatic change (Ferris, Cernea, and Petz, 2011, pp. 3, 5, 19). In the wake of sea-level rise, "the citizens of Kiribati, Tuvalu, Tokelau and the Marshall Islands will most likely have to be resettled by 2050" (Butros, Gyberg, and Kaijser, 2021, p. 843). The government of Kiribati, a remote Pacific island less than 6 feet above sea level, has proactively purchased several thousand acres of land in Fiji, 1000 miles away as a potential relocation site for its 100,000 citizens. In the Maldives, where islands in the Indian Ocean barely clear sea level, the government has dedicated substantial sums and commenced the relocation of thousands of residents from outer atolls to Hulhumalé (see Muller, 2022).[9] A study of alternative scenarios for the Marshall Islands reported by Nakayama et al. (2022, p. 323) concludes that while migration is and will be happening, other options, such as land reclamation and raising, merit simultaneous consideration (particularly in light of relocation inertia). They also found that "none of the atoll countries in the Pacific (e.g., Kiribati, RMI and Tuvalu) have made a firm decision about the way they manage anticipated sea level rise by climate change."

We expect that members of vulnerable populations, especially persons living in coastal megacities and densely settled delta areas, increasingly will resort to migration as a "proactive diversification strategy" in anticipation of climate-change impacts; others will be forced to move abruptly and reluctantly in the wake of climate-influenced disasters (Bardsley and Hugo, 2010, pp. 239, 242, 244–245, 248; Martin, Bergmann, Rigaud, and Yameogo, 2021, p. 145; Hauer, et al., 2020; Pierre-Louis, 2019). Actual movement occurs when "people believe they no longer have the capacity to adapt to ... [environmental] hazards or anticipate worsening conditions in the future" (Aleinikoff and Martin, 2022, p. 5; also Bardsley and Hugo, 2010). As James Morrissey (2008) shows in the case of Ethiopian highlanders stressed by drought, people consider a range of individual, environmental, economic, and structural factors when "calculating the relative advantages of moving against the relative advantages of remaining behind" (also see Etana, Snelder, Van Wesenbeeck, and Buning, 2022). The mobility of aging and disabled family members, children, pets, and the type of structure one calls home are among the factors potential climate migrants take into account. Policy makers also need to take emotional attachments to one's living place into consideration.

Many among the poorest and most vulnerable to climate-induced disasters often lack the resources and capacity needed to move. As Anna Rhodes and Max Besbris (2022) report, "encouraging mobility will require better information on the risks of staying put and [about] the [enhanced] resources residents would have access to in less-flood-prone neighborhoods." Both those who move and those left behind merit our attention (see George, 2022) and would benefit from TC preparation.

Displacement Contexts

The number of people vulnerable to sea-level rise continues to grow in the face of population growth, in-migration to coastal cities, land subsidence, storm surges, and small island encroachments (Ionesco, Mokhnacheva, and Gemenne, 2017, pp. 50–53; Griggs, 2018). In *The Water Will Come*, Jeff Goodell (2017, pp. 178, 13–14) looks ahead and asks: "What do rich industrialized nations like the United States and the European Union owe them?" "Will we [the North] welcome people who flee submerged coastlines and sinking islands – or will we imprison them?" As Mohamed Nasheed, former Maldives President, challenged the leaders of wealthy Northern GHG-emitting countries:

> 'You can drastically reduce your greenhouse-gas emissions so that the seas do not rise so much … Or, when we show up on your shores in our boats, you can let us in … Or, when we show up on your shores in our boats, you can shoot us. You pick.'
>
> (cited in ibid., pp. 187–188)

John Sullivan and Keeley Townsend (2022, pp. 914–916, 920) contend that the growing resource pressures and competition associated with flooding, drought, and (in particular) water scarcity, all three induced by climate change expand global vulnerability to a "cascade of [inter-state and intra-state] unrest, conflict, crime, and terrorism" associated with forced migration (also see White House, 2021, p. 7; Matlin, et al., 2018, p. 7; Hamlin, 2021, p. 4). Contrary to popular notions about "water wars," there is no evidence that countries would have gone to war due to water availability — largely because there can hardly be any winners (Pearse-Smith, 2012; Wolf, 2007). At the local level, however,

> findings from the growing body of rigorous research in economics, as well as from political science and other disciplines that use modern

econometric analytical approaches, indicate that adverse climatic events increase the risk of violence and conflict, at both the interpersonal level and the intergroup level, in societies around the world and throughout history.

(Burke, Hsiang and Miguel, 2015, p. 610)

In addition, the risk that mass environmental displacements will result in violent conflict is heightened when linked to existing tensions and failed policies (Ionesco, Mokhnacheva, and Gemenne, 2017, pp. 82–83).

Following the practice applied in determining whether someone is an official *Convention* refugee, climate change need not be the *main* reason responsible for the cross-border displacement of someone defined as a climate or environmental migrant (see Dun and Gemenne, 2008, p. 10). Although not afforded legal recognition or automatically guaranteed the right of *non-refoulement* (Butros, Gyberg, and Kaijser, 2021, p. 844; Aleinikoff and Martin, 2022, pp. 5–6, 23; White House, 2021, pp. 17, 21) and referred to by UNHCR as "persons displaced in the context of climate change" (cited in Karl and Karl, 2022, p. 388), the U.N. Human Rights Committee recognized in a 2020 ruling that "international refugee law is applicable in the context of climate change and disaster displacement." The Committee supported its decision with reference to findings that

[UNHCR] has consistently stressed that people fleeing adverse effects of climate change … may have valid claims for refugee status under the 1951 Refugee Convention or regional refugee frameworks. This includes but is not limited to situations where climate change and disasters are intertwined with conflict and violence.

(cited in Sullivan and Townsend, 2022, p. 916)[10]

Interconnected conditions include lack of access to life-sustaining resources by persons targeted or marginalized by conflict, disproportionate impacts on "already marginalized communities',"[11] inability to seek safety in one's country of origin (Aleinikoff and Martin, 2022, p. 17), withholding of relief "in a manner and to a degree amounting to persecution" (White House, 2021, p. 17), and the absence of functioning dispute resolution institutions (ibid., pp. 8, 15) – including peace builders endowed with TC.

Whether the outcome is refuge in the North or South, the magnitude of the resettlement challenge is daunting when the prospective numbers of climate migrants is superimposed alongside the lack of measurable progress across the planet in meeting essential emission-reduction goals (Fountain, 2022a). Given that flood prevention in the face of sea-level rise is prohibitively expensive (Tanner and Horn-Phathanothai, 2014, p. 77), emergency responders can be expected increasingly to resort to evacuations. However, evacuation of urban populations and industries and their relocation in newly built communities is mind-boggling in terms of logistics, costs,[12] housing, demands for sustainable resettlement space, reemployment and training needs, resistance by host communities, and increased stress and public health threats. Considering the transportation and rebuilding required, mass migration, resettlement, and reconstruction also would exacerbate GHG emissions (see Aguirre, 2022). Finally, evacuation invasions are burdensome for hosts.

The UNHCR's (2021) *Strategic Framework for Climate Action* adopts objectives endorsing operations that "'prevent and mitigate environmental damage in operation settings, and enhance the resilience of displaced persons and host communities to environmental risks, and support protection and solutions for displaced persons and host communities'" (Aleinikoff and Martin, 2022, p. 18). UN-Habitat favors a capacity-building approach to housing and urban services in situations of climate-induced migrations that recognizes that authorities in receiving cities are "often strained and need support to manage rapid urbanization" (ibid., p. 22; also see p. 34). TC preparation would enhance such endeavors.

Settings

Currently, the "level of preparedness to handle CIM [climate-induced migration] is low globally" (Butros, Gyberg, and Kaijser, 2021, p. 841). The world's most populous cities are likely to experience the greatest burdens from climate-change stressors and climate migration (Sullivan and Townsend, 2022, p. 919; White House, 2021, p. 4). Sullivan and Townsend (2022, p. 917) foresee that "as the scale and locations of climate migration expand, conflicts between native populations (or persons who view themselves as natives) and new migrants are likely to grow, leaving more and more migrants vulnerable to inhumane anti-migrant sentiments and policies." The Sphere Project's *Humanitarian Charter*, initiated by concerned NGOs and the International Federation of Red Cross and Red Crescent Societies (IFRC), asserts the primacy of the humanitarian imperative that "'action should be taken to prevent or alleviate human suffering arising out of disaster or conflict'" on a non-discriminatory and non-political basis determined only by needs (cited in Chan, 2017, pp. 22–23).[13] The Sphere standards intended to guide humanitarian responders always include involving beneficiaries and focusing on building local self-support capacity (Hyslop, 2020). TC preparation nicely complements these objectives for persons affected by climate-induced displacement.

Responders and Stakeholders

The governments of Norway and Switzerland launched the Nansen Initiative in 2012 for the explicit purpose of addressing "the protection and assistance needs of persons displaced across borders in the context of disasters, including the adverse effects of climate change" (Nansen Initiative, 2015, p.

8). At a global intergovernmental consultation in Geneva in October 2015, 109 governmental delegations endorsed the *Agenda for the Protection of Cross-Border Displaced Persons in the Context of Disasters and Climate Change*. Specifically, the *Protection Agenda*, focused on preparedness, endorses the voluntary admission and enhanced protection of disaster-displaced persons based on "humanitarian considerations and international solidarity with disaster-affected countries and communities" and supports effective practices that will reduce risks of being displaced by disaster in countries of origin (ibid., pp. 8, 16–17). The subsequent (May 2016) *Platform on Disaster Displacement* (PDD), a group of states and other stakeholders (including universities) working in partnership to forge durable solutions (White House, 2021, p. 25), aims to "promote measures to address the protection and assistance of persons displaced across borders due the adverse effects of climate change" (Aleinikoff and Martin, 2022, pp. 18, 42). One of the PDD's four priorities calls for "facilitating the exchange of knowledge" in the interest of capacity-building (ibid., p. 18), a strategic objective that TC education and training are positioned to advance.

The Pentagon has long considered climate change to be one of the main security threats to the USA, including because of prospects for increased conflict and refugee flows (see Klare, 2019). In 2021, President Joe Biden directed the National Security Advisor to prepare a report in which, for the first time, the U.S. Government officially addressed the impact of climate change on migration (White House, 2021). The White House report captures a wide range of issues concerning climate migration and highlights existing U.S. responses for foreign assistance devoted to risk reduction, building resilience, and integrated humanitarian and development aid (ibid., pp. 10, 12–14). The report further acknowledges that current U.S. funding levels are "inadequate" and recognizes that the financial challenges brought about by climate-induced population displacement extend "far beyond the resources of the United States alone" (ibid., pp. 5, 6). Its concluding recommendations call for improved coordination among multilateral agencies, the private sector, and civil-society actors representing affected populations; and

> [the] establishment of a standing interagency policy process on Climate Change and Migration to coordinate U.S. Government efforts to mitigate and respond to migration resulting from the impacts of climate change that brings together representatives across the scientific, development, humanitarian, and peace and security elements of the U.S. Government.

The proposed interagency policy process would contribute a "holistic view of opportunities to address climate migration" that includes assistance to displaced persons and destination-host communities (ibid., pp. 6, 30–31). TC preparation constitutes a vital component of such assistance.

Along with self-interest, Earth's principal GHG emitters have a special moral responsibility for enabling climate migrants to enjoy humane security and maintain personal health (McMichael, Barnett, and McMichael, 2012, p. 652; Butros, Gyberg, and Kaijser, 2021, p. 847; White House, 2021, p. 5). In Lustgarten's (2020b) formulation of the conundrum, "Northern nations can relieve pressures on the fastest-warming countries by allowing more migrants to move north across their borders, or they can seal themselves off, trapping hundreds of millions of people in places that are increasingly unlivable." Collaborative responses to climate-induced migration are enhanced by adherence to the principle of common but differentiated responsibilities (see Butros, Gyberg, and Kaijser, 2021, p. 843). This principle has been embedded in the *U.N. Framework Convention on Climate Change*.[14] The challenge is to avoid "overwhelming the places they move to, deepening divisions and exacerbating inequalities" (Lustgarten, 2020b).[15] Therefore, the needs of host communities must receive parallel attention among humanitarian responders. The most promising relocation approaches take into account people's need for sustained livelihood opportunities, basic services, inter-personal competence (including TC), social networks, equivalent lands, and housing that protects their health (Nansen Initiative, 2015, p. 18; McMichael, Barnett, and McMichael, 2012, p. 649).

Given the urgency of locating and arranging proximate sites in the wake of climate displacements (Ahmed, 2018, p. 20), most immediate resettlement contexts will be in the South and require the involvement and empowerment of multiple stakeholders drawn from local experts and community interests (Ospina, 2000, p. 39), host governments at all levels (Hoffman, 2021, p. 125), the U.N. development system (Browne and Weiss, 2021),[16] non-profit NGOs, informal unpaid volunteers,[17] the World Bank's Global Facility for Disaster Reduction and Recovery (Aleinikoff and Martin, 2022, p. 20), and the for-profit sector (Thabrew, Wiek, and Ries, 2009, p. 68). Humanitarian NGOs – including Médecins Sans Frontières, IFRC, Oxfam, Save the Children, and Merlin[18] – perform crucial roles during complex humanitarian emergencies (Davies, 2010, p. 50; Chan, 2017, p. 135).[19] Given the number of responders involved, such contexts typically are "characterised by decentralised and pluralistic decision-making" (Whittaker, McLennan, and Handmer, 2015, p. 365). Consequently, "improving stakeholder participation, coordination, and commitment beyond narrow self-interest is required" (Thabrew, Wiek, and Ries, 2009, p. 67; also Baker, 2016, pp. 52–53; Anghel and Grierson, 2020, p. 488). Field participants recognize an increasing need for improved coordination of assistance among the many involved inter-governmental organizations, humanitarian agencies, and faith-based and other international and local NGOs (Martin and Zetter, 2012, p. 32). Thabrew, Wiek, and Ries (2009, pp. 68–69, Figure 1) commend the United Nations Environmental Programme's (UNEP) *Initiative on Capacity Building for Integrated Assessment and Planning for Sustainable Development* as an example of an approach that develops collaborative projects involving all cross-sectoral stakeholders in a focal context and provides a post-disaster redevelopment model of an integrated planning and facilitation scenario.

Stakeholder functional TC along the lines detailed in Chapters 5 and 6 facilitates such initiatives.

Anticipatory Climate Migration

The challenge of reducing the vulnerability of (particularly poverty-stricken) populations and societies to the impacts of climate change necessitates urgent action (Uitto and Shaw, 2006, p. 94; Hoffman, 2021, pp. 125, 130) that engages future preparation. In some last-resort circumstances, it will be necessary to facilitate anticipatory climate migration in order to "enhance well-being and maximize social and economic development in both the places of origin and destination" (McMichael, Barnett, and McMichael, 2012, p. 652; Black, et al., 2011, p. 1). *Agenda 2030* calls on all humanitarian responders to "work with one another and with counterparts in development" to reduce vulnerability to climate change by "moving people out of crisis" (cited in Hoffman, 2021, p. 124; also p. 130). In climate-threatened contexts, pro-active, pre-crisis resettlement accompanied by targeted TC training can "ease people out of situations of vulnerability" and enable "long-term resilience" in ways that maximize benefits to "the individual and both source and destination communities" (Black, et al., 2011, p. 2; also Martin, et al., 2021, pp. 144–145; Tempus, 2021; Sengupta and Lee, 2020, p. A7; White House, 2021, p. 22).[20] In such situations, moreover, "planned and well-managed migration ... can reduce the chance of later humanitarian emergencies and [sudden] displacement" (Black, et al., 2011, p. 1). Further, proactive investment in protective adaptation measures, including planning and training initiatives, is cost-effective over the long term due to reductions in displacement, mobility, resettlement, deaths, disease, and disabilities. In this connection, the Global Commission on Adaptation calls for a revolution in planning and in mainstreaming climate risk into strategy development, budget formulation, and investment decisions (GCA, 2019).

The most promising approaches to climate adaptation and resilience building are infused by TC and incorporate community-centered concerns and methods, "nonassimilationist" Indigenous knowledge and leadership (Mustonen and Feodoroff, 2018, pp. 116–117), local capacity strengthening (Sovacool, Tan-Mullins, Ockwell, and Newell, 2017, p. 1264), and multi-sectoral/multi-stakeholder partnerships (Uitto and Shaw, 2006, pp. 97–101). Nature-based solutions can provide "cost-effective measures that support climate change mitigation and adaptation while simultaneously addressing land degradation and biodiversity loss" (Bierbaum, 2020). Physical moves should be followed by "a transitional period during which time the livelihoods and standards of living of relocated persons are restored and any adverse impacts on other groups are mitigated" (Brookings Institution, Georgetown University's School of Foreign Service, and UNHCR, 2015, p. 6). In partnered contexts, it is important that adaptation planning avoids any negative consequences associated with the "politics of adaptation"

(Sovacool, et al., 2017, pp. 1250, 1254, 1263) by, in part, resolving governance and coordination issues in advance, particularly "who should most usefully tackle which area, with which risk management intervention" (Heine and Petersen, 2008, pp. 48, 50). Transnationally competent stakeholders can greatly facilitate effective collaborative responses.

Adaptive policies and practices that address the flow of environmental migrants also "must not lose sight of the positive potential of human mobility" (Ionesco, Mokhnacheva, and Gemenne, 2017, p. 95, 119). People often "keep their assets in more than one place" and temporary migration can allow a family to supplant lost incomes and resources (Heine and Petersen, 2008, p. 50). Moreover, TC-endowed migrants and their diaspora associates can play critical roles in adapting to climate change dislocations. In the face of the new threats involving frequent hazard encounters, the spread of infectious disease, food insecurity, and unavailability of clean water associated with climate change (see, e.g., Schmall and Sharma, 2022), supported migration to protected areas can diminish health risks and facilitate access to health services for both migrants and their hosts (Ionesco, Mokhnacheva, and Gemenne, 2017, p. 87; Popkin, 2022).

Health Challenges

Like the conflict-driven population movements considered in Chapter 2, migrants fleeing climate change disasters and risks will be vulnerable to emerging pathogens and prone to suffer maladies, malnutrition, injuries, mental anguish, and loss of life (McMichael, Barnett, and McMichael, 2012, pp. 649, 651; Davies, 2010, p. 134; Carballo, Smith, and Pettersson, 2008, p. 33). Trauma caused by natural disasters can lead to long-standing psychological damage and a changed perception of the external world (Surjan, Kudo, and Uitto, 2016, pp. 41–43). In addition, people on the move "not only take with them their own immediate health status but also introduce a new statistical and biological component into the places and populations they join" (McCracken and Phillips, 2017, pp. 310–311, 326).

In many cases, moreover, *immobility* increases personal and family vulnerability to hazards, stress, and risks of morbidity and mortality (Ionesco, Mokhnacheva, and Gemenne, 2017, p. 28).[21] Being trapped in immobility "is most often the case for individuals with low socio-economic status, few material and financial assets, or limited social support networks" (ibid., pp. 28–29). Older and disabled individuals face fewer prospects of exiting and are particularly vulnerable during and after climate-induced disasters and emergencies (McCracken and Phillips, 2017, pp. 326–327; Chan, 2017, p. 175). Following floods, moreover, many structures remain standing although they are uninhabitable, resulting in additional disorientation and mental health challenges (Carey, 2017). In a thoughtful contribution to the responder's toolkit, Kristie Ebi (2015, p. 239) presents a framing and scoping process for vulnerability assessment designed to identify susceptibility to health risks and to reveal recommended "avoid, prepare for, respond to, and recover from impacts" interventions that can increase resilience in emergency contexts.

In rapid-onset disasters, "the most immediate health issues facing displaced populations typically concern access to food, water and shelter, and adequate sanitation to avoid spread of disease" (Ager and Hermosilla, 2012, p. 81; also Chan, 2017, pp. 92–94). Additional challenging disruptions to health care among dislocated survivors include loss of medical records, termination of relationships with familiar care providers, care avoidance, rupture of support networks, and interruptions in drug treatments (Uscher-Pines, 2009, pp. 2, 17; Dankelman, et al., 2008). Studies suggest that prevailing relocation efforts are not protective of these and other newly encountered risks to physical health and often are associated with an uptick in depression and other mental illnesses (Uscher-Pines, 2009, pp. 6, 17; McMichael, Barnett, and McMichael, 2012, pp. 649–650; Carballo, Smith, and Pettersson, 2008, p. 33).[22]

Prolonged climate-affected displacement poses particularly acute mental health stresses (Bell, 2010, p. 35). Migrants experiencing protracted displacement also tend to "become increasingly vulnerable with time, as assistance and resources deplete after the completion of the emergency phase of the disaster response" (Ionesco, Mokhnacheva, and Gemenne, 2017, pp. 22–23).[23] Ruth Wells, et al. (2018, p. 2) offer insights of considerable value to humanitarian responders who are concerned with psychosocial impacts and supporting individual and community resilience. They specifically address the reciprocal and cumulative interactions of environmental stressors and psychological stressors "pre, during and post displacement."

When properly planned and executed as an adaptive response to climate change, "the move to a new location can alleviate health deficits from undernutrition or freshwater shortages, avoid the physical dangers of extreme weather events and degraded physical environments, and enhance access to medical facilities" (McMichael, Barnett, and McMichael, 2012, p. 648). The "healthy" response to actual and prospective climate migration involves contextually applied adaptation policies that help build resilience and place demographically sensitive health concerns at the center of action (ibid., pp. 647, 650–651; Dankelman, et al., 2008). Consultation with, and influential participation in health-care planning by, those relocated (particularly women) and by host communities, "with full respect of the rights of affected people" (Nansen Initiative, 2015, p. 18), are particularly critical initiative components (Haysom, Pantuliano, and Davey, 2012, pp. 125–127). TC facilitates such participation.

To minimize negative impacts on health and well-being, promising interventions include encouraging disaster-displaced individuals to take advantage of their social networks when making relocation decisions and to select close and safe destinations that are "most culturally similar" to the sending site (Uscher-Pines, 2009, p. 20). The vulnerability of climate migrants is further reduced and the health and social costs of relocation minimized by allowing adequate time for community consultations and planning, paying compensation at a level equal to the standard of housing and materials in the host community, ensuring that the money and resources made available to assist communities to relocate is spent on those communities, ... employing the people being moved wherever labor is required, and providing support for housing, health services, mental health services, employment, and education.

(McMichael, Barnett, and McMichael, 2012, p. 651)

Provision of cargo bikes offers a useful and "fun" transportation option for resettled climate migrants that is not operated by fossil fuel and can carry both passengers and goods (Mohn, 2022).

The Promise of Transnational Competence Training and Education

Earth's principal GHG emitters bear special moral responsibility for assisting climate migrants. Evacuations and resettlements are burdensome to those displaced, those invaded, those impacted, and those who provide help. Adequate funding needs to be dedicated now to ensure that relocation and other forthcoming climate change adaptation measures will be addressed in a proactive, equitable, ethically responsible, healthy, and TC-informed manner. Reframing complex humanitarian emergencies as sustainable-development, TC-training, and resilience-building opportunities for both the displaced and their hosts offers promise as a unifying long-term strategic response (Poole, Willitts-King, Hammond, and Zetter, 2012, pp. 201–204; Astier, 2008, p. S9). New roles, new social bonds, and new identities feature in resilience building and TC preparation among the dislocated and their hosts (Wells, et al., 2018, p. 2).

Along with opportunities to access resources and acquire skills tailored to available employment and volunteer opportunities (ibid., p. 2), TC preparation promises to facilitate adaptation to proactive and reactive climate-generated migration. TC training is important for migrants, their hosts, "the front-line workers who deal directly with people in transit and on reception," providers of physical and mental health, and "a wide range of other professionals" who interact with dislocated persons, "including social, welfare, legal and employment bureau staff and interpreters" (Matlin, et al., 2018, p. 22; also p. 43; also Kagawa-Singer and Kassim-Lakha, 2003, pp. 584–585). Chapter 4 elaborates on the TC training needs of the diverse stakeholders affected by or responding to climate-induced and conflict-induced displacement.

Notes

1 https://climate.nasa.gov/global-warming-vs-climate-change/
2 https://blogs.worldbank.org/climatechange/when-poverty-meets-climate-change-critical-challenge-demands-cross-cutting-solutions#:~:text=The%20connection%20between%20climate%20change,their%20own%20countries%20by%202050.

3 In Pakistan, a country that emits a tiny fraction of global GHGs, in 2022, flooding caused by climate change resulted in more than 1,000 deaths, the damage or destruction of more than one million homes, loss of two million acres of farmland, widespread displacement, and food shortages (Bearak and Zhong, 2022; Mir, 2022; Bhutto, 2022; Zhong, 2022c). In Iraq, an unpopular exodus to towns and cities by farmers and fishermen swelled in the face of unprecedented extreme heat and drought (Loveluck and Salim, 2022).

4 At the same time, wealthy and technologically advanced cities have more options to cope with the effects of climatic change than do coastal megacities such as Dhaka or Lagos that have grown in an unplanned manner.

5 In commenting on the Paris Accord, former President Barack Obama said: "'There's gonna have to be some adaptation … the oceans will be rising and that is going to displace people. And so we're going to [have to] anticipate and care for some of the consequences of that, including large-scale migration and disruptions that are going to be very costly'" (*Missoulian*, December 14, 2019). Also see Raymond Zhong's (2022b) summary of the main findings reported in the Intergovernmental Panel on Climate Change's 2022 report.

6 Space-based technology can "contribute to assessments of the vulnerability of communities to climate change" and enhance "a nation's ability to predict sea level rise at the local scale" (White House, 2021, pp. 6, 10).

7 http://www.un.org/waterforlifedecade/scarcity.shtml (accessed September 25, 2016).

8 https://data.worldbank.org/indicator/EN.ATM.CO2E.PC

9 In 2022, the Biden Administration funded an innovative program "specifically designed to help relocate communities threatened by climate change." Five Native American reservations along the Olympic Peninsula applied for relocation grants under this initial program (Flavelle, 2022).

10 Statistical analysis reveals that the interconnection of "climate shocks, conflict, and subsequent migration" is contextual rather than "everywhere" (Abel, Brottrager, Cuaresma, and Muttarak, 2019; White House, 2021, p. 8; also p. 7).

11 In this context, marginalized populations include "indigenous peoples, women and girls, youth, persons with disabilities" (White House, 2021, pp. 15, 22). Moreover, "xenophobia, prejudice, and stigmatization toward people in vulnerable situations further aggravate their ability to respond to climate change pressures" (ibid., p. 22).

12 One proposal for building a 10-km sea wall to protect New York City comes with a $120 billion cost estimate (Cohen, 2020).

13 On the minimum standards required to support population health in the wake of disasters suggested by the Sphere Project, see Chan (2017, pp. 121–124). They include emphasis on access to integrated and effective patient-centered health care, providing evidence-based health information, and reducing mortality and morbidity (Hyslop, 2020). For specific approaches to addressing the needs of dislocated populations, see Chan (2017, pp. 133–141).

14 https://unfccc.int/topics/climate-finance/the-big-picture/introduction-to-climate-finance/introduction-to-climate-finance

15 Some hosts misperceive climate-induced migrants as merely economic opportunists.

16 The United Nations Development Programme (UNDP), for instance, has incorporated a focus on "addressing displacement related to climate and environmental events" into the international organization's migration-and-development projects (Aleinikoff and Martin, 2022, p. 21). The International Labour Organization (ILO) views safe labor migration as one important adaptive response in its strategic approach to enhancing protection and empowering migrants affected by climate change (ibid., p. 21).

17 Whittaker, McLennan, and Handmer (2015, p. 358; also see pp. 360–361, 366) point out that "ordinary citizens are usually first on the scene in an emergency …

often play vital roles in helping those affected to respond and recover, and can provide invaluable assistance to official agencies." Citizen volunteers also often identify needs not recognized and being met by other responders (ibid., p. 365).

18 See the list of key international-disaster-response stakeholders found in Chan (2017, pp. 183–184).

19 However, the health-supporting roles of NGOs often are heavily influenced by self-interest and donor/state pressures (Davies, 2010, p. 133).

20 In coastal Alaska, 15 Native villages are working "to design a culturally sensitive process for relocating communities" (Tempus, 2021).

21 Yarimar Bonilla (2022), Director of the Center for Puerto Rican Studies at Hunter College, faults the relocation and rebuilding responses of emergency management in the wake of Hurricanes Maria and Fiona. Puerto Ricans, he asserts, are tired of celebrating personal resilience, "our ability to endure, of being creative in the face of adversity and of surviving despite state neglect … We need our government infrastructure to be as resilient as we are forced to be."

22 Lori Uscher-Pines' literature search found that concern with physical health often is tangential in post-disaster relocation studies (2009, pp. 2, 5).

23 Avoiding this outcome requires early attention to sustainable approaches to complex-humanitarian crises (see Martin and Zetter, 2012, p. 32).

References

Abel, Guy J.; Brottrager, Michael; Cuaresma, Jesus C.; and Muttarak, Raya. 2019. "Climate, Conflict and Forced Migration." *Global Environmental Change* 54 (January): 239–249.

Adger, W. Neil; et al. 2001. "Asia: Contribution of Working Group II to the Third Assessment Report of the Intergovernmental Panel on Climate Change." In *Climate Change 2001: Impacts, Adaptation, and Vulnerability*, edited by James J. McCarthy; Osvaldo F. Canziani; Neil A. Leary; David J. Dokken; and Kasey S. White. Cambridge: Cambridge University Press, pp. 533–590.

Ager, Alastair; and Hermosilla, Sabrina. 2012. "Health on the Move: The Impact of Forced Displacement on Health." In *World Disasters Report 2012*, edited by Roger Zetter. Geneva: International Federation of Red Cross and Red Crescent Societies (IFRC), pp. 81–110.

Aguirre, Jessica C. 2022. "Buildings Contribute Nearly 40 Percent of the World's Carbon Emissions." *New York Times*, October 21, pp. B1, B6–B8.

Ahmed, Bayes. 2018. "Who Takes Responsibility for the Climate Refugees?" *International Journal of Climate Change Strategies and Management* 10 (1): 5–26.

Aleinikoff, T. Alexander; and Martin, Susan. 2022. *The Responsibility of the International Community in Situations of Mobility Due to Environmental Events*. Zolberg Institute Working Paper Series 2022–2021. New York: Zolberg Institute on Migration and Mobility, The New School.

Anghel, Roxana; and Grierson, J. 2020. "Addressing Needs in Liminal Space: The Citizen Volunteer Experience and Decision-Making in the Unofficial Calais Migrant Camp – Insights for Social Work." *European Journal of Social Work* 23 (3): 486–499.

Astier. M. Almedom. 2008. "Resilience Research and Policy/Practice Discourse in Health, Social, Behavioral, and Environmental Sciences Over the Last Ten Years." *African Health Sciences* 8 (December): S1–S13.

Baker, Camille. 2021. "Amid Climate-Change Trauma, Care Concerns for Mental Health." *Washington Post*, September 8.

Baker, Susan. 2016. *Sustainable Development*, 2nd edition. London: Routledge.

Bardsley, Douglas K.; and Hugo, Graeme J. 2010. "Migration and Climate Change: Examining Thresholds of Change to Guide Effective Adaptation Decision-Making." *Population and Environment* 32: 238–262.

Batra, Geeta; and Norheim, Trond. 2022. "Staying Small and Beautiful: Enhancing Sustainability in the Small Island Developing States." In *Transformational Change for People and the Planet: Evaluating Environment and Development*, edited by Juha I. Uitto and Geeta Batra. Cham, Switzerland: Springer, pp. 73–91.

Bearak, Max; and Popovich, Nadja. 2022. "The World Is Falling Short of Its Climate Goals. The Actions of Four Big Emitters Show Why." *New York Times*, November 10, p. A8.

Bearak, Max; and Zhong, Raymond. 2022. "Relentless Downpours Turn Deadly in Pakistan." *New York Times*, August 30, pp. A1,A6.

Bell, Erica J. 2010. "Climate Change: What Competencies and Which Medical Education and Training Approaches?" *BMC Medical Education* 10 (31): 1–9.

Bhutto, Fatima. 2022. "What Is Owed to Pakistan, Now One-Third Underwater." *New York Times*, September 6, p. A20.

Bierbaum, Rosina. 2020. *Nature-based Solutions and the GEF*. Advisory Document. Washington, D.C.: Scientific and Technical Advisory Panel to the Global Environment Facility.

Black, Richard; Adger, Neil; Arness, Nigel; Dercon, Stefan; Geddes, Andrew; and Thomas, David. 2011. *Foresight: Migration and Global Environmental Change*. Final Project Report. London: The Government Office for Science.

Blackburn, Sophie; and Marques, Cesar. 2013. "Mega-Urbanisation and the Coast." In *Megacities and the Coast: Risk, Resilience and Transformation*, edited by Mark Pelling and Sophie Blackburn. London: Routledge, pp. 1–21.

Bonilla, Yarimar. 2022. "Why Must Puerto Ricans Be Resilient in Each Storm's Wake?" *New York Times*, October 12, p. A22.

Bradshaw, Corey J.; Ehrlich, Paul R., et al. 2021. "Underestimating the Challenges of Avoiding a Ghastly Future." *Frontiers in Conservation Science*, January 13. https://doi.org/10.3389/fcosc.2020.615419.

Bradsher, Keith. 2009. "American Officials Press China on Efforts to Curb Greenhouse Gases." *New York Times*, July 16, p. A10.

Bradsher, Keith; and Krauss, Clifford. 2022. "China Keeps Burning More Coal." *New York Times*, November 9, p. B1.

Brookings Institution, Georgetown University's School of Foreign Service, and UNHCR. 2015. *Guidance on Protecting People from Disasters and Environmental Change through Planned Relocation*. Washington, D.C.: Brookings Institution.

Browne, Stephen; and Weiss, Thomas G. 2021. "Reflections: Prospects for the UN Development System." In *Routledge Handbook on the UN and Development*, edited by Stephen Browne and Thomas G. Weiss. London: Routledge, pp. 286–292.

Burke, Marshall; Hsiang, Solomon M.; and Miguel, Edward. 2015. "Climate and Conflict." *Annual Review of Economics* 7: 577–617.

Butros, Deniz; Gyberg, Veronica B.; and Kaijser, Anna. 2021. "Solidarity Versus Security: Exploring Perspectives on Climate Induced Migration in UN and EU Policy." *Environmental Communication* 15 (6): 842–856.

Carballo, Manuel; Smith, Chelsea B.; and Pettersson, Karen. 2008. "Health Challenges." *Forced Migration Review* 31 (October): 32–33.

Carey, Benedict. 2017. "Katrina and Its Hard-Learned Lessons." *New York Times,* September 12, pp. D1, D6.

Chan, Emily Ying Yang. 2017. *Public Health Humanitarian Responses to Natural Disasters.* London: Routledge.

Cohen, Steve. 2020. "The Politics and Cost of Adapting to Climate Change in New York City." In *State of the Planet.* News from the Columbia Climate School.

Dankelman, Irene; Alam, Khurshid; Ahmed, Wahida B.; Gueye, Yacine D.; Fatenia, Naureen; and Mensah-Kutin, Rose. 2008. "What It Means for Women." *Forced Migration Review* 31 (October): 56.

Davies, Sara. 2010. *Global Politics of Health.* Cambridge: Polity Press.

Dun, Olivia; and Gemenne, François. 2008. "Defining 'Environmental Migration.'" *Forced Migration Review* 31 (October): 10–11.

Ebi, Kristie I. 2015. "Vulnerability and Adaptation Assessment." In *Climate Change and Public Health,* edited by Barry S. Levy and Jonathan A. Patz. Oxford: Oxford University Press, pp. 239–241.

Etana, Dula; Snelder, Denyse J.R.M.; van Wesenbeeck, Cornelia F.A.; and Buning, Tjard DeCock. 2022. "Climate Change, In-situ Adaptation, and Migration Decisions of Smallholder Farmers in Central Ethiopia." *Migration and Development* 11 (3): 737–761.

Ferris, Elizabeth; Cernea, Michael M.; and Petz, Daniel. 2011. *On the Front Line of Climate Change and Displacement: Learning from and with Pacific Island Countries.* Washington, D.C.: Brookings Institution.

Filho, Walter L. et al. 2022. "An Analysis of Climate Change and Health Hazards: Results from an International Study." *International Journal of Climate Change Strategies and Management* 14 (4): 375–398.

Flavelle, Christopher. 2022. "As Waters Rise, U.S. Quietly Tests a New Strategy." *New York Times,* November 3, p. A12.

Fountain, Henry. 2022a. "Carbon Dioxide Levels in Atmosphere Reach 4-Million-Year High and Continue to Climb." *New York Times,* June 4, p. A29.

Fountain, Henry. 2022b. "The Monsoon Is Becoming More Extreme. And Harder to Predict. And More Deadly" *New York Times,* October 10, pp. A10–A12.

Fuchs, Roland; Conran, Mary; and Louis, Elizabeth. 2011. "Climate Change and Asia's Coastal Urban Cities: Can They Meet the Challenge?" *Environment and Urbanization Asia* 2 (1): 13–28.

George, Susannah. 2022. "Thousands Refuse to Flee Submerged Pakistani Villages." *Washington Post,* September 10, p. A8.

Gillis, Justin. 2017. "Antarctic Dispatches," *New York Times,* May 20, pp. A11–A12.

Global Commission on Adaptation (GCA). 2019. *Adapt Now: A Global Call for Leadership on Climate Resilience.* Washington, D.C.: Global Center on Adaptation and World Resources Institute.

Goodell, Jeff. 2017. *The Water Will Come: Rising Seas, Sinking Cities, and the Remaking of the Civilized World.* New York: Little, Brown.

Griggs, Troy. 2018. "Sea Is Rising, and the Land Is Sinking." *New York Times,* March 8, p. A20.

Hamlin, Rebecca. 2021. *Crossing: How We Label and React to People on the Move.* Stanford, CA: Stanford University Press.

Hauer, Mathew E.; Fussell, Elizabeth; Mueller, Valerie; Burkett, Maxine; Call, Maia; Abel, Kali; McLeman, Robert; and Wrathall, David. 2020. "Sea-Level Rise and Human Migration." *Nature Reviews Earth & Environment* 1: 28–39.

Haysom, Simone; Pantuliano, Sara; and Davey, Eleanor. 2012. "Forced Migration in an Urban Context: Relocating the Humanitarian Agenda." In *World Disasters Report 2012*, edited by Roger Zetter. Geneva: International Federation of Red Cross and Red Crescent Societies (IFRC), pp. 113–143.

Heine, Britta; and Petersen, Lorenz. 2008. "Adaptation and Cooperation." *Forced Migration Review* 31 (October): 48–50.

Hellegatte, Stephane; Vogt-Schilb, Adrien; Bangalore, Mook; and Rozenberg, Julie. 2017. *Unbreakable: Building the Resilience of the Poor in the Face of Natural Disasters*. Washington, D.C.: International Bank for Reconstruction and Development.

Hoffman, Peter J. 2021. "What Does 'Leave No One Behind' Mean for Humanitarians?" In *Routledge Handbook on the UN and Development*, edited by Stephen Browne and Thomas G. Weiss. London: Routledge, pp. 121–134.

Hyslop, Chris. 2020. "Public Health in Humanitarian Emergencies." Public lecture presented at the University of Montana, October 6.

Ionesco, Dina; Mokhnacheva, Daria; and Gemenne, François. 2017. *The Atlas of Environmental Migration*. London: Routledge.

IPCC (Intergovernmental Panel on Climate Change). 2021. *Climate Change 2021: The Physical Science Basis. Sixth Assessment Report, Working Group I Summary for Policymakers*. Cambridge: Cambridge University Press.

IPCC (Intergovernmental Panel on Climate Change). 2022. *Climate Change 2022: Impact, Adaptation and Vulnerability. Sixth Assessment Report, Working Group II Summary for Policymakers*. Cambridge: Cambridge University PressIves, Mike. 2017. "Study Finds Dire Effects from a Tad More Heat." *New York Times*, June 9, p. A7.

Kagawa-Singer, Marjorie; and Kassim-Lakha, Shaheen. 2003. "A Strategy to Reduce Cross-Cultural Miscommunication and Increase the Likelihood of Improving Health Outcomes." *Academic Medicine* 78 (6): 577–587.

Karl, Alexandre A.; and Karl, Julia S. 2022. "Human Rights for Refugees: Enhancing Sustainable Supply Chain to Guarantee a Health Environment in Refugee Settlements." *Journal of Humanitarian Logistics and Supply Chain Management* 12 (3): 382–403.

Kelman, Ilan. 2015. "Difficult Decisions: Migration from Small Island Developing States under Climate Change." *Earth's Future* 3: 133–142.

Klare, Michael T. 2019. *All Hell Breaking Loose: The Pentagon's Perspective on Climate Change*. New York: Metropolitan Books.

Leonhardt, David. 2017. "The Storm that Humans Helped Cause." *New York Times*, August 29, p. A27.

Loveluck, Louisa; and Salim, Mustafa. 2022. "Climate Migration in Iraq's South Brings Crisis to Cities." *Washington Post*, September 29, p. A8.

Lustgarten, Abrahm. 2020a. "How Climate Migration Will Reshape America." *New York Times Magazine*, September 15.

Lustgarten, Abrahm. 2020b. "The Great Climate Migration." *New York Times Magazine*, July 23.

Martin, Susan F.; Bergmann, Jonas; Rigaud, Kanta; and Yameogo, Nadege D. 2021. "Climate Change, Human Mobility, and Development." *Migration Studies* 9 (1): 142–149.

Martin, Susan F.; and Zetter, Roger. 2012. "Forced Migration: The Dynamics of Displacement and Response." In *World Disasters Report 2012*, edited by Roger Zetter. Geneva: International Federation of Red Cross and Red Crescent Societies (IFRC), pp. 13–46.

Matlin, Stephen A.; Depoux, Anneliese; Schutte, Stefanie; Flahault, Antoine; and Saso, Luciano. 2018. "Migrants' and Refugees' Health: Towards an Agenda of Solutions." *Public Health Reviews* 39 (27): 1–55.

McCracken, Kevin; and Phillips, David R. 2017. *Global Health: An Introduction to Current and Future Trends*. London: Routledge.

McMichael, Anthony J. 2013. "Globalization, Climate Change, and Human Health." *New England Journal of Medicine* 368: 1335–1343.

McMichael, Celia; Barnett, Jon; and McMichael, Anthony J. 2012. "An Ill Wind? Climate Change, Migration, and Health." *Environmental Health Perspectives* 120 (5): 646–654.

Mir, Hamid. 2022. "By No Fault of Its Own, Pakistan Is Paying Dearly on Climate Change." *Washington Post*, September 14, p. A21.

Mohn, Tanya. 2022. "Bike Built to Carry Goods, and Passengers, Takes Off." *New York Times*, July 6, p. B4.

Mooney, Chris. 2022. "Study: No Stopping Sea-Level Rise." *Washington Post*, August 30.

Morrissey, James. 2008. "Rural-Urban Migration in Ethiopia." *Forced Migration Review* 31 (October): 28–29.

Muller, Nicholas. 2022. "Seeking Higher Ground: Climate Resilience in the Maldives." *The Diplomat*, February 16.

Mustonen, Tero; and Feodoroff, Pauliina. 2018. "Skolt Sami and Atlantic Salmon Collaborative Management of Naatamo Watershed, Finland as a Case of Indigenous Evaluation and Knowledge in the Eurasian Artic." In *Indigenous Evaluation: New Directions for Evaluation*, 159, edited by F. Cram; K.A. Tibbets; and J. LaFrance. Wiley Online Library, pp. 107–120.

Nakayama, Mikiyasu; Fujikura, Ryo; Okuda, Rie; Fujii, Mai; Takashima, Ryuta; Murakawa, Tomoya; Sakai, Erika; and Iwama, Hiroaki. 2022. "Alternatives for the Marshall Islands to Cope with the Anticipated Sea Level Rise by Climate Change." *Journal of Disaster Research* 17 (3): 315–326.

Nansen Initiative. 2015. "Global Consultation Conference Report: Geneva, 12–13 October 2015." Available at: https://nanseninitiative.org (accessed October 21, 2017).

Nishio, Akihiko. 2021. "When Poverty Meets Climate Change: A Critical Challenge that Demands Cross-Cutting Solutions." In *Development and a Changing Climate*. Washington, D.C.: The World Bank.

Ospina, Gustavo L. 2000. "Education for Sustainable Development: A Local and International Challenge." *Prospects* 30 (1): 31–40.

Pearse-Smith, Scott W.D. 2012. "'Water War' in the Mekong Basin?" *Asia Pacific Viewpoint* 53 (2): 147–162.

Penney, Veronica. 2020. "5 Things We Know about Climate Change and Hurricanes." *New York Times*, November 10, p. A19.

Pierre-Louis, Kendra. 2018. "Antarctica Is Melting at a Much Faster Pace." *New York Times*, June 14, p. A13.

Pierre-Louis, Kendra. 2019. "As the Earth Warms, Duluth Is Looking Pretty Cool." *New York Times*, April 16, p. A11.

Plumer, Brad. 2020. "Rising Seas Could Menace Millions Beyond Shorelines, Study Finds." *New York Times*, July 31, p. B3.

Plumer, Brad; and Popovich, Nadja. 2017. "Tracking Possible Trajectory of a World of Sweltering Days." *New York Times*, June 23, p. A10.

Poole, Lydia; Willitts-King, Barnaby; Hammond, Laura; and Zetter, Roger. 2012. "Who Pays? Who Profits? The Costs and Impacts of Forced Migration." In *World Disasters Report 2012*, edited by Roger Zetter. Geneva: International Federation of Red Cross and Red Crescent Societies (IFRC), pp. 175–211.

Popkin, Gabriel. 2022. "The D.C. Area Can Be a Refuge for People Fleeing Climate Instability, One Resident Writes." *Washington Post*, July 3, p. C5.

Rhodes, Anna; and Besbris, Max. 2022. "Why Won't Texans Leave After Hurricane Harvey?" *New York Times*, August 25, p. A19.

Rigaud, Kanta K.; de Sherbinin, Alex; Jones, Bryan; Bergmann, Jonas; Clement, Viviane; Ober, Kayly; Schewe, Jacob; Adamo, Susana; McCusker, Brent; Heuser, Silke; and Midgley, Amelia. 2018. *Groundswell: Preparing for Internal Climate Migration*. Washington, D.C.: World Bank.

Samet, Jonathan M.; and Zhang, Junfeng. 2014. "Climate Change and Health." In *Routledge Handbook of Global Public Health in Asia*, edited by Sian M. Griffiths, Jin Ling Tang, and Eng Kiong Yeoh. London: Routledge, pp. 281–298.

Schmall, Emily; and Sharma, Bhadra. 2022. "Kathmandu Finally Got Tap Water. After a Climate Disaster, It Was Gone." *New York Times*, October 7, p. A4.

Sengupta, Somini; and Lee, Chang W. 2020. "Sea at the Front Door: Climate Projections Become a Perilous Reality for Coastal Cities." *New York Times*, February 15, pp. A5–A7.

Skeldon, Ronald. 2021. *Advanced Introduction to Migration Studies*. Cheltenham: Edward Elgar.

Sovacool, Benjamin K.; Tan-Mullins, May; Ockwell, David; and Newell, Peter. 2017. "Political Economy, Poverty, and Polycentrism in the Global Environmental Facility's Least Developed Countries Fund (LDCF) for Climate Change Adaptation." *Third World Quarterly* 38 (6): 1249–1271.

Sullivan, John P.; and Townsend, Keeley. 2022. "Climate Migration: Adding Fuel to the Ethnocentric Fire." *Terrorism and Political Violence* 43 (5): 914–925.

Surjan, Akhilesh; Kudo, Shinpei; and Uitto, Juha I. 2016. "Risk and Vulnerability." In *Sustainable Development and Disaster Risk Reduction* , edited by Juha I. Uitto and Rajib Shaw. Tokyo: Springer, pp. 37–55.

Tanner, Thomas; and Horn-Phathanothai, Leo. 2014. *Climate Change and Development*. London: Routledge.

Tempus, Alexandra. 2021. "The Great Climate Migration Era Is Dawning." *New York Times*, September 1, p. A23.

Thabrew, Lanka; Wiek, Arnim; and Ries, Robert. 2009. "Environmental Decision Making in Multi-stakeholder Contexts: Applicability of Life Cycle Thinking in Development Planning and Implementation." *Journal of Cleaner Production* 17: 67–76.

Uitto, Juha I. 2021. "Surviving the Anthropocene: How Evaluation Can Contribute to Knowledge and Better Policymaking." *Evaluation* 27 (4): 1–17.

Uitto, Juha I.; and Shaw, Rajib. 2006. "Adaptation to Changing Climate: Promoting Community-based Approaches in the Developing Countries." *SANSAI: An Environmental Journal for the Global Community* 1: 93–107.

UNHSP (United Nations Human Settlements Programme). 2011. *Cities and Climate Change: Global Report on Human Settlements 2011*. London: Earthscan.

Uscher-Pines, Lori. 2009. "Health Effects of Relocation Following Disaster: A Systematic Review of the Literature." *Disasters* 33 (1): 1–22.

Walsh, Declan. 2022. "Warfare and Drought Hurl Somalia Toward Famine." *New York Times*, November 22, pp. A6–A7.

Wells, Ruth; Lawsin, Catalina; Hunt, Caroline; Youssef, Omar Said; Abujado, Fayzeh; and Steel, Zachary. 2018. "An Ecological Model of Adaptation to Displacement: Individual, Cultural and Community Factors Affecting Psychological Adjustment among Syrian Refugees in Jordan." *Global Mental Health* 5: 1–13. doi:10.1017/gmh.2018.30

White House. 2021. *Report on the Impact of Climate Change on Migration.* Washington, D.C.: The White House.

Whittaker, Joshua; McLennan, Blythe; and Handmer, John. 2015. "A Review of Informal Volunteerism in Emergencies and Disasters: Definition, Opportunities and Challenges." *International Journal of Disaster Risk Reduction* 13: 358–368.

Wolf, Aaron T. 2007. "Shared Waters: Conflict and Cooperation." *Annual Review of Environment and Resources* 32: 241–269.

Zhong, Raymond. 2022a. "Climate Change Raises Risk of Major Wildfires." *New York Times*, February 23, p. A6.

Zhong, Raymond. 2022b. "5 of the Main Findings from the U.N.'s Report." *New York Times*, March 1.

Zhong, Raymond. 2022c. "Study of Pakistan's Floods Shows Signs of Climate Change at Work." *New York Times*, September 16, p. A13.

4 TC Development for the Needs of Displaced Populations

This chapter applies training-needs assessment with specific reference to the diverse stakeholders directly or indirectly affected by, or responding to, population displacement. The stakeholders of special interest in the contexts of conflict displacement and climate dislocation are migrants, members of host communities, national and local government authorities, development actors, and international and local humanitarian responders.[1] Casting a wide stakeholder training net ensures the diversity, redundancy, and flexibility of capabilities associated with risk-mitigating, resilient endeavors in the types of multifaceted and unpredictable circumstances that characterize conflict-induced and climate-induced population displacements and relocations (Schroeder and Hatton, 2012, pp. 412–413).

The TC initiatives highlighted in this book will be embedded in a multinational and multisectoral environment that also requires modifying interventions and resource investments in the glocal context. The overriding process objective for responders is immediate and long-term "ethical placemaking," a key component of an "enabling, or capabilities-oriented, conception of justice" for resettled populations. Constructively, ethical placemaking "facilitates the formulation of an account of what ecological subjects generally and refugees particularly need to flourish and to be treated fairly as they await settlement (and eventually within a new given society) …" (Eckenwiler and Wild, 2021, p. 234; also pp. 242, 245).

At the initial stage of needs assessment, it is helpful to prepare a map of the stakeholder landscape (both individuals and groups). Robert Moran, et al. (2009, pp. 294–295) provide one useful mapping method based on stakeholders' principal intention (block or support) and contextual power (high or low). The needs and intentions of high-power blockers merit special attention since they possess considerable, but unrealized, power to remove barriers and support humanitarian interventions. High-power supporters who already are inclined to facilitate the work of humanitarian-aid providers "should be fully supported … as they have the greatest potential for adding significant value" (ibid., p. 215). Low-power blockers need to be "listened to in order to identify and avoid or mitigate potential project risks" (ibid.). The focus of interaction with low-power supporters (e.g., most displaced

DOI: 10.4324/9781003330493-5

persons) should be on "learning and acquiring new skills and abilities" (ibid.) so they are able to contribute more effectively to well-being and sustainable development.[2]

Here, we distinguish conflict-displacement and climate-displacement stakeholders by background characteristics relevant to training and by prevailing skill needs. Stakeholder distinctions enable the building blocks needed for training needs analysis (Taylor, 2003, pp. 71, 82). Identifying assets and deficiencies along with intended training outcomes and impacts by applying theory-of-change methods opens up pathways to promising TC development interventions and well-being.

Needs Assessment: Training Conflict-Displacement Stakeholders

TC development requires establishing a conducive context for learning. Camps are commonly located in remote, segregated, obscured (Eckenwiler and Wild, 2021, p. 239; Jahre, Kembro, Adjahossou, and Altay, 2018, p. 324), and "ecologically marginal areas" where conflict-displaced populations are deprived of access to productive agricultural land and forced to "rely heavily on [limited] natural resources to meet their basic livelihood needs" (Horst, 2006, p. 84; also see Karl and Karl, 2022, pp. 390, 392). Preventing and mitigating camp-related impacts on the local environment and providing inhabitants with healthy and sustainable livelihood options and alternatives for daily living require "the integration of sustainable management practices" in all dimensions of humanitarian operations (Karl and Karl, 2022, p. 383; also pp. 389–393).[3] Camp sites typically fail to consider the needs of refugees for nonresidential buildings "such as economic enterprises, schools, clinics, warehouses, administrative offices, and community centers" along with durable housing (Jahre, et al., 2018, pp. 325–326).

In addition, the drastic changes in resources and social connections along with the stresses that accompany displacement (see Almoshmosh, et al., 2020, p. 22; Pincock, Betts, and Easton-Calabria, 2020, p. 112) can differentially shape the resilience and adaptive capabilities of male and female camp residents (Wells, et al., 2018, p. 9). Providing healthy places of solace within settlement environs, where displaced persons experience "safety and a sense of security" along with social support, is a critical emotional and social restorative and renewal facilitator (Sampson and Gifford, 2010, pp. 123, 126, 128–129; also see Giles, 2018, p. 174; Stewart, 2014, pp. 91, 93; Karam, Monaghan, and Yoder, 2017, p. 456; Beiser, 2014, pp. 73, 86; Jones, 2020, p. 352). Sport fields and opportunities for safe and playful sport activities at different proficiency levels can fill the non-gendered "medicine," educational, and belonging needs of camp populations (Michelini, 2022, pp. 1, 7–8; Nunn, Spaaij, and Luguetti, 2022; Spaaij, Luguetti, and Ugolotti, 2022, p. 411; Sampson and Gifford, 2010, p. 123). Responders trained in TC also can establish a refugee therapy center with a clinical zone where they provide one-on-one counseling sessions along with various therapeutic methods (Negm and Mayer, 2022, p. 48; also Pincock, Betts, and Easton-Calabria,

2020, p. 114). Post-settlement stressors further require attention to employment, generating capital, educational opportunities, language barriers, discrimination and resentment experiences, resilience reinforcement, community building, and other non-clinical interventions (Almoshmosh, et al., 2020, pp. 22–23, 27; Perouse de Montclos and Kagwanja, 2000, p. 208).

Although the potential for individual and community self-sufficiency often is present in camps, humanitarian responders "are likely to supply handouts continuously without providing the refugees with the responsibility and chance to establish their own livelihoods" (Horst, 2006, p. 206). Moreover, NGO-initiated income-generating projects typically have "limited impact" (Horst, 2006, p. 85). In some cases, however, refugees pool and rotate financial resources for small business start-up purposes (Horst, 2006, p. 85; Pincock, Betts, and Easton-Calabria, 2020, p. 2). Comparing two Syrian refugee camps in Jordan, Davies (2020, p. 68) notes how in one an unplanned market has given rise to vibrancy, while, in the second, central planning by the Jordanian authorities and UNHCR has stifled it. In the unplanned market, "[s]ome of the refugees have used the employment and resources ... to satisfy Maslow's final need, 'self-actualization', expressing their own potential, talent and individuality."[4] For good reason, then, Kate Pincock, et al. (2020, p. 119) advocate application of the principle of subsidiarity to participatory camp governance; that is, allowing decisions to "take place at the smallest level of governance except where clashes of interest cannot be reconciled, or unless levels of efficiency and competence in [service] delivery justify a greater external role." Promoting decentralized needs identification, coupled with transparency, also facilitates accurate identification of, and response to, emerging and unexpected risks of critical importance to local beneficiaries (Schroeder and Hatton, 2012, pp. 413–414).

At the same time, policies and providers "need to support host communities, and the relationship between refugees and hosts" (Betts, 2021, p. 2; Kihato and Landau, 2016, p. 409; Jahre, et al., 2018, pp. 326, 331, 333–334; Anderson and Woodrow, 1998, pp. 72–73; Milner, 2021, p. 423; Perouse de Montclos and Kagwanja, 2000, p. 214; Fajth, Bilgili, Loschmann, and Siegel, 2019, pp. 1–2, 17). Jahre, et al. (2018, pp. 324, 326, 335–337) suggest a flexible approach to camp design based on long-term spatial planning and natural resource sustainability where "refugees and the local community actively participate in camp development and operation." One dimension of their mutually beneficial approach to camp design calls for "building hospitals, schools, and markets at strategic points accessible by all, and no longer at the center of the camp" (ibid., p. 327). In camp operations, stakeholders' commitment to policies of ethical placemaking and shared-use practices promises to "mitigate some of the harms of encampment and, at the same time, serve as a catalyst" in advancing peaceful co-existence, integration, and, ultimately, "global social justice" (Eckenwiler and Wild, 2021, pp. 235, 244; also see Murdoch-Eaton, Redmond, and Bax, 2011, p. 562). In the Bur-Amino camp in Ethiopia, for instance, UNHCR has welcomed the host community "to use water taps, health services, and schools in the camp" and "constructed primary schools, solar street lighting, and sanitations [sic] facilities in the host community." In addition, "local materials, trucks, and communication networks are increasingly used in the camp operations" and "there is an exchange of food and workers between the camp and the host community" (Jahre, et al., 2018, p. 330; also see regarding Kakuma camp, Pincock, Betts, and Easton-Calabria, 2020, p. 89). In the case of Congolese refugees in Rwanda, Veronika Fajth, et al. (2019, p. 1; also pp. 2, 17) found that "greater (economic) interaction between the two populations helps increase trust between refugees and host communities over time."

Displaced populations residing in urban settings and their responders possess a different set of needs. To meet dispersed populations' needs, responding humanitarians will need to identify shared interests and "build solidarities with 'local' constituencies facing similar marginalization" (Kihato and Landau, 2016, pp. 408–409, 421). They will need "local institutional literacy" that includes understanding the subnational politics of urban development and poverty reduction (ibid., pp. 416–417). They will need to mobilize high-power supporters on behalf of such inclusive policy changes as free and unhindered access to social services, providing employment and network-building opportunities for the conflict-displaced, and expanded resources for health providers (ibid., pp. 418–421; Eckenwiler and Wild, 2021, pp. 244–245; Kirmayer, Kronick, and Rousseau, 2018, p. 119; White House, 2021, p. 31). They will need skill in resisting market-based pressures associated with new public-management pressures to treat the displaced as clients and to focus on quantified measures of efficiency in delivery and number of beneficiaries (Kihato and Landau, 2016, p. 414).

The *Global Compact on Refugees* explicitly recognizes these sustainable development imperatives. The *Compact* calls for cooperation among humanitarian and development actors, additionality in migration and development resource commitments to host and refugee communities (and to countries of origin when that would facilitate repatriation), local ownership, and integration of refugees who contribute to sustainable development and environmental protection "through new jobs and livelihoods" (see Micinski, 2021, p. 145).

Education and Training

Karen Mundy and Sarah Dryden-Peterson (2011, p. 11) point to the centrality of refugee academic and social learning for "coping" in the present and "hoping" for the future. When successfully implemented, education and training programs can prepare young camp residents for satisfying and productive livelihoods (Giles, 2018, p. 179; Pincock, Betts, and Easton-Calabria, 2020, p. 93) and build resilience (Sleijpen, Boeije, Kleber, and Mooren, 2016, p. 175). In spite of the 1990 *Jomtien Declaration on Education for All*, children fleeing conflict zones are prone to receive little if any quality education that provides a promising bridge to sustainable livelihoods, an avenue for personal well-being, and an alternative to joining in armed conflict (Mundy and Dryden-Peterson, 2011, pp. 2, 6–7; Pincock, Betts, and Easton-Calabria, 2020, pp. 93, 112; Karam, Monaghan, and Yoder, 2017, pp. 449–450, 452).

According to UNESCO, "less than 2% of all humanitarian aid is directed to education" (cited in Mundy and Dryden-Peterson, 2011, p. 9). NGOs commonly assume decision-making authority for refugee education initiatives (Karam, Monaghan, and Yoder, 2017, pp. 450–451). The Borderless Higher Education for Refugees Project's experience in Dadaab camp further "indicates that education for refugees at all levels cannot be implemented without the support of the local community and the host country government" (Giles, 2018, p. 175; also see Karam, Monaghan, and Yoder, 2017, pp. 451, 461; Dryden-Peterson, 2016, pp. 135, 138–139). Subnational governments often play or fail to play a critical education role, given the informal urban settlement of many conflict-displaced migrants (see Karam, Monaghan, and Yoder, 2017, p. 450; Dryden-Peterson, 2016, pp. 138–139).

Background Considerations Relevant to Training

UNESCO's guide to "Conflict-Sensitive Education"[5] provides helpful preparatory site-adaptable advice for humanitarian responders intent on introducing education/training for conflict-displaced populations and other affected persons. The following factors should be taken into consideration:

- *When?* Commencement date. Observed holidays. Length of external intervention. Exit strategy.
- *Where?* Site characteristics. Outside conflict zone. Avoids land disputes. Harmonized with national education system.
- *What?* Deliverables. Resources to be brought in (vehicles, computers, radios, books, videotapes,[6] etc.). Languages of instruction.
- *With whom will you partner?* Selection criteria. Selection process. Reasons for any exclusions. Short-term vs long-term.

The following process components also should be taken into consideration:

- *Assess.* Conduct conflict analysis (education mitigates? conflict interferes?).
- *Do no harm.* Education "is not manipulated to promote exclusion and hate"; "does not reflect and perpetuate gender and social inequities"; engages community participation and responds to community priorities.
- *Prioritize prevention.* Protect trainers and students. Provide engaging alternative opportunities for youth. Build emergency preparedness.
- *Development partners.* Sustainable financing. Coordinate with local/national education system. Donors devote "some element of humanitarian funding to support assessment and advocacy" (Kihato and Landau, 2016, p. 421). Jointly prepare exit strategy. Partners stay engaged after external responders depart.

In sharp contrast to "medicalization" – "describing refugees as medical, mechanical objects that impose medical and financial burdens on health facilities in host countries" (Van den Bos, Sabar, and Tenenboim, 2019, p. 203; also p. 210) – the developmental approach to training is based on the assumption that "refugees have many skills and capabilities" (Anderson and Woodrow, 1998, p. 326; also Baraldi and Gavioli, 2021, p. 1059; Ramsay and Baker, 2019, p. 67). They find themselves in a "between and betwixt transitional" place that is simultaneously "a stressful experience of ambiguity, uncertainty and loss of meaning, but also of intense creativity and self-awareness, with potential for transformation" (Anghel and Grierson, 2020, p. 488). Often, they are positioned to "leverage transnational networks to expand their available resources for meeting health needs" (Villa-Torres, et al., 2017, p. 77).

Front-line community health-care workers are positioned to "take on a critical bridging function" between the needs of conflict-displaced migrants and professional humanitarian responders and to act in overlapping roles as community representatives and semi-professionals (Falge, Ruzza, and Schmidtke, 2012, pp. 181–182). Provided that channels of communication exist that can transmit the insights of TC-prepared community health workers regarding migrant vulnerabilities and assets, their small-scale local inputs "can trigger a momentous institutional learning process" (ibid., p. 182).

Skill Deficiencies

Lack of skills needed for empowerment and sustainable development among humanitarian responders, the conflict-displaced, and hosts poses special challenges. For instance, refugees typically lack understanding of the newly encountered health system and skill in navigating its access barriers (Rashid, Cervantes, and Goez, 2020, p. 477; Van den Bos, Sabar, and Tenenboim, 2019, pp. 201, 210). At the same time, international volunteers typically lack key competencies (Tiessen and Lough, 2019, p. 304), health-care providers "often are unprepared to manage refugees' health-related challenges" (Pechak, Howe, Padilla, and Frietze, 2020, p. e131), and most humanitarian responders lack background preparation in culturally responsive mental health and trauma care (Diaków, 2021, pp. 108–113).

The local and foreign staff of international humanitarian organizations who respond to conflict-displacement situations also need to address TC gaps. High staff turnover in organizations that serve displaced persons, including UNHCR, means that younger, less-experienced personnel lack training in the inter-sectoral, policy, management, evaluation, and related skills needed to operate effectively in the field (Martin, Davis, Benton, and Waliany, 2017, p. 114). Needed, for instance, is dedication to "increasing local capacities and reducing vulnerabilities" (Anderson and Woodrow, 1998, p. 97). This objective requires ensuring that affected participants are encouraged and enabled to provide an "active voice" in health-care policies in displaced-population contexts (Kirmayer, Kronick, and Rousseau, 2018, p. 119; Anghel and Grierson, 2020, p. 494; Van den Bos, Sabar, and Tenenboim, 2019, p. 202) and in encounters among "one set of people who need services and another who have been entrusted to deliver them" (Frenk, et al., 2010, p. 1925; also Koehn, 2006). Further, responders' skill in arranging sustainable economic opportunities enhances resilience and relieves mental health stresses (Kirmayer, Kronick, and Rousseau, 2018, pp. 119–120) among populations in camps, persons who informally settle, and host communities (Betts, 2021, p. 2). The ability to collaborate interprofessionally and transnationally is another key asset that requires development and/or enhancement (see Pechak, et al., 2020, p. e135).

When international responders withdraw or are evacuated from camps and informal settlements, the tasks of aid provision must be entirely assumed by local and national staff who often lack the requisite skill sets. In preparation for this eventuality, humanitarian responders need to devote early attention to overcoming barriers to collaboration among international and national aid providers, including language utilization, different priorities, and local organizations' hesitancy to engage with international NGOs. In Greece, for instance, national responders commonly used English in official meetings that aimed to address urgent issues of safety, sanitation, violence, etc. for the first 5 minutes and then switched to Greek and regularly told off international responders who did not speak Greek even though on-site non-profit and governmental organizations required providers to speak communicative English as one of the working languages. In Bulgaria, Iraq, Poland, and Ukraine, Diaków encountered similar issues associated with limited transnational skill on the part of national aid workers to foster an inclusive working environment where decisions can be made swiftly and all on-site providers can have equal access to information.

Thus, to ensure that providers of aid and skill development to the Global South are not "left behind" (Hoffman, 2021, p. 132), ongoing training-of-trainers programs need to be introduced shortly after the internationals arrive. Transnational humanitarian responders need to be specifically prepared for the special training-of-trainers aspect of their field responsibilities and given time to engage in this continuous and periodically reviewed and adjusted activity (Oakley, et al., 1991, pp. 231, 233).

Needs Assessment: Training Climate-Displaced Stakeholders

In Chapter 3 of this book, we discuss the advantages of pro-active, pre-crisis resettlement in climate-threatened contexts. Based on thorough background work, the Brookings Institution, in collaboration with Georgetown University's School of Foreign Service, and UNHCR, prepared a "Guidance on Planned Relocation" document that identifies the "specific rights, needs, circumstances, and vulnerabilities" of relocated persons, host communities, and other affected persons (2015, pp. 12–13).[7] The guidance provided in this document is of considerable value for the process of preparing for planned climate-induced relocation. We draw on this document in the interest of identifying helpful relocation processes and practices for climate-displacement stakeholders.

The recommended process steps for planned relocation are: (1) ascertaining that it is necessary;[8] (2) formulating a relocation plan based on relevant baseline studies and needs analysis;[9] (3) preparing conditions (including land, infrastructure, health and education services) for the physical move; (4) carrying out a resilience-building relocation;[10] (5) improving or maintaining the skills and livelihoods of displaced persons and host populations; and (6) mitigating effects on others (ibid., pp. 5–6, 12, 20–22). These planned relocation steps should be "conceived and executed within a sustainable development framework" (ibid., p. 18) for all stakeholders and in partnership with affected communities (White House, 2021, pp. 5, 23, 28).[11] If successful, relocated persons will be fully integrated into the new setting by the final stage of what can amount to a long process.

The outcomes of planned relocation initiatives will depend on the extent to which all stakeholders "actively engage in all aspects of the process" (Brookings Institution, Georgetown University's School of Foreign Service, and UNHCR, 2015, p. 6; also White House, 2021, p. 31) and participate in TC preparation. In particular, "the agency, resilience, and empowerment of Relocated Persons should be recognized, promoted, and enhanced throughout a Planned Relocation" (Brookings Institution, Georgetown University's School of Foreign Service, and UNHCR, 2015, p. 12). In addition, civil-society organizations "are often the first to respond when a disaster strikes and play a pivotal role … [in] understanding displacement by climate change" and in "bringing innovative thinking to the table" (White House, 2021, p. 28). By engaging with civil-society organizations and local leaders, humanitarian responders can access timely data that enhance "understanding the context and intricacies of communities impacted by climate change" and "allows for a more accurate and targeted response" (ibid., p. 28).

Needs of Populations Affected by Climate Displacement

At the initial stage of the climate-displacement needs assessment, it is helpful to prepare a map of the stakeholder landscape. The needs of high-power blockers and supporters and low-power blockers and supporters (see Moran, Youngdahl, and Moran, 2009, pp. 294–295) all merit attention (see above discussion).

Vulnerability, adaptation, and resilience assessments together offer a useful approach for identifying the needs of populations dislodged by disturbances induced by climate change – particularly "the magnitude and pattern of possible health risks" and "the effectiveness of the health systems designed to protect populations from those risks" (Ebi, 2015, p. 239). Such assessment data are likely to be particularly useful when humanitarian responders apply the guidelines and "toolbox on planned relocation in the context of environmental change" developed by the World Bank's Global Knowledge Partnership on Migration and Development (KNOMAD), Georgetown University, Brookings Institution, and UNHCR (Martin, Bergmann, Rigaud, and Yameogo, 2021, p. 147; Aleinikoff and Martin, 2022, p. 20). Under the cluster approach, moreover, the IOM (International Organization for Migration), the lead agency responsible for undertaking needs assessments in situations where people are dislocated by environmental drivers, including climate change, has developed a "Displacement Tracking Matrix, which collects and analyses data on the needs of those who have been displaced ..." (Aleinikoff and Martin, 2022, p. 15). Following the immediate rehabilitation phase of climate-provoked resettlement, the objective of humanitarian responders shifts to "aiding the population to regain their pre-disaster standard of living – or even better standard of living than before, if possible" (Karl and Karl, 2022, p. 396). The education needs of climate-displaced children received attention at the 2016 World Humanitarian Summit. One of the adopted initiatives, *Education Cannot Wait*, calls for funding quality education in safe places for school-aged children displaced by disasters (Hoffman, 2021, pp. 124–125).

Background Considerations Relevant to Training

Health-service managers who respond to global health needs in emergency contexts increasingly engage in highly mobile careers that require transnational competencies (Harrison, Meyer, Chauhan, and Agaliotis, 2019, p. 2). Responders focused on managing sustainable development following climate-induced displacement require a host of competencies that parallel those elaborated in Chapter 1 of this book (see Galleli, Hourneaux, and Munck, 2019, Tables IV and V). Among climate-displaced populations, enhanced social-ecological resilience enables beneficial adaptation and transformation outcomes in the wake of environmental vulnerability and in advance of future threats (Plastina, 2022, pp. 593, 609).

In the immediate aftermath of complex humanitarian emergencies, the challenge of coordinating a multiplicity of responders can overwhelm the delivery of health services to dislocated people (Heymann and Chand, 2013, p. 135). Arriving inexperienced citizen volunteers lack even basic aid-relief training, although they bring transferable professional knowledge, skills, and contacts (Anghel and Grierson, 2020; Whittaker, McLennan, and Handmer, 2015, p. 366; Jones, 2020, p. 15). Further, citizen volunteers can provide "rich, contextual" emergency-related information, often via social media, that is updated with dispatch (Whittaker, McLennan, and Handmer, 2015, p. 364). Through trial and error, and relevant training, they "gradually accumulate situational and contextual knowledge" and spontaneously develop projects suited to their skills (Anghel and Grierson, 2020, pp. 489–490, 494–497).

Skill Deficiencies

The skills needed for emergency care are "likely to be reshaped by the pressures of climate change" (Bell, 2010, p. 3). Specifically, the eco-medical capabilities and procedures required for "implementing disaster plans, as well as [for] retrospective analysis and development, may need to change rapidly" in the wake of events induced by climate change (ibid., pp. 3, 6). Rural and remote communities that already lack quality services will be especially disadvantaged and require in-depth analysis of context (ibid., pp. 4–5).

Humanitarian responders in urban areas encountering an influx of rural migrants will need skills to deal with "a convergence of challenges from population growth, climate stressors, and ethnic tensions" (Sullivan and Townsend, 2022, p. 918; also p. 921). They will need to be able to "think flexibly" about ill-defined problems and to respond creatively to "multi-faceted, novel issues" (Grotzer and Lincoln, 2007, p. 274). In clinical histories and diagnostic reasoning, health-care providers will need to develop analytic competence in capturing detailed understanding of environmental determinants of health and regarding how disrupted eco-systems "operate to shape disease" (Bell, 2010, pp. 3, 5) and how people are coping with climate displacement. Clearly, then, responders to climate displacement will require interprofessional learning that facilitates collaborative action with other practitioners, including "those in the voluntary and community sectors" (Hammick and Anderson, 2009, pp. 209, 213–214; also Barr, 2009, pp. 10–11; *Global Compact on Migration*, cited in Aleinikoff and Martin, 2022, p. 13). Hammick and Anderson (2009, p. 214) conclude that "only when professionals have the ability to reflect interprofessionally can they ever seek to become transformative in all aspects of practice."[12]

Even when local health services are provided on a temporary or partial basis, ethnicity, gender, income, and mobility independently and unequally affect health risks and access (Lyttleton, 2014, p. 185). Therefore, existing training approaches need to be modified in order to equip responders and collaborating specialists for "climate-influenced emergencies" (Bell, 2010, p. 4). In particular, new "clinical and non-clinical competencies" will be needed to respond to the needs and capabilities of Indigenous peoples, given that their special relationships with place and unique methods of responding and adapting will "shape the effects of climate change on their health" (ibid., pp. 4–5). Their anchoring in place and local knowledge offer important assets in building resilience (Ford, et al., 2020). In sum, medical responders need to "inquire about the patient's own capacity for self-healing and encounter how migrants are endeavoring to heal themselves" (Mollica, 2006, p. 105).

At the same time, many health-compromised migrants remain unaware of available services and providers remain ignorant regarding pre-departure and host-environment social determinants, individual and family needs, chronic health conditions, and culturally specific approaches (Lyttleton, 2014, p. 119;

Koehn, 2006). For instance, "following a disaster, with a compromised immune system, a person living with HIV may not be able to recover from a simple chest infection if he/she cannot get his/her usual antiretroviral drugs to manage the underlying conditions" (Chan, 2017, pp. 152–153). In addition, climate-displaced persons will need competence to (re)build capabilities to adapt socially and economically that employ sustainable technologies (Sovacool, Tan-Mullins, Ockwell, and Newell, 2017, p. 1263; Fohrer, Erne, and Finlay, 2019, p. 17).

Theory-of-Change Applications

In the interests of meaningful project design and evaluation rigor, this chapter introduces theory-of-change (ToC) methodology and applies it to training initiatives and stakeholders' TC development in the contexts of displacement associated with conflict and climate change. According to John Mayne (2017, p. 158), a robust ToC "would support a well-designed plausible intervention design, and would provide a solid basis both for monitoring and for theory-based evaluations."

Theory of change calls for backward mapping when designing a program or a project. Backward mapping involves starting with identifying intended outcomes and impacts and, then, working backward to identify steps or actions required to achieve the targeted outcomes and impacts. Backward mapping also allows for aligning implementation and evaluation.

The theory-of-change approach begins with monitoring and iteratively moves on to evaluation (see Ebi, 2015, p. 240). Monitoring involves the frequent and ongoing tracking of changes in training inputs, processes, outputs, and preliminary outcomes in order to inform program implementation and improvement (Zint, 2011, p. 332; Giles, 2018, p. 181).

The most helpful evaluation processes are relevant and of practical utility, ongoing, and trigger remedial actions. Utilization-focused evaluation is one approach to achieve this. It is intended to assist various groups of stakeholders to make informed decisions about the intervention (Patton, 2008, pp. 37–38). Comprehensive training evaluations need to cover inputs, objectives, processes, outputs, outcomes, and impacts. An *output* is a "tangible product (including services) of an intervention that is directly attributable to the initiative" (UNDP, 2011). Outputs relate to the extent (amount, volume) of completion of the objectives that actors set for themselves (Hardi, 2007, p. 26; Poister, Aristigueta, and Hall, 2015, p. 58). *Process* refers to the means by which activities are conducted. In the training context, an *outcome* is the actual change in stakeholder capabilities. *Impact* involves high-level improvements in human well-being that encompass, but extend beyond, the direct project stakeholders. Who (and what) are directly and indirectly better off and worse off (Thabrew, Wiek, and Ries, 2009, p. 71)? Under what circumstances, and why?

Theory-based approaches (Stame, 2004; Weiss, 1997) identify the impact pathways through which the intervention is intended to deliver its outcomes and impacts; they offer a promising way of arranging implementation steps and evaluating the outcomes of TC-training initiatives. As every intervention takes place in a complex context and interacts with all other parts in the system, the ToC should not be narrowly constrained to the internal logic of the intervention. First, one needs to define the system boundaries that inform the evaluation design (Garcia and Zazueta, 2015, pp. 32–33). Although the interlinkages are usually extensive, for practical purposes there is a need to limit the evaluation scope so that it is not too unwieldy, but still meaningful and flexible enough to account for activities that are constantly in flux.

The theory of change for a training initiative "is the logical sequence of conditions and factors that are necessary to deliver its ultimate impact" (Todd and Craig, 2021, p. 111). It is particularly difficult to determine attribution for training's ultimate impacts. Impacts typically are clouded when evaluated early on and specific contributions are more difficult to distinguish from other influences as one comes closer in time to observable ultimate impacts. Impact pathways are complex, time lags often lengthy, and there are multiple intervening factors and actors that can facilitate or hinder impact. For these reasons, some evaluators treat the issue of impact attribution by comparing intervention results with counterfactual values (conditions sans intervention) or by comparing before-after situations.

Theory-of-change applications commence with "mapping the hypothesized results chain" (Ssosse, Wagner, and Hopper, 2021, p. 7). The results chain maps intended causality among inputs (including behavioral drivers), processes (see, for instance, Karam, Monaghan, and Yoder, 2017, p. 456), activities ("the set of educational interventions responsible for transforming inputs into outputs"), outputs (numbers trained), and final outcomes ("the concrete results visible in behavioral change applied 'in real life' and visible at the individual … level)" (Ssosse, Wagner, and Hopper, 2021, p. 8).[13] Given that the generation of outputs provides "no guarantee that outcomes will result" (Poister, Aristigueta, and Hall, 2015, p. 58) and in light of the complexity surrounding impact assessment, an initial focus on outcomes is most relevant and helpful in TC training contexts.

Outcomes of TC Development

Intended TC development *outcomes* are: (1) to equip humanitarian responders with TC skill sets relevant for assisting dislocated persons who possess diverse nationality and ethnic backgrounds; (2) to equip dislocated persons with TC skill sets relevant for advancing personal/family integration[14] and health/resilience promotion in a new location and for contributing to local adaptation and sustainable development; (3) to equip hosts and other affected persons with TC skill sets relevant for contributing to local adaptation and sustainable development; and (4) to ensure that initiated TC training programs incorporate lessons learned and become self-sustaining.

Once specific training outcomes are identified, the theory-of-change approach articulates plausible causal hypotheses with explicit assumptions, baselines, and key indicators (Uitto, 2014, p. 8). From a process perspective, we can expect that "more comprehensive training and longer postings" will enhance the capabilities of humanitarian responders (Hyndman, 2000, p. 191). We would expect humanitarian responders to conflict-induced and climate-induced disasters who are trained in TC to develop contextually helpful analytic, emotional, creative, communicative, and functional competence. Among other outcomes, they would "reinforce synergies with other public health initiatives"; "ensure community participation"; "promote intersectoral cooperation and collaboration"; and engage in "advocacy at the national and international levels" (Ebi, 2015, p. 241; also Kirmayer, Kronick, and Rousseau, 2018). We also would expect both displaced persons and hosts who are trained in TC to develop contextually helpful analytic, emotional, creative, communicative, and functional competence.

Impacts of TC Development

Intended TC development *impacts* are: (1) dislocated individuals/families use their new transnational competencies to enhance resiliency, health, and well-being, and achieve integration and belonging, in a new location; (2) dislocated individuals/families and hosts use their new transnational competencies to contribute to health promotion, adaptation, and sustainable development; (3) humanitarian responders employ their new transnational competencies to advocate successfully for policies and approaches that enhance resiliency, health, and well-being, and achieve integration and belonging, among dislocated populations; (4) humanitarian responders use their new transnational competencies to advocate successfully for policy changes that mitigate persecution, conflict-induced migration, or climate-generated dislocations. During the TC development implementation phase, trainers should be prepared to "assess impact on a small scale" and to envision "next steps towards scaling the solution to the societal [and transnational] level" (Rowe and Hiser, 2016, p. 327).

ToC impact applications commence with mapping the hypothesized results chain (Ssosse, Wagner, and Hopper, 2021, p. 7). We would expect TC-trained humanitarian responders to succeed in preparing displaced populations for local integration, resettlement, and/or repatriation; in training local trainers; in advancing sustainable community development; and in withdrawing on the basis of a sustainable exit strategy. We would expect TC-trained displaced persons to succeed in local (re)integration and to contribute to sustainable community development. We would expect TC-trained hosts to support the local integration of displaced persons, to adapt to an increasingly diverse socio-economic context, and to contribute to sustainable community development.

Outcomes-Impacts Pathways

Evaluation is a "continuous process" (Oakley, 1991, p. 264). After the training program has been completed and outcomes evaluated, it is time to carry out a "detailed Theory of Change between outcomes and impacts, referred to as *outcomes-impacts pathways*" (Todd and Craig, 2021, p. 112; emphasis in original) in order to discover whether initial assumptions "have in fact held true in the longer term" (ibid., p. 133). The challenge is to formulate precise questions that will test the hypotheses underlying the theory of change (Ssosse, Wagner, and Hopper, 2021, p. 8).[15] This procedure allows "assessment of progress, even in cases where the duration of the change process may be many years" (Todd and Craig, 2021, p. 133). Clearly, outcome-impact pathway evaluations cannot be completed by a team of evaluators "merely spending a week or ten days at the project area" (Oakley, 1991, p. 264). Participatory evaluation, which shifts the locus of activity away from external actors to the grassroots and unfolds in stages over time (ibid., pp. 264–265), must be cultivated and facilitated.

Key elements in outcomes-impacts pathways are intermediate targets and states ("the transitional conditions between a project's outcomes and impacts that must be achieved in order to deliver the intended impacts"), impact drivers ("factors that, if present, are expected to contribute to the ultimate realization of project impacts and that are within the ability of the project to influence"), and assumptions ("factors that, if present, are expected to contribute to the ultimate realization of project impacts but are largely beyond the ability of the project to influence or address") (Todd and Craig, 2021, p. 112; also Ssosse, Wagner, and Hopper, 2021, p. 8). In the case of climate dislocation, the latter set of assumptions would include estimates regarding additional socioeconomic burdens, constraints, and future health risks under "a range of climate change scenarios" along with expectations concerning the availability of critical human and financial resources, reinforcing and undermining policy and actions implemented by other actors, and unintended consequences (Ebi, 2015, p. 240).

Evaluation Methods

Theory-of-change evaluations favor "mixed methods of data collection" (Ssosse, Wagner, and Hopper, 2021, p. 12), or what Patton (2019, pp. 114–116) calls "bricolage." Impact measures can be prospective and retrospective; qualitative and quantitative (ibid., p. 12). Triangulation with mixed methods, including field-level verification, observations, interviews, focus groups, policy analysis, and other more traditional evaluation tools is particularly useful in outcome evaluations because "confidence in the validity of observations and findings is proportional to the extent that information from different sources is congruent and compatible" (Green and Tones, 2010, 503; also Ssosse, Wagner, and Hopper, 2021, p. 12). For evaluations of TC outcomes, we recommend triangulated inter-subjective interviewing regarding participant behavior along the analytic-functional continuum. In health-care contexts, uniform, but independent and privately conducted, interviews with patients, providers (most commonly physicians), and support professionals (nurses, MHPSS providers, and/or social workers) enable scaled identification and comparison of each participant's level of transnational competence (see Koehn, 2005, pp. 50–69).

Pathways to Promising Interventions for Skill Development

Humanitarian responders with various professional backgrounds "have special obligations and responsibilities to acquire competencies and to undertake functions beyond purely technical tasks" (Frenk, et al., 2010, p. 1951). In the fluid and often under-resourced contexts of population displacement, transdisciplinary preparation (Taylor, 2008, pp. 94–95)[16] facilitates "task shifting and task sharing" among specialists (Frenk, et al., 2010, p. 1951). The health concerns that arise in population displacement contexts engage responders charged with, among other challenges, "surveillance, immunisation, containment, treatment, and interventions to modify social determinants such as absence of access to clean water and sanitation" (ibid., p. 1944). Particularly important for health-care delivery, capacity building, and leveraging resources, therefore, is transnational ability to "collaborate not only across [multi-disciplinary] health care teams but also with patients, other services and other sectors" (Harrison, et al., 2019, p. 6; also Hu and Zhang, 2020, pp. 235, 240). Such TC-facilitated teamwork collaborations include advocacy for policy and structural changes that enhance the well-being of local populations, that transform the social and environmental determinants of inequality, health, and dispossession (Kirmayer, Kronick, and Rousseau, 2018, pp. 119–120; Ozkazanc-Pan, 2019, p. 96; Taylor, 2008, p. 98), and that address drivers of conflict and climate displacement.

The key practical skills required of effective "boundary riding" managers of emergency health services who work "across multiple countries" on interconnected health challenges include the ability to initiate changes, to "collaborate with a range of stakeholders both internally and externally," to "listen to others and take feedback from them," and to relate authentically to dislocated health seekers "with compassion" (Harrison, et al., 2019, pp. 4, 6–7). The pathway to promising TC development embraces a common core of transprofessional education and training designed to promote transformative learning

> *from* fact memorisation *to* searching, analysis, and synthesis of information for decision making; *from* seeking professional credentials *to* achieving core competencies for effective teamwork …; and *from* non-critical adoption of educational models *to* creative adaptation of global resources to address local problems.
> (Frenk, et al., 2010, p. 1924; emphasis added; also pp. 1929, 1943–1944)

Peter Walker and colleagues' survey of aid workers and relevant academics highlighted the need for core competencies in TC-related domains of empathy, adaptability, teamwork, diversity, integrity, communication, and technological mastery. The survey respondents highlighted the need for skills related to "working in teams, working with less-than-perfect data, and working in insecure and dangerous environments" (Walker, et al., 2010, p. 2228).

As repositories of unmatched knowledge infrastructure, including research findings on migrant health and development beyond the reach of fully occupied practitioners, universities are positioned to play a central role in the preparation of transnationally competent humanitarian responders (see Edwards, 1996, p. 20). To be prepared beyond a purely local and immediate context, professional humanitarian responders will be well served by initial TC skill development through rigorous "academic education and training" (Edwards, 1996, p. 21). In most cases, this requires the transformation of higher-education institutions through top-level commitment and support and "the redesign of university courses to involve more practice-based involvement and ... development of practical problem-solving skills" (Edwards, 1996, pp. 23–24). Walker, et al. (2010, pp. 2224, 2228) recommend establishment of an "international accreditation body" that could complement higher-education preparation by certifying core individual transnational competence. Importantly, "certified training from accredited institutions in countries such as Ethiopia, Thailand, and Venezuela would carry the same weight as that from institutions in Europe and North America" (ibid. p. 2229).

The next two chapters elaborate the objectives and approaches to TC training. Chapter 5 focuses on preparing humanitarian responders for conflict and climate displacements. Chapter 6 is devoted to training displaced persons and their hosts.

Notes

1 Including volunteers (see Tiessen and Lough, 2019; Jones, 2020, pp. 89, 91), civil-society organizations, and local leaders (see White House, 2021, p. 28).

2 To be avoided is "disempowerment": "the tendency to picture refugees as lacking knowledge of and agency in pursuing the right health services" (Van den Bos, Sabar, and Tenenboim, 2019, p. 203; also p. 210; also Valtonen, 1998, p. 57). The 2016 World Humanitarian Summit recognized "crisis-affected people themselves as important first responders." In most cases, however, it is "almost impossible" without extensive training and capacity-building for community-based organizations "to be recognized as implementing partners or operational partners in their own right by UNHCR" (Pincock, Betts, and Easton-Calabria, 2020, pp. 3, 13, 120).

3 For instance, the NGO GOAL, in partnership with UNHCR, introduced a camp program "focused on women which was related to energy-efficient [mud] stove technology, cooking techniques, environmental awareness and the use of a renewable source of firewood" (Karl and Karl, 2022, p. 394).

4 In the centrally controlled camp for Syrian refugees that Richard Davies visited, the refugees

do not go cold and they do not go hungry, [but] they are left wanting. What they are missing are all the higher needs that are satisfied when trade arises organically, firms are set up as a matter of choice, products bought as a matter of taste. On this deeper view, markets are not just a means to an end but ends in themselves that provide agency, vocation and life satisfaction.

(Davies, 2020, p. 71)

5 iiep.unesco.org/sites/default/files/inee_csc_graphics.pdf (accessed February 20, 2021).

6 Videotapes contributed by the community can be particularly helpful for health education in displaced contexts (Lipson and Meleis, 1999, p. 99; Clabots and Dolphin, 1992).

7 The White House Report (2021, p. 5) asserts that planned relocations "must respect and maintain household, community, social cohesion, and kinship ties and avoid separating families."

8 Relocation is accompanied by risks. Planned permanent relocation should be "a measure of last resort" once a threshold is reached "beyond which it is no longer considered safe for people to remain in place" (ibid., p. 23).

9 Among other considerations, the plan should allow affected persons sufficient time to make informed decisions about participating; specify timelines; ensure sufficient and sustainable funding for all phases; identify available and suitable sites; be "sufficiently flexible to accommodate changing needs, circumstances, and requests from Relocated Persons that may arise"; identify other affected persons and include measures aimed at avoiding adverse impacts to them (Brookings Institution, Georgetown University's School of Foreign Service, and UNHCR, 2015, pp. 18–19, 21).

10 See the package of resilience-building measures highlighted in Hellegatte, Vogt-Schilb, Bangalore, and Rozenberg (2017, pp. 14–15).

11 Vanuatu, São Tomé and Principe, and New Zealand have utilized participatory decision making by including affected communities "at every step of the planned relocation process" (White House, 2021, p. 23).

12 For responders working in remote areas who have limited access to professional support, this need can be fulfilled via online networking and/or participation in online courses taught by qualified persons with diverse professional backgrounds.

13 In their study of the transnational and interdisciplinary Caring Society project, Teunissen, et al. (2023, pp. 50–60) devote special attention to the outcome-shaping input and activities steps of the theory of change – including project management (organization, information, agenda and role communications, hybrid meetings and other socialization and team-building functions, time and scheduling clarifications, workplace facilities and ICT infrastructure, internal support, team links), commitment to clear and shared objectives, and participant selection.

14 Including political participation (Eckenwiler and Wild, 2021, pp. 243–244).

15 Ssosse, et al. (2021, pp. 8–9) recognize that "while the research question will need to remain largely unchanged throughout the impact assessment process, the theory of change may need to be modified to accommodate surprises in the data."

16 *Trans*disciplinarity "goes 'beyond disciplines', focusing on solving real-world problems, often with the participation of non-academic stakeholders" (Ursic, et al., 2022, p. 3).

References

Aleinikoff, T. Alexander; and Martin, Susan. 2022. *The Responsibility of the International Community in Situations of Mobility Due to Environmental Events*. Zolberg Institute Working Paper Series 2022–2021. New York: Zolberg Institute on Migration and Mobility, The New School.

Almoshmosh, Nadim; Bahloul, Hussam J.; Barkil-Oteo, Andres; Hassan, Ghayda; and Kirmayer, Laurence J. 2020. "Mental Health of Resettled Syrian Refugees: A Practical Cross-cultural Guide for Practitioners." *Journal of Mental Health Training, Education and Practice* 15 (1): 20–32.

Anderson, Mary B.; and Woodrow, Peter J. 1998. *Rising from the Ashes: Development Strategies in Times of Disaster*. Boulder, CO: Lynne Rienner.

Anghel, Roxana; and Grierson, J. 2020. "Addressing Needs in Liminal Space: The Citizen Volunteer Experience and Decision-Making in the Unofficial Calais Migrant Camp – Insights for Social Work." *European Journal of Social Work* 23 (3): 486–499.

Baraldi, Claudio; and Gavioli, Laura. 2021. "Effective Communication and Knowledge Distribution in Healthcare Interaction with Migrants." *Health Communication* 36 (9): 1059–1067.

Barr, Hugh. 2009. "Interprofessional Education as an Emerging Concept." In *Interprofessional Education: Making It Happen*, edited by Patricia Bluteau and Ann Jackson. New York: Palgrave Macmillan, pp. 3–23.

Beiser, Marion. 2014. "Personal and Social Forms of Resilience: Research with Southeast Asian and Sri Lankan Tamil Refugees in Canada." In *Refuge and Resilience: Promoting Resilience and Mental Health among Resettled Refugees and Forced Migrants*, edited by Laura Simich and Lisa Andermann. New York: Springer, pp. 73–90.

Bell, Erica J. 2010. "Climate Change: What Competencies and Which Medical Education and Training Approaches?" *BMC Medical Education* 10 (31): 1–9.

Betts, Alexander. 2021. "Refugees: Overcoming Prejudices." *UNESCO Courier*, 4.

Brookings Institution, Georgetown University's School of Foreign Service, and UNHCR. 2015. *Guidance on Protecting People from Disasters and Environmental Change through Planned Relocation*. Washington, D.C.: Brookings Institution.

Chan, Emily Ying Yang. 2017. *Public Health Humanitarian Responses to Natural Disasters*. London: Routledge.

Clabots, Renee B.; and Dolphin, Diane. 1992. "The Multilingual Videotape Project: Community Involvement in a Unique Health Education Program." *Public Health Reports* 107 (1): 75–80.

Davies, Richard. 2020. *Extreme Economies: What Life at the World's Margins Can Teach Us About Our Own Future*. London: Transworld Publishers.

Diaków, Diana M. 2021. "Humanitarian Workers' Perspectives on Mental Health and Resilience of Refugee Youth: Implications for School Psychology." PhD dissertation, University of Montana.

Dryden-Peterson, Sarah. 2016. "Refugee Education in Countries of First Asylum: Breaking Open the Black Box of Pre-Resettlement Experiences." *Theory and Research in Education* 14 (2): 131–148.

Ebi, Kristie I. 2015. "Vulnerability and Adaptation Assessment." In *Climate Change and Public Health*, edited by Barry S. Levy and Jonathan A. Patz. Oxford: Oxford University Press, pp. 239–241.

Eckenwiler, Lisa; and Wild, Verina. 2021. "Refugees and Others Enduring Displacement: Structural Injustice, Health, and Ethical Placemaking." *Journal of Social Philosophy* 52: 234–250.

Edwards, Michael. 1996. "The Getting of Wisdom: Educating the Reflective Practitioner." In *Educating for Real: The Training of Professionals for Development Practice*, edited by Nabeel Hamdi and Amr El-Sherif. London: Intermediate Technology Publications.

Fajth, Veronika; Bilgili, Ozge; Loschmann, Craig; and Siegel, Melissa. 2019. "How Do Refugees Affect Social Life in Host Communities? The Case of Congolese Refugees in Rwanda." *Comparative Migration Studies* 7 (33): 1–21.

Falge, Christiane; Ruzza, Carlo; and Schmidtke, Oliver. 2012. *Migrants and Health: Political and Institutional Responses to Cultural Diversity in Health Systems.* Farnham: Ashgate.

Fohrer, Bianca; Erne, Roland; and Finlay, Graham. 2019. "Transnational Competence: A Transformative Tool?" *Labor Studies Journal* 46 (1): 1–31.

Ford, James D.; King, Nia; Galappaththi, Eranga K.; Pearce, Tristan; McDowell, Graham; and Harper, Sherilee L. 2020. "The Resilience of Indigenous Peoples to Environmental Change." *One Earth* 2: 532–543.

Frenk, Julio; et al. 2010. "Health Professionals for a New Century: Transforming Education to Strengthen Health Systems in an Interdependent World." *Lancet* 376 (December 4): 1923–1958.

Galleli, Barbara; Hourneaux, Flavio Jr.; and Munck, Luciano. 2019. "Sustainability and Human Competences: A Systematic Literature Review." *Benchmarking: An International Journal* January. doi:10.108/BIJ-12-2018-0433.

Garcia, Jeneen R.; and Zazueta, Aaron. 2015. "Going Beyond Mixed Methods to Mixed Approaches: A Systems Perspective for Asking the Right Questions." *IDS Bulletin* 46 (1): 30–43.

Giles, Wenona. 2018. "The Borderless Higher Education for Refugees Project: Enabling Refugee and Local Kenyan Students in Dadaab to Transition to University Education." *Journal on Education in Emergencies* 4 (1): 164–184.

Green, Jackie; and Tones, Keith. 2010. *Health Promotion: Planning and Strategies.* Thousand Oaks, CA: Sage.

Grotzer, Tina; and Lincoln, Rebecca. 2007. "Educating for 'Intelligent Environmental Action' in an Age of Global Warming." In *Creating a Climate for Change: Communicating Climate Change and Facilitating Social Change,* edited by Susanne C. Moser and Lisa Dilling. Cambridge: Cambridge University Press, pp. 266–280.

Hammick, Marilyn; and Anderson, Elizabeth. 2009. "Sustaining Interprofessional Education in Professional Award Programmes." In *Interprofessional Education: Making It Happen,* edited by Patricia Bluteau and Ann Jackson. New York: Palgrave Macmillan, pp. 202–226.

Hardi, Peter. 2007. "The Long and Winding Road of Sustainable Development Evaluation." In *Impact Assessment and Sustainable Development: European Practice and Experience,* edited by Clive George and Colin Kirkpatrick. Cheltenham: Edward Elgar, pp. 15–30.

Harrison, Reema; Meyer, Lois; Chauhan, Ashfaq; and Agaliotis, Maria. 2019. "What Qualities Are Required for Globally-Relevant Health Service Managers? An Exploratory Analysis of Health Systems Internationally." *Globalization and Health* 15 (11): 1–9.

Hellegatte, Stephane; Vogt-Schilb, Adrien; Bangalore, Mook; and Rozenberg, Julie. 2017. *Unbreakable: Building the Resilience of the Poor in the Face of Natural Disasters.* Washington, D.C.: International Bank for Reconstruction and Development.

Heymann, David L.; and Chand, Sudeep. 2013. "Diplomacy and Global Health Security." In *Global Health Diplomacy: Concepts, Issues, Actors, Instruments, Fora and Cases,* edited by Ilona Kickbusch; Graham Lister; Michaela Told; and Nick Drager. New York: Springer, pp. 125–139.

Hoffman, Peter J. 2021. "What Does 'Leave No One Behind' Mean for Humanitarians?" In *Routledge Handbook on the UN and Development,* edited by Stephen Browne and Thomas G. Weiss. London: Routledge, pp. 121–134.

Horst, Cindy. 2006. *Transnational Nomads: How Somalis Cope with Refugee Life in the Dadaab Camps of Kenya.* New York: Berghahn Books.

Hu, Qian; and Zhang, Haibo. 2020. "Incorporating Emergency Management into Public Administration Education: The Case of China." *Journal of Public Affairs Education* 26 (2): 228–249.

Hyndman, Jennifer. 2000. *Managing Displacement: Refugees and the Politics of Humanitarianism.* Minneapolis, MN: University of Minnesota Press.

Jahre, Marianne; Kembro, Jaokim; Adjahossou, Anicet; and Altay, Nezih. 2018. "Approaches to the Design of Refugee Camps: An Empirical Study in Kenya, Ethiopia, Greece, and Turkey." *Journal of Humanitarian Logistics and Supply Chain Management* 8 (3): 323–345.

Jones, Lynne. 2020. *The Migrant Diaries.* New York: Refuge Press.

Karam, Fares J.; Monaghan, Christine; and Yoder, Paul J. 2017. "'The Students Do Not Know Why They Are Here': Education Decision-Making for Syrian Refugees." *Globalisation, Societies and Education* 15 (4): 448–463.

Karl, Alexandre A.; and Karl, Julia S. 2022. "Human Rights for Refugees: Enhancing Sustainable Humanitarian Supply Chain to Guarantee a Health [sic] Environment in Refugee Settlements." *Journal of Humanitarian Logistics and Supply Chain Management* 12 (3): 382–401.

Kihato, Caroline W.; and Landau, Loren B. 2016. "Stealth Humanitarianism: Negotiating Politics, Precarity and Performance Management in Protecting the Urban Displaced." *Journal of Refugee Studies* 30 (3): 407–425.

Kirmayer, Laurence J.; Kronick, Rachel; and Rousseau, Cecile. 2018. "Advocacy as Key to Structural Competency in Psychiatry." *JAMA Psychiatry* 75 (2): 119–120.

Koehn, Peter. 2005. "Medical Encounters in Finnish Reception Centres: Asylum-Seeker and Clinician Perspectives." *Journal of Refugee Studies* 18 (1): 47–75.

Koehn, Peter. 2006. "Health-Care Outcomes in Ethnoculturally Discordant Medical Encounters: The Role of Physician Transnational Competence in Consultations with Asylum Seekers." *Journal of Immigrant and Minority Health* 8 (2): 137–147.

Lipson, Juliene G.; and Meleis, Afaf I. 1999. "Research with Immigrants and Refugees." In *Handbook of Clinical Nursing Research,* edited by Ada S. Hinshaw; Suzanne L. Feetham; and Joan L. Shaver. Thousand Oaks, CA: Sage, pp. 87–106.

Lyttleton, Chris. 2014. *Intimate Economies of Development: Mobility, Sexuality and Health in Asia.* London: Routledge.

Martin, Susan F.; Bergmann, Jonas; Rigaud, Kanta; and Yameogo, Nadege D. 2021. "Climate Change, Human Mobility, and Development." *Migration Studies* 9 (1): 142–149.

Martin, Susan F.; Davis, Rochelle; Benton, Grace; and Waliany, Zoya. 2017. *Responsibility Sharing for Refugees in the Middle East and North Africa: Perspectives from Policymakers, Stakeholders, Refugees and Internally Displaced Persons.* Report 2017:8. Stockholm: Delmi, The Migration Studies Delegation.

Mayne, John. 2017. "Theory of Change Analysis: Building Robust Theories of Change." *Canadian Journal of Program Evaluation / La Revue canadienne d'évaluation de programme* 32 (2): 155–173.

Michelini, Enrico. 2022. "Organized Sport in Refugee Sites: An Ethnographic Research in Niamey." *European Journal for Sport and Society* 19 (1): 1–17.

Micinski, Nicholas R. 2021. "Migration and Development in the UN Global Compacts." In *Routledge Handbook on the UN and Development,* edited by Stephen Browne and Thomas G. Weiss. London: Routledge, pp. 135–147.

Milner, James. 2021. "Refugees and International Development Policy and Practice." In *Introduction to International Development: Approaches, Actors, Issues, and Practice*, edited by Paul Haslam; Jessica Shafer; and Pierre Beaudet. Oxford: Oxford University Press, pp. 408–425.

Mollica, Richard. 2006. *Healing Invisible Wounds: Paths to Hope and Recovery in a Violent World*. Orlando, FL: Harcourt, Inc.

Moran, Robert T.; Youngdahl, William E.; and Moran, Sarah V. 2009. "Intercultural Competence in Business Leading Global Projects: Bridging the Cultural and Functional Divide." In *The Sage Handbook of Intercultural Competence*, edited by Darla K. Deardorff. Los Angeles, CA: Sage, pp. 287–303.

Mundy, Karen; and Dryden-Peterson, Sarah. 2011. "Educating Children in Zones of Conflict: An Overview and Introduction." In *Educating Children in Conflict Zones: Research, Policy, and Practice for Systemic Change – A Tribute to Jackie Kirk*. New York: Teachers College Press, pp. 1–12.

Murdoch-Eaton, Deborah; Redmond, Anthony; and Bax, Nigel. 2011. "Training Healthcare Professionals for the Future: Internationalism and Effective Inclusion of Global Health Training." *Medical Teacher* 33: 562–569.

Negm, Lena; and Mayer, Aida. 2022. "Proposal to Establish Refugees Therapy Center." *Civil Engineering and Architecture* 10 (3A): 43–49.

Nunn, Caitlin; Spaaij, Ramon; and Luguetti, Carla. 2022. "Beyond Integration: Football as a Mobile, Transnational Sphere of Belonging for Refugee-Background Young People." *Leisure Studies* 41 (1): 42–55.

Oakley, Peter. 1991. *Projects with People: The Practice of Participation in Rural Development*. Geneva: International Labour Office.

Ozkazanc-Pan, Banu. 2019. *Transnational Migration and the New Subjects of Work: Transmigrants, Hybrids and Cosmopolitans*. Bristol: Bristol University Press.

Patton, Michael Q. 2008. *Utilization-Focused Evaluation*. 4th edition. Thousand Oaks, CA: Sage.

Patton, Michael Q. 2019. *Blue Marble Evaluation: Premises and Principles*. New York: The Guilford Press.

Pechak, Celia; Howe, Vicki; Padilla, Margie; and Frietze, Gabriel A. 2020. "Preparing Students to Serve a Refugee Population through a Health-Focused Interprofessional Education Experience ." *Journal of Applied Health* 49 (3): e131–e138.

Perouse de Montclos, Marc-Antoine; and Kagwanja, Peter M. 2000. "Refugee Camps or Cities: The Socio-Economic Dynamics of the Dadaab and Kakuma Camps in Northern Kenya." *Journal of Refugee Studies* 13 (2): 205–222.

Pincock, Kate; Betts, Alexander; and Easton-Calabria, Evan. 2020. *The Global Governed? Refugees as Providers of Protection and Assistance*. Cambridge: Cambridge University Press.

Plastina, Anna F. 2022. "Changing Discourses of Climate Change: Building Social-Ecological Resilience Cross-Culturally." *Text & Talk* 42 (4): 591–612.

Poister, Theodore H.; Aristigueta, Maria P.; and Hall, Jeremy L. 2015. *Managing and Measuring Performance in Public and Nonprofit Organizations: An Integrated Approach*, 2nd edition. San Francisco, CA: Jossey-Bass.

Ramsay, Georgina; and Baker, Sally. 2019. "Higher Education and Students from Refugee Backgrounds: A Meta-Scoping Study." *Refugee Survey Quarterly* 38: 55–82.

Rashid, Marghalara; Cervantes, Andrea D.; and Goez, Helly. 2020. "Refugee Health Curriculum in Undergraduate Medical Education (UME): A Scoping Review." *Teaching and Learning in Medicine* 32 (5): 476–485.

Rowe, Debra; and Hiser, Krista. 2016. "Higher Education for Sustainable Development in the Community and through Partnerships." In *Routledge Handbook of Higher Education for Sustainable Development*, edited by Matthias Barth; Gerd Michelsen; Marco Rieckmann; and Ian Thomas. London: Routledge, pp. 315–330.

Sampson, Robyn; and Gifford, Sandra M. 2010. "Place-Making, Settlement and Well-Being: The Therapeutic Landscapes of Recently Arrived Youth with Refugee Backgrounds." *Health & Place* 16: 116–131.

Schroeder, Kent; and Hatton, Michael. 2012. "Rethinking Risk in Development Projects: From Management to Resilience." *Development in Practice* 22 (3): 409–416.

Sleijpen, Marieke; Boeije, Hennie R.; Kleber, Rolf J.; and Mooren, Trudy. 2016. "Between Power and Powerlessness: A Meta-Ethnography of Sources of Resilience in Young Refugees." *Ethnicity & Health* 21 (2): 158–180.

Sovacool, Benjamin K.; Tan-Mullins, May; Ockwell, David; and Newell, Peter. 2017. "Political Economy, Poverty, and Polycentrism in the Global Environmental Facility's Least Developed Countries Fund (LDCF) for Climate Change Adaptation." *Third World Quarterly* 38 (6): 1249–1271.

Spaaij, Ramon; Luguetti, Carla; and Ugolotti, Nicola M. De. 2022. "Forced Migration and Sport: An Introduction." *Sport in Society* 25 (3): 405–417.

Ssosse, Quentin; Wagner, Johanna; and Hopper, Carina. 2021. "Assessing the Impact of ESD: Methods, Challenges, Results." *Sustainability* 13 (2854): 1–26. doi:10.3390/su13052854.

Stame, Nicoletta. 2004. "Theory-Based Evaluation and Types of Complexity." *Evaluation* 10 (1): 58–76.

Stewart, Miriam J. 2014. "Social Support in Refugee Resettlement." In *Refuge and Resilience: Promoting Resilience and Mental Health among Resettled Refugees and Forced Migrants*, edited by Laura Simich and Lisa Andermann. New York: Springer, pp. 91–107.

Sullivan, John P.; and Townsend, Keeley. 2022. "Climate Migration: Adding Fuel to the Ethnocentric Fire." *Terrorism and Political Violence* 43 (5): 914–925.

Taylor, Peter. 2003. *How to Design a Training Course: A Guide to Participatory Curriculum Development*. London: Continuum.

Taylor, Peter. 2008. "Higher Education Curricula for Human and Social Development." In *Higher Education in the World 3: New Challenges and Emerging Roles for Human and Social Development*. London: Palgrave Macmillan, pp. 89–101.

Teunissen, R. A.; Dierx, J. A.; Venter, T.; Young, C. T.; and Titus, S. 2023. "Managing International, Intercultural, and Interdisciplinary Collaboration in Health and Well-being Capacity Building: Lessons Learned within the CASO Higher Education Project." *Studies in Higher Education* 48 (1): 49–62.

Thabrew, Lanka; Wiek, Arnim; and Ries, Robert. 2009. "Environmental Decision Making in Multi-Stakeholder Contexts: Applicability of Life Cycle Thinking in Development Planning and Implementation." *Journal of Cleaner Production* 17: 67–76.

Tiessen, Rebecca; and Lough, Benjamin J. 2019. "International Volunteering Capacity Development: Volunteer Partner Organization Experiences of Mitigating Factors for Effective Practice." *Forum for Development Studies* 46 (2): 299–320.

Todd, David; and Craig, Rob. 2021. "Assessing Progress towards Impacts in Environmental Programmes Using the Field Review of Outcomes to Impacts Methodology." In *Evaluating Environment in International Development*, 2nd edition, edited by Juha I. Uitto. London: Routledge, pp. 111–136.

Uitto, Juha I. 2014. "Evaluating Environment in International Development." In *Evaluating Environment in International Development*, edited by Juha I. Uitto. London: Routledge, pp. 3–16.

UNDP. (United Nations Development Programme). 2011. *Evaluation Policy*. New York: UNDP. Available at: http://www.undp.org/evaluation/policy.htm.

Ursic, Luka; et al. 2022. "Factors Influencing Interdisciplinary Research and Industry-Academia Collaborations at Six European Universities: A Qualitative Study." *Sustainability* 14: 1–24.

Valtonen, Kathleen. 1998. "Resettlement of Middle Eastern Refugees in Finland: The Elusiveness of Integration." *Journal of Refugee Studies* 11 (1): 38–60.

Van den Bos, Nellie; Sabar, Galia; and Tenenboim, Shiri. 2019. "Healthcare Providers' Images of Refugees and Yheir Use of Health Services: A Exploratory Study." *International Journal of Migration, Health and Social Care* 15 (3): 201–213.

Villa-Torres, Laura; Gonzalez-Vazquez, Tonatiuh; Fleming, Paul J.; Gonzalez-Gonzalez, Edgar L.; Infante-Xibille, Cesar; Chavez, Rebecca; and Barrington, Clare. 2017. "Transnationalism and Health: A Systematic Literature Review on the Use of Transnationalism in the Study of the Health Practices and Behaviors of Migrants." *Social Science & Medicine* 183: 70–79.

Walker, Peter; Hein, Karen; Russ, Catherine; Bertleff, Greg; and Caspersz, Dan. 2010. "A Blueprint for Professionalizing Humanitarian Assistance." *Health Affairs* 29 (December): 2223–2230.

Weiss, Carol H. 1997. "Theory-Based Evaluation: Past, Present and Future." *New Directions for Evaluation* 76: 41–55.

Wells, Ruth; Lawsin, Catalina; Hunt, Caroline; Youssef, Omar Said; Abujado, Fayzeh; and Steel, Zachary. 2018. "An Ecological Model of Adaptation to Displacement: Individual, Cultural and Community Factors Affecting Psychological Adjustment among Syrian Refugees in Jordan." *Global Mental Health* 5: 1–13. doi:10.1017/gmh.2018.30

White House. 2021. *Report on the Impact of Climate Change on Migration*. Washington, D.C.: The White House.

Whittaker, Joshua; McLennan, Blythe; and Handmer, John. 2015. "A Review of Informal Volunteerism in Emergencies and Disasters: Definition, Opportunities and Challenges." *International Journal of Disaster Risk Reduction* 13: 358–368.

Zint, Michaela. 2011. "Evaluating Education for Sustainable Development Programs." In *World Trends in Education for Sustainable Development*, edited by Walter L. Filho. Frankfurt: Peter Lang, pp. 329–347.

5 Guidelines for TC Training
Humanitarian Responders

Today's humanitarian responders have "broadened the scope of their mission beyond the … 'saving' and protection of others to include strengthening capacity and … setting the foundation for development" (Eckenwiler and Wild, 2021, p. 241). They shoulder ethical responsibility for acquiring competencies and undertaking functions "beyond purely technical tasks" (Frenk, et al., 2010, p. 1951). This chapter provides detailed TC skill development guidelines for contemporary humanitarian responders to populations dislocated by conflict and climate change. Incorporating insights drawn from field experience, the authors elaborate practical approaches for adaptable site-based training and higher-education programs as well as mental health and psychosocial support (MHPSS) interventions aimed at equipping responders with TC skill sets that will enhance their capacity-strengthening capabilities in conflict-dislocation and climate-dislocation contexts.[1] Health care, resilience-building, and sustainable development feature in this connection.

Education and Training Contexts

Given the immediate challenges that confront humanitarian responders in most crisis situations, it is important to initiate transnational-competence preparation during the windows of opportunity that precede engagement. These windows can be long-term, in which case, higher-education can be involved, or short-term, which utilize an initial pre-departure or on-arrival training program.

Higher-Education Initiatives

Higher-education institutions in the North and South are positioned to offer a comprehensive and skill-reinforcing TC curriculum to students intending to support displaced populations and improve health outcomes.[2] Southern educational institutions play an indispensable role in the recruitment, training, and sustaining of local TC responders.[3] Moreover, transcontinental partnerships offer vast potential for educating global humanitarian

DOI: 10.4324/9781003330493-6

responders (see Koehn, 2019, Chapter 8). Michaela Hynie et al. (2014, pp. 3–4) provide a South-North list of 12 research centers focused on migration and refugee issues that could fulfill this role.

The comprehensive set of analytic, emotional, creative, communicative, and functional skills that form the core of a transnational-competence curriculum (see Chapter 1 for details) promise to reinforce new educational initiatives and redirect traditional medical school and health education in ways that promote context-sensitive migrant health in "ethnically and socially discordant … encounters" (Matlin, et al., 2018, p. 43). Nursing educators and trainers, for instance, can incorporate TC preparation in identifying and addressing upstream determinants of migrant health (Kim, 2010, p. 568), in emphasizing that competent interpretation must be available, in learning ways to engage in careful and open-minded listening to patient narratives (Jones, 2020, p. 350), in recognizing the need for appropriate interprofessional referrals, and in advocating for migrant needs for equitable resource allocation, health-care treatment, and access to social and economic services (see Commodore-Mensah, Shaw, and Ford, 2021, pp. e41–e42; Koehn and Sainola-Rodriguez, 2005; Flaskerud, 1987, p. 156). Fordham University could showcase TC in its multidisciplinary International Diploma in Humanitarian Affairs.[4] Humanitarian U could integrate TC into its face-to-face and remote training programs (Teitelbaum, 2019). And, the U.S. State Department could include TC preparation in its online course on migration and climate change available to academic and government institutions and incorporated into training curricula and workshops (White House, 2021, p. 13). In such educational ventures, interprofessional-team projects and opportunities to practice the TC skills being learned should be maximized (Taylor, 2003, pp. 130–132; Frenk, et al., 2010, p. 1944; Mohamedbhai, 2008, pp. 200–201; Rashid, Cervantes, and Goez, 2020, pp. 478, 484).

To date, specialized academic training opportunities focused on providing for refugees' mental health, trauma, and recovery that could feature TC remain limited world-wide. Relevant higher-education programs available to students, professionals, and practitioners (e.g., the Global Mental Health: Trauma and Recovery Certificate Program offered by Harvard Medical School) impose insurmountable financial barriers for many prospective participants. Therefore, it also is important to locate TC preparation among agencies and organizations that can reach a wider audience by providing training and operational opportunities that are financially inclusive.

Pre-Departure Training

Humanitarian and community-partner organizations "consistently cite the importance of [expanded and enhanced] pre-departure training" that prepares highly skilled responders with additional needed competencies (Tiessen and Lough, 2019, pp. 307, 312; also Fox, 1999, p. 428) prior to deployment.[5] TC learning can be incorporated into pre-fieldwork courses and workshops[6] (Pilkington and Mbai, 2016, p. 10) offered as part of an internationally accepted set of core competencies by a recognized Southern or Northern training organization (Walker, et al., 2010, pp. 2228–2229) or by an appropriately staffed NGO devoted to humanitarian operations. Ideally, TC training also would be an ongoing feature of a robust International Health Service Corps (see Kerry, Auld, and Farmer, 2010) or a Global Health and Migration Corps (see Koehn, 2019, Chapter 8, for details).

Pre-departure training is enhanced by the development of a competency profile that clearly identifies the essential transnational competencies that trainees should possess upon completion of the course/workshop (Taylor, 2003, p. 80). Pre-departure training can range from one week to several months (Oakley, et al., 1991, p. 234) and be offered by academic or practitioner specialists in TC education (Edwards, 1996, pp. 23–24). TC-based education and training involve a "highly individualised learning process" (Frenk, et al., 2010, p. 1043). Thus, experiential learning (Rashid, Cervantes, and Goez, 2020, pp. 476, 478, 482) would feature in TC pre-departure trainings.

On-Arrival Training

Humanitarian responders' TC preparation also needs to be adapted to specific local contexts (Frenk, et al., 2010, p. 1951; Taylor, 2008, p. 94).[7] Training programs on arrival are positioned to incorporate the benefits of "participatory curriculum development" and "participatory action research" involving "trainers, learners and other stakeholders" (Taylor, 2003, pp. 1, 70; Taylor, 2008, pp. 93, 98; Whittaker, McLennan, and Handmer, 2015, p. 364; Warriner, 2021, p. 57) prior to engagement and continuously (Karam, Monaghan, and Yoder, 2017, p. 456) when field time permits. In this collaboratively negotiated and arranged scenario, "the curriculum evolves in response to and engaged with specific experiences of mobility and migration ... [and] attends simultaneously to the 'global' and the 'local' (along with the dynamic relationship between them)" (Warriner, 2021, p. 57).

Informative participatory needs assessment and priority-setting techniques such as "mapping, ranking and transect walks" can be incorporated into the on-site learning process (Taylor, 2003, pp. 71, 73). Mapping, for instance, can "make visible and legible the range and diversity of refugee-led social protection initiatives and the ways in which they currently relate to the formal humanitarian system" (Pincock, Betts, and Easton-Calabria, 2020, p. 119; also see Giles, 2018, Map 2, p. 167). By engaging with civil-society organizations and local leaders, therefore, humanitarian responders can access timely and context-specific data that otherwise would be lost (White House, 2021, p. 28) while building on "expertise gained elsewhere" (Anderson and Woodrow, 1998, p. 83). In short, humanitarian responders need to bear in mind that "the learning process in disasters is two-way – for the project participant and for the relief/development worker" (ibid., p. 83).

Ongoing On-Site Training

Given the importance of responder resilience in the face of the psychological and physical obstacles that characterize displacement circumstances (Hannibal and Lawrence, 1999, p. 411), mental health sustainability is a key factor to consider and address while delivering on-site trainings. Humanitarian responders employed by well-established international humanitarian organizations typically only receive operational debriefing at the end of their assignment. Grassroots organizations and community-led initiatives are unlikely to possess sufficient resources to ensure their staff and volunteers' psychological well-being. Even if on-site supervisors are available, humanitarian responders often are reluctant to seek debriefing within their organizations for symptoms of second-hand trauma (Sualp, Okumus, and Molina, 2022, p. 321). Additionally, on-site supervisors themselves can struggle with the accumulation of mental health challenges.

When debriefing resources are offered on an opt-in basis, humanitarian workers hesitate to admit their vulnerabilities and seek professional support. Humanitarian responders tend to struggle with allowing themselves to step back in order to rejuvenate their mental resources. Diana Diaków (2021, pp. 116–117) found that some humanitarian workers perceive seeking mental health support for their burnout symptoms as a sign of weakness and incompetence. The delivery of on-site debriefing programs also can be hindered by potential conflicts of interests and confidentiality concerns. For instance, responders are likely to experience discomfort discussing in-team dynamics as a factor contributing to psychological distress when the field coordinator provides debriefing to the team members. It is important, therefore, that ongoing TC training be a recurring theme in the debriefers' toolkit in order to reduce misinterpretations of symptoms and needs, conflicts of interests, and violations of confidentiality as well as to protect responders' (and interpreters') psychosocial well-being (Sualp, Okumus, and Molina, 2022, pp. 323, 329).

Transnational Learning Networks

In all education and training efforts, transnational learning networks will be called upon for internet-supplemented and continuous TC learning. One approach that can be employed for emergency situations calls for initial in-person training sessions followed by proximate and/or remote supervised experiential learning (Walker, et al., 2010, p. 2228) along with systematic and integrated action/reflection (Edwards, 1996, pp. 20, 22–23; Taylor, 2008, p, 98; Warriner, 2021, p. 55). Extended responder self-learning can be facilitated by e-skilling (Omelaniuk, 2016, p. 31), off-site video and text-based consultation, transnational online professional sharing (Dahya and Dryden-Peterson, 2017, p. 294), and mobile mentoring.[8] Further, the training and experiences of transnationally competent diaspora professionals constitute a valuable additional resource that can be mobilized for ongoing humanitarian responder TC preparation (see, for instance, Tejada, 2016, pp. 197, 199; Whittaker, McLennan, and Handmer, 2015, p. 364).

One of the challenges faced by humanitarian responders is finding time for training while actively delivering assistance in crisis situations. Nevertheless, this constraint does not obviate the need to enhance the competencies of humanitarian-aid workers (see Teitelbaum, 2019). At the same time that eLearning "affords field workers a certain level of flexibility both with accessing education anytime and anywhere," responders often encounter technical constraints "resulting from available bandwidth and broadband connectivity" (ibid.). Fortuitously, social media platforms can be utilized to supplement on-site TC-based training programs by allowing field workers in remote areas to access resources (e.g., infographics, short videos, recorded webinars) asynchronously. In the Balkan and Mediterranean regions, for instance, refugee educators launched an online network featured on social media: "Refugee Educator's Network – Eastern/Southern Europe." The purpose of this group is to bring all teachers and informal educators working with forcibly displaced people (FDPs) in or outside of camps in Eastern/ Southern Europe into one online group where they can share experiences, insights, resources, and advice with one another. Through collaboration and communication, the network aims to facilitate the delivery of educational services to FDPs. Such networks and online communities are positioned to incorporate remote TC learning.[9]

Training of Trainers

As part of an exit strategy that is articulated early on, responsible humanitarian responders strive to ensure that many more care providers are "trained locally" (Crisp, 2010, pp. 65, 206; also Frenk, et al., 2010, p. 1950) and adequately prepared for task shifting (Mbai, Mangeni, Abuelaish, and Pilkington, 2017, pp. 164–165, 169, 176, 178). The transnational "chain of training" for humanitarian responders extends to willing and respected members of camp and settlement populations (ibid., p. 165), host communities, and informal volunteers.[10] In refugee camps, for instance, providing TC training to informal or community organization leaders with primary or secondary education enables them to impart similar skills to others and, thereby, promote self-reliance (Anderson and Woodrow, 1998, p. 85; Giles, 2018, p. 169; Frenk, et al., 2010, p. 1948; Whittaker, McLennan, and Handmer, 2015, p. 365; Dryden-Peterson, 2016, p. 135; Toole, 2019, p. 75), to manage camp schools (Karam, Monaghan, and Yoder, 2017, pp. 449–450, 452), and/or personally to share the workload of providing services in a locally informed and transnationally competent manner (El-Gamal and Hanefeld, 2020, p. 37; Pincock, Betts, and Easton-Calabria, 2020, pp. 25, 92–93; Toole, 2019, p. 75; Frenk, et al., 2010, pp. 1947–1949; Matlin, et al., 2018, p. 43). In Dadaab camp, Beryl Pilkington and Isabella Mbai (2016, pp.

4, 5, 11) found that theoretically informed training and education for community health workers that address "the broad determinants of health [are] more likely to improve health outcomes than a narrow focus on clinical care." TC preparation satisfies this theory need.

The emergency nature of humanitarian work often forces small-size and medium-size NGOs to employ people who are immediately available, but not formally equipped to work with traumatized and diverse populations in, for instance, refugee camps. The urgent need to bridge language barriers in the provision of MHPSS reinforces the need to recruit humanitarian-aid workers from the refugee community. On one hand, this action can bolster refugee resilience and leadership by offering employment opportunities and providing meaningful service. However, grassroots NGOs often lack sufficient expertise and resources to ensure effective training to employees and volunteers from the refugee community; in the long term, this limitation can exacerbate those partners' mental health conditions by exposing them to re-traumatization and vicarious traumatization (Diaków, 2021, pp. 111, 116; Martine Crezee, Jülich, and Hayward, 2011, pp. 260–261). It is important, therefore, that TC preparation incorporates a trauma-informed lens that both prepares trainees to serve FDPs and mitigates potential barriers to learning by addressing trainees' own mental health needs.

Emergency care-providers will need to be trained in how to teach TC. The teachers' training-of-teachers guidelines crafted by Columbia University's Mary Mendenhall for emergency contexts[11] can be usefully applied by transnational humanitarian responders. All trainees would participate in initial and extended training tracks. Initial training of local responders would consist of "a four-day training followed by two months of peer coaching and two months of mobile mentoring." The extended training involves continued training workshops plus 6 months of mobile mentoring and 11 months of peer coaching. Members of each training cohort can apply to be coaches. If selected, they would receive coaching training. In addition to on-site transnational humanitarian responders, mentors could include TC-prepared and experienced volunteers and diaspora professionals from around the world who engage with mentees about specific problems that arise or broader challenges of working with displaced populations and other affected persons through WhatsApp or other accessible technology (see, for instance, Whittaker, McLennan, and Handmer, 2015, p. 364; Chikanda, Crush, and Walton-Roberts, 2016, pp. 5, 11; Krystallidou and Braun, 2023, p. 135).

In training-of-trainers contexts, trainers should "draw on the extensive experience, strengths and resiliency which migrants bring with them when designing, conducting and evaluating training programs."[12] Thus, TC skill training can be "more effectively accomplished" when humanitarian responders "work in partnership with a team of local volunteers" (Tiessen and Lough, 2019, p. 312) who are trusted and seen as credible.[13] At the same time, preparing local partners for collaborative, learning "from others and with others" (Hammick and Anderson, 2009, p. 212) initiatives is mutually rewarding "as local volunteers [and employed staff] can help contextualize ... the application of interventions to local conditions" (Tiessen and Lough, 2019, p. 307; Whittaker, McLennan, and Handmer, 2015, pp. 363, 366; Anghel and Grierson, 2020, p. 496; Krystallidou and Braun, 2023, pp. 138–139, 141–142). In response to human resource-constrained climate and conflict dislocations, preparing, task shifting, supervising, and mentoring "peers, teachers, parents, clergy, health workers and other [frontline] nonspecialists" to provide mental health support simultaneously empowers affected persons and communities "to bolster their own emotional resilience and mental health" (Baker, 2021; also Silove, Ventevogel, and Rees, 2017, pp. 132, 134–135, 137). Success in task shifting among nonprofessionals "is contingent upon having the correct mix of skills, supervision and support structures in place" (Sidibe and Campbell, 2015).

TC Preparation: Current and Prospective Humanitarian Responders

The specific TC development guides for analytic, emotional, creative, communicative, and functional competence elaborated in this section apply both in the preparation that international humanitarian responders receive and transmit to local responders and local teachers/trainers through classroom and in learning encounters in the field based on training needs assessments. The TC training of resettled and host populations is the subject of Chapter 6.

In the discussions that follow, we identify valuable components of TC preparation for responders who serve in displaced population contexts. Although educators and trainers hold no expectation that students and trainees will master all five TC skills or all dimensions of a skill component, the hypothesized results chain is that humanitarian responders who demonstrate deep and extensive TC capabilities will be viewed as effective in assisting dislocated individuals, hosts, and other affected persons who possess diverse nationality, ethnic, and migration backgrounds and in contributing to local integration and sustainable development in diverse contexts.

Analytic Competence

When working with refugees, other conflict-affected persons, and those displaced by phenomena induced by climate change, the TC-prepared responder will have learned about the specific causes and history of the displacement, the actors involved, and possible future impacts.[14] In this connection, Banu Ozkazanc-Pan (2019, p. 22) cautions transnational responders that "by analytically segregating groups by ethnicity or other dimensions of difference ... we risk adopting a myopic approach that cannot fully account for shared experiences and interrelated social dynamics." TC-prepared humanitarian-aid providers will recognize that displaced persons possess multiple identities and diverse perspectives shaped, in large part, by their social experiences.

Understanding the socio-ecological, (multi)cultural, economic, educational, service delivery, and political context of displaced populations and their hosts constitutes an important TC analytic skill for successful capability development (Tiessen and Lough, 2019, pp. 306–307; Betts, 2021, p. 3; Oakley, et al., 1991, pp. 230, 234; Wells, et al., 2018, p. 1). This preparation includes awareness of global health disparities and inequities, the limitations of Western treatment approaches and assessment tools (Rogers-Sirin, 2017, p. 3), how social determinants influence health and migration outcomes, and the connection of climate change abatement and adaptation to health and migration (McMichael, 2013, p. 1342). Active, self-directed learning constitutes a particularly important component of analytical-competence preparation, given its utility for humanitarian responders who are frequently challenged to adapt to rapidly changing contextual circumstances (Morris, 2021; Ssosse, Wagner, and Hopper, 2021, p. 19). On-site interviewing constitutes the "most common tool used" for securing useful information about individual training needs (Taylor, 2003, p. 75).

Enhancing the resilience and well-being of people of concern, particularly those informally settled in urban areas, also requires insight into "intergovernmental relations [and] everyday bureaucratic practices" as well as global connections (Kihato and Landau, 2016, pp. 408–409, 413, 416, 418; also Oakley, et al., 1991, pp. 236). This preparation includes developing critical appraisal competence (Murdoch-Eaton, Redmond, and Bax, 2011, p. 566) for variable, complex, and translocal (Galipo, 2019, p. 153) displacement contexts. Prior research and participation in group and peer-led exercises with responders recently returned from the same or similar situation are likely to be helpful in this connection (Murdoch-Eaton, Redmond, and Bax, 2011, p. 567).

In clinical histories and diagnostic reasoning, health-care providers will need to develop analytic competence in capturing detailed understanding of environmental determinants of health, how disrupted eco-systems "operate to shape disease" (Bell, 2010, pp. 3, 5), how people are coping with climate displacement, and the connection of climate change abatement and adaptation to health and migration (McMichael, 2013, p. 1342). Responding health-care professionals also need to develop understanding of how the interacting glocal roots of health disparities affect populations of immediate concern (Murdoch-Eaton, Redmond, and Bax, 2011, p. 563; Kickbusch, 1999, p. 451) and the ability to ascertain how individual health issues can "manifest at different stages and show different progression over time" (Matlin, et al., 2018, p. 7). Clearly, then, responders to climate displacement will require interprofessional learning that facilitates collaborative action with other practitioners, including "those in the voluntary and community sectors" (Hammick and Anderson, 2009, pp. 209, 213–214).

A diverse set of analytic abilities and co-learning strategies provides useful TC preparation for humanitarian responders in contexts of conflict and climate dislocation. Here, captured from literature review, we provide an encompassing picture of particularly valuable analytic competencies for such contexts:

- ability to locate and utilize relevant information from multiple (including local, international, indigenous, narrative, and digital) sources, perspectives, and approaches (Murdoch-Eaton, Redmond, and Bax, 2011, p. 566; Ozkazanc-Pan, 2019, p. 25; Ssosse, Wagner, and Hopper, 2021, p. 19; Whittaker, McLennan, and Handmer, 2015, p. 363; Hanesova and Theodoulides, 2022, p. 29);
- ability to recognize and analyze social, economic, political, and environmental drivers and connections (Trad, 2019, p. 294);
- ability to undertake accurate assessments of [economic, social, and emotional] resource losses (Silove, Ventevogel, and Rees, 2017, p. 133);
- ability to comprehend how displacement(s) and prior educational and cultural experiences contribute to receptivity to TC preparation (Ramsay and Baker, 2019, p. 81);
- ability to identify physical and mental health problems, health-care barriers including factors hindering the provision of and access to specialized care, and challenges commonly experienced by dislocated persons across all migration stages (Pechak, Howe, Padilla, and Frietze, 2020, p. e135; Rashid, Cervantes, and Goez, 2020, pp. 478, 484; Jones, 2020, p. 360);
- ability to understand specific health conditions "from the patient's point of view" (Andermann, 2014, p. 63);
- ability to identify a wide variety of comorbid conditions that frequently affect refugees (Almoshmosh, et al., 2020, p. 28; Silove, Ventevogel, and Rees, 2017, p. 134);
- ability to determine "the cumulative impacts of different determinants [of health] at different stages and phases" (Matlin, et al., 2018, p. 7);
- ability to discern both the roots of mobile persons' practices and "what happens [to those practices] when they arrive in different places" (Ozkazanc-Pan, 2019, p. 25);
- ability to identify and assess individual health strengths, resilience factors, and coping strategies (Almoshmosh, et al., 2020, p. 25);
- ability to identify the (cross-border) contacts that displaced persons maintain with their families and communities of origin and to distinguish their relative intensity and importance (Faist, Fauser, and Reisenauer, 2013, pp. 6–7, 16; also see Galipo, 2019, p. 19);
- ability to assess which stakeholders possess authority, power, and resources needed to improve conditions for displaced populations and other affected persons (Kihato and Landau, 2016, pp. 411, 416);
- ability to discern the host community's (un)willingness and (in)ability to support particular displaced populations, for instance, survivors of gender-based violence, LGBTI persons (Cherepanov, 2019b, p. 12);

- ability to comprehend relevant "values, attitudes and practices of the host society" (Baarnhielm, et al., 2017, p. 572);
- ability to discern the "array of interventions" available for responding to the physical and mental health needs of dislocated persons (Silove, Ventevogel, and Rees, 2017, p. 134).

Emotional Competence

TC responders encourage prior ethical consideration and contextualization of one's humanitarian role and responsibilities (Murdoch-Eaton, Redmond, and Bax, 2011, p. 567; Hyndman and Giles, 2017, p. 13). Recognition of the emotional context of humanitarian work and the emotional competence required for social justice work with displaced persons prepares responsible humanitarian-aid providers to "engage with our hearts as well as our heads and hands" (Finn, 2021, p. 201). In addition, acting with humility during interactions with displaced and host populations is necessary for overcoming barriers associated with socio-economic disparities (Tiessen and Lough, 2019, p. 308; Rashid, Cervantes, and Goez, 2020, pp. 481–482) and power differentials (Asgary and Lawrence, 2020, p. 7).

Empathy is a key element of emotional competence in the TC framework. Just engagement calls for empathy as the foundation of compassion in humanitarian contexts. At the subjective level, humanitarian-aid workers should seek to identify with the experiences and emotions of the individuals they serve. At the objective level, humanitarian-aid providers should practice critical curiosity about questions of meaning, power, context, and history when endeavoring to comprehend the care seekers' internal frame of reference and emotional experiences. At the interpersonal level, humanitarian responders should seek to grasp the care seekers' situation and convey understanding and emotional connection (see Clark and Butler, 2020, pp. 170–175). Preparation for working in displacement contexts further requires "anticipatory empathy," which involves considering "the resilience, capabilities, and strengths of people and communities" and resisting "the pull of problem-saturated preconceptions … Anticipatory empathy is also a time for getting in touch with our own feelings and biases" (Finn, 2021, pp. 200–201).

A diverse set of emotional abilities provide useful TC preparation for humanitarian responders[15] in conflict-dislocation and climate-dislocation contexts. Here, we provide a snapshot of particularly valuable emotional competencies for such contexts:

- ability to approach dislocated care-seekers with "open, inclusive, non-stigmatizing images" (Van den Bos, Sabar, and Tenenboim, 2019, p. 210; also D'souza, Blatman, Wier, and Patel, 2022, p. 358) that are sensitive to racial and other privileges (Diaków, 2021, p. 149);

- ability to acknowledge the partiality of one's understanding and to open oneself to "honoring" the care-seeker's story. By approaching challenges

  from a place of cultural humility, one tries to apprehend meaning systems, values, ways of perceiving the world, and ways of constructing fundamental concepts such as personhood, family, wellness, and healing in ways that may be very different from one's own.

  (Finn, 2021, p. 60)

- ability to avoid "othering" classifications where refugees are "either invisible or hypervisible, but rarely just visible. Most of the time we do not see the other or see right through them" (Nguyen, 2019, p. 15);
- ability to "identify barriers that prevent learners from integrating learning into their [new] way of life" (Landler-Pardo, Elyashiv, Levi-Keren, and Weinberger, 2022, p. 393);
- ability to empathize with persons affected by displacement and to "demonstrate authenticity of motivation" (Anghel and Grierson, 2020, p. 495);
- ability to engage in social solidarity; to share in the migrants' struggle for "material, social and psychological wellbeing" (Jones, 2020, p. 397);
- ability to empower and enhance the resilience and empathetic skills of persons affected by displacement (Landler-Pardo, et al., 2022, p. 394; D'souza, et al., 2022, pp. 358–359). Reaffirming individuality and dignity through focused attention and support enhances the recipient's "courage and resilience to deal with whatever comes next" (Jones, 2020, p. 97).
- ability to evoke emotionally relieving discussions with displaced persons regarding the "somatic components of reactions to trauma" and "common, non-stigmatized manifestations of stress like changes in concentration, sleep and appetite" (Almoshmosh, et al., 2020, p. 26);
- ability to generate "positive emotions such as optimism, hope and enjoyment; increased self-esteem and sense of identity; and increased inspiration and opportunities for meaning making" (Matlin, et al., 2018, p. 21);
- ability to serve as a modest role model without a savior mentality;
- ability to empathize with other stressed responders (Anghel and Grierson, 2020, p. 495);
- ability to maintain one's own resilience and to respond effectively to early-stage care provider burnout.

Creative Competence

TC preparation for dislocated situations introduces a "plurality of visions" and encourages creative, context-specific linkages of "the spiritual, emotional and ecological" (Taylor, 2008, p. 98). TC responders are prepared to "improvise and innovate" (Whittaker, McLennan, and Handmer, 2015, pp.

362, 365; also Anghel and Grierson, 2020, p. 495). Therefore, TC humanitarian responders demonstrate "willingness to be a learner ... in the local context" (Anderson and Woodrow, 1998, p. 86; Anghel and Grierson, 2020, p. 495). Further, training local volunteers opens up prospects for the "bidirectional exchange" of contextually insightful ideas for sustainable capacity development (Tiessen and Lough, 2019, pp. 307, 312; Anghel and Grierson, 2020, pp. 496–497).

A diverse set of creative abilities provides useful TC preparation for humanitarian responders in conflict-dislocation and climate-dislocation contexts. Here, we provide a snapshot of particularly valuable creative competencies for such contexts:

- ability to generate insights regarding ways to reduce vulnerability among men, women, and children on the move due to climate displacement (McMichael, Barnett, and McMichael, 2012, p. 652);
- ability to discover creative ways of integrating displaced persons into host programs and enhancing such programs in ways that benefit all participants (Kihato and Landau, 2016, pp. 408–409);
- ability to envision a diverse range of tools and interventions, including those that reflect the ethnic backgrounds and folk rituals of displaced communities (Moore, 2017);
- ability to design, develop, and creatively apply relevant and useful digital content (Hanesova and Theodoulides, 2022, p. 29);
- ability to identify "new strengths" that are likely to emerge when dislocated individuals and other affected persons are "afforded new opportunities" (Kirmayer, 2014, p. ix);
- ability to engage in anticipatory thinking (Trad, 2019, p. 295).

Communicative Competence

At least minimal language training is a valuable TC asset for humanitarian responders engaged in capacity development among displaced persons and their hosts (Tiessen and Lough, 2019, p. 307). When anticipation of the need for interpreters and translators trained in the many language pairs and dialects required in crisis situations cannot be fulfilled, international humanitarian responders will need to ensure the availability and selection of, and be able to work proficiently with, trained local interpreters, translators, and culture brokers who are "familiar with the 'language' of their people and the 'language' of the development agency" (Galipo, 2019, p. 89; also O'Brien and Federici, 2020, pp. 130–132, 135, 137–138); Almoshmosh, et al., 2020, p. 27; Rashid, Cervantes, and Goez, 2020, p. 481; Andermann, 2014, p. 63; O'Conor, Roan, Cushner, and Metcalf, 2010, pp. 17–18).[16]

TC communicative competence, including encouragement and support for patient participation and active and careful listening, is needed to foster mutual understanding by health-care providers, the administrative-assistant workforce, and interpreters (Baraldi and Gavioli, 2021, pp. 1059–1060, 1066; also Anderson and Woodrow, 1998, pp. 84, 86). Using inter-cultural group conversations during training sessions that "verbalize logical reasoning together" enables "joint understanding of not only actions but also values, feelings and teamwork functions" (Heldal, Sjovold, and Stalsett, 2020, p. 224). In on-site training circumstances, communicating transcontinentally by email mitigates time differences, but transmitting messages via text is not ideal for clarity (Pilkington and Mbai, 2016, p. 17).

A diverse set of communicative abilities provide useful TC preparation for humanitarian responders in conflict-dislocation and climate-dislocation contexts. Here, we provide a snapshot of particularly valuable communicative competencies for such contexts:

- learning to communicate with care-seekers, other care providers, and families whose dominant language is not yours (Murdoch-Eaton, Redmond, and Bax, 2011, p. 566);
- learning to discern and incorporate culture-specific and other nonverbal communication skills (Roter and Hall, 1992, p. 138);
- learning to anticipate how migrants of diverse backgrounds are likely to understand and receive one's messages (Colvin and Edwards, 2018, p. 10);
- learning to use language and arguments that resonate and establish rapport with local stakeholders (Kihato and Landau, 2016, p. 419);
- learning to "allow refugees to tell their story at their own pace" (Almoshmosh, et al., 2020, p. 27; Harwood, 1981, p. 499);
- learning to follow the migrant's lead while adjusting the number and nature of questions to those that are necessary to be asked by a responder in order to provide meaningful support and prevent re-traumatization (Tufnell, 2003);
- learning to hear the migrant's explanations of personal "behavioural changes, emotional feelings and previous experiences" (Jackson, Blaxter, and Lewando-Hundt, 2003, p. 536);
- learning to listen carefully to the wishes and perspectives of displaced persons seeking help (Almoshmosh, et al., 2020, p. 20; Harwood, 1981, p. 499);
- learning respectfully and successfully to ask displaced persons to "tell us your strengths;"
- learning to adjust one's communication style to the developmental, mental health, and cultural needs of displaced persons;
- learning to hear the voices of dislocated persons themselves through collaboration with transnationally competent interpreters (Matlin, et al., 2018, p. 43; Harwood, 1981, p. 497; D'souza, et al., 2022, p. 359) who provide "meaningful, reliable, sensitive, multilingual and multilateral translation" (Blumczynski and Wilson, 2023, p. 4);
- learning to recognize and respond to "*intercultural discourse*" in which the prior experience of interlocutors blends with features created ad hoc

in the interaction in a synergetic way that results in mutual transformation of knowledge and communicative behaviors (Ngai, 2021, p. 21);

- learning to use language in ways that move discourse in the direction of "solidarity and a humanitarian paradigm" (Anghel and Grierson, 2020, p. 495);
- learning to identify and utilize "appropriate technology and media to communicate with diverse audiences" (Mansilla and Jackson, 2013, p. 16)

Functional Competence

The preparation of transnationally competent humanitarian responders emphasizes the importance of developing relationships built upon personal interest, commitment, and trust as a precondition for exercising functional competence (Murdoch-Eaton, Redmond, and Bax, 2011, p. 563; Pechak, et al., 2020, p. e137; Anghel and Grierson, 2020, p. 495; Pilkington and Mbai, 2016, p. 18; Ramsay and Baker, 2019, p. 75). For instance, TC-prepared front-line health facilitators "create a safe therapeutic environment which nurtures trust, mutual care and community-wide respect" (Silove, Ventevogel, and Rees, 2017, p. 136; also Baarnhielm, et al., 2017, p. 572; Cherepanov, 2019a, p. 82).

Community engagement is an "emerging strength in humanitarian responsiveness" (Eckenwiler and Wild, 2021, p. 243). Functionally TC responders ensure that affected populations join in resettlement planning and livelihood (sustainable development) strategies based on self-reliance principles (see Milner, 2021, p. 423). Specifically, affected populations would "participate in nearly all aspects of shelter and settlement planning, construction, maintenance, monitoring, and evaluation" (Eckenwiler and Wild, 2021, p. 243) and would be assisted to establish "new businesses that contribute to local economies" (Micinski, 2021, p. 145).

A diverse set of functional abilities provide useful TC preparation for humanitarian responders in conflict-dislocation and climate-dislocation contexts. Here, we provide an encompassing picture of particularly valuable action-oriented operational competencies for such contexts:

- ability to avoid over-diagnosing mental disorders and psychiatric labeling, to foster coping skills, to enhance individual and community resilience, to utilize mindfulness techniques and testimony therapy, and to provide intensive clinical interventions when required and requested (Almoshmosh, et al., 2020, pp. 20–22, 24–25, 27; Silove, Ventevogel, and Rees, 2017, p. 134);
- ability to show interest in the care-seeker as a person (Harwood, 1981, p. 499; Roter and Hall, 1992, p. 138), in the beneficiary's family's well-being (O'Conor, et al., 2010, p. 18), and in the care-receiver's current challenges;
- ability to establish a trusting relationship and to promote health empowerment by actively involving patients in decision making regarding the intervention plan (Almoshmosh, et al., 2020, pp. 24, 27);

- ability to utilize a trauma-informed approach across all dimensions of humanitarian aid;
- ability to create a participatory, inclusive, supportive, and context-appropriate learning environment (Karam, Monaghan, and Yoder, 2017, p. 456);
- ability to problem-solve in diverse settings (Murdoch-Eaton, Redmond, and Bax, 2011, p. 566; Taylor, 2008, p. 95);
- ability to "engage diverse professionals who complement one's own professional expertise" (Pechak, et al., 2020, p. e137; also Kihato and Landau, 2016, p. 408);
- "transpositional competence"[17] to collaborate effectively in multi-national, inter-professional, and community-engaged teams (Murdoch-Eaton, Redmond, and Bax, 2011, p. 566; Pechak, et al., 2020, pp. e131, e137; Jackson and Bluteau, 2009, p. 200; Barr, 2009, p. 11; Rashid, Cervantes, and Goez, 2020, p. 478; Andermann, 2014, p. 63; Frenk, et al., 2010, pp. 1944, 1948; D'souza, et al., 2022, pp. 359, 361);
- ability to construct service-enhancing and policy-improving alliances and coalitions with other humanitarian responders, transnational and local development actors, and community-based organizations (Kihato and Landau, 2016, pp. 408, 411, 417; Milner, 2021, p. 423; Kirmayer, Kronick, and Rousseau, 2018, p. 120);
- ability to ensure that displaced persons (including minors) and their representatives have an "active voice" in local health and welfare policy making (ibid., p. 119; also Eckenwiler and Wild, 2021, p. 238);
- ability to mobilize and catalyze community participation in collective action (Oakley, et al., 1991, pp. 230–231);
- ability to demonstrate to host governments and communities how displaced populations can be an economic asset (Kihato and Landau, 2016, p. 408) and to advocate for refugee rights to exercise entrepreneurship;
- ability to address identified barriers to care, health justice, "human flourishing," and sustainable development (Eckenwiler and Wild, 2021, p. 241; Pechak, et al., 2020, pp. e132, e135; Kihato and Landau, 2016, p. 413);
- ability and commitment, in collaboration with other professionals and stakeholders, to address the root glocal "social, cultural, environmental, behavioral, political, and economic factors" that drive and contribute to dislocation and associated (mental) health problems and constitute "impediments to recovery" (Kirmayer, Kronick, and Rousseau, 2018, p. 119; also Matlin, et al., 2018, p. 11; Zarowsky, 2000, p. 387; Kerry, Auld, and Farmer, 2010, p. 1200).[18] Instead of a narrow focus on clinical learning, prospective practitioners who will be addressing upstream, midstream, and downstream manifestations are best served by "the development of unique, broad-based, interprofessional global health competencies" (Melby, et al., 2016, p. 634). Lynne Jones (2020, p. 288) observes that "providing individual psychological or biological treatments is less

complicated than helping your patients think through the consequences of engaging in political action. But if you are fleeing for your life, every action to save it is political."

- ability to advocate for transnationally competent health care, social support, access to education and meaningful employment, and self-help resources for persons of concern (Almoshmosh, et al., 2020, pp. 21, 27; Andermann, 2014, p. 63; Rashid, Cervantes, and Goez, 2020, p. 482);
- ability to mobilize transnational networks and harness and move resources across borders (Villa-Torres, et al., 2017, p. 77; Frenk, et al., 2010, p. 1951);
- ability to suggest appropriate referral pathways (Pechak, et al., 2020, pp. e132, e135). For instance, "more complex trauma-related cases" require "longer-term rehabilitation"; "the severely mentally ill" need "an array of mainstream interventions"; "special groups such as women exposed to domestic violence" require "a gender-sensitive approach to care" (Silove, Ventevogel, and Rees, 2017, p. 136);
- ability to advance peace through health (see Buhmann and Pinto, 2008, pp. 293–296; Koehn, 2019, Chapter 8);
- ability to formulate a sustainable exit strategy that will guide external involvement and planned withdrawal in ways that avert dependency;

Laurence Kirmayer, et al. (2018, p. 119) distinguish three levels of functional-advocacy competence:

(1) recognizing and understanding the structural determinants of health and incorporating this knowledge into professional education, clinical practice, and community intervention; (2) supporting coalitions and collective action that aim to change policy and practice; and (3) initiating, mobilizing, and organizing action to challenge social injustice.

Responder skill in arranging sustainable economic opportunities mitigates the impact of prolonged displacement, enhances resilience, and relieves mental health stresses (ibid., 2018, pp. 119–120) among camp, informally settled, and host populations (Betts, 2021, p. 2; Milner, 2021, p. 424). Consistent with the *New York Declaration for Refugees and Migrants*, TC-prepared humanitarian responders endeavor to eliminate or mitigate "the drivers and root causes of large movements of refugees and migrants" (cited in Milner, 2021, p. 422). As part of an overall commitment by humanitarian responders to advocacy work aimed at opening up educational pathways for dislocated persons (Ramsay and Baker, 2019, p. 82), another valuable dimension of functional competence is skill in arranging long-term capacity-building partnerships and agreements with in-country and foreign higher-education institutions (Tiessen and Lough, 2019, p. 308).

Suggested Training Approaches and Methods for Developing TC among Humanitarian Responders

It is critically important that trainers pay attention to approaches and methods that facilitate TC development among humanitarian responders. A rewarding first approach is conducting a pre-training needs assessment that identifies trainees' preliminary TC strengths and potential areas of growth along with qualified co-trainers who can be recruited from the displaced or host populations. In order for progress to occur, professional trainers need to focus on establishing trusting relationships with trainees before activities commence. Early attention also needs to be devoted to motivating humanitarian-aid providers to become TC learners. To stimulate motivation, the benefits of TC learning should be made explicit, intrinsic to the competency interests of trainees, interesting and engaging, and quickly observable. Contextually appropriate teaching strategies and instructional methods will be distinguished in advance. Whenever available, the transitional interaction of outgoing team members with incoming responders allows for sharing lessons learned. Sustained mentoring and periodic follow-up trainings are a huge asset. Outcome and impact skill-based assessments and programmatic evaluations will be conducted (see Chapter 7).[19]

In this section, we offer potentially valuable suggestions regarding multiple methods for TC training among humanitarian responders. Some of these illustrative methods are likely to be particularly appropriate for analytic, emotional, creative, communicative, and/or functional TC training. In general, integrating experiential activities helps foster increased transnational competence through the process of applying didactic learning to practice. Experiential learning has four stages: (1) concrete experience; (2) reflective observation; (3) abstract conceptualization; and (4) active experimentation. In the responder training process, concrete experiences could involve role-playing and exposure to diverse populations. Reflective observations could involve viewing training videos and writing hypothetical displacement autobiographies. Abstract conceptualization might involve case studies. Active experimentation could involve performing multi-stakeholder interviews (Houseknecht and Swank, 2019, p. 130; also see O'Conor, et al., 2010, pp. 24. 31).

When direct exposure to displaced persons is not possible during training, viewing video interviews and reflecting on the experiences reported can enhance transnational competence. For instance, interviews with diverse populations of refugees can be accessed via YouTube. Using the search term "interview with a refugee" results in over 300,000 videos. To narrow down results, trainers and trainees can identify a specific dislocation, ethnic group, or age group within the search term. The trainer should encourage trainees to select interviews that they believe would be valuable to their TC development. While emphasizing trainee reflections on the viewed videos, trainers can guide deconstructing discourses on migrant victimization, integration, and belonging (Allegri, et al., 2020, p. 533). The following are sample guiding questions for self-reflection (adapted from Houseknecht and Swank, 2019, p. 131):

- What are my initial reactions to the refugees in the videos?
- What assumptions did I make about particular types of refugees and their backgrounds?
- What do these realizations tell me about my own beliefs, values, and assumptions?
- What cultural, economic, political, social, and/or psychological factors are at stake in the videos?
- How do I best communicate to refugee care-seekers that I understand and empathize with the experiences, thoughts, and feelings they have shared with me?
- What aspects of my own beliefs, values, or world-view do I anticipate might be challenged or in conflict in my work with different types of displaced persons?
- How might changes in my own TC development facilitate or hinder the capability of refugee care-seekers in attaining their goals?

Such critical self-reflection serves to promote awareness of the trainee's TC along with deeper appreciation of the care-seeker's situation and perspectives as a foundation for building constructive working alliances.

Analytic competence can be enhanced by authentically derived case analysis (O'Conor, et al., 2010, pp. 31, 33). Learners should be prepared to "define what the core problem is and what data are relevant for possible solutions" (ibid., p. 33). For instance, clinicians can present clinical cases followed by group discussion. During the discussion, which could be facilitated by experienced humanitarian practitioners, trainees are invited to contribute actively to the creation of enhanced case formulation by asking questions and providing comments, impressions, and insights to the presenters (Johnson-Lafleur, Nadeau, and Rousseau, 2022, p. 395). A discourse-based learning environment encourages reflection and consideration of multiple perspectives (O'Conor, et al., 2010, p. 33).

Critical incident case analysis can be used in training to generate transnational awareness for working with displaced persons and their hosts. A critical incident is "a snapshot, vignette, brief episode, or situation of interest followed by a reflective examination of the incident" (Houseknecht and Swank, 2019, p. 132). The reflective examination involves "exploring the incident on both cognitive and affective levels. The goal of reflection is to reach a transformative understanding of the experience" (ibid., p. 132). A post-migration critical incident could involve racism and micro-aggressions experienced by migrants in real-life humanitarian settings. Incorporating critical incident analysis can facilitate TC development among responders by enlightening personal experience and reflection and by facilitating transformation of knowledge and meaning (ibid., p. 132; see also Collins and Pieterse, 2007, pp. 14–18).

On-site TC training with local and international humanitarian responders can usefully adopt the group-based Community of Practice (CoP) approach. The CoP approach addresses both knowledge transmission and the role of group dynamics, contextual elements, identity, and social positioning in learning. This approach offers a modality of training where the group provides access to shared and locally embedded experiential knowledge and to potential collaboration and support networks among participants. The co-presence of different identities, knowledges, and socio-political orientations brings "implicit cultural representations and social positioning to light while the group works on a common story" (Johnson-Lafleur, Nadeau, and Rousseau, 2022, p. 408). Local and international humanitarian workers involved in the training can represent the "others." Participants can "challenge, reinforce, transgress, and negotiate certain representations and norms." Emergent variations in "emotional reactions to certain discourses reveal what is at stake in a given context" (ibid., p. 408).

On-site TC training for humanitarian responders also can usefully involve a process of anticipatory empathy preparation "through critical reflection on the possible situations, concerns, and interests of the participants in the change effort" (Finn, 2021, pp. 200–201). At the same time, "the structural violence confronting refugees ... pummel our emotions and wrench our guts" (ibid.). Thus, anticipatory-empathy training

> requires time and space to feel and to be honest with ourselves about what we feel, especially difficult emotions such as fear, anger, or courage ... It is a process of readying ourselves for an encounter with others, focusing our energies and attention, and opening ourselves to new learning.
>
> (ibid.)

Self-care and burnout prevention are critical for humanitarian-aid providers. The daunting professional and personal challenges associated with complex emergencies often disturb the mental stability of responders. Humanitarian work with displaced persons exposes care providers to "mass suffering and mortality which may create a perception that life has no value, resulting in neglecting self-care and/or taking unnecessary risks" (Cherepanov, 2019a, p. 82). This is why prioritizing safety and self-care in all decisions must be regarded as an ethical responsibility in the TC training of humanitarian workers. The recommended steps for developing trauma stewardship set forth in Laura van Dernoot Lipsky's (2009) *Trauma Stewardship: An Everyday Guide to Caring for Self While Caring for Others* are particularly useful in such TC training – including mapping one's response to trauma exposure (e.g., identifying stress responses), creating change from the inside out by bolstering coping strategies that are an integral part of TC training, such as reconnecting with the present moment (e.g., mindfulness, breathing exercises), fostering self-introspection and curiosity (e.g., journaling), building compassion and community (e.g., identifying support groups, seeking supervision, practicing guided meditations, engaging in spiritual practices), finding balance (e.g., setting clear boundaries and practicing assertive communication), and creating routines that are paramount when working in emergencies as they provide a sense of grounding and safety.

Special TC training on how to work collaboratively with multi-sector interpreters is a particularly valuable communicative-competence preparation for humanitarian responders in displacement contexts. The first part of such a training activity is a discussion about the need to include interpreters as part of the response team. The trainer asks: (1) how does meaningful interaction result when using an interpreter?; (2) how is a responder's ability to "assess a service-user's thoughts, emotions, and behaviors, as expressed by the [care-seeker's] facial expressions, tone of voice, and body language, changed by using an interpreter?"; and (3) how is a care-provider's ability to assess a care-seeker's progress "changed by using an interpreter?" The trainer also introduces the use of pre- and post-session briefings when working with interpreters. Pre-session briefing involves the responder and interpreter and occurs prior to the counseling session. The goal of pre-session briefings is to agree on a joint plan for the engagement that will "enhance collaboration" between the humanitarian-aid provider and the interpreter and "minimize communication errors." During the briefing, the care provider and interpreter: (1) "discuss the interpreter's knowledge of counseling"; (2) "review the tenets of confidentiality"; (3) "identify the goal of the counseling session" (Houseknecht and Swank, 2019, pp. 133–134); (4) reach agreement that the trainer's informational messages and concerns should be conveyed authentically without the interpreter interjecting his/her opinion or taking charge; and (5) discuss the role of debriefing in terms of time management, accuracy of translation, and mention of concerns (O'Conor, et al., 2010, pp. 17–18). Then, the training program shifts to skill development. "Small group role-play that involves trainees simulating" a humanitarian-responder counseling session using an interpreter that employs lessons learned comes into play here (Houseknecht and Swank, 2019, p. 133; also McDonald, et al., 2021, p. 10). The post-session briefing reviews the interpreter's performance and any need for rectification. The interpreters, who preferably are members of the targeted population(s) and of shared gender and religion, also can debrief regarding cultural meanings embedded in the translation to help sharpen the humanitarian-responder trainees' analytic and emotional competence and enhance continuous learning about the beneficiaries' worldview and perspectives concerning needs and challenges.

Scenario role-playing constitutes a useful functional competence training method for humanitarian responders.[20] We illustrate this approach here by reference to three hypothetical scenarios:

1   A refugee describes domestic violence in his family and explains it as a cultural tradition, adding that his wife doesn't mind.

2   A refugee whose child displays symptoms of serious mental health issues declines referral to a psychiatrist and informs the provider that they will be using herbal remedies and traditional healers.

The first two scenarios are examples of the dilemmas that arise when traditions conflict with universal human rights or local laws. In such situations, "local law typically has precedence. Cultural sensitivity and respect for cultural traditions cannot replace the requirement to be law-abiding citizens." On the other hand, "mandated reporting must be exercised if there are any reasons to believe that a displaced person could be in harm's way" (Cherepanov, 2019b, p. 9). Ethics training comes into play here. Functional competence preparation should include opportunities for humanitarian-aid workers to practice intercultural ethical decision-making and the ethical algorithm formula based on meta-ethics contextualization (Ting-Toomey and Chung, 2012, pp. 253–254). A TC care provider who enjoys the service-seeker's trust can be instrumental in "destigmatizing mental-health issues, helping [displaced persons] reconcile traditional and contemporary values, and in educating them about the law; these learnings are an important part of a safe adjustment and, simultaneously, build skills in problem-solving and conflict resolution" (Cherepanov, 2019b, p. 9).

Confidence for applying TC (i.e., self-efficacy) is developed through immersion, service learning, and/or simulation exercises (Jeffreys, 2016, pp. 84, 321). Videos can be used for role-play and simulation exercises. For instance, trainees watch videos of specific service-providing situations with the accompanying transcripts and, then, critically reflect and complete tasks as guided by questions such as: During which moments do you think the humanitarian worker questions, challenges, or affirms the care receiver's values? How would you ask questions differently to elicit more of the service-seeker's lived experiences (Lee, Kourgiantakis, and Hu, 2022, pp. 829–830)? A filmed role-play activity demonstrating TC interventions and approaches can complement open-ended exercises.

3   A care provider suggests that a displaced person "leave her abusive and unemployed husband and offers support in placing her in a safe place."

Giving life-changing advice in a care-providing setting is never a good idea. First, such advice often comes across as imperative for a displaced person because it originates with an expert who possesses special privileges and actual and perceived power (racial, socio-economic, institutional, credential, and/or governance). When care-seekers feel pressured to follow, the communication becomes "clearly unethical." In response, the care-seeker might either "follow the recommendation without questioning it" or put herself in further danger by "limiting future disclosures." Awareness of power and privileges helps TC-prepared providers to communicate recommendations in a responsible and sensitive manner, which means that displaced persons are enabled to make their own informed decisions. The accountability principle underscores the importance of "engaging beneficiaries in any decision-making about them: 'nothing about us without us'" (Cherepanov, 2019b, p. 9).

Potential Impacts of TC-Prepared Responders

Education and training approaches, curricula, and methods need to equip humanitarian responders, collaborating specialists, and hosts with transnational competencies for conflict-induced and climate-induced displacements. This chapter has offered detailed suggestions for TC development across the analytic, emotional, creative, communicative, and functional domains. These guidelines can inform continuous university-led education, pre-departure and on-site trainings, and training of trainers. TC development enables responders to act sensitively and effectively on behalf of the needs of the displaced and other affected persons within a framework of sustainable development for all.

Furthermore, engagement informed by TC in peace-making and conflict-resolution initiatives constitutes a bridge to forestalling further violence and population displacement, preventing dire health consequences (Rushton, 2008, pp. 16, 18), and promoting cooperative "environmental peacebuilding" and sustainable development practices (Conca, 2015, pp. 102, 115, 116–117, 212–213). As a common and transcendent goal, TC-prepared health-care providers and collaborating parties can work toward uniting conflicting forces (Davies, 2010, p. 121). There is peace-building value in Oxfam's "safe programming" (do-no-harm) approach; i.e., ensuring that water, sanitation, and hygiene projects "'do not inadvertently put affected populations in further danger and that aid does not negatively impact on conflict dynamics'" (cited in Zetter and Horst, 2012, p. 59).[21] Prospects for reversion to violence can be greatly diminished by early investments in health care accompanied by

> bringing groups together to plan the health system, forming multiethnic teams for this task and for subsequent health delivery, making care equally accessible to all, and respecting the cultural needs of all groups in the design of health care and its facilities.
> (MacQueen and Santa Barbara, 2008, pp. 39–42; also Davies, 2010, pp. 121–122)

Notes

1 Although not specifically addressed, the competencies set forth in this chapter also merit mastery for service in migrant detention centers (see, for instance, Kellezi, Wakefield, Bowe, Stevenson, and McNamara, 2021).

2 However, existing education programs typically are inadequate for preparing physicians who expect to care for refugees in complex field conditions (Rashid, Cervantes, and Goez, 2020, p. 477). Further, "eco-medical literacy" and related

competencies for identifying and addressing "the health effects of climate change have, generally, not been integrated into medical education and training systems" (Bell, 2010, p. 1).

3 Southern-trained providers often are particularly well positioned to address the needs of migrants who seek health care (Frenk, et al., 2010, p. 1942).

4 https://www.fordham.edu/info/23454/institute_of_international_humanitarian_affairs

5 Some technical training prior to or during service also facilitates skill transfer (Tiessen and Lough, 2019, p. 312).

6 Guided post-fieldwork reflective sessions would contribute to continuous learning.

7 Lynne Jones' approach to the on-site training of volunteers "starts with a brainstorm on how their experiences resemble those of the people they are trying to help" (2020, p. 98).

8 Mobile mentoring is built into Columbia University's Teachers for Teachers initiative. Global mentors "are selected based on their experiences in teaching, working in developing world contexts, and knowledge of the education in emergencies field." Through WhatsApp, global mentors provide new on-location trainers (paired mentees) with "ongoing, real time support on teaching challenges that arise on a regular basis." Available at: https://www.te.columbia.edu/refugeeeducation/projects/teachers-for-teachers/training/ (accessed February 20, 2021). Also see Negin Dahya, "A Socio-Technical Approach to Refugee Education: Connected Networks and ICTs in Kenyan Refugee Camps," on YouTube, available at: https://www.youtube.com/watch?v=pBL2-QyQjuw (accessed September 1, 2022).

9 While providing remote training to various NGO social media initiatives, such as TeamUp2Teach, Diaków observed that one of the needs repetitively voiced by participants pertains to cultural responsiveness in conjunction with a trauma-informed perspective.

10 On the latter and their training needs, see Whittaker, McLennan, and Handmer (2015, pp. 361–363, 366). On the "upskilling" of citizen volunteers through supervised field experience, see Anghel and Grierson (2020, pp. 495–496).

11 https://www.te.columbia.edu/refugeeeducation/projects/teachers-for-teachers/training/ (accessed February 20, 2021).

12 iom.int/sites/default/files/migrated_files/What-We-Do/docs/Best-Practices-in-Migrant-Training.pdf (accessed June 28, 2021).

13 On local hiring processes and education strategies in conflict-displaced situations, see iiep.unesco.org/sites/default/files/inee_csc_graphics.pdf (accessed February 20, 2021).

14 iiep.unesco.org/sites/default/files/inee_csc_graphics.pdf (accessed February 20, 2021).

15 Including non-specialist assistants to health providers (see Chen, 2011).

16 In some cases, technologies such as "machine translation" also can be helpful (see O'Brien and Federici, 2020, p. 132).

17 University of Montana President Seth Bodar suggested this term.

18 For health-care providers, such actions include "raising the alarm about the dire mental health effects of prolonged detention of refugees," calling for an end to the detention of children, and advocating for changes in policies and service practices that would "mitigate the health consequences of forced migration" (Kirmayer, Kronick, and Rousseau, 2018, p. 120).

19 The insights regarding the approach to training humanitarian responders presented above are adapted from the literature search and informed interview findings reported in the context of the training and mentoring preparation of military advisors (O'Conor, et al., 2010, pp. v–vi, 2, 14–15, 27, 30, 33, 36). In their study, interviewed soldiers reported they had received "no [prior] training in effective teaching and presentation skills" (ibid., p. 3).

20 These and similar scenarios also are useful in preparing care-seekers with functional TC (see Chapter 6).
21 On psychosocial healing in post-war contexts, see Gutlove (2008).

References

Allegri, Elena; Eve, Michael; Mazzola, Roberto; Perino, Maria; and Pogliano, Andrea. 2020. "Other 'Lenses': A Training Programme for Social Workers and Others Working with Asylum Seekers and Migrants in Italy," *European Journal of Social Work* 23 (3): 529–540.

Almoshmosh, Nadim; Bahloul, Hussam J.; Barkil-Oteo, Andres; Hassan, Ghayda; and Kirmayer, Laurence J. 2020. "Mental Health of Resettled Syrian Refugees: A Practical Cross-Cultural Guide for Practitioners." *Journal of Mental Health Training, Education and Practice* 15 (1): 20–32.

Andermann, Lisa. 2014. "Reflections on Using a Cultural Psychiatry Approach to Assessing and Fortifying Refugee Resilience in Canada." In *Refuge and Resilience: Promoting Resilience and Mental Health among Resettled Refugees and Forced Migrants*, edited by Laura Simich and Lisa Andermann. New York: Springer, pp. 61–71.

Anderson, Mary B.; and Woodrow, Peter J. 1998. *Rising from the Ashes: Development Strategies in Times of Disaster*. Boulder, CO: Lynne Rienner.

Anghel, Roxana; and Grierson, J. 2020. "Addressing Needs in Liminal Space: The Citizen Volunteer Experience and Decision-Making in the Unofficial Calais Migrant Camp – Insights for Social Work." *European Journal of Social Work* 23 (3): 486–499.

Asgary, Ramin; and Lawrence, Katharine. 2020. "Evaluating Underpinning, Complexity and Implications of Ethical Situations in Humanitarian Operations: Qualitative Study through the Lens of Career Humanitarian Workers." *BMJ Open* 10 (9): 1–11.

Baarnhielm, Sofie; Laban, Kees; Schouler-Ocak, Meryam; Rousseau, Cecile; and Kirmayer, Laurence J. 2017. "Mental Health for Refugees, Asylum Seekers and Displaced Persons: A Call for a Humanitarian Agenda." *Transcultural Psychiatry* 54 (5–6): 565–574.

Baker, Camille. 2021. "Amid Climate-Change Trauma, Care Concerns for Mental Health." *Washington Post*, September 8.

Baraldi, Claudio; and Gavioli, Laura. 2021. "Effective Communication and Knowledge Distribution in Healthcare Interaction with Migrants." *Health Communication* 36 (9): 1059–1067.

Barr, Hugh. 2009. "Interprofessional Education as an Emerging Concept." In *Interprofessional Education: Making It Happen*, edited by Patricia Bluteau and Ann Jackson. New York: Palgrave Macmillan, pp. 3–23.

Bell, Erica J. 2010. "Climate Change: What Competencies and Which Medical Education and Training Approaches?" *BMC Medical Education* 10 (31): 1–9.

Betts, Alexander. 2021. "Refugees: Overcoming Prejudices." *UNESCO Courier*, 4.

Blumczynski, Piotr; and Wilson, Steven. 2023. "Are We All in This Together?" In *The Languages of COVID-19: Translational and Multilingual Perspectives on Global Healthcare*, edited by Piotr Blumczynski and Steven Wilson. New York: Routledge, pp. 1–11.

Buhmann, Caecilie; and Pinto, Andrew D. 2008. "Students and Peace through Health: Education, Projects, and Theory." In *Peace through Health: How Health Professionals*

Can Work for a Less Violent World, edited by Neil Arya and Joanna Santa Barbara. Sterling, VA: Kumarian Press, pp. 290–312.

Chen, Pauline W. 2011. "Doctor and Patient: Unsung Heroes at the Front Lines of Patient Care." *New York Times*, July 5, p. D5.

Cherepanov, Elena. 2019a. "Ethical Dilemmas in Global Mental Health." *BJPsych International* 16 (4): 81–83.

Cherepanov, Elena. 2019b. *Ethics for Global Mental Health*. London: Routledge. Chikanda, Abel; Crush, Jonathan; and Walton-Roberts, Margaret. 2016. "Introduction: Disaggregating Diasporas." In *Diasporas, Development and Governance*, edited by Abel Chikanda; Jonathan Crush; and Margaret Walton-Roberts. New York: Springer, pp. 1–18.

Clark, Authur; and Butler, Carrie. 2020. "Empathy: An Integrated Model in Clinical Social Work." *Social Work* 65 (2): 169–177.

Collins, Noah M.; and Pieterse, Alex L. 2007. "Critical Incident Analysis Based Training: An Approach for Developing Active Racial/Cultural Awareness ." *Journal of Counseling and Development* 85: 14–23.

Colvin, Richard L.; and Edwards, Virginia. 2018. *Teaching for Global Competence in a Rapidly Changing World*. Paris: OECD/New York: Asia Society.

Commodore-Mensah, Yvonne; Shaw, Barbara; and Ford, Miriam. 2021. "A Nursing Call to Action to Support the Health of Migrants and Refugees." *Journal of Advanced Nursing* 77 (12): e41–e43.

Conca, Ken. 2015. *An Unfinished Foundation: The United Nations and Global Environmental Governance*. Oxford: Oxford University Press.

Crisp, Nigel. 2010. *Turning the World Upside Down: The Search for Global Health in the 21st Century*. London: Royal Society of Medicine Press.

Dahya, Negin; and Dryden-Peterson, Sarah. 2017. "Tracing Pathways to Higher Education for Refugees: The Role of Virtual Support Networks and Mobile Phones for Women in Refugee Camps." *Comparative Education* 51 (2): 284–301.

Davies, Sara. 2010. *Global Politics of Health*. Cambridge: Polity Press.

Diaków, Diana M. 2021. "Humanitarian Workers' Perspectives on Mental Health and Resilience of Refugee Youth: Implications for School Psychology." PhD dissertation, University of Montana.

Dryden-Peterson, Sarah. 2016. "Refugee Education in Countries of First Asylum: Breaking Open the Black Box of Pre-Resettlement Experiences." *Theory and Research in Education* 14 (2): 131–148.

D'souza, Finola; Blatman, Zachary; Wier, Samuel; and Patel, Mitesh. 2022. "The Mental Health Needs of Lesbian, Gay, Bisexual, and Transgender (LGBT) Refugees: A Scoping Review." *Journal of Gay & Lesbian Mental Health* 26 (4): 341–366.

Eckenwiler, Lisa; and Wild, Verina. 2021. "Refugees and Others Enduring Displacement: Structural Injustice, Health, and Ethical Placemaking." *Journal of Social Philosophy* 52: 234–250.

Edwards, Michael. 1996. "The Getting of Wisdom: Educating the Reflective Practitioner." In *Educating for Real: The Training of Professionals for Development Practice*, edited by Nabeel Hamdi. London: Intermediate Technology Publications.

El-Gamal, Salma; and Hanefeld, Johanna. 2020. "Access to Health-Care Policies for Refugees and Asylum-Seekers." *International Journal of Migration, Health and Social Care* 16 (1): 22–45.

Faist, Thomas; Fauser, Margit; and Reisenauer, Eveline. 2013. *Transnational Migration*. Cambridge: Polity.

Finn, Janet. 2021. *Just Practice: A Social Justice Approach to Social Work*. 4th edition. New York: Oxford University Press.

Flaskerud, Jacquelyn H. 1987. "A Proposed Protocol for Culturally Relevant Nursing Psychotherapy." *Clinical Nurse Specialist* 1 (4): 150–157.

Fox, Renee. 1999. "Medical Humanitarianism and Human Rights: Reflections on Doctors Without Borders and Doctors of the World." In *Health and Human Rights: A Reader*, edited by Jonathan M. Mann; Sofia Gruskin; Michael A. Grodin; and George J. Annas. London: Routledge, pp. 417–438.

Frenk, Julio, et al. 2010. "Health Professionals for a New Century: Transforming Education to Strengthen Health Systems in an Interdependent World." *Lancet* 376 (December 4): 1923–1958.

Galipo, Adele. 2019. *Return Migration and Nation Building in Africa: Reframing the Somali Diaspora*. London: Routledge.

Giles, Wenona. 2018. "The Borderless Higher Education for Refugees Project: Enabling Refugee and Local Kenyan Students in Dadaab to Transition to University Education." *Journal on Education in Emergencies* 4 (1): 164–184.

Gutlove, Paula. 2008. "Psychosocial Healing." In *Peace through Health: How Health Professionals Can Work for a Less Violent World*, edited by Neil Arya and Joanna Santa Barbara. Sterling, VA: Kumarian Press, pp. 225–231.

Hammick, Marilyn; and Anderson, Elizabeth. 2009. "Sustaining Interprofessional Education in Professional Award Programmes." In *Interprofessional Education: Making It Happen*, edited by Patricia Bluteau and Ann Jackson. New York: Palgrave Macmillan, pp. 202–226.

Hanesova, Dana; and Theodoulides, Lenka. 2022. *Mastering Transversal Competences in a Higher Education Environment: Through Processes of Critical Thinking and Reflection*. Banska Bystrica, Slovakia: Belianum. doi:10.24040/2022.9788055720159.

Hannibal, Kari; and Lawrence, Robert. 1999. "The Health Professional as Human Rights Promoter: Ten Years of Physicians for Human Rights." In *Health and Human Rights: A Reader*, edited by Jonathan M. Mann; Sofia Gruskin; Michael A. Grodin; and George J. Annas. London: Routledge, pp. 404–416.

Harwood, Alan. 1981. "Guidelines for Culturally Appropriate Health Care." In *Ethnicity and Medical Care*, edited by Alan Harwood. Cambridge, MA: Harvard University Press, pp. 482–507.

Heldal, Frode; Sjovold, Endre; and Stalsett, Kenneth. 2020. "Shared Cognition in Intercultural Teams: Collaborating Without Understanding Each Other." *Team Performance Management* 26 (3): 211–226.

Houseknecht, Alisa; and Swank, Jacqueline. 2019. "Preparing Counselors to Work with Refugees: Integration of Experiential Activities." *Journal of Creativity in Mental Health* 14 (1): 127–136.

Hyndman, Jennifer; and Giles, Wenona. 2017. *Refugees in Extended Exile: Living on the Edge*. London: Routledge.

Hynie, Michaela; McGrath, Susan; Young, Julie E.E.; and Banerjee, Paula. 2014. "Negotiations of Engaged Scholarship and Equity through a Global Network of Refugee Scholars." *Scholarly and Research Communication* 5 (3): 1–18.

Jackson, Ann; Blaxter, Loraine; and Lewando-Hundt, Gillian. 2003. "Participating in Medical Education: Views of Patients and Carers Living in Deprived Communities." *Medical Education* 37: 532–538.

Jackson, Ann; and Bluteau, Patricia. 2009. "Creating a Model: Overcoming the Challenges of Implementing Interprofessional Education." In *Interprofessional*

Education: Making It Happen, edited by Patricia Bluteau and Ann Jackson. New York: Palgrave Macmillan, pp. 183–201.

Jeffreys, Marianne R. 2016. *Teaching Cultural Competence in Nursing and Health Care: Inquiry, Action, and Innovation*, 3rd edition. New York: Springer.

Johnson-Lafleur, Janique; Nadeau, Lucie; and Rousseau, Cecile. 2022. "Intercultural Training in Tense Times: Cultural Identities and Lived Experiences Within a Community of Practice of Youth Mental Health Care in Montréal." *Culture, Medicine, and Psychiatry* 46: 391–413.

Jones, Lynne. 2020. *The Migrant Diaries*. New York: Refuge Press.

Karam, Fares J.; Monaghan, Christine; and Yoder, Paul J. 2017. "'The Students Do Not Know Why They Are Here': Education Decision-Making for Syrian Refugees." *Globalisation, Societies and Education* 15 (4): 448–463.

Kellezi, Blerina; Wakefield, Juliet; Bowe, Mhairi; Stevenson, Clifford; and McNamara, Niamh. 2021. "Healthcare Provision Inside Immigration Removal Centres: A Social Identity Analysis of Trust, Legitimacy and Disengagement." *Applied Psychology Health and Well-Being* 13: 578–601.

Kerry, Vanessa B.; Auld, Sara; and Farmer, Paul. 2010. "An International Service Corp for Health – An Unconventional Prescription for Diplomacy." *New England Journal of Medicine* 363 (13): 1199–1202.

Kickbusch, Ilona. 1999. "Global + Local = Glocal Public Health." *Journal of Epidemiological Public Health* 53: 451–452.

Kihato, Caroline W.; and Landau, Loren B. 2016. "Stealth Humanitarianism: Negotiating Politics, Precarity and Performance Management in Protecting the Urban Displaced." *Journal of Refugee Studies* 30 (3): 407–425.

Kim, Hyun-Sil. 2010. "Social Integration and Health Policy Issues for International Marriage Migrant Women in South Korea." *Public Health Nursing* 27 (6): 561–570.

Kirmayer, Laurence J. 2014. "Foreword." In *Refuge and Resilience: Promoting Resilience and Mental Health among Resettled Refugees and Forced Migrants*, edited by Laura Simich and Lisa Andermann. New York: Springer, pp. vii–ix.

Kirmayer, Laurence J.; Kronick, Rachel; and Rousseau, Cecile. 2018. "Advocacy as Key to Structural Competency in Psychiatry." *JAMA Psychiatry* 75 (2): 119–120.

Koehn, Peter H. 2019. *Transnational Mobility and Global Health: Traversing Borders and Boundaries*. New York: Routledge.

Koehn, Peter H.; and Sainola-Rodriguez, Kirsti. 2005. "Clinician/Patient Connections in Ethnoculturally Nonconcordant Encounters with Political-Asylum Seekers: A Comparison of Physicians and Nurses." *Journal of Transcultural Nursing* 16 (4): 298–311.

Krystallidou, Demi; and Braun, Sabine. 2023. "Risk and Crisis Communication during COVID-19 in Linguistically and Culturally Diverse Communities." In *The Languages of COVID-19: Translational and Multilingual Perspectives on Global Healthcare*, edited by Piotr Blumczynski and Steven Wilson. New York: Routledge, pp. 128–144.

Landler-Pardo, Gabriella; Elyashiv, Rinat A.; Levi-Keren, Machal; and Weinberger, Yehudith. 2022. "Being Empathic in Complex Situations in Intercultural Education: A Practical Tool." *Intercultural Education* 33 (4): 391–405.

Lee, Eunjung; Kourgiantakis, Toula; and Hu, Ran. 2022. "Developing Holistic Competence in Cross-Cultural Social Work Practice: Simulation-Based Learning Optimized by Blended Teaching Approach ." *Social Work Education* 41 (5): 820–836.

MacQueen, Graeme; and Santa Barbara, Joanna. 2008. "Mechanisms of Peace through Health." In *Peace through Health: How Health Professionals Can Work for a*

Less Violent World, edited by Neil Arya and Joanna Santa Barbara. Sterling, VA: Kumarian Press, pp. 38–45.

Mansilla, Veronica B.; and Jackson, Anthony. 2013. "Educating for Global Competence: Learning Redefined for an Interconnected World." In *Mastering Global Literacy: Contemporary Perspectives*, edited by Heidi Jacobs. New York: Solution Tree, pp. 1–26.

Martine Crezee, Ineke H.; Jülich, Shirley; and Hayward, Maria. 2011. "Issues for Interpreters and Professionals Working in Refugee Settings." *Journal of Applied Linguistics and Professional Practice* 8 (3): 253–273.

Matlin, Stephen A.; Depoux, Anneliese; Schutte, Stefanie; Flahault, Antoine; and Saso, Luciano. 2018. "Migrants' and Refugees' Health: Towards an Agenda of Solutions." *Public Health Reviews* 39 (27): 1–55.

Mbai, Isabella I.; Mangeni, Judith N.; Abuelaish, Izzeldin; and Pilkington, F. Beryl. 2017. "Community Health Worker Training and Education in a Refugee Context." In *Science Research and Education in Africa: Proceedings of a Conference on Science Advancement*, edited by Alain L. Fymat and Joachim Kapalanga. Newcastle Upon Tyne: Cambridge Scholars Publishing, pp. 163–186.

McDonald, Jordanos T.; Dahlin, Marie; and Bäärnhielm, Sofie. 2021. "Cross-Cultural Training Program on Mental Health Care for Refugees – A Mixed Method Evaluation." *BMC Medical Education* 21 (533): 1–14.

McMichael, Anthony J. 2013. "Globalization, Climate Change, and Human Health." *New England Journal of Medicine* 368: 1335–1343.

McMichael, Celia; Barnett, Jon; and McMichael, Anthony J. 2012. "An Ill Wind? Climate Change, Migration, and Health." *Environmental Health Perspectives* 120 (5): 646–654.

Melby, Melissa K.; Loh, Lawrence C.; Evert, Jessica; Prater, Christopher; Lin, Henry; and Khan, Omar A. 2016. "Beyond Medical 'Missions' to Impact-Driven Short-Term Experiences in Global Health (STEGHs): Ethical Principles to Optimize Community Benefit and Learner Experience." *Academic Medicine* 91 (5): 633–639.

Micinski, Nicholas R. 2021. "Migration and Development in the UN Global Compacts." In *Routledge Handbook on the UN and Development*, edited by Stephen Browne and Thomas G. Weiss. London: Routledge, pp. 135–147.

Milner, James. 2021. "Refugees and International Development Policy and Practice." In *Introduction to International Development: Approaches, Actors, Issues, and Practice*, edited by Paul Haslam; Jessica Shafer; and Pierre Beaudet. Oxford: Oxford University Press, pp. 408–425.

Mohamedbhai, Goolam. 2008. "The Role of Higher Education for Human and Social Development in Sub-Saharan Africa." In *Higher Education in the World 3: New Challenges and Emerging Roles for Human and Social Development*. London: Palgrave Macmillan, pp. 191–202.

Moore, Temple. 2017. "Strengths-Based Narrative Storytelling as Therapeutic Intervention for Refugees in Greece." *World Federation of Occupational Therapists Bulletin* 73 (1): 45–51. https://doi.org/10.1080/14473828.2017.1298557.

Morris, Thomas H. 2021. "Meeting Educational Challenges of Pre- and Post-COVID-19 Conditions through Self-Directed Learning: Considering the Contextual Quality of Educational Experience Necessary." *On the Horizon* 29 (2): 52–61.

Murdoch-Eaton, Deborah; Redmond, Anthony; and Bax, Nigel. 2011. "Training Healthcare Professionals for the Future: Internationalism and Effective Inclusion of Global Health Training." *Medical Teacher* 33: 562–569.

Ngai, Phyllis. 2021. "Discourse Analysis for Intercultural Competence Development." *International Journal of Bias, Identity and Diversities in Education* 6 (1): 17–30.

Nguyen, Viet Thanh. 2019. "Introduction." In *The Displaced: Refugee Writers on Refugee Lives*, edited by Viet Thanh Nguyen. New York: Abrams Press, pp. 11–22.

Oakley, Peter. 1991. *Projects with People: The Practice of Participation in Rural Development*. Geneva: International Labour Office.

O'Brien, Sharon; and Federici, Frederico M. 2020. "Crisis Translation: Considering Language Needs in Multilingual Disaster Settings." *Disaster Prevention and Management* 29 (3): 129–143.

O'Conor, Andi; Roan, Linda; Cushner, Kenneth; and Metcalf, Kimberly A. 2010. *Cross-Cultural Strategies for Improving the Teaching, Training, and Mentoring Skills of Military Transition Team Advisors*. Technical Report 1264. Arlington, VA: U.S. Army Research Institute for the Behavioral and Social Sciences.

Omelaniuk, Irena. 2016. "The Global Forum on Migration and Development and Diaspora Engagement." In *Diasporas, Development and Governance*, edited by Abel Chikanda; Jonathan Crush; and Margaret Walton-Roberts. New York: Springer, pp. 19–32.

Ozkazanc-Pan, Banu. 2019. *Transnational Migration and the New Subjects of Work: Transmigrants, Hybrids and Cosmopolitans*. Bristol: Bristol University Press.

Pechak, Celia; Howe, Vicki; Padilla, Margie; and Frietze, Gabriel A. 2020. "Preparing Students to Serve a Refugee Population through a Health-Focused Interprofessional Education Experience." *Journal of Applied Health* 49 (3): e131–e138.

Pilkington, F. Beryl; and Mbai, Isabella. 2016. "Researching the Gap between the Existing and Potential Community Health Worker Education and Training in the Refugee Context: An Intersectoral Approach." Final Interim Report to IDRC. Toronto: York University, July 31.

Pincock, Kate; Betts, Alexander; and Easton-Calabria, Evan. 2020. *The Global Governed? Refugees as Providers of Protection and Assistance*. Cambridge: Cambridge University Press.

Ramsay, Georgina; and Baker, Sally. 2019. "Higher Education and Students from Refugee Backgrounds: A Meta-Scoping Study." *Refugee Survey Quarterly* 38: 55–82.

Rashid, Marghalara; Cervantes, Andrea D.; and Goez, Helly. 2020. "Refugee Health Curriculum in Undergraduate Medical Education (UME): A Scoping Review." *Teaching and Learning in Medicine* 32 (5): 476–485.

Rogers-Sirin, L. 2017. "Psychotherapy from the Margins: How the Pressure to Adopt Evidence-Based-Treatments Conflicts with Social Justice-Oriented Practice." *Journal for Social Action in Counseling and Psychology* 9 (1): 1–13.

Roter, Debra L.; and Hall, Judith A. 1992. *Doctors Talking with Patients/Patients Talking with Doctors: Improving Communication in Medical Visits*. Westport, CT: Auburn House.

Rushton, Simon. 2008. "History of Peace through Health." In *Peace through Health: How Health Professionals Can Work for a Less Violent World*, edited by Neil Arya and Joanna Santa Barbara. Sterling, VA: Kumarian Press, pp. 15–20.

Sidibe, Michel; and Campbell, James. 2015. "Reversing a Global Workforce Crisis." *Bulletin of the World Health Organization* 93 (3).

Silove, Derrick; Ventevogel, Peter; and Rees, Susan. 2017. "The Contemporary Refugee Crisis: An Overview of Mental Health Challenges." *World Psychiatry* 16 (2): 130–138.

Ssosse, Quentin; Wagner, Johanna; and Hopper, Carina. 2021. "Assessing the Impact of ESD: Methods, Challenges, Results." *Sustainability* 13 (2854): 1–26. doi:10.3390/su13052854.

Sualp, Kenan; Okumus, F. Elif E.; and Molina, Olga. 2022. "Group Work Training for Mental Health Professionals Working with Syrian Refugee Children in Turkey: A Needs Assessment Study." *Social Work with Groups* 45 (3–4): 319–335.

Taylor, Peter. 2003. *How to Design a Training Course: A Guide to Participatory Curriculum Development*. London: Continuum.

Taylor, Peter. 2008. "Higher Education Curricula for Human and Social Development." In *Higher Education in the World 3: New Challenges and Emerging Roles for Human and Social Development*. London: Palgrave Macmillan, pp. 89–101.

Teitelbaum, Pamela. 2019. *Pilot Evaluation to Assess the Impact of eLearning on Humanitarian Aid Work: Final Report*. Geneva: Medair, Humanitarian Leadership Academy.

Tejada, Gabriela. 2016. "Knowledge Transfers through Diaspora Transnationalism and Return Migration: A Case Study of Indian Skilled Migrants." In *Diasporas, Development and Governance*, edited by Abel Chikanda; Jonathan Crush; and Margaret Walton-Roberts. New York: Springer, pp. 187–203.

Tiessen, Rebecca; and Lough, Benjamin J. 2019. "International Volunteering Capacity Development: Volunteer Partner Organization Experiences of Mitigating Factors for Effective Practice." *Forum for Development Studies* 46 (2): 299–320.

Ting-Toomey, Stella; and Chung, Leeva C. 2012. *Understanding Intercultural Communication*. New York: Oxford University Press.

Toole, Mike. 2019. "Health in Humanitarian Crises." In *The Health of Refugees: Public Health Perspectives from Crisis to Settlement*, 2nd edition, edited by Pascale Allotey and Daniel D. Redpath. Oxford: Oxford University Press, pp. 54–84.

Trad, Sloan P. 2019. "A Framework for Mapping Sustainability Within Tertiary Curriculum." *International Journal of Sustainability in Higher Education* 20 (2): 288–308.

Tufnell, Guinevere. 2003. "Refugee Children, Trauma and the Law." *Clinical Child Psychology and Psychiatry* 8 (4): 431–443.

van den Bos, Nellie; Sabar, Galia; and Tenenboim, Shiri. 2019. "Healthcare Providers' Images of Refugees and Their Use of Health Services: An Exploratory Study." *International Journal of Migration, Health and Social Care* 15 (3): 201–213.

van Dernoot Lipsky, Laura. 2009. *Trauma Stewardship: An Everyday Guide to Caring for Self While Caring for Others*. Oakland, CA: Berrett-Koehler Publishers, Inc.

Villa-Torres, Laura; Gonzalez-Vazquez, Tonatiuh; Fleming, Paul J.; Gonzalez-Gonzalez, Edgar L.; Infante-Xibille, Cesar; Chavez, Rebecca; and Barrington, Clare. 2017. "Transnationalism and Health: A Systematic Literature Review on the Use of Transnationalism in the Study of the Health Practices and Behaviors of Migrants." *Social Science & Medicine* 183: 70–79.

Walker, Peter; Hein, Karen; Russ, Catherine; Bertleff, Greg; and Caspersz, Dan. 2010. "A Blueprint for Professionalizing Humanitarian Assistance." *Health Affairs* 29 (December): 2223–2230.

Warriner, Doris. 2021. "Theorizing the Spatial Dimensions and Pedagogical Implications of Transnationalism." In *Curriculum of Global Migration and Transnationalism*, edited by Elena Toukan; Ruben Gaztambide-Fernandez; and Sardar Anwaruddin. London: Routledge, pp. 52–61.

Wells, Ruth; Lawsin, Catalina; Hunt, Caroline; Youssef, Omar Said; Abujado, Fayzeh; and Steel, Zachary. 2018. "An Ecological Model of Adaptation to Displacement: Individual, Cultural and Community Factors Affecting Psychological Adjustment among Syrian Refugees in Jordan." *Global Mental Health* 5: 1–13. doi:10.1017/gmh.2018.30.

White House. 2021. *Report on the Impact of Climate Change on Migration*. Washington, D.C.: The White House.

Whittaker, Joshua; McLennan, Blythe; and Handmer, John. 2015. "A Review of Informal Volunteerism in Emergencies and Disasters: Definition, Opportunities and Challenges." *International Journal of Disaster Risk Reduction* 13: 358–368.

Zarowsky, Christina. 2000. "Trauma Stories: Violence, Emotion and Politics in Somali Ethiopia." *Transcultural Psychiatry* 37 (3): 383–402.

Zetter, Roger; and Horst, Cindy. 2012. "Vulnerability and Protection: Reducing Risk and Promoting Security for Forced Migrants." In *World Disasters Report 2012*, edited by Roger Zetter. Geneva: International Federation of Red Cross and Red Crescent Societies (IFRC), pp. 46–79.

6 Guidelines for TC Training

Displaced Persons and Host Communities

Prospects for positive migrant health outcomes are greatly enhanced when care-seekers as well as providers are transnationally competent (Koehn, 2005a; 2005b, pp. 65–69; WHO, 2010, pp. 15, 66–67). This chapter elaborates practical guidelines for adaptable site-based and remote training aimed at preparing displaced populations and their hosts with TC skill sets that will enhance their capabilities in conflict- and climate-dislocation contexts as well as for eventual "flexible" return to the country of origin.[1] Health care, resilience-building, social justice, and sustainable development feature in this connection.

Specifically, this chapter provides detailed training goals and guides aimed at equipping persons dislocated and otherwise affected by armed conflict, persecution, or climatic events with useful TC skill sets for advancing coping and rebuilding capabilities,[2] personal/family integration and belonging,[3] and agency in a new location. As Mary Anderson and Peter Woodrow (1998, p. 83) observe, "disasters open up special, short-term opportunities for training and learning … In the aftermath of a disaster, people are open to … learning new ways of doing things which offer greater security" (also Jahre, Kembro, Adjahossou, and Altay, 2018, p. 337).

For affected persons, the dislocation disaster initiates a series of stops and starts that activate an ongoing struggle between hope and despair, between the desire to be active, useful, and empowered and becoming dependent, passive, and disempowered (Tomlinson & Egan, 2002, p. 1031). TC training for dislocated persons needs to address individual skill development relevant to "transnational life circumstances." This includes preparation helpful for one's current migration status and living situation along with the mobilization of capabilities and resources that can be transferred from home and applied in transit countries (James, Seidel, Kilian, and Trostmann, 2022, p. 561). Of course, contacts with agencies and providers that lead to training opportunities involve an element of chance and do not always directly result in employment or professional development (Burkardt, et al., 2019, p. 2).

Without education, however, refugees and other displaced persons "are at risk of exploitation, abuse and further disadvantage" (Ramsay and Baker, 2019, p. 56). With education and TC training, displaced persons of all ages

DOI: 10.4324/9781003330493-7

can contribute to ending existing conflicts, post-conflict reconstruction, and preventing future armed conflicts from arising (Dryden-Peterson, Dahya, and Adelman, 2017, pp. 1012, 1043–1044; Montero-Sieburth and Giralt, 2021, p. 10). TC-prepared migrants and hosts are centrally positioned to contribute to adaptation, resilience,[4] and sustainable development.

Education and Training Contexts

In mass displacement situations, "training and education are probably the most valuable tools for development and they can be applied in almost every situation, regardless of the level of disruption" (Anderson and Woodrow, 1998, p. 83). It is important to recognize, however, that the education and training of the displaced and other affected persons take place in multiple and diverse contexts. Here, we consider the common settings of TC preparation for refugees and other displaced populations and members of host communities.

Displaced People

Free education offers a particularly empowering source of resilience and facilitator of enhanced living and upward mobility among young refugees (Sleijpen, Boeije, Kleber, and Mooren, 2016, pp. 158, 169; Dryden-Peterson, Dahya, and Adelman, 2017, p. 1040). In line with overall progress toward universal primary education,[5] the three first-line educational facilities available for add-on TC preparation for displaced youth are "refugee-only schools in refugee camps; in national schools, primarily in urban areas of countries of first asylum; and in informal schools, in camps or urban areas, initiated by refugee communities" (Dryden-Peterson, 2016, pp. 138–139; Dryden-Peterson, Dahya, and Adelman, 2017, p. 1036). While integration in formal education systems increases employment opportunities after graduation, only small numbers of displaced young people typically can be accommodated in Southern educational contexts (Karam, Monaghan, and Yoder, 2017, p. 452; Giles, 2018, p. 178). Fortuitously, "access to a phone and mobile network" serves as a key component creating capability-advancing "higher education pathways in refugee camps" (Dahya and Dryden-Peterson, 2017, p. 288; also see Ramsay and Baker, 2019, p. 70; Granato, 2022).

In refugee camps, informal settlements, and evacuation settings, "people have time to study" and they are looking for and "ready to acquire" new and non-traditional skills (Anderson and Woodrow, 1998, p. 86). In this context, capacity-building refers to the ability of refugees to self-organize (Tomlinson and Egan, 2002, p. 1037). Dislocated situations can become places of "new beginnings" where "old habits and structures no longer make much sense [and] new identity positions are made possible" (Turner, 2015, p. 144). Regrettably, however, "little attention has been paid to developing appropriate pedagogical models that work for most of the globally displaced—refugees stuck in under-resourced and over-burdened refugee camps in poor and fragile states" (Lovey, O'Keeffe, and Petignat, 2021, p. 2).

Tutors, school counselors, and social workers (particularly those from one's own community) are respected teachers (Sleijpen, et al., 2016, p. 168; Dryden-Peterson, Dahya, and Adelman, 2017, pp. 1035–1037). Refugee-selected and refugee-run management boards, committees, secretaries, and sector heads[6] along with refugee-led community organizations (see Pincock, Betts, and Easton-Calabria, 2020, pp. 1–2, 89–90, 94, 103; Agier, 2011, p. 156) can be engaged for TC co-training. Provision of a safe, tranquil, and equipped place for inclusive, context-appropriate TC preparation enables participation and encourages openness to sharing and exploring challenging experiences and conundrums (Sleijpen, et al., 2016, p. 175; Dahya and Dryden-Peterson, 2017, pp. 287, 289; Silove, Ventevogel, and Rees, 2017, p. 136; Almoshmosh, et al., 2020, p. 25; Sampson and Gifford, 2010, pp. 123, 126; Giles, 2018, p. 170; Pincock, Betts, and Easton-Calabria, 2020, p. 114). Camp situations can benefit from the demarcation of "educational" zones for learning activities and "social" or "enterprise" zones where TC skills are practiced (Negm and Mayer, 2022, p. 48; Jahre, Kembro, Adjahossou, and Altay, 2018, pp. 327, 332; Almoshmosh, et al., 2020, p. 25; Cohen and Van Hear, 2020, p. 41). Playgrounds and sports facilities offer particularly conducive sites for TC learning.

TC Training for Economic Well-being and Health

When successfully implemented, TC education and training programs can prepare camp residents, the informally and planned (anticipatory) resettled, and hosts of all ages for satisfying and productive livelihoods in host communities.[7] In most cases, these trainings will be delivered on-site[8] utilizing group-project work (Sualp, Okumus, and Molina, 2022, pp. 326; Colvin and Edwards, 2018, pp. 25–26), exploratory questioning, and well-planned experiential interactions with permeable surroundings[9] (Warriner, 2021, pp. 55, 57; also Taylor, 2003, p. 130; Ssosse, Wagner, and Hopper, 2021, p. 19),[10] although ties to university-education initiatives sometimes can be arranged for both displaced populations and hosts (e.g., Giles, 2018, pp. 171–172; Rashid, Cervantes, and Goez, 2020, p. 477; Dahya and Dryden-Peterson, 2017, pp. 289, 293, 296; Mbai, Mangeni, Abuelaish, and Pilkington, 2017, p. 179; Granato, 2022). In addition to generic TC preparation that equips learners for productive contributions, attention also is devoted to requirements for employment – skills, certificates, and references that help resolve ambiguities that employers often associate with refugees (Tomlinson and Egan, 2002, p. 1032).

The front-line position of women in health care and education and the need to prepare community health workers in resettlement contexts should receive attention in future-oriented training programs (Koehn, 1994a, pp. 73, 83–85; Almoshmosh, et al., 2020, p. 26). Pairing TC training with therapeutic and socially appealing vertical gardening activity offers one promising avenue for enhancing the participation of refugee (and other displacement-affected) women (Talhouk, et al., 2021). Similarly, participation in safety-assured group projects, such as art therapy and sports, which give trauma-exposed children their childhood back, can build resilience and confidence and strengthen communication, collaboration, and emotional competencies (Sualp, Okumus, and Molina, 2022, pp. 321, 326, 330) while simultaneously building relationships with members of host communities.

TC for Social Integration and Belonging

In resettlement contexts, displaced communities typically have lost "their informal social networks and social associations" and, consequently, end up with weakened social strength (Uttam and Bipin, 2020, p. 43) and a growing sense of alienation (Fathi, et al., 2018, p. 2). Some degree of acculturation and psychological preparation is likely to be necessary (ibid., p. 2). According to John Berry's (1997) model of acculturation, there are four main acculturation strategies: (1) integration (i.e., retention of the heritage culture as well as attainment of the new culture); (2) separation (i.e., retention of the heritage culture but no attainment of the new one); (3) assimilation (i.e., abandonment of the heritage culture and adoption of the new culture); and (4) marginalization (i.e., abandonment of the heritage culture as well as failure to adapt to the new culture). TC training and education aim to support *integration*.

Migrants typically develop and maintain a "complex web" of bicultural and multi-cultural and transnational identities (Toukan, Gaztambide-Fernandez, and Anwaruddin, 2021, p. 10).[11] To promote integration, there is a need to provide new arrivals with "adequate social services and support in the biographical and institutional transitions they undergo during their life course, which are accelerated, condensed, heightened, and more complex" (Raithelhuber, 2018, p. 251) in resettlement contexts. TC training helps build and reinforce skill in accessing local networks that refugees can draw on in promoting acceptance and belonging in host communities.

Belonging is enhanced when displaced persons are equipped to contribute to their host communities. For instance, TC training for professional, intercultural communicative-competence development aids educated refugees integrate into the receiving community's labor market (Schukking and Kircher, 2022, p. 31). Given the right resources and support, displaced persons can contribute to the improvement and development of health care in their communities (Lovey, O'Keeffe, and Petignat, 2021, p. 1). In addition, migrants often are employed as service providers and work as caseworkers, interpreters, or in other mental health, education, and resettlement roles. With TC training, they can become valuable brokers and advocates within and between the arriving and receiving systems. These roles often entail mediating among refugees and other service providers, providing information, and encouraging integration (Shaw, 2014, p. 285).

TC for Sustainable Development

Successful integration enables refugees and other dislocated persons to advance sustainable community development as well as to benefit themselves. For instance, displaced persons who worked as professionals in their sending place (Ganassin and Young, 2020, p. 125) can make a positive contribution to the host economy by participating in the local labor market and, at the same time, ameliorate host-community challenges of demographic deficits and workforce shortages (Schukking and Kircher, 2022, p. 34).

TC analytic competence training is useful for analyzing complex social and environmental issues that arise in the wake of unexpected population dislocation. Mass population influx can "put the local wildlife and the entire ecosystem at risk" and fuel socio-economic tensions between those who have arrived and the receivers (Sajib, Islam, and Sohad, 2022, p. 89). For instance, Rohingya refugees in Bangladesh

> inhabited locals' cultivable land for their settlements and also occupied the enriched hill and forest landscapes on which the area's local poor are mainly dependent for their supportable earnings by trading the good quality of furniture wood and selling the firewood.

Increased pressure on socio-economic life and the local labor market angered the locals (ibid., p. 96). TC training for leaders of dislocated and host communities that emphasizes means of addressing the intersecting social, political, economic, and environmental issues created by displacement promotes sustainable development for all parties.

Conditions surrounding refugee repatriation require special attention. Programs directed toward training health-sector personnel and promoting sustainable development for future participation in the sending country should commence at an early date in the dislocation experience (Koehn, 1994a, pp. 6–7, 83–85; Martin, et al., 2017, p. 108; Karam, Monaghan, and Yoder, 2017, pp. 456, 459; Toole, 2019, p. 75). To maximize prospects for successful repatriation that supports long-term sustainable development in the sending country, refugee participation needs to be ensured at all stages of decision making and implementation regarding training and repatriation (Koehn, 1994b, p. 104; also 1991, p. 385).[12]

Members of Host Communities

It is essential that the services provided by humanitarian responders in displacement situations be available to host communities as well as to displaced persons. Therefore, this chapter includes TC training for members of host communities.

TC for Helping

Members of host communities drawn from civil society, including "social or religious organizations, grassroots initiatives, civil society networks ... [along with] individual helpers" and educators can be mobilized for humanitarian assistance when dislocated persons arrive (Raithelhuber, 2018, p. 251). The kinds of help they can offer include accessing social services and support and transitioning to social and economic integration. Members of host communities who dedicate themselves to improving life conditions for vulnerable and marginalized displaced individuals are especially likely to benefit from TC training.

For members of host communities who like to offer helping hands to newcomers, TC training can enhance their contributions. TC allows host community volunteers to "engage diversity competently across boundaries" (Koehn and Rosenau, 2010, p. 76). For instance, teachers who work with refugee youths should have emotional competence "training related to trauma" and "cultural awareness"; functional competence "training on culturally focused responsive practices"; and communicative competence "training for working with English language learning" youths (Damaschke-Deitrick, et al., 2022, pp. 5–8). In addition to offering help at the micro and mezzo levels, host community members can contribute to mutual problem solving that addresses drivers of displacement.

TC for Social Justice

Members of host communities who step forward to support the integration or sustainable-development contributions of refugees and other displaced persons often are motivated by a commitment to social justice. Generally speaking,

> notions of social justice ... embrace values such as the equal worth of all citizens, their equal right to meet their basic needs, the need to spread opportunity and life chances as widely as possible, and finally the requirement that we reduce and, where possible, eliminate unjustified inequalities.
>
> (Finn, 2021, p. 13)

Further, social justice is concerned with "the structuring of societal institutions to guarantee human rights and dignity and ensure opportunities for free and meaningful social participation" (ibid., p. 14).

Social justice work occurs in "the halls of government and in the streets"; "in family homes, schools, women's shelters, food pantries, ... youth centers, clinics, ... [and in] social service agencies and organizations" (ibid., p. 22). The social justice contributions that host community members can make involve employment, the environment, food security, health, and many other aspects of individual and family well-being. TC training that enhances host community members' abilities to support displaced persons at the micro, mezzo, and macro levels in the complex, multi-faceted, and diverse contexts of transition and resettlement is a powerful asset.

TC-prepared helping professionals and volunteers also "confront injustices that, increasingly, are locally and globally interconnected." Thus, they "need to take this action commitment to a new level where borders are removed from their thinking about social action and policy" and strive to "empower diverse individuals and groups for full societal inclusion and participation, enjoyment of their legal and human rights" (Koehn and Rosenau, 2010, p. 82). At the macro level, host civil-society actors who want to help need to advocate for "transforming the inequities and injustices that burden individuals, communities, societies and the world through reflective, proactive practice and through advocacy for the people with whom they work"; they need to "challenge negative discrimination and unjust policies and practices particularly when such … perpetuate global economic and environmental inequities" that often are the root causes of migration (ibid., p. 82).

TC Preparation: Displaced Persons and Host Communities

The individualized, adaptable, and portable nature of TC preparation ensures that skills "are not lost when additional moves become necessary" (Anderson and Woodrow, 1998, p. 327). Health, education,[13] integration,[14] and sustainable development needs, identified through careful future-sensitive assessments that involve refugees themselves, should drive the planning and implementation of TC training programs.

The specific TC development guides for analytic, emotional, creative, communicative, and functional competence elaborated in this section apply in the preparation of persons affected by climate displacement and conflict displacement. In the discussions that follow, we identify valuable components of transnational-competence preparation to be imparted by trainers who serve in displaced-population contexts. Among trainees, the integrated components of transnational competence can be viewed in pyramidal fashion, with analytic competence at the base, with each subsequently treated skill building on the prior domain(s), and with meaningful action (functional competence) being the culminating point.

Given the volatility of prevailing conditions in most involved locales, there can be no expectation that trainees will master all five TC skills or all dimensions of a skill component. Thus, the hypothesized results chain is TC-equipped trainers will be effective in preparing dislocated individuals, hosts, and other affected persons who possess diverse nationality, ethnic, and migration backgrounds with sufficient transnational competence to enable them to attain local (re-)integration and belonging in diverse resettled and/or repatriated contexts and to contribute to sustainable community development (see Milner, 2021, pp. 422, 424; Karam, Monaghan, and Yoder, 2017, p. 460; Pilkington and Mbai, 2016, p. 12; Tejada, 2016, p. 188; Mbai, et al., 2017, pp. 165–166, 179). Displaced persons and hosts who form meaningful and sustainable relationships with well-endowed (financially and/or educationally) trainers through TC preparation are likely to experience especially positive competency impacts (see Miller, Katz, Paris, and Bhatia, 2022; Dryden-Peterson, Dahya, and Adelman, 2017, pp. 1014–1015; Brooks, 2022).

Two principal approaches to developing the TC of the displaced and other affected persons are available: formal and informal/non-formal learning. Formal TC learning can occur through higher-education courses or short training courses focused on particular components of TCs and through formalized experiential learning opportunities (e.g., on-the-job training). Informal and non-formal learning opportunities occur through exchanges, shadowing, forums, media technology, and so on. Informal learning also occurs through "daily lived experience in interacting with those who differ in age, gender, religion, ethnicity, socio-economic status, political beliefs, or physical abilities, to name a few differences" (UNESCO, 2015, p. 14). Both approaches to developing TC encompass the three main domains of learning: cognitive, socio-emotional, and behavioral. To engage displaced and other affected persons in ways that promote TC learning, the International Organization for Migration's (IOM) respectful, learner-centric, interactive, and peer-to-peer training methodology is especially useful. This approach "takes into account participants' different learning styles and provides ample opportunity for learners to express themselves as part of their learning process."[15] With the use of technology, trainers can now make learning materials available and accessible to displaced persons and host community members who do not have access to or time for formal training, but are motivated to engage in self-directed learning.

Analytic Competence

Analytic competence provides the foundation for TC development among those displaced, their hosts, and other affected persons. Contextually sensitive training in analytic TC must bear in mind that "knowledge traditions interact and collide with" one another "in complex and unpredictable ways" (Toukan, Gaztambide-Fernandez, and Anwaruddin, 2021, p. 11). Learner-centered teaching methods need to accommodate "goals of cognitive mobility that accompany long-term uncertainty" and "consistently re-imagined futures" (Dryden-Peterson, 2021, p. 21).

Enhancing resilience and well-being of migrants and hosts requires analytic insight into "intergovernmental relations [and] everyday bureaucratic practices" as well as global connections. This navigating TC skill is especially valuable for conflict-displaced and climate-displaced people informally settled in urban areas (Kihato and Landau, 2016, pp. 408–409, 413, 416, 418).

Active, self-directed learning constitutes an important component of analytic-competence preparation. A diverse set of analytic abilities provides useful TC preparation for life in contexts of conflict and climate dislocation. Here, captured from literature review, we provide a picture of particularly valuable analytic competencies for such contexts:

- ability to combine various sources and types of knowledge in the learning process (Plastina, 2022, p. 594);
- ability to link the new with the familiar;
- ability to access and utilize digital technologies (Ramsay and Baker, 2019, p. 75; Dryden-Peterson, Dahya, and Adelman, 2017, p. 1033);
- ability to access "COVID online information [and study] platforms, COVID webinars, online … and virtual workshops, as well as … virtual meetings and initiatives transcending geographic divides" (McAuliffe, Freier, Skeldon, and Blower, 2021, p. 19);
- ability to ascertain and understand basic health information, available services, and procedures in one's new location (Warriner, 2021, p. 56; Stewart, 2014, p. 103);
- ability to unravel linkages among physical and mental health and post-migration constraints and stressors associated with local reception practices;
- ability to discern the "array of interventions" available for responding to physical and mental health needs (Silove, Ventevogel, and Rees, 2017, p. 134);
- ability to describe how events and conditions in the country of origin often continue to affect one's mental health and physical well-being;
- ability to identify and assess one's health strengths, resilience factors, and coping skills (Almoshmosh, et al., 2020, p. 25);
- ability to assess which stakeholders possess authority, power, and resources needed to enhance well-being and promote sustainable development (Kihato and Landau, 2016, pp. 411, 416);
- ability to comprehend relevant "values, attitudes and practices of the host society" (Baarnhielm, et al., 2017, p. 572).

Emotional Competence

Emotionally skillful participants appreciate that every care encounter is a multidimensional interaction among the care receiver, the humanitarian responder or other care provider, any support staff, and the dislocated care context that surrounds them. The bases for displaced-population resilience include hopeful vision for the future; religious faith; self-reliance; personal history of overcoming adversity; finding meaning/purpose in life; and community assistance and support groups (see, for instance, Pickren, 2014, p. 20;

Finell, Tiilikainen, Jasinskaja-Lahti, Hasan, and Muthana, 2021, p. 16; Marume, January, and Maradzika, 2018, pp. 381–384; Dryden-Peterson, 2021, p. 20). Social support from the host society can exert considerable effect on "minimizing acculturative stress and empower individuals to handle the difficulties of living" in the new environment (Fathi, El-Awad, Reinelt, and Petermann, 2018, p. 9).

A sense of personal, family, and/or group efficacy constitutes a powerful determinant of the adoption and maintenance of health-promoting actions and is associated with a host of outcomes that enhance health and prevent illness (Bandura, 1995, pp. 25–28, 35; Ballard-Kang, 2020, pp. 24–25). Developing empathy also enables displaced persons to "play a critical interpersonal and societal role in conflict situations, which are complex and highly emotional" (Landler-Pardo, Elyashiv, Levi-Keren, and Weinberger, 2022, p. 394).

A diverse set of emotional capabilities provide useful TC preparation for affected persons in conflict-dislocation and climate-dislocation contexts. Here, we provide a snapshot of particularly valuable emotional competencies for such contexts:

- ability to engage in critical self-appraisal and promote one's emotional growth (Salovey, Woolery, and Mayer, 2001, pp. 280–281);
- ability to move beyond tolerance and be fully inclusive based on willingness to take responsibility for being personally connected with, learning from, and caring about those who are unlike ourselves (Pusch, 2009, p. 76);
- ability to interact with humility that allows for taking the role of learner, rather than expert, in order to understand people who have different social identities and experiences than one's own (Finn, 2021, p. 60);
- ability to develop receptive attitudes that encourage establishing and maintaining contact with diverse others, seeing from other perspectives/world-views (UNESCO, 2013, p. 16);
- ability to engage in discussions that relieve emotions regarding the "somatic components of reactions to trauma" and "common, non-stigmatized manifestations of stress like changes in concentration, sleep and appetite" (Almoshmosh, et al., 2020, p. 26);
- ability to develop sufficient emotional stability to cope with the stress of unfamiliar transnational interactions (Hofhuis, Schilderman, and Verdooren, 2020, p. 814);
- ability to nurture self-esteem and confidence (Ramsay and Baker, 2019, p. 56);
- ability to perceive changes as opportunities that can be managed (Williams and Berry, 1991, p. 635);
- ability to develop confidence in one's capability to empathize with and care for others (Dryden-Peterson, 2021, p. 20);
- ability to "revive a sense of connectedness [and confidence to] re-establish social networks" (Silove, Ventevogel, and Rees, 2017, pp. 135–136)

that enhance emotional support and efficacy feelings for oneself and one's peers (Dryden-Peterson, Dahya, and Adelman, 2017, pp. 1014, 1043; Stewart, 2014, p. 93; Gupta, 2022);

- ability to cultivate and maintain reflection, remediation of stereotyping/ bias, and cultural humility (Tervalon and Murray-Garcia, 1998, pp. 118–119);
- ability to engage in self-awareness and self-reflection that allows for evaluating and critiquing one's own values, beliefs, convictions, and assumptions, and discerning how they shape one's world view and influence one's interactions with others (Finn, 2021, p. 75; Pusch, 2009, p. 80).

Creative Competence

The freeing-up of creative capacities is a powerful force for positive outcomes in transnational humanitarian encounters. In the migrant health arena, for instance, innovative approaches to managing treatment and health protection include complementary integrations of biomedical, alternative, and ethnocultural explanatory frameworks and health-related practices (Pachter, 2000, pp. 36–39; Seto-Nielsen, et al., 2012, pp. 2719, 2724–2725).

TC preparation for dislocated situations requires a "plurality of visions" and encourages creative, context-specific linkages of "the spiritual, emotional and ecological" (Taylor, 2008, p. 98). Dislocated and otherwise affected individuals need to be prepared to provide valuable input and feedback for humanitarian actions (Hoffman, 2021, p. 122). With TC training, conflict-affected and climate-affected individuals and communities will be prepared to "improvise and innovate" (Whittaker, McLennan, and Handmer, 2015, pp. 362, 365) and engage in the "bi-directional exchange" of contextually insightful co-created ideas for sustainable capacity development (Tiessen and Lough, 2019, pp. 307, 312; also Anghel and Grierson, 2020, pp. 495–497; Murdoch-Eaton, Redmond, and Bax, 2011, p. 564).

In the health domain, TC training emphasizes patient contributions. The medical consultation is approached as a partnership, with the patient participating as teacher as well as learner. The patient's voice is treated as an indispensable source of experiential insight (Gerrish, Husband, and Mackenzie, 1996, p. 36; Popay and Williams, 1996, pp. 760–762). As Melanie Tervalon and Jann Murray-Garcia (1998, p. 121) point out:

> only the patient is uniquely qualified to help the physician understand the intersection of race, ethnicity, religion, class, and so on in forming his (the patient's) identity and to clarify the relevance and impact of this intersection on the present illness or wellness experience [that is] how little or how much culture has to do with that particular clinical encounter.

Thus, TC preparation for transnational health encounters focuses on the ability to offer uniquely tailored suggestions.

A diverse set of creative abilities provide useful TC preparation for affected persons in conflict-dislocation and climate-dislocation contexts. Here, we provide a snapshot of particularly valuable creative competencies for such contexts:

- ability to generate insights regarding ways to reduce vulnerability among men, women, and children on the move due to climate displacement (McMichael, Barnett, and McMichael, 2012, p. 652);
- ability to discover creative ways of integrating displaced persons into host programs and enhancing such programs in ways that benefit all participants (Kihato and Landau, 2016, pp. 408–409);
- ability to initiate, activate, reinforce, and incorporate one's own ideas, suggestions, resources, and ingenuity into a mutually supported health plan (Seto-Nielsen, et al., 2012, p. 2726; Baraldi and Gavioli, 2021, pp. 1059, 1065);
- ability to contribute to a health plan based on a complementary combination of biomedical and personal ethnocultural/mixed cultural health-care beliefs/practices that is neither clinically nor culturally contra-indicated (CMHS, 2001, pp. III, 5, 10; Tervalon, 2003, p. 573);
- ability to forge synergetic and congruent linkages between what the care-seeker believes and what the care provider believes;
- ability to engage in brainstorming, sharing ideas, and problem-solving (Wellman and Bey, 2015, p. 40) with diverse others;
- ability to "self-organize" and adapt to ongoing changes (Plastina, 2022, p. 594);
- ability to "imagine a meaningful future" (Turner, 2015, p. 145);
- ability to design multilevel and multilocational linkages of individual, family, and community strengths;
- ability to participate in the adaptation of "global resources to address local priorities" (Frenk, et al., 2010, p. 1952).

Communicative Competence

Transnationally sensitive communication promises to contribute to substantial improvements in the well-being of affected populations. At least minimal "other language" (most commonly English) training is a valuable TC asset for displaced persons and their hosts (Tiessen and Lough, 2019, p. 307; Karam, Monaghan, and Yoder, 2017, pp. 456–457; Baraldi and Gavioli, 2021, p. 1065; Torun, et al., 2018, p. 604). Using inter-cultural group conversations during training sessions that "verbalize logical reasoning together" enables "joint understanding of not only actions but also values, feelings and teamwork functions" (Heldal, Sjovold, and Stalsett, 2020, p. 224). In addition, communication recovery skills, such as humor, apology, and admission that one does not know everything, "reinforce confidence as well as competence because, when it is known that there is something to fall back on, one is less likely to avoid interactions that may prove difficult" (Kavanagh, 1999, p. 245; also see Tervalon and Murray-Garcia, 1998, p. 119).

The reticence of patients to share their explanatory model presents a serious challenge to practitioners in migrant/provider health-care interactions (e.g., Seto-Nielsen, et al., 2012, p. 2725). Training in patient communication both enables care seekers "to exhibit greater control" in medical interactions and facilitates improvement in health outcomes (Post, Cegala, and Miser, 2002, pp. 345, 350). In addition, involving community intercultural mediators and "patient navigators" can provide humanitarian responders with invaluable insights and indispensable support for care recommendations that respect a patient's explanatory framework (WHO, 2010, pp. 14, 44).

A diverse set of communicative abilities provide useful TC preparation for affected persons in conflict-dislocation and climate-dislocation contexts. Here, we provide a synthesis of particularly valuable communicative competencies for such contexts:

- learning to communicate with care providers and other affected persons whose first language is not yours (Murdoch-Eaton, Redmond, and Bax, 2011, p. 566);
- learning to use language that resonates with local stakeholders (Kihato and Landau, 2016, p. 419) and to adjust communication styles and approaches in response to the practice of others (Ting-Toomey and Chung, 2022, pp. 1–10);
- skill in interpreting, translating, and cultural transferring "through oral, signing, written or multimodal channels" (O'Brien and Federici, 2020, pp. 130, 132);
- ability to engage in in-depth information and insight sharing (Finell, et al., 2021, p. 16; Roter and Hall, 1992, pp. 5, 9–10, 105, 138) and to facilitate self-disclosure;[16]
- ability to maintain (cross-border) contacts with families and communities of origin (Warriner, 2021, p. 52);
- ability to open up conversations about cultural bereavement (Gupta, 2022);
- ability to share details regarding the role of ethnocultural and other nonstandard health-related beliefs, values, practices, and challenges;
- ability and willingness to articulate serious questions, doubts, concerns,[17] and disagreements;
- learning to be assertive when seeking medical care or other services (Ferguson and Candib, 2002, p. 36) while employing a positive and collaborative demeanor when engaging with care providers (Roter and Hall, 1992, p. 16);
- ability to demonstrate proficiency in nonverbal communication (see, for instance, Post, Cegala, and Miser, 2002, p. 344);

- ability to engage in active and careful listening that advances mutual understanding with care providers;
- ability to engage in deep-structure communication that "addresses values, norms, and interpersonal scripts that go beyond language and phenotypic similarity" and shape behavior (Vega and Cherfas, 2012, pp. 330–331, 337);
- ability to comprehend a transnational provider's verbal diagnosis and instructions (Warriner, 2021, p. 56);
- ability to develop facility with mobile and wireless technologies; to demonstrate digital literacy and to engage in rewarding digital interactions (McAuliffe, Freier, Skeldon, and Blower, 2021, p. 19; Hanesova and Theodoulides, 2022, p. 29); to access and participate in personalized online communication (Giles, 2018, p. 176) that uses social media to "engage attention and empathy" while countering misinformation and false claims (Ostherr, 2023, pp. 200–204);
- ability to frame community needs through the discourse of international development and humanitarianism (Pincock, Betts, and Easton-Calabria, 2020, p.47);[18] learning to use language in ways that move discourse in the direction of "solidarity and a humanitarian paradigm" (Anghel and Grierson, 2020, p. 495).

Functional Competence

Developing positive inter-personal relationships built upon respect, trust (see Pincock, Betts, and Easton-Calabria, 2020, pp. 41, 115), and commitment is a precondition for exercising functional competence. The key to success in building trusted and fruitful interpersonal relationships involves demonstrating personal interest in the humanitarian care-provider or teacher as an individual; that is, showing that one sincerely is interested in, respects, and cares about the other's current situation and aspirations.

Functional competence entails the interpersonal ability to accomplish tasks and achieve objectives. Affected populations should be prepared to participate meaningfully in resettlement planning and livelihood (sustainable development) strategies based on self-reliance principles (see Milner, 2021, p. 423). For young persons, functional TC enhances potential to acquire a meaningful role, and to serve as a role model, in changed and diverse contexts (Sleijpen, et al., 2016, p. 175; Dahya and Dryden-Peterson, 2017, p. 294; Dryden-Peterson, Dahya, and Adelman, 2017, p. 1037). Skill in arranging suitable and sustainable economic opportunities mitigates the impact of prolonged displacement, enhances resilience, and relieves mental health stresses (Kirmayer, Kronick, and Rousseau, 2018, pp. 119–120) among camp, informally settled, and host populations (Betts, 2021, p. 2; Milner, 2021, p. 424).

Playing teamwork games (Colvin and Edwards, 2018, p. 25) and participating in sports can provide a welcome avenue to learning functional TC skills[19] and a vital pathway to experiencing transnational belonging. For instance, a Football Festival at the Kara Tepe refugee camp on the island of Lesvos, Greece, demonstrated the "unifying power of sport" among boys and girls from Syria, Iraq, Afghanistan, and Eritrea (Cohen and Van Hear, 2020, p. 66; also see Koehn and Koehn, 2016). The universal appeal and practice of football (and football fandom) offer a particularly powerful vehicle (and resource) for dislocated persons to develop and employ practical transnational functional skills through bridging sociocultural relationships and attachments with hosts (Nunn, Spaaij, and Luguetti, 2022, pp. 43–45, 52). By itself, the informal "everyday practice of kicking around – individually or in small groups; in yards, on streets, or in parks – provides an opportunity for embodied, affective belonging that is accessible and affordable" (ibid., pp. 44–45).

Enhanced migrant resilience and competence simultaneously enable host society citizens to participate more deeply and effectively in shared projects and to interact confidently with authoritative decision makers. In integrated educational settings, "by discussing lived experiences and challenges they have encountered, [both sets of] learners might begin to identify and/or debate different ways of responding to or engaging with such challenges" (Warriner, 2021, p. 55).

In the transnational therapeutic alliance, "the process of negotiation between practitioner and patient involves developing courses of action that are consistent with the patient's values and goals and that also satisfy the physician's values and goals" (DiMatteo, 1997, p. 13). For many migrants, transculturally sustainable agreements necessitate involvement by (extended) family and/or migrant community support networks (Kleinman, Eisenberg, and Good, 1978, p. 257). Negotiating a mutually agreed upon and situationally tailored health/treatment plan involves learning how to resolve differences between the provider's professional agenda and expectations and one's personal/family agenda and expectations. Migrant TC preparation should incorporate counseling regarding how to augment biomedical treatments with safe and complementary alternative and transnational health-care practices, including familiar nutritional supplements (Kovandzic, et al., 2012, pp. 537, 543).

A diverse set of functional abilities provide useful TC preparation for affected populations in conflict-dislocation and climate-dislocation contexts. Here, we provide an encompassing picture of particularly valuable action-oriented operational competencies for such contexts:

- ability to cope with uncertainty and change (Plastina, 2022, p. 594) and to "persevere with dignity" in the face of deprivation and discrimination (DeSantis, 1997, p. 27);
- ability to solve problems in diverse and resource-constrained settings (Murdoch-Eaton, Redmond, and Bax, 2011, pp. 566, 567; Taylor, 2008, p. 95; Almoshmosh, et al., 2020, p. 26; Ramsay and Baker, 2019, p. 56);

- ability to apply relevant insights from the other four TC domains in ways that accomplish tasks and achieve objectives;
- ability to access facilities and services and promote self-help activities in unfamiliar locations (Silove, Ventevogel, and Rees, 2017, pp. 133, 135; Pincock, Betts, and Easton-Calabria, 2020, p. 94; Almoshmosh, et al., 2020, p. 26; Torun, et al., 2018, p. 604);
- ability to construct service-enhancing and policy-improving alliances and coalitions with other displaced persons of diverse backgrounds, humanitarian responders, transnational and local development actors, and community-based organizations (Kihato and Landau, 2016, pp. 408, 411, 417; Milner, 2021, p. 423; Pincock, Betts, and Easton-Calabria, 2020, pp. 14, 105, 112);
- ability to manage interpersonal conflicts in stressful, chaotic humanitarian contexts (Pusch, 2009, p. 72);
- ability to manage intergroup conflicts involving displaced populations and host communities;
- ability to bring about intergroup reconciliation (Nadler, Malloy, and Fisher, 2008, pp. 1–10);
- ability to participate in and contribute to teamwork (Ramsay and Baker, 2019, p. 56);
- ability to engage in peer support and mentoring (Stewart, 2014, pp. 102–103);
- ability to mobilize and catalyze community participation in collective action (Oakley, et al., 1991, pp. 230–231);
- ability to exercise agency in ways that bring about positive changes in one's resettlement situation (Valtonen, 1998, p. 57);
- ability to demonstrate to host governments and communities how displaced populations can be an economic asset (Kihato and Landau, 2016, p. 408);
- ability to maintain an "active voice" in local health and welfare policymaking (Kirmayer, Kronick, and Rousseau, 2018, p. 119; also Eckenwiler and Wild, 2021, p. 238; Silove, Ventevogel, and Rees, 2017, p. 137);
- ability to apply transnational analytic, emotional, creative, and communicative skills toward mobilizing specific resources and support that will empower displaced persons and others affected by their dislocation;
- ability to negotiate competent health care, social support, access to education and meaningful employment, and self-help resources (Almoshmosh, et al., 2020, pp. 21, 27; DeSantis, 1997, p. 27; Roter and Hall, 1992, p. 13);
- ability to increase one's advocacy competence; that is, recommendations/actions that will facilitate upstream and downstream changes in domestic and international economic, social, institutional, and policy conditions that produce the systemic disparities that preclude the realization of health and well-being for displaced persons and other affected persons;

- ability to address site-specific barriers to care, conflict aversion, health justice, "human flourishing," and sustainable development (Eckenwiler and Wild, 2021, p. 241; Kihato and Landau, 2016, p. 413);[20]
- ability to address oppressive systems created by institutional racial, gender, and class discrimination (Stephan and Stephan, 2013, p. 281);
- ability to address "the social, cultural, environmental, behavioral, political, and economic factors" that contribute to (mental) health problems and constitute "impediments to recovery" (Kirmayer, Kronick, and Rousseau, 2018, p. 119);
- ability to build and activate societal resources that are likely to enhance migrant health and well-being by mitigating or removing existing socioeconomic inequities, power differentials, exclusion policies, and other institutionalized constraints (Mohan and Clark Prickett, 2010, p. 199);
- simultaneous ability to link and mediate the priorities of international responders and community needs (Pincock, Betts, and Easton-Calabria, 2020, p. 115);
- ability to mobilize transnational networks and resources (Villa-Torres, et al., 2017, pp. 72; Pincock, Betts, and Easton-Calabria, 2020, pp. 50, 114–115; Dryden-Peterson, Dahya, and Adelman, 2017, p. 1014).[21]

The defining and unifying feature of authentic contemporary citizenship is functional TC participation in shared deterritorialized projects (Koehn and Ngai, 2006; Nicolaidis, 2006, p. 199). Because unifying projects and collective efforts are not confined to nation-state borders, preparation for civil-society citizenship is inescapably transnational. Numerous studies emphasize that "the distinct experiences of refugees need to be recognized as assets rather than deficits" (Ramsay and Baker, 2019, p. 67). As a result of their transnationally lived experiences and the practical lessons they learn through the process of spatial transition, the displaced bring valuable skills and commitments to the contemporary civil-society citizenship table.

Suggested Training Approaches and Methods for Developing TC among Dislocated Persons and Hosts

A range of training methods and approaches are available for building and enhancing the transnational competence of the displaced and others affected by climate and conflict dislocation. Here, we offer suggestions and guidelines for educators and trainers that relate to one or more of the five domains of TC.

A rewarding first step is conducting a pre-training needs assessment that identifies trainees' preliminary TC strengths and potential areas of growth, along with qualified co-trainers who can be recruited from the displaced or host populations. In order for progress to occur, trainers need to focus on establishing trusting relationships with trainees before activities commence. Early attention also needs to be devoted to motivating persons affected by displacement to become TC learners. To stimulate motivation, the benefits of TC learning should be made explicit, intrinsic to the competency interests of trainees, interesting and engaging, and quickly observable. Sustained mentoring and periodic follow-up trainings are a huge asset. Outcome and impact skill-based assessments and programmatic evaluations should be conducted (see Chapter 7).

Analytic Competence

A range of training tools and approaches are useful for learning aspects of analytic competence. Case studies, simulations, experiential learning, cultural discourse analysis, and inquiry-based learning are discussed here.

The "Intercultural Sensitizer" has received strong empirical validation for its effectiveness (Albert, 1983; 1995; Brislin, Brandt, and Landis, 1983) in increasing cross-cultural sensitivity and understanding and overcoming stereotyping. This training tool involves using case studies, called "critical incidents," that depict interactions between persons from two or more cultures followed by alternative attributions for their behaviors (Houseknecht and Swank, 2019, p. 133). A programmed learning format is used and participants from culture A are asked to select the attribution they believe that members of culture B typically would select. After each choice, trainers give members instant feedback on their answers and invite them to continue until they select the answer given by members of culture B. Ten episodes administered in less than 20 minutes had the effect of reducing negative reactions to unfamiliar behaviors and practices (Yook and Albert, 1999, p. 5). The critical incidents and responses are easily programmed into an interactive software format; they also can be used along with other methods such as role play or discussion in person.

Simulation-based learning (SBL) is a training method that can be used in person or virtually to develop analytic competence. This experiential-training approach features simulated encounters among refugees and members of their host communities. Simulation-based learning guides trainees to use a scaffolded approach that includes case-based-transcript analysis, role-play with peers, and videotaped simulated scenarios for trainees to observe and analyze (Lee, Kourgiantakis, and Hu, 2022, pp. 824–826).

Trainers can use theatre-based experiential learning activities (Garcia, et al., 2019, p. 669) and participatory action learning activities such as photovoice (Kim, et al., 2019, p. 1036; Peabody, 2013, p. 251) to help displacement-affected persons comprehend the formation of diverse social identities and understand systemic power and oppression (Lee, Kourgiantakis, and Hu, 2022, p. 827).

Cultural discourse analysis is an ethnographic approach to studying how transnational and intercultural interactions are shaped by socio-cultural, political, historical, relational, and personal factors in specific contexts and situations (Carbaugh, 2005, pp. 2, 10). Trainees practice the D.A.E. steps.

Step D stands for observe and *describe* without judgement. Step A involves *analysis* through hypothesizing in cultural terms. Step E involves *evaluation* or verifying/refuting the hypotheses that emerged. Ten cultural terms are useful for this stage of discourse analysis (see Table 1 in Ngai, 2021, p. 24). These cultural terms, abstracted from taxonomies developed by Edward Hall, Geert Hofstede, and Robert House and colleagues' GLOBE Dimensions, capture a nearly exhaustive range of cultural orientations in the form of useful continua for cultural discourse analysis. Trainees can use the continua to help hypothesize about possible cultural influences shaping observed interaction and practices. They evaluate their hypotheses using insights gained from: (1) a review of valid and reliable research about the relevant culture and context or situation; (2) observational data collected over time; and/or (3) an emic perspective shared in interviews. Trainees need to assess the degree of typicality of the observed discourse patterns and unlearn tendencies to over-generalize or essentialize while focusing on illuminating potentially unique combinations of cultural influences and "fragments of culture" manifested in spheres of interculturality (Ngai, 2021, p. 21; Abdallah-Pretceille, 2006, p. 479).

Inquiry-Based Learning (IBL) is associated with real-world, problem-based, project-based, and place-based learning. IBL is a "learner-centered approach based on problem scenarios that encourage trainees to interrogate themselves, their communities, and the nature of the problems they are confronting" (Leite, 2022, p. 408). Training in collaborative inquiry "can also serve a first step toward transformative learning, which involves making deep shifts in the way we think and act in the world. In an unpredictable world, this ability to ask ongoing questions and adapt to new situations" can be a key attribute of a TC-prepared migrant and host (ibid., p. 409).

Critical Digital Pedagogy (CDP) is a training approach that encourages learners to choose and investigate the issues they want to respond to. CDP guides investigation of transformative ways to access and engage critically with digital tools. The approach allows for developing the analytic competence required to identify specific underlying ideologies within the digital environment and to recognize disinformation (Dooly and Darvin, 2022, p. 360).[22]

Emotional Competence

In this section, we offer guidance regarding emotional competence applications of the strengths-based training approach, intercultural sensitivity development, group training, and intergroup training.

To nurture resilience, humanitarian respondents can apply the *strengths-based approach* based on empowerment perspectives. The basic premises of strengths-based training (adapted from Finn, 2021, p. 157) are:

• individuals, families, groups, and communities possess many strengths;
• migrant motivation is activated by the prospect of fostering one's strengths;

- taking learner aspirations seriously precludes setting limits on their potential to grow;
- humanitarian responders are collaborators with the displaced and other affected persons;
- camp and settlement environments are replete with different types of tangible and intangible resources;
- a focus on strengths challenges a victim mindset.

An emotional competence training approach based on the empowerment perspective promotes belonging, healing, and empathy-building through dialogue and collaboration. Rather than focusing on "what's wrong?" the training provides space for exploring "what's possible?" The resulting outcome includes development of a "more powerful sense of self" (ibid., p. 158).

For both displaced persons and their hosts, *intercultural sensitivity development* is crucial for emotional competence. Trainers can use the Developmental Model of Intercultural Sensitivity (DMIS) to identify appropriate training approaches for trainees who are at different stages of intercultural sensitivity development: the *ethnocentric* stages (i.e., denial, defense, and minimization) where one's own world is experienced as "central to reality" and the *ethnorelative* stages (i.e., acceptance, adaptation, and integration) where one's worldview is experienced in the context of others (Hammer, Bennett, & Wiseman, 2003, p. 424).

Trainees who deny the existence of meaningful interpersonal differences can benefit from the following training activities:

- activities that simply increase awareness (e.g., music, dance, food, costumes, etc.)
- travelogues, history, lectures, newsletter articles
- differentiation of general categories of cultural, within-culture, and other differences
- avoidance of premature discussion of potentially conflict-/trauma-exacerbating differences.

Training participants at the stage of defensiveness about differences that threaten their own world views can benefit from the following training activities:

- Increase self-esteem – discussion of what is "good" about one's own culture and background, followed by discussions of what is "good" about another person's or persons' culture and background.
- Emphasizing commonality in terms of what is generally "good" in all cases rather than simply different.

Training participants at the minimization stage who tend to trivialize differences can benefit from the following training activities:

- Use of simulations, reports of personal experience, and other illustrations of substantial differences in the interpretation of behavior.
- Show how differences have definite practical significance for emotional outcomes.
- Use "representatives" of diverse backgrounds as resource persons (e.g., in a small facilitated discussion group).
- Increase familiarity with what diversity encompasses.
- Highlight the value and importance of diversity.

Training participants at the acceptance stage who respect and acknowledge cultural differences without judgment can benefit from the following training activities:

- Explain difference as part of a person's overall organization of the world.
- Connect perspective differences to behavioral manifestations.
- Stress recognition and non-evaluative respect for behavioral variation.

Training participants at the adaption stage who are ready to act outside of their own world view can benefit from the following training activities:

- Provide opportunities for applying knowledge of cultural and other differences to actual face-to-face interactions (e.g., transnational partnerships, facilitated multicultural-group discussions, interviewing people from other backgrounds).
- Practice empathy through activities involving real-life interactions with persons of multiple diverse backgrounds (the above adapted from Bennett, 1986, pp. 180–190).

Group work provides multidimensional benefits for dislocated children and young persons. Participation in group projects helps build resilience, confidence, and other emotional competencies (Sualp, Okumus, and Molina, 2022, pp. 321, 326, 330). Children respond enthusiastically to recreational projects, especially those including music, movement, dance, drawing, and play. Practical and simple activities can simultaneously support individual emotional growth and introduce trainees to peers who have different social identities, experiences, and perspectives (Kuriansky, 2019, pp. 355, 361). Experiential learning, combined with reflective writing and metacognitive strategies, is a particularly promising approach for developing intercultural humility.

Story circles allow for the development of multiple dimensions of emotional competence required for *intergroup work*, including respect, listening, curiosity, self- and other awareness, reflection, sharing, and empathy. Both the displaced and members of host communities are at "the place of needing to explore similarities with those they perceive to be different from them" (Deardorff, 2020, p. 14).[23] Circle processes provide a non-threatening way in which individuals can share personal experiences and explore similarities as well as differences with one another. The key objective of story circles is to achieve emotional connections with other participants. In addition,

> creating a perception of shared fate and common identity with an individual member of the group can both facilitate the development of empathy and enhance the impact of the empathy that is aroused on responses to the person and to the group.
>
> (Nadler, Malloy, Fisher, 2008, p. 145)

Along these lines, intergroup dialog is a competency model designed to create self-awareness of prejudicial attitudes; the pedagogy aims to enhance learners' progressive ability to identify, and thereby reduce and remove, social-identity prejudices and biases (see Bibus and Koh, 2021, p. 22).

Creative Competence

Exposure to diversity provides one key to the development of transnational creative/innovative competence. Exposure to multicultural stimuli, simultaneous internalization of two or more perspectives, and/or activation of thinking about other outlooks and insights can increase transnational creative abilities. Learning about other perspectives facilitates flexible thinking and helps avoid fixedness (Groyeckaa, et al., 2020, p. 2).

Useful TC training for creative competence, therefore, should provide space for a diverse set of participants to converse about their cultures and countries of origin, share migration experiences and lessons, and explore common ground as well as differences (James, et al., 2020, p. 561). Creative competence training built upon multidimensional learning should provide opportunities for trainees to adopt and massage multiple perspectives by exceeding common barriers (Groyeckaa, et al., 2020, p. 1). Further, stereotype-reducing interventions serve to increase creative thinking. Exposure to and/or elaboration on counter-stereotypical stimuli can "suppress stereotype activation and therefore leads to 'thinking outside of the box' that allows more flexible idea generation" (ibid., p. 2). Thus, the emotional competence training for increasing intercultural sensitivity described above also can indirectly boost creative competence.

A training activity called Creativity Compass builds upon the interplay of creativity and intercultural sensitivity. It aims to trigger creativity in children by enriching their exposure to the diversity of the world. Creative competence can be developed through exercises that engage "all aspects of divergent thinking, question thinking (e.g., ability to form questions and re-define their form and content), creative imagination, creative thinking operations, and creative attitude such as openness, independence, and perseverance" (ibid., p. 6) in conjunction with learning about different viewpoints, transnational differences, self-awareness, and diverse identities.

Communicative Competence

Among displaced persons, communicative deficiencies often constrain social integration, belonging, health status, and ability to contribute to sustainable development (Capstick, 2020, p. 213). Local-language learning, coupled with intercultural communication training, can serve as a pathway to integration and as a vehicle promoting resilience. A course in *Transcultural Pragmatics: English for Intercultural Communication*, builds upon the synergy of discourse analysis, instructional-pragmatics pedagogy, and the ethnographic approach. The overarching objective is to bring about transcultural-pragmatics awareness, which is the ability to decipher how cultures, cultural mixing, and contextual factors shape language use and communication in spheres of interculturality (Ngai, 2021, p. 23).

The suggested communicative competence training approach focuses on helping trainees connect language learning to their transnational communication encounters in the humanitarian assistance context. This method of TC training incorporates a cycle of progressive steps:

1   *Noticing*: To develop the sensitivity and awareness of how socio-cultural and situational factors shape language use and communication.
2   *Cross-cultural comparison*: To develop an awareness of cross-cultural and within-culture differences and similarities in language usage for various types of communication.
3   *Real-world discovery*: To learn as participant observers in practical, real-world transnational-communication situations.
4   *Comparative analysis*: To reflect on one's own orientation, perceptions, and interpretations as shaped by one's background and experiences in contrast to those that surface in another's communication style and language use in specific transnational contexts and situations.
5   *Real-world application*: To reflect on the extent to which it will be helpful to make adjustments that comply with the socio-cultural-communication patterns of speakers of the necessary language(s) and practice making the desired adjustments in real-world interactions (above adapted from Ngai, 2021, p. 24).

The cycle repeats itself as training/practicing moves from one type of speech act to the next and from one context to the next.

Speech acts covered in the training could include, but not be limited to, basic interpersonal-communication tasks such as: (1) criticism, complaints, expressing opinions (in the inter-agency context); (2) expressing sympathy, invitations, and apologies (in the social and community context); (3) compliments, questioning, providing feedback (in the teaching/learning context); and (4) making suggestions, requesting, and thanking (in the workplace context). Speech acts required for achieving the communicative competencies listed above can be incorporated into this training; for instance, assertive when seeking medical care or other services; able to open up conversations and offer supportive communication about bereavement; able to comprehend and talk about the role of ethnocultural and other nonstandard health-related beliefs, values, practices, and challenges; and effectiveness in framing host-community needs through the discourses of international development and humanitarianism. A needs assessment completed by displaced people and members of the host communities determines the contexts and immersion sites for communicative competence training.

Transnational communicative competence also is crucial for understanding and connecting displaced populations and host communities and for inter-personal construction of the new social world. Training aimed at bridging differences among these populations could include the following communication processes that research has demonstrated are effective in bringing about the positive impact of intergroup dialogues (Stephan and Stephan, 2013, pp. 281–282):

- Focus on how people talk with each other.
- Appreciate differences through listening and learning from others' experiences, feelings, and beliefs.
- Engage in intergroup dialogues through reciprocal sharing and disclosing personal experiences.
- Practice critical collective reflection by talking with others in the group about the ways in which power and privilege operate in the humanitarian response context.

Functional Competence

In this section, we differentiate TC functional training for displaced and other affected persons according to three distinct needs: (1) inter-personal well-being; (2) professional-skill development; and (3) intergroup reconciliation/sustainable development.

Since functional competence draws upon the other four transnational competencies, most of the training approaches identified above also will be useful for negotiation, problem-solving, teamwork, and alliance-building. For instance, case studies provide concrete situations that engage participants through the exploration of possible solutions. Simulations involve experiential learning that allows participants to experience differences and practice inter-personal functional skills in a safe setting. Role plays provide a mechanism for generating feedback on applications. Group activities (games, discussions, structured learning exercises) can engage migrants and members of host communities face-to-face with guidance and feedback from trained facilitators. These TC training tools often take place in a more formal learning setting, such as a workshop or course, and are usually facilitated by "outside experts" (Deardorff, 2020, p. 7). For TC functional competence development, incorporating contextualized inter-personal training that builds on emic knowledge and peer support is likely to be essential.

The peer-support approach, coupled with modeling, offers useful methods for helping displaced people develop professional skills for the roles of caseworkers, interpreters, and paraprofessionals in mental health, education, resettlement, etc. (Shaw, 2014, p. 286). Displaced persons themselves who have successfully navigated through the migration experience are likely to possess special ability to understand the needs of people facing similar circumstances. Thus, they can be successfully incorporated into a modeling role for newly arriving families and individuals. Trainees also can be prepared to perform as inter- and intra-community brokers and advocates within and between their community of origin and the new environment in the place of transition/resettlement. This role often entails mediating among the conflict-displaced and climate-displaced and members of host communities who are service providers, project/program partners, and neighbors (ibid., p. 285). Regular supervision, training, and ongoing dialogue to promote critical reflection and address stress are necessary to ensure these professional bridge builders continue to develop the skills necessary to work empathically among displaced populations and host communities (ibid., p. 293).

Mere contact among displaced populations and host communities is not sufficient to improve more challenging intergroup relations. Indeed, contact among the different populations without deliberate operational preparations can increase rather than reduce inter-group tensions. The characteristics of contact required for constructive contact in the contexts of concern in this book include perceived equal status by the displaced population and members of the host community, cooperative rather than competitive interactions among outgroup members, opportunities for building deep trust among members of the different populations, and connections between the displaced population and the host communities that are encouraged by local authorities and supported by law and custom (Pettigrew and Tropp, 2006, p. 761). To start breaking down barriers to trust, a platform that encourages the mutual sharing of food and recipes with the aim of introducing migrants and refugees to the host community and helping the displaced population integrate into the local community can serve as a tool for intercultural mediation (Todorova, 2022, abstract).

Intergroup reconciliation is further advanced by the frequency of positive interactions with outgroup members and the degree to which participants experience positive emotions in intergroup settings (Stephan and Stephan, 2013, p. 284). Intergroup contact that succeeds in accomplishing first minor and then major tasks and projects advances intergroup reconciliation. In best-case scenarios, such training interventions will result in development of a common group identity that serves as a critical mediating pulse (Nadler, Malloy, and Fisher, 2008, pp. 233–234). The *Common Ingroup Identity Model* emphasizes the process of recategorization, whereby members of different groups are induced to conceive of themselves as a single, more inclusive superordinate group rather than as two completely separate groups. As a consequence, attitudes toward former out-group members become more positive through processes involving pro-in-group bias.

(ibid., p. 234)

One approach to achieving common in-group identity among displaced persons and host communities is "recategorization." There are two forms of this approach. One involves combining two distinct social or cultural entities to form a single superordinate category and thus transforming two separate groups into one inclusive group. The other form is one in which members maintain their initial in-group identity, but do so within the context of a superordinate category (ibid., p. 234).

Transnational Learning Networks

Transnational learning networks increasingly will be called upon for internet-supplemented and continuous TC learning. Initial in-person training sessions for the displaced and other affected persons can be continuously reinforced and augmented by proximate and/or remote supervised simulation-based (Landler-Pardo, Elyashiv, Levi-Keren, and Weinberger, 2022, p. 394) and experiential learning (Walker, et al., 2010, p. 2228) and by mobile mentoring.[24] Transnational networks, eHealth, mHealth, smartphones, tablets, telemedicine, and other features of virtual transnational social space and support are particularly valuable in the physical and mental health-care and self-care lives of migrants who are prevented from accessing educational opportunities and other vital services in their place of residence (Villa-Torres, et al., 2017, pp. 71, 76; WHO, 2010, p. 64; Dahya and Dryden-Peterson, 2017, p. 297; Sampson and Gifford, 2010, p. 126; Giles, 2018, pp. 172, 180; Hyndman and Giles, 2017, p. 91; Villa-Torres, et al., 2017, p. 71; Marume, January, and Maradzika, 2018, pp. 378, 382).[25] Mobile connectivity for educational pursuits, including peer consultations, instant messaging group chats,[26] and use by children of parental phones, has rapidly expanded in rural and remote places in the South (Bergin, 2017; Dahya and Dryden-Peterson, 2017, pp. 286, 289, 292). The advantage of easily fixed, upgradable, and sustainable mobile devices coupled with off-line sharing is that they enable learning breakthroughs and support collective resilience in displaced contexts that do not support reliable internet connectivity or require higher costs, technical support, and training for users (Bergin, 2017; Dahya and Dryden-Peterson, 2017, pp. 287, 289; Plastina, 2022, p. 592).[27] Mobile phones also afford women increased access, control, and privacy of educational usage in comparison to public venues (Dahya and Dryden-Peterson, 2017, pp. 295–296). The learning advantage of transnational information and communication technologies (ICTs) is that they allow pivoting among locations, "presence" in multiple locations at the same time, and long-distance sharing of transnational experiences (Villa-Torres, et al., 2017, p. 71).

Technological methods like using web-based or phone devices, e-conferencing, WhatsApp messages, and emailing also can be explored for training professional health-care skills, technology skills, business skills, social work skills, sustainable development administration skills, etc., among displaced populations and local volunteers (Kuriansky, 2019, p. 362). In TC-training efforts, transnational learning networks and platforms such as iEARN (Colvin and Edwards, 2018, p. 25) should be called upon for remote support and continuous learning. In low-resource settings, E-learning has advantages in supporting the delivery of outcome-based TC education/training programs. E-learning formats can be either text-led webpages, blended learning programs, massive-open-online-courses (MOOCs), or online clinical simulations (Burkardt, et al., 2019 p. 2). Learning materials can be the Khan Academy videos followed by the WhatsApp group forum (Lovey, O'Keeffe, and Petignat, 2021, p. 8). North-South and South-to-South partnerships can collaborate on offering professional skill training using a Moodle platform (Davcheva, 2011, p. 122). To bypass internet connectivity issues, training can be delivered that provides each trainee with a Universal Serial Bus (USB) stick that contains all readings and exercises. Such remote training can be complemented by face-to-face teaching support from locals or via e-tutorials on WhatsApp (Burkardt, et al., 2019 p. 3).

Contextualized blended learning offered by accredited higher-education institutions can provide migrants and refugees with the credentials required for future employment in settlement sites or after repatriation. For example, the InZone learning ecosystem takes a learner-centered approach where materials and lectures are delivered through the web and facilitated by a refugee management team in a refugee camp. Students receive pedagogical support from web-based tutors from the University of Geneva, who meet the students through online tutorials via WhatsApp instant messaging for a designated amount of time each week throughout the course. Students also are supported by trained on-site facilitators in the learning hub, who assist the tutors in managing the class and the learning process (Lovey, O'Keeffe, and Petignat, 2021, p. 8).

Further, the training and experiences of transnationally competent diaspora responders constitute a valuable additional resource that can be mobilized for ongoing migrant and host community TC preparation (Dryden-Peterson, Dahya, and Adelman, 2017, pp. 1015, 1019). With proven skill portability, bicultural and multicultural individuals have a head start on transnational competence that endows them with valuable personal assets for contributing in today's socially, politically, economically, culturally, technologically, and environmentally interconnected dislocated spaces. Transmigrants often possess valuable process expertise – critical awareness of the sending country's political culture, bureaucratic rules, the history of conflicts and coalitions, likely sources of support and resistance – and astuteness in translating and fitting insights garnered abroad in ways that are compelling domestically. In an historic advance from the Millennium Development Goals (MDGs), U.N. members integrated "the role of migrants, their communities and diasporas" into the Sustainable Development Goals (SDGs) adopted at the 2015 Sustainable Development Summit (Ionesco, Mokhnacheva, and Gemenne, 2017, p. 95).

As Farhad Manjoo (2016, p. B1) reports, "what has often gone unnoticed in the politics of migration are the shifting dynamics of migrant life – particularly the surprising and subtle ways in which technology, especially smartphones and social networks, has altered the immigrant experience" (also McAuliffe, et al., 2021, p. 18; Perouse de Montclos and Kagwanja, 2000, p. 216; Dahya and Dryden-Peterson, 2017, p. 286). The simplicity of WhatsApp has made it a particularly popular choice for remaining connected with "an old life" for millions of migrants, including those who are "neophytes to digital technology" (Manjoo, 2016, pp. B1, B7). Free and secure, WhatsApp initially became "the lingua franca among people who, whether by choice or force, have left their homes for the unknown" (Manjoo, 2016, p. B1; also Pincock, Betts, and Easton-Calabria, 2020, p. 45). By 2021, however, WhatsApp became a disputable source of communication due to changes in encryption. Many NGOs have opted to incorporate alternative tools (e.g., Signal, Skype, Facebook) (Giles, 2018, p. 174; Pincock, Betts, and Easton-Calabria, 2020, p. 50). Facebook is the "primary means of communicating with peers" used by female refugees in Dadaab camp (Dahya and Dryden-Peterson, 2017, pp. 292, 296–297).[28] In any case, the most effective training practices use technology "alongside [and reinforced by] face-to-face learning and interactions," integrate appealing and illustrative local content and references, and utilize appropriate language (Bergin, 2017; also Dryden-Peterson, Dahya, and Adelman, 2017, pp. 1029, 1032–1033, 1038–1039, 1042; Dahya and Dryden-Peterson, 2017, p. 293).

The Promise of TC Development for Dislocated Individuals, Hosts, and Other Affected Persons

This chapter has offered detailed guidelines for TC development across the analytic, emotional, creative, and communicative domains that can inform continuous on-site and remote training for dislocated populations and host communities. The hypothesized results chain is that gaining TC capabilities will facilitate psychosocial belonging (Matlin, et al., 2018, p. 21) and enable dislocated individuals, hosts, and other affected persons to contribute to sustainable development in multiple contexts.

Individual and societal benefits and conditions supporting sustainable development for all are most fully realized when all participants are transnationally competent. TC-informed participation by conflict-dislocated and climate-dislocated persons is universally beneficial because "all members of a community" are negatively affected by dependence and lack of capability to unlock supportive agency (see, e.g., Smedley, Stith, and Nelson, 2003, p. 37).

Notes

1 On the latter, see Galipo (2019, pp. 9, 117).
2 Long-term resilience and coping are objectives set forth for displaced migrants in the Global Compact on Migration (Aleinikoff and Martin, 2022, p. 13).
3 On the importance of attaining a sense of belonging, a multifaceted condition that exceeds integration (Nunn, Spaaij, and Luguetti, 2022, pp. 44, 52) and a "much more complex and nuanced understanding of experiences related to inclusion," see Ozkazanc-Pan (2019, p. 483).
4 Resilience in this context refers to "both the capacity of the individual to withstand experiences of trauma and stress and ... the capacity to remain vigorously engaged with life's tasks" (Silove, Ventevogel, and Rees, 2017, p. 133).
5 By 2022, 68 percent of refugee children had access to some sort of primary education versus more than 90 percent of their non-dislocated peers (Granato, 2022).
6 See, for instance, http://bhutanesrefugees.com/ (accessed January 28, 2019).
7 Around 40 percent of Hope of Children and Women Victims of Violence's (HOCW) trainees in Kampala, Uganda, are "Ugandans, encouraging interaction between refugees and the host community" (Pincock, Betts, and Easton-Calabria, 2020, p. 1).
8 The Health Secretariat of Columbia, for instance, offers day courses for relocated populations (White House, 2021, pp. 23–24).
9 For instance, linked "to contexts of transnationalism and intercultural communication as experienced in a health care setting" (Warriner, 2021, p. 57).
10 In contrast to the TC pedagogical approach (see Koehn and Rosenau, 2010, Chapter 11), the prevailing method of refugee education suffers from heavy reliance on didactic presentations, memorization and regurgitation, disproportionate time spent learning languages, and failure to consider pre-resettlement educational experiences (Dryden-Peterson, 2016, pp. 142–143, 133).
11 On the fluid transitional process of transnational in-between identity self-formation, see Wang (2022, abstract).
12 On CARE's Refugee Self-Management approach, see Hyndman (2000, pp. 138, 142).
13 Susan Martin, et al. (2017, p. 112) find that "greater emphasis on livelihoods and education, with the concomitant funding needed to support such initiatives, could help dispel both the perception and the reality of hopelessness for many who are unable to return home or be resettled elsewhere."
14 Including time-management, goal-setting, and job interview skills as well as ways to navigate transportation systems and social services, available at: iom.int/sites/default/files/migrated_files/What-We-Do/docs/Best-Practices-in-Migrant-Training.pdf (accessed June 28, 2021).
15 iom.int/sites/default/files/migrated_files/What-We-Do/docs/Best-Practices-in-Migrant-Training.pdf (accessed June 28, 2021).
16 When migrant perspectives on personal health and illness are withheld from or incongruent with the perceptions of host clinicians, their health-care needs cannot be addressed fully and effectively.
17 See the list of useful questions to raise with an attending physician found in Perry (2001, pp. 48–51).
18 For instance, references to "accountability," "human rights," "good governance," and "accountability" (Pincock, Betts, and Easton-Calabria, 2020, p. 47).
19 For instance, trust-building, collective goal-setting, and collaborative solution realization (Colvin and Edwards, 2018, p. 25).
20 Also iiep.unesco.org/sites/default/files/inee_csc_graphics.pdf (accessed February 20, 2021).
21 Including medications from places of origin and access to traditional healers (Villa-Torres, et al., 2017, p. 72; Tiilikainen and Koehn, 2011; Mutiso, et al., 2019, pp. 210, 215).

22 See, for example, #BeyondTheClick toolkit, available at: https://toolkit.8020.ie/using-this-toolkit/
23 The Manual for facilitating story circles is available on this UNESCO website: https://en.unesco.org/themes/intercultural-dialogue/competencies
24 https://www.te.columbia.edu/refugeeeducation/projects/teachers-for-teachers/training/ (accessed February 20, 2021). Also see Negin Dahya, "A Socio-Technical Approach to Refugee Education: Connected Networks and ICTs in Kenyan Refugee Camps," on YouTube, available at: https://www.youtube.com/watch?v=pBL2-QyQjuw (accessed September 1, 2022).
25 However, the limitations of technological advances are striking when a distant "crisis of care" confronts the transnational migrant. These precarious situations, which typically involve a physical or mental health crisis involving an (often elderly) family member left behind, are common and emotionally taxing experiences for cross-border displaced persons.
26 Negin Dahya, "A Socio-Technical Approach to Refugee Education: Connected Networks and ICTs in Kenyan Refugee Camps." on YouTube, available at: https://www.youtube.com/watch?v=pBL2-QyQjuw (accessed September 1, 2022); also Dryden-Peterson, Dahya, and Adelman (2017, p. 129).
27 In Uganda's Nakivale camp, mobile phone usage is "above the national average" and refugees "buy credit (scratch cards) to ensure internet connectivity" (Mwangu, 2022, p. 444). In Tongogara refugee camp, Zimbabwe, 75 percent of study respondents owned a mobile phone (Marume, January, and Maradzika, 2018, p. 382).
28 Aggregating calling and messaging tools like Nimbuzz also prove helpful in camps with limited proximate resources (Dahya and Dryden-Peterson, 2017, pp. 296, 298; Dryden-Peterson, Dahya, and Adelman, 2017, p. 1044).

References

Abdallah-Pretceille, Martine. 2006. "Interculturalism as a Paradigm for Thinking about Diversity." *Intercultural Education* 17 (5): 475–483.

Agier, Michel. 2011. *Managing the Undesirables: Refugee Camps and Humanitarian Government.* Cambridge: Polity.

Albert, Rosita D. 1983. "The Intercultural Sensitizer or Culture Assimilator: A Cognitive Approach." In *Handbook of Intercultural Training*, edited by D. Landis and R. W. Brislin. New York: Pergamon Press, pp. 196–217.

Aleinikoff, T. Alexander; and Martin, Susan. 2022. *The Responsibility of the International Community in Situations of Mobility Due to Environmental Events.* Zolberg Institute Working Paper Series 2022–2021. New York: Zolberg Institute on Migration and Mobility, The New School.

Almoshmosh, Nadim; Bahloul, Hussam J.; Barkil-Oteo, Andres; Hassan, Ghayda; and Kirmayer, Laurence J. 2020. "Mental Health of Resettled Syrian Refugees: A Practical Cross-Cultural Guide for Practitioners." *Journal of Mental Health Training, Education and Practice* 15 (1): 20–32.

Anderson, Mary B.; and Woodrow, Peter J. 1998. *Rising from the Ashes: Development Strategies in Times of Disaster.* Boulder, CO: Lynne Rienner.

Anghel, Roxana; and Grierson, J. 2020. "Addressing Needs in Liminal Space: The Citizen Volunteer Experience and Decision-Making in the Unofficial Calais Migrant Camp – Insights for Social Work." *European Journal of Social Work* 23 (3): 486–499.

Baarnhielm, Sofie; Laban, Kees; Schouler-Ocak, Meryam; Rousseau, Cecile; and Kirmayer, Laurence J. 2017. "Mental Health for Refugees, Asylum Seekers and

Displaced Persons: A Call for a Humanitarian Agenda." *Transcultural Psychiatry* 54 (5–6): 565–574.

Ballard-Kang, Jennifer L. 2020. "Using Culturally Appropriate, Trauma-informed Support to Promote Bicultural Self-Efficacy among Resettled Refugees: A Conceptual Model." *Journal of Ethnic and Cultural Diversity in Social Work* 29 (1–3): 23–42.

Bandura, Albert. 1995. "Exercise of Personal and Collective Efficacy in Changing Societies." In *Self-Efficacy in Changing Societies*, edited by Albert Bandura. Cambridge: Cambridge University Press, pp. 1–45.

Baraldi, Claudio; and Gavioli, Laura. 2021. "Effective Communication and Knowledge Distribution in Healthcare Interaction with Migrants." *Health Communication* 36 (9): 1059–1067.

Bennett, Milton J. 1986. "A Developmental Approach to Training for Intercultural Sensitivity." *International Journal of Intercultural Relations* 10: 179–195.

Bergin, Charlotte. 2017. *Promising Practices in Refugee Education: Synthesis Report by Save the Children International and UNHCR.* New York: Pearson Publishers.

Berry, John W. 1997. "Immigration, Acculturation, and Adaptation." *Applied Psychology* 46 (1): 5–6.

Betts, Alexander. 2021. "Refugees: Overcoming Prejudices." *UNESCO Courier*, 4.

Bibus, Anthony A.; and Koh, Bibiana D. 2021. "Intercultural Humility in Social Work Education." *Journal of Social Work Education* 57 (1): 16–27.

Brislin, R.; Landis, D.; and Brandt, M.E. 1983. "Conceptualizations of Intercultural Behavior and Training." In *Handbook of Intercultural Training*, edited by D. Landis and R.W. Brislin. New York: Pergamon Press, pp. 1–35.

Brooks, David. 2022. "What Is It about Friendships that Is So Powerful?" *New York Times*, August 2, p. A20.

Burkardt, Aude D.; Krause, Nicerine; and Velarde, Minerva C. 2019. "Critical Success Factors for the Implementation and Adoption of E-learning for Junior Health Care Workers in Dadaab Refugee Camp Kenya." *Human Resources for Health* 17 (98): 1–10.

Capstick, Tony. 2020. *Language and Migration.* London: Routledge.

Carbaugh, Donal. 2005. *Cultures in Conversation.* Mahwah, NJ: Lawrence Erlbaum Associates.

CMHS (Center for Mental Health Services). 2001. *Cultural Competence Standards in Managed Care Mental Health Services: Four Underserved/Underrepresented Racial/ Ethnic Groups.* U.S. Department of Health and Human Services. Available at; www.mentalhealth.samhsa.gov/publications/allpubs/SMA00-3457/default.asp

Cohen, Robin; and Van Hear, Nicholas. 2020. *Refugia: Radical Solutions to Mass Displacement.* London: Routledge.

Colvin, Richard L.; and Edwards, Virginia. 2018. *Teaching for Global Competence in a Rapidly Changing World.* Paris: OECD/New York: Asia Society.

Dahya, Negin; and Dryden-Peterson, Sarah. 2017. "Tracing Pathways to Higher Education for Refugees: The Role of Virtual Support Networks and Mobile Phones for Women in Refugee Camps." *Comparative Education* 51 (2): 284–301.

Damaschke-Deitrick, Lisa; Galegher, Ericka; Davidson, Petrina M.; and Wiseman, Alexander W. 2022. "Teaching Refugee and Forced Immigrant Youth: Lessons from the United States." *Teachers and Teaching, Theory and Practice* [ahead-of-print]: 1–14.

Davcheva, Leah. 2011. "Mobility as an Intercultural Training Agenda: An Awareness-raising Programme for Youth Workers and Educators." *Intercultural Education* 22 (1): 121–122.

Deardorff, Darla K. 2020. *The UNESCO Manual for Developing Intercultural Competencies: Story Circles*. Paris: UNESCO.

DeSantis, Lydia. 1997. "Building Healthy Communities with Immigrants and Refugees." *Journal of Transcultural Nursing* 9 (1): 20–31.

DiMatteo, M. Robin. 1997. "Health Behaviors and Care Decisions." In *Handbook of Health Behavior Research* II: *Provider Determinants*, edited by David S. Gochman. New York: Plenum Press, pp. 5–22.

Dooly, Melinda; and Darvin, Ron. 2022. "Intercultural Communicative Competence in the Digital Age: Critical Digital Literacy and Inquiry-Based Pedagogy." *Language and Intercultural Communication* 22 (3): 354–366.

Dryden-Peterson, Sarah. 2016. "Refugee Education in Countries of First Asylum: Breaking Open the Black Box of Pre-resettlement Experiences." *Theory and Research in Education* 14 (2): 131–148.

Dryden-Peterson, Sarah. 2021. "Refugee Education: Education for an Unknowable Future." In *Curriculum of Global Migration and Transnationalism*, edited by Elena Toukan; Ruben Gaztambide-Fernandez; and Sardar Anwaruddin. London: Routledge, pp. 14–24.

Dryden-Peterson, Sarah; Dahya, Negin; and Adelman, Elizabeth. 2017. "Pathways to Educational Success among Refugees: Connecting Locally and Globally Situated Resources." *American Educational Research Journal* 54 (6): 1011–1047.

Eckenwiler, Lisa; and Wild, Verina. 2021. "Refugees and Others Enduring Displacement: Structural Injustice, Health, and Ethical Placemaking." *Journal of Social Philosophy* 52: 234–250.

Fathi, Atefeh; El-Awad, Usama; Reinelt, Tilman; and Petermann, Franz. 2018. "A Brief Introduction to the Multidimensional Intercultural Training Acculturation Model (MITA) for Middle Eastern Adolescent Refugees." *International Journal Environmental Research and Public Health* 15 (7): 1–14.

Ferguson, Warren J.; and Candib, Lucy M. 2002. "Culture, Language, and the Doctor-Patient Relationship." *Family Medicine* 34 (May): 353–361.

Finell, Eerika; Tiilikainen, Marja; Jasinskaja-Lahti, Inga; Hasan, Nasteho; and Muthana, Fairuz. 2021. "Lived Experiences Related to the COVID-19 Pandemic among Arabic-, Russian- and Somali-Speaking Migrants in Finland." *International Journal of Environmental Research and Public Health* 18. doi:10.31234/osf.io/o2v7r.

Finn, Janet. 2021. *Just Practice: A Social Justice Approach to Social Work*, 4th edition. New York: Oxford University Press.

Frenk, Julio; et al. 2010. "Health Professionals for a New Century: Transforming Education to Strengthen Health Systems in an Interdependent World." *Lancet* 376 (December 4): 1923–1958.

Galipo, Adele. 2019. *Return Migration and Nation Building in Africa: Reframing the Somali Diaspora*. London: Routledge.

Ganassin, Sara; and Young, Tony J. 2020. "From Surviving to Thriving: 'Success Stories' of Highly Skilled Refugees in the UK." *Language and Intercultural Communication* 20 (2): 125–140.

Garcia, Betty; Crifasi, Elizabeth; and Dessel, Adrienne B. 2019. "Oppression Pedagogy: Intergroup Dialogue and Theatre of the Oppressed in Creating a Safe Enough Classroom." *Journal of Social Work Education* 55 (4): 669–683.

Gatt, Justine M.; Alexander, Rebecca; Emond, Alan; Foster, Kim; Hadfield, Kristin; … Wu, Qiaobing. 2020. "Trauma, Resilience, and Mental Health in Migrant and Non-Migrant Youth: An International Cross-Sectional Study Across Six Countries."

Frontiers in Psychiatry 10. https://www.frontiersin.org/articles/10.3389/fpsyt.2019. 00997/full.

Gerrish, Kate; Husband, Charles; and Mackenzie, Jennifer. 1996. *Nursing for a Multiethnic Society*. Buckingham: Open University Press.

Giles, Wenona. 2018. "The Borderless Higher Education for Refugees Project: Enabling Refugee and Local Kenyan Students in Dadaab to Transition to University Education." *Journal on Education in Emergencies* 4 (1): 164–184.

Granato, Rebecca. 2022. "Migration, Refugees, and Education." Webinar sponsored by the Council on Foreign Relations, November 2.

Groyeckaa, Agata; Gajdab, Aleksandra; Jankowskab, Dorota M.; Sorokowskia, Piotr; and Karwowskic, Maciej. 2020. "On the Benefits of Thinking Creatively: Why Does Creativity Training Strengthen Intercultural Sensitivity Among Children?" *Thinking Skills and Creativity* 37 (100693): 1–8.

Gupta, Alisha H. 2022. "Uprooted from Home, Migrants Often Pine for the Little Things." *New York Times*, October 24, p. A13.

Hammer, Mitchell R.; Bennett, Milton J.; and Wiseman, Richard. 2003. "Measuring Intercultural Sensitivity: The Intercultural Development Inventory." *International Journal of Intercultural Relations* 27 (4): 421–443.

Hanesova, Dana; and Theodoulides, Lenka. 2022. *Mastering Transversal Competences in a Higher Education Environment: Through Processes of Critical Thinking and Reflection*. Banska Bystrica, Slovakia: Belianum. doi:10.24040/2022.9788055720159.

Heldal, Frode; Sjovold, Endre; and Stalsett, Kenneth. 2020. 'Shared Cognition in Intercultural Teams: Collaborating Without Understanding Each Other." *Team Performance Management* 26 (3): 211–226.

Hoffman, Peter J. 2021. "What Does 'Leave No One Behind' Mean for Humanitarians?" In *Routledge Handbook on the UN and Development*, edited by Stephen Browne and Thomas G. Weiss. London: Routledge, pp. 121–134.

Hofhuis, Joep; Schilderman, Marike F.; and Verdooren, Arjan. 2020. "Multicultural Personality and Effectiveness in an Intercultural Training Simulation: The Role of Stress and Pro-active Communication." *International Journal of Psychology* 55 (5): 812–821.

Houseknecht, Alisa; and Swank, Jacqueline. 2019. "Preparing Counselors to Work with Refugees: Integration of Experiential Activities." *Journal of Creativity in Mental Health* 14 (1): 127–136.

Hyndman, Jennifer. 2000. *Managing Displacement: Refugees and the Politics of Humanitarianism*. Minneapolis, MN: University of Minnesota Press.

Hyndman, Jennifer; and Giles, Wenona. 2017. *Refugees in Extended Exile: Living on the Edge*. London: Routledge.

Ionesco, Dina; Mokhnacheva, Daria; and Gemenne, François. 2017. *The Atlas of Environmental Migration*. London: Routledge.

Jahre, Marianne; Kembro, Jaokim; Adjahossou, Anicet; and Altay, Nezih. 2018. "Approaches to the Design of Refugee Camps: An Empirical Study in Kenya, Ethiopia, Greece, and Turkey." *Journal of Humanitarian Logistics and Supply Chain Management* 8 (3): 323–345.

James, Sigrid; Seidel, Franziska A.; Kilian, Juri; and Trostmann, Julian. 2020. "Labor Market Integration of Young Adult Refugees in Germany: Triangulating Perspectives Toward Program Development." *Research on Social Work Practice* 30 (5): 553–563.

Jeffreys, Marianne R. 2016. *Teaching Cultural Competence in Nursing and Health Care: Inquiry, Action, and Innovation*, 3rd edition. New York: Springer.

Karam, Fares J.; Monaghan, Christine; and Yoder, Paul J. 2017. "'The Students Do Not Know Why They Are Here': Education Decision-Making for Syrian Refugees." *Globalisation, Societies and Education* 15 (4): 448–463.

Kavanagh, Kathryn H. 1999. "Transcultural Perspectives in Mental Health." In *Transcultural Concepts in Nursing Care*, 3rd edition, edited by Margaret M. Andrews and Joyseen S. Boyle. Philadelphia, PA: Lippincott, pp. 223–261.

Kihato, Caroline W.; and Landau, Loren B. 2016. "Stealth Humanitarianism: Negotiating Politics, Precarity and Performance Management in Protecting the Urban Displaced." *Journal of Refugee Studies* 30 (3): 407–425.

Kim, Suk-Hee; Canfield, James; and Harley, Dana. 2019. "Using Photovoice as a Method to Examine Microaggressions: Conceptualizing Culturally Competent Practice and Curriculum with Asian Americans." *Journal of Human Behavior in the Social Environment* 29 (8): 1036–1043.

Kirmayer, Laurence J.; Kronick, Rachel; and Rousseau, Cecile. 2018. "Advocacy as Key to Structural Competency in Psychiatry." *JAMA Psychiatry* 75 (2): 119–120.

Kleinman, Arthur; Eisenberg, Leon; and Good, Byron. 1978. "Culture, Illness, and Care: Clinical Lessons from Anthropologic and Cross-Cultural Research." *Annals of Internal Medicine* 88: 251–258.

Koehn, Justin; and Koehn, Jason. 2016. "Beach Volleyball with Refugees: A Testimonial." *Jeanette Rankin Peace Center Newsletter* (Winter/Spring): 4.

Koehn, Peter H. 1991. *Refugees from Revolution: U.S. Policy and Third-World Migration.* Boulder, CO: Westview Press.

Koehn, Peter H. 1994a. *Final Report of the International Symposium "Refugees and Development Assistance: Training for Voluntary Repatriation."* Missoula: Office of International Programs, The University of Montana, April.

Koehn, Peter H. 1994b. "Refugee Settlement and Repatriation in Africa: Development Prospects and Constraints." In *African Refugees: Development Aid and Repatriation*, edited by Howard Adelman and John Sorenson. Boulder, CO: Westview Press, pp. 97–116.

Koehn, Peter H. 2005a. "Improving Transnational Health-Care Encounters and Outcomes: The Challenge of Enhanced Transnational Competence for Migrants and Health Professionals." In *Proceedings of the Hospitals in a Culturally Diverse Europe Conference on Quality-Assured Health Care and Health Promotion for Migrants and Ethnic Minorities*, Amsterdam, December 9–11, 2004.

Koehn, Peter H. 2005b. "Medical Encounters in Finnish Reception Centres: Asylum-Seeker and Clinician Perspectives." *Journal of Refugee Studies* 18 (1): 47–74.

Koehn, Peter H.; and Ngai, Phyllis B. 2006. "Citizenship Education for an Age of Population Mobility and Glocally Interconnected Destinies." *Finnish Journal of Ethnicity and Migration* 1 (1): 26–33.

Koehn, Peter H.; and Rosenau, James N. 2010. *Transnational Competence: Empowering Professional Curricula for Horizon-Rising Challenges.* Boulder, CO: Paradigm Press.

Kovandzic, Marija; et al. 2012. "The Space of Access to Primary Mental Health Care: A Qualitative Case Study." *Health & Place* 18: 536–551.

Kuriansky, Judy. 2019. "A Model Psychosocial Support Training and Workshop during a Medical Mission for Syrian Refugee Children in Jordan: Techniques, Lessons Learned and Recommendations." *Journal of Infant, Child, and Adolescent Psychotherapy* 18 (4): 352–366.

Landler-Pardo, Gabriella; Elyashiv, Rinat A.; Levi-Keren, Machal; and Weinberger, Yehudith. 2022. "Being Empathic in Complex Situations in Intercultural Education: A Practical Tool." *Intercultural Education* 33 (4): 391–405.

Lee, Eunjung; Kourgiantakis, Toula; and Hu. Ran. 2022. "Developing Holistic Competence in Cross-Cultural Social Work Practice: Simulation-Based Learning Optimized by Blended Teaching Approach." *Social Work Education* 41 (5): 820–836.

Leite, Stephanie. 2022. "Using the SDGs for Global Citizenship Education: Definitions, Challenges, and Opportunities." *Globalisations, Societies and Education* 20 (3): 401–413.

Lovey, Thibault; O'Keeffe, Paul; and Petignat, Ianis. 2021. "Basic Medical Training for Refugees via Collaborative Blended Learning: Quasi-Experimental Design." *Journal of Medicine Internet Research* 23 (3): 1–14.

Manjoo, Farhad. 2016. "A Shared Lifeline for Millions of Migrants." *New York Times*, December 22, pp. B1, B7.

Martin, Susan F.; Davis, Rochelle; Benton, Grace; and Waliany, Zoya. 2017. *Responsibility Sharing for Refugees in the Middle East and North Africa: Perspectives from Policymakers, Stakeholders, Refugees and Internally Displaced Persons*. Report 2017:8. Stockholm: Delmi, The Migration Studies Delegation.

Marume, Anesu; January, James; and Maradzika, Julita. 2018. "Social Capital, Health-Seeking Behavior and Quality of Life among Refugees in Zimbabwe: A Cross-Sectional Study." *International Journal of Migration, Health and Social Care* 14 (4): 377–386.

Matlin, Stephen A.; Depoux, Anneliese; Schutte, Stefanie; Flahault, Antoine; and Saso, Luciano. 2018. "Migrants' and Refugees' Health: Towards an Agenda of Solutions." *Public Health Reviews* 39 (27): 1–55.

Mbai, Isabella I.; Mangeni, Judith N.; Abuelaish, Izzeldin; and Pilkington, F. Beryl. 2017. "Community Health Worker Training and Education in a Refugee Context." In *Science Research and Education in Africa: Proceedings of a Conference on Science Advancement*, edited by Alain L. Fymat and Joachim Kapalanga. Newcastle Upon Tyne: Cambridge Scholars Publishing, pp. 163–186.

McAuliffe, Marie; Freier, Luisa F.; Skeldon, Ronald; and Blower, Jenna. 2021. "The Great Disrupter: COVID-19's Impact on Migration, Mobility and Migrants Globally." In *World Migration Report 2022*, edited by Marie McAuliffe and A. Triandafyllidou. Geneva: International Organization for Migration.

McMichael, Celia; Barnett, Jon; and McMichael, Anthony J. 2012. "An Ill Wind? Climate Change, Migration, and Health." *Environmental Health Perspectives* 120 (5): 646–654.

Miller, Claire C.; Katz, Josh; Paris, Francesca; and Bhatia, Aatish. 2022. "Wealthy Friends May Be Ticket Out of Poverty." *New York Times*, August 2, pp. A1, A15.

Milner, James. 2021. "Refugees and International Development Policy and Practice." In *Introduction to International Development: Approaches, Actors, Issues, and Practice*, edited by Paul Haslam; Jessica Shafer; and Pierre Beaudet. Oxford: Oxford University Press, pp. 408–425.

Mohan, Brij; and Clark Prickett, Julia E. 2010. "Macro Social Work Practice with Transmigrants." In *Transnational Social Work Practice*, edited by Nalini J. Negi and Rich Furman. New York: Columbia University Press, pp. 191–204.

Montero-Sieburth, Martha; and Giralt, Rosa M. 2021. "Introduction." In *Family Practices in Migration: Everyday Lives and Relationships*, edited by Martha Montero-Sieburth; Rosa Giralt; Noemi Garcia-Arjona; and Joaquin Eguren. London: Routledge, pp. 1–23.

Murdoch-Eaton, Deborah; Redmond, Anthony; and Bax, Nigel. 2011. "Training Healthcare Professionals for the Future: Internationalism and Effective Inclusion of Global Health Training." *Medical Teacher* 33: 562–569.

Mutiso, Victoria; Warsame, Abdulkadir H.; Bosire, Edna; Musyimi, Christine; Musau, Abednego; Isse, Maimuna M.; and Ndetei, David M. 2019. "Intrigues of Accessing Mental Health Services among Urban Refugees Living in Kenya: The Case of Somali Refugees Living in Eastleigh, Nairobi." *Journal of Immigrant and Refugee Studies* 17 (2): 204–221.

Mwangu, Alex R. 2022. "An Assessment of Economic and Environmental Impacts of Refugees in Nakivale, Uganda." *Migration and Development* 11 (3): 433–449.

Nadler, Arie; Malloy, Thomas; and Fisher, Jeffrey (Eds.). 2008. *The Social Psychology of Intergroup Reconciliation*. New York: Oxford University Press.

Negm, Lena; and Mayer, Aida. 2022. "Proposal to Establish Refugees Therapy Center." *Civil Engineering and Architecture* 10 (3A): 43–49.

Ngai, Phyllis. 2021. "Discourse Analysis for Intercultural Competence Development." *International Journal of Bias, Identity and Diversities in Education* 6 (1): 17–30.

Nicolaidis, Kalypso. 2006. "We, the Peoples of Europe ..." In *Globalization and State Power: A Reader*, edited by Joel Krieger. New York: Pearson, pp. 194–200.

Nunn, Caitlin; Spaaij, Ramon; and Luguetti, Carla. 2022. "Beyond Integration: Football as a Mobile, Transnational Sphere of Belonging for Refugee-Background Young People." *Leisure Studies* 41 (1): 42–55.

Oakley, Peter. 1991. *Projects with People: The Practice of Participation in Rural Development*. Geneva: International Labour Office.

O'Brien, Sharon; and Federici, Frederico M. 2020. "Crisis Translation: Considering Language Needs in Multilingual Disaster Settings." *Disaster Prevention and Management* 29 (3): 129–143.

Ostherr, Kirsten. 2023. "The Visual Language of COVID-19: Narrative, Data and Emotion in Online Health Communications." In *The Languages of COVID-19: Translational and Multilingual Perspectives on Global Healthcare*, edited by Piotr Blumczynski and Steven Wilson. New York: Routledge, pp. 199–216.

Ozkazanc-Pan, Banu. 2019. "'Superdiversity': A New Paradigm for Inclusion in a Transnational World." *Equality, Diversity and Inclusion* 38 (4): 477–490.

Pachter, L.M. 2000. "Working with Patients' Health Beliefs and Behaviors: The Awareness-Assessment-Negotiation Model in Clinical Care." In *Child Health in the Multicultural Environment: Report of the 31st Ross Roundtable on Critical Approaches to Common Pediatric Problems*, edited by E. Silverman. Columbus, OH: Ross Products Division, Abbott Laboratories, pp. 36–43.

Peabody, Carolyn G. 2013. "Using Photovoice as a Tool to Engage Social Work Students in Social Justice." *Journal of Teaching in Social Work* 33 (3): 251–265.

Perouse de Montclos, Marc-Antoine; and Kagwanja, Peter M. 2000. "Refugee Camps or Cities: The Socio-Economic Dynamics of the Dadaab and Kakuma Camps in Northern Kenya." *Journal of Refugee Studies* 13 (2): 205–222.

Perry, Angela. 2001. *Guide to Talking to Your Doctor*. New York: John Wiley & Sons.

Pettigrew, Thomas F.; and Tropp, Linda R. 2006. "A Meta-Analytic Test of Intergroup Contact Theory." *Journal of Personality and Social Psychology* 90: 751–783.

Pickren, Wade E. 2014. "What Is Resilience and How Does It Relate to the Refugee Experience? Historical and Theoretical Perspectives." In *Refuge and Resilience: Promoting Resilience and Mental Health among Resettled Refugees and Forced Migrants*, edited by Laura Simich and Lisa Andermann. New York: Springer, pp. 7–26.

Pilkington, F. Beryl; and Mbai, Isabella. 2016. *Researching the Gap between the Existing and Potential Community Health Worker Education and Training in the Refugee Context: An Intersectoral Approach.* Final Interim Report to IDRC. Toronto: York University, July 31.

Pincock, Kate; Betts, Alexander; and Easton-Calabria, Evan. 2020. *The Global Governed? Refugees as Providers of Protection and Assistance.* Cambridge: Cambridge University Press.

Plastina, Anna F. 2022. "Changing Discourses of Climate Change: Building Social-Ecological Resilience Cross-Culturally." *Text & Talk* 42 (4): 591–612.

Popay, Jennie; and Williams, Gareth. 1996. "Public Health Research and Lay Knowledge." *Social Science and Medicine* 42 (5): 759–768.

Post, Douglas M.; Cegala, Donald J.; and Miser, William F. 2002. "The Other Half of the Whole: Teaching Patients to Communicate with Physicians." *Family Medicine* 34 (5): 344–352.

Pusch, Magaret. 2009. "The Interculturally Competent Global Leaders." In *The Sage Handbook of Intercultural Competence*, edited by Darla Deardorff. Thousand Oaks, CA: Sage, pp. 66–84.

Raithelhuber, Eberhard. 2018. "How 'Godparents' Are Made for 'Unaccompanied Refugee Minors': An Ethnographic View into the Training of Future Youth Mentors." *Child & Youth Services* 39 (4): 250–283.

Ramsay, Georgina; and Baker, Sally. 2019. "Higher Education and Students from Refugee Backgrounds: A Meta-Scoping Study." *Refugee Survey Quarterly* 38: 55–82.

Rashid, Marghalara; Cervantes, Andrea D.; and Goez, Helly. 2020. "Refugee Health Curriculum in Undergraduate Medical Education (UME): A Scoping Review." *Teaching and Learning in Medicine* 32 (5): 476–485.

Roter, Debra L.; and Hall, Judith A. 1992. *Doctors Talking with Patients/Patients Talking with Doctors: Improving Communication in Medical Visits.* Westport, CT: Auburn House.

Sajib, Sadat al; Islam, Ziaul; and Sohad, Muhammad K.N. 2022. "Rohingya Influx and Socio-Environmental Crisis in Southeastern Bangladesh." *The International Journal of Community and Social Development* 4 (1): 89–103.

Salovey, Peter; Woolery, Alison; and Mayer, John D. 2001. "Emotional Intelligence: Conceptualization and Measurement." In *Blackwell Handbook of Social Psychology: Interpersonal Processes*, edited by Garth J.O. Fletcher and Margaret S. Clark. Oxford: Blackwell, pp. 278–307.

Sampson, Robyn; and Gifford, Sandra M. 2010. "Place-Making, Settlement and Well-being: The Therapeutic Landscapes of Recently Arrived Youth with Refugee Backgrounds." *Health & Place* 16: 116–131.

Schukking, Anna F; and Kircher, Ruthorcid. 2022. "Professional Intercultural Communicative Competence and Labour Market Integration Among Highly-Educated Refugees in the Netherlands." *European Journal of Applied Linguistics* 10 (1): 31–56.

Seto-Nielsen, Lisa; Angus, Jan E.; Lapum, Jennifer; Dale, Craig; Kramer-Kile, Marnie; Abramson, Beth; Marzolini, Susan; Oh, Paul; Price, Jennifer; and Clark, Alex. 2012. "'I Can't Just Follow Any Particular Textbook': Immigrants in Cardiac Rehabilitation." *Journal of Advanced Nursing* 68 (12): 2719–2729.

Shaw, Stacey A. 2014. "Bridge Builders: A Qualitative Study Exploring the Experiences of Former Refugees Working as Caseworkers in the United States." *Journal of Social Service Research* 40 (3): 284–296.

Silove, Derrick; Ventevogel, Peter; and Rees, Susan. 2017. "The Contemporary Refugee Crisis: An Overview of Mental Health Challenges." *World Psychiatry* 16 (2): 130–138.

Sleijpen, Marieke; Boeije, Hennie R.; Kleber, Rolf J.; and Mooren, Trudy. 2016. "Between Power and Powerlessness: A Meta-Ethnography of Sources of Resilience in Young Refugees." *Ethnicity & Health* 21 (2): 158–180.

Smedley, Brian D.; Stith, Adrienne Y.; and Nelson, Alan R. (Eds.). 2003. *Unequal Treatment: Confronting Racial and Ethnic Disparities in Health Care.* Washington, D. C.: National Academy Press.

Ssosse, Quentin; Wagner, Johanna; and Hopper, Carina. 2021. "Assessing the Impact of ESD: Methods, Challenges, Results." *Sustainability* 13 (2854): 1–26. doi:10.3390/su13052854.

Stephan, Walter G; and Stephan, Cookie W. 2013. "Designing Intercultural Education and Training Programs: An Evidence-Based Approach." *International Journal of Intercultural Relations* 37: 277–286.

Stewart, Miriam J. 2014. "Social Support in Refugee Resettlement." In *Refuge and Resilience: Promoting Resilience and Mental Health among Resettled Refugees and Forced Migrants,* edited by Laura Simich and Lisa Andermann. New York: Springer, pp. 91–107.

Sualp, Kenan; Okumus, F. Elif E.; and Molina, Olga. 2022. "Group Work Training for Mental Health Professionals Working with Syrian Refugee Children in Turkey: A Needs Assessment Study." *Social Work with Groups* 45 (3–4): 319–335.

Talhouk, S.N.; Chalak, A.; Kamareddine, Z.; Fabian, M.; Itani, M.; and Ferguson, N. 2021. "Vertical Gardening and Syrian Women Refugees in Lebanon: An Exploratory Study on Motivation for Gardening and Depression Relief." *Local Environment* 26 (10): 1235–1249.

Taylor, Peter. 2003. *How to Design a Training Course: A Guide to Participatory Curriculum Development.* London: Continuum.

Taylor, Peter. 2008. "Higher Education Curricula for Human and Social Development." In *Higher Education in the World 3: New Challenges and Emerging Roles for Human and Social Development.* London: Palgrave Macmillan, pp. 89–101.

Tejada, Gabriela. 2016. "Knowledge Transfers through Diaspora Transnationalism and Return Migration: A Case Study of Indian Skilled Migrants." In *Diasporas, Development and Governance,* edited by Abel Chikanda; Jonathan Crush; and Margaret Walton-Roberts. New York: Springer, pp. 187–203.

Tervalon, Melanie. 2003. "Components of Culture in Health for Medical Students' Education." *Academic Medicine* 78 (6): 570–576.

Tervalon, Melanie; and Murray-Garcia, Jann. 1998. "Cultural Humility versus Cultural Competence: A Critical Distinction in Defining Physician Training Outcomes in Multicultural Education." *Journal of Health Care for the Poor and Underserved* 9 (2): 117–125.

Tiessen, Rebecca; and Lough, Benjamin J. 2019. "International Volunteering Capacity Development: Volunteer Partner Organization Experiences of Mitigating Factors for Effective Practice." *Forum for Development Studies* 46 (2): 299–320.

Tiilikainen, Marja; and Koehn, Peter H. 2011. "Transforming the Boundaries of Healthcare: Insights from the Transnational Outlooks and Practices of Somali Migrants." *Medical Anthropology* 30 (5): 1–27.

Ting-Toomey, Stella; and Chung, Leeva C. 2022. *Understanding Intercultural Communication,* 3rd edition. New York: Oxford University Press.

Todorova, Marija. 2022. "Translating Refugee Culinary Cultures: Hong Kong's Narratives of Integration." *Translation and Interpreting Studies* 17 (1): 88–110.

Tomlinson, Frances; and Egan, Sue. 2002. "From Marginalization to (Dis)empowerment: Organizing Training and Employment Services for Refugees." *Human Relations* 55 (8): 1019–1043.

Toole, Mike. 2019. "Health in Humanitarian Crises." In *The Health of Refugees: Public Health Perspectives from Crisis to Settlement*, 2nd edition, edited by Pascale Allotey and Daniel D. Reidpath. Oxford: Oxford University Press, pp. 54–84.

Torun, Perihan; Karaaslan Mücaz, Maltem; Sendikli, Büşra; Acar, Ceyda; Shurtleff, Ellyn; Dhrolia, Sophia; and Herek, Bülent. 2018. "Health and Health Care Access for Syrian Refugees Living in Istanbul." *International Journal of Public Health* 63 (5): 601–608. https://doi.org/10.1007/s00038-018-1096-4.

Toukan, Elena V.; Gaztambide-Fernandez, Ruben; and Anwaruddin, Sardar. 2021. "Shifting Borders and Sinking Ships: What (and Who) Is Transnationalism 'Good' For?" In *Curriculum of Global Migration and Transnationalism*, edited by Elena Toukan; Ruben Gaztambide-Fernandez; and Sardar Anwaruddin. London: Routledge, pp. 1–13.

Turner, Simon. 2015. "What Is a Refugee Camp? Explorations of the Limits and Effects of the Camp." *Journal of Refugee Studies* 29 (2): 139–147.

UNESCO. 2013. *Intercultural Competencies: Conceptual and Operational Framework.* Paris: UNESCO.

UNESCO. 2015. *Global Citizenship Education: Topics and Learning Objectives.* Paris: UNESCO.

Uttam, Sahoo; and Bipin, Jojo. 2020. "Examining Displacement, Resettlement and Rehabilitation Processes: The Case of Rengali Dam Displaced Communities in Odisha, India." *The International Journal of Community and Social Development* 2 (1): 29–50.

Valtonen, Kathleen. 1998. "Resettlement of Middle Eastern Refugees in Finland: The Elusiveness of Integration." *Journal of Refugee Studies* 11 (1): 38–60.

Vega, Miriam Y.; and Cherfas, Lina. 2012. "The Landscape of Latina HIV Prevention Interventions and Their Implementation: Cultural Sensitivity in Community-based Organizations." In *HIV Prevention with Latinos: Theory, Research, and Practice*, edited by Kurt C. Organista. Oxford: Oxford University Press, pp. 329–349.

Villa-Torres, Laura; Gonzalez-Vazquez, Tonatiuh; Fleming, Paul J.; Gonzalez-Gonzalez, Edgar L.; Infante-Xibille, Cesar; Chavez, Rebecca; and Barrington, Clare. 2017. "Transnationalism and Health: A Systematic Literature Review on the Use of Transnationalism in the Study of the Health Practices and Behaviors of Migrants." *Social Science & Medicine* 183: 70–79.

Walker, Peter; Hein, Karen; Russ, Catherine; Bertleff, Greg; and Caspersz, Dan. 2010. "A Blueprint for Professionalizing Humanitarian Assistance." *Health Affairs* 29 (December): 2223–2230.

Wang, Suyang. 2022. "The Transnational In-Between Identity of Chinese Student Returnees from the UK: Mobility, Variations and Pathways." *British Educational Research Journal* 48 (3): 536–555.

Warriner, Doris. 2021. "Theorizing the Spatial Dimensions and Pedagogical Implications of Transnationalism." In *Curriculum of Global Migration and Transnationalism*, edited by Elena Toukan; Ruben Gaztambide-Fernandez; and Sardar Anwaruddin. London: Routledge, pp. 52–61.

Wellman, Sascha; and Bey, Sharif. 2015. "Refugee Children and Art Teacher Training: Promoting Language, Self-Advocacy, and Cultural Preservation." *Art Education* 68 (6): 36–44.

White House. 2021. *Report on the Impact of Climate Change on Migration*. Washington, D.C.: The White House.

Whittaker, Joshua; McLennan, Blythe; and Handmer, John. 2015. "A Review of Informal Volunteerism in Emergencies and Disasters: Definition, Opportunities and Challenges." *International Journal of Disaster Risk Reduction* 13: 358–368.

WHO (World Health Organization). 2010. *Health of Migrants: The Way Forward: Report of a Global Consultation held in Madrid, Spain, March, 3–5*. Geneva: WHO.

Williams, Carolyn L.; and Berry, J.W. 1991. "Primary Prevention of Acculturative Stress among Refugees: Application of Psychological Theory and Practice." *American Psychologist* 46 (6): 632–641.

Yook, Eunkyong Lee; and Albert, Rosita D. 1999. "Perceptions of International Teaching Assistants: The Interrelatedness of Intercultural Training, Cognition, and Emotion." *Communication Education* 48 (1): 1–17.

7 Framework for Evaluating Conflict-Displaced and Climate-Displaced TC Development and Impacts

Given the likelihood of increased displacement induced by climate change and conflicts, reliable evaluations of responses and effects assume special importance (Baarnhielm, et al., 2017, p. 572). To date, however, prevailing humanitarian organization evaluations of training initiatives have been "limited and non-systematic" (Teitelbaum, 2019). There are initiatives that focus on evaluation and learning in the humanitarian-aid sector, most notably ALNAP (Active Learning Network for Accountability and Performance).[1] The Environmental Peacebuilding Association also has a monitoring and evaluation interest group, which has been advancing the practice since around 2018.[2] The UNHCR established an independent evaluation function in 2016 to enhance accountability and learning in the organization. Nevertheless, "evidence-based knowledge sharing or transfer of learning into the ecosystem of humanitarian field work" merits additional attention (ibid.).

Meaningful evaluation involves a rigorous, systematic, transparent, and evidence-based process of collecting, analyzing, and interpreting information to answer specific questions. Evaluation is carried out for multiple purposes, including generating new insights, action-pathway identification and confirmation, improvement and scaling-up of program interventions, shared and continuous individual, initiator, and stakeholder learning (Gibson, 2005, p. 155), and accountability for results achieved and resources used. An entire strand of evaluation has developed, focusing on the utility and actual use of evaluation findings and processes by "real people in the real world" (Patton, 2008, p. 37).

Most definitions of evaluation incorporate the notion of "making a judgment of the value or worth of the subject of the evaluation" (Morra-Imas and Rist, 2009, p. 8). Unlike research or monitoring, therefore, evaluation is not value-free. Although evaluation involves an important accountability dimension for results (not) achieved and resources used, it is most valuable when utilized by stakeholders for program improvement (or conclusion) and in connection with learning lessons for future application.

Drawing on experience with international development evaluation and insights derived from the prior chapters of this book, this chapter sets forth specific recommendations for conducting evaluations of TC preparation. Specifically, the chapter provides an adaptable TC assessment scheme

DOI: 10.4324/9781003330493-8

centered on process, outcomes, and impacts at individual and grassroots levels, along with recommendations for the evaluation process when conducting tailored TC development and TC training outcome and impact evaluations. Developing capabilities to evaluate the consequences of displacement will require concerted effort along with face-to-face, online, and blended continuing education on the part of humanitarian organizations and institutions of higher learning.

The capabilities needed to conduct TC development evaluations will vary and depend on the specific situation. Evaluators should start with ensuring that the intervention design is evaluable and that the monitoring process can be linked with the evaluation plan. According to the widely accepted definition of the OECD Development Assistance Committee, *evaluability* refers to "the ability to assess effectiveness, impact, coherence and sustainability" (OECD, 2021, p. 58). An evaluability assessment of the intervention to be evaluated is conducted to verify whether the project design, including its theory of change, allows for its evaluation and whether data, systems, and capacities are available (Davies, 2013, p. 7).

To link design with evaluation and monitoring means that program or project proponents be prepared upfront to identify success factors for the intervention and how to measure them. Necessary training components can be identified in the context of the intervention's theory of change, which spells out the essential steps for the achievement of the intervention goals along with the barriers, risks, and assumptions involved. Success factors include indicators for monitoring progress. However, indicators are not sufficient for evaluation. Given that the purpose of evaluation not only is to measure achievement of milestones, but to provide explanations for success or failure, to identify what works, for whom, under what circumstances and why, and to be alert for unintended or unanticipated consequences (Uitto, 2021, p. 445; Ssosse, Wagner, and Hopper, 2021, p. 21; Sykes, 2014, p. e40), it is fundamentally important that participants are able to articulate program theories that will provide a basis against which meaningful process (Brundiers, et al., 2014, p. 203), outcome, and impact evaluations can be conducted.

Humanitarian interventions are "*never* neutral in their developmental impact" (Anderson and Woodrow, 1998, p. 93). TC preparation evaluations are anchored in specific outcome and impact objectives. In the wake of conflict and climate displacement, evaluation capacity needs are expanded when we move from evaluating the outcomes of individual humanitarian-responder training initiatives to evaluating the catalytic impact of interventions on broader adoption and behavioral change in the long-term interest of population well-being, belonging, and sustainable development (Uitto, 2016, p. 109; Martin, Bergmann, Rigaud, and Yameogo, 2021, pp. 145–146). Evaluating transformational change requires a creative and holistic way of looking at the context in which the intervention takes place. Experimental designs will seldom be useful in the challenging contexts of TC development outcome and impact evaluations.

The initially developed theory of change forms the basis for subsequent evaluations, including the final (or terminal) evaluation and possible ex-post evaluations. The first step in theory-of-change impact analysis is to "reconstruct the expected causal pathway" of the training design, beginning with the hypothesized impact(s), considering intermediate outcome indicators, "then working backwards through the pattern of effects and causes to the inputs and learning activities ... meant to set the overall process in motion" (Ssosse, Wagner, and Hopper, 2021, pp. 7–8, 11). At the summative post-intervention (TC preparation) point, theory-of-change assumptions (e.g., how risk and opportunity perceptions have changed; whether barriers addressed by specific training activities proved actually limiting; how available resources changed approaches, outcomes, and impacts) are tested.

Understanding outcome to impact pathways in complex systems can be facilitated by theory-based approaches that identify the assumptions and risks that will affect how training interventions lead to lasting change. Outcome-to-impact analysis is conducted with special attention to understanding the effect of impact drivers and intermediate states (Todd and Craig, 2014, p. 64). Key questions to ask at this evaluation stage are:[3] What was the TC training initiative ultimately trying to achieve? How accurate were the initiative's original underlying assumptions (Oakley, 1991, p. 264)? Which barriers to intended training outcomes and impacts were overcome or not overcome? What did the training intervention actually achieve at completion? What were the reasons for successes or failures in delivering the intended impacts? Are there external factors or unforeseen causal pathways that contributed to or better explain observed impacts (Norgbey and Spilsbury, 2014, pp. 144–145; Zint, 2011, pp. 332–337)? What else needs to happen to deliver the intended impacts? Are necessary follow-up interventions introduced and on track eventually to contribute toward the originally intended impacts? Are the support systems for the necessary continuation strong enough to ensure that TC training activities will move forward toward realizing intended outcome and impact objectives?

TC Evaluations

In this chapter we recognize that humanitarian agencies, civil-society organizations, and universities will employ variable and tailored applications of any framework for TC development evaluation. To avoid haphazard applications, however, we suggest here a core set of illustrative evaluation guidelines that can serve as a practical foundation with widespread utility. First, we enumerate core process principles.

Evaluation Process Principles

Meaningful evaluations depend in the first instance on getting multiple process components right. Independent (external) as well as internal evaluators with diverse, transboundary expertise (Thomas and Tominaga, 2013, p. 69) need to be assembled, engaged, and supplied with material and staff resources that enable successful implementation of the practical evaluation plan. Before starting, it is important to understand the context in which the evaluation takes place. Linda Morra-Imas and Ray Rist (2009, pp. 142–143) provide a comprehensive list of questions to be included in the "front-end analysis," starting with understanding who the main client for evaluation is and who the other stakeholders are. Front-end analysis also includes a study to understand what prior literature and other evaluations of similar programs report about the problem. Front-end analysis is needed to answer critical questions about the evaluation, including "timing, time to complete, people involved, resources, design, program theory and logic, and existing knowledge" (ibid., p. 171).

Common steps in the evaluation process involve: (1) the identification of questions, relevant criteria, stakeholders, and target audiences; (2) identifying and arranging the evaluators; (3) developing a research design that will guide the collection and analysis of collected data; (4) analyzing and disseminating results; and (5) disseminating and promoting the use of findings (Zint, 2011, p. 332). Each of these steps requires careful preparation. Box 7.1 presents 12 helpful principles aimed at guiding TC preparation evaluations in a promising direction.

Box 7.1 TC Development Evaluations: Process Principles

1 Ensure top-level commitment and support.
2 Make decisions informed by theory of change all along the way.
3 Allocate sufficient resources to formative and summative, internal and external, evaluation practice (Teitelbaum, 2019).
4 Evaluation should encompass curricula, teaching approaches, e-learning, outreach, partnerships, and participants and be linked to training operations.
5 Commitment to moving beyond inputs and outputs.[4] Incorporate process, demonstrated outcomes associated with defined competencies, and impact assessments (Hollenbeck, McCall, and Silzer, 2006, pp. 404, 412).
6 Impact evaluation should be contextually centered and be near-term and long-term.
7 Utilize multiple methods and triangulate whenever possible. Evaluation questions must drive the choice of appropriate methods rather than vice versa.
8 Establish a participatory evaluation process that engages students, stakeholders, and partners on an equitable footing.
9 Promote collective learning (da Silva, et al., 2018, p. 12) and implement lessons learned.

10 Ensure transparency of the evaluation process and wide dissemination of findings (share results with all trainees and stakeholders). Report findings in a timely and concise manner of strategic value to decision makers at all levels.

11 Findings from ongoing monitoring of relocation activities and from outcome and impact evaluations "should be shared, in a timely manner, with Relocated Persons and Other Affected Persons as applicable" (Brookings Institution, Georgetown University's School of Foreign Service,, and UNHCR, 2015, p. 22).

12 Identify and secure recognition for contextual and generic attainments and pursue external certification that will enable TC training and education contributions to human and social development in dislocated situations to be sustained in the long run (Taylor, 2008, pp. 97, 100; Hammick and Anderson, 2009, p. 220).

Evaluators will be challenged to emphasize integrated outcome and impact assessments. Systematic TC evaluations progress from process to capability-building outcomes and, then, from local to national and transnational (glocal) impacts. The conduct of integrated evaluations addresses near-term and inter-generational ecological, social, and sustainable-development impacts; the process is contextually driven, but cognizant of common criteria. The needed type of evaluation response to specific framework inquiries determines the research methods and complementary strategies that evaluators use and the triangulation possibilities pursued (Ssosse, Wagner, and Hopper, 2021, p. 11; da Silva, et al., 2018, p. 12).

TC-Specific Evaluation Approaches

All evaluation initiatives must involve key stakeholders (including trainees) from the beginning in the evaluation process. Indeed, the participatory bases of the TC approach would be contradicted if the sole contributors to the evaluation process are internal or external professional evaluators (Oakley, 1991, p. 263). In particular, beneficiaries need to inform development of the evaluation tools in ways that maximize community responsiveness and contextual insights. As Michael Patton points out, "one of the negative connotations often associated with evaluation is that it is something done *to* people. Participatory evaluation, in contrast, involves working *with* people" (2002, p. 183; emphases added). Through participation in the overall evaluation process, trainees and other stakeholders simultaneously engage in ongoing learning that further develops their transnational competencies (Oakley, 1991, p. 263).

Participatory evaluation builds upon principles outlined in techniques such as Participatory Rural Appraisal (Chambers, 1994). This will require early contact with stakeholders to inform them of the goals and intentions of the intervention and to secure their feedback. Early contact can take the form of interviews, meetings, and participatory workshops where stakeholders discuss their issues and felt problems and explore ways to solve them. It is important to ensure that all voices are heard; this might require splitting stakeholders into different groups. For example, in settings where women are discouraged from voicing their opinions or there is an ethnic group that is in the minority, it might be necessary to meet with them separately. Youth is another important group that needs to be reached. In this regard, schools (informal or formal), sports clubs, and the like can be useful venues. Methods of data collection might involve storytelling and personal accounts of change using techniques such as Most Significant Change (Davies and Dart, 2005).

It is important for evaluators to position themselves as open listeners and facilitators and not to come across as directing the stakeholders or as advocates of the intervention. It can be quite helpful in this regard to engage TC-prepared interpreters. Equally important is that the evaluators communicate findings necessary for course correction to the intervention proponents while protecting the confidentiality of individual stakeholders, and that the stakeholders understand that this is happening.

The suggested multi-level TC evaluation process builds from being focused on participants and agencies to partners and stakeholders and, then, to societal considerations. In a displacement context where power relations typically are quite uneven, it is particularly important to include voices from all stakeholders equally, including those of the displaced persons themselves and impacted host community members. Stakeholder involvement can take different forms at different stages of evaluation. At the start, stakeholders should be engaged in setting the evaluation questions and criteria in order to ensure that the evaluation addresses questions that are relevant and of use to them. Similarly, the stakeholders should have an opportunity to review evaluation conclusions and recommendations before they are finalized so that what is suggested is realistic and implementable.

Strategic feedback, continuous learning, and transformational change are central features of meaningful approaches to evaluating TC development activity. Transparency suffuses all stages of the evaluation process. There is full disclosure of data collection and verification methods along with the people involved in evaluating (da Silva, et al., 2018, p. 8). Consolidated evaluation findings from diverse perspectives are integrated into recommendations (Thomas and Tominaga, 2013, p. 66) and disseminated internally among stakeholders and partners, to other educators and humanitarian responders, and to the evaluation community.

Rather than relying exclusively on technical knowledge or on numerical output indicators such as the attainment of qualifying credentials, evaluations of human capabilities emphasize comprehensive outcomes (Frenk, et al., 2010, pp. 1949, 1952) and performance impacts. A useful approach to evaluating TC training and education in contexts of displacement by climate change or conflict initially centers on preparatory training, enhancement of individual human capabilities, addressing challenges, and problem-solving.

Preparatory learning should be skill-based and informed by relevant experience. Evaluations begin by exploring the process utilized. Did a broad range of stakeholders, along with transnationally competent educators, trainees, and experienced practitioners, participate in developing and refining training objectives and approaches (Guerra, et al., 2018, p. 1676; da Silva, et al., 2018, p. 8)? Among other advantages, external stakeholder input provides "a means of validating the relevance of competencies and ensuring key domains are not neglected" (Gruppen, Mangrulkar, and Kolars, 2012, p. 45).

Other process-focused inquiries shed further light on the outcome of preparatory learning. Behavioral change can be influenced through various "levers" (Metternicht, Carr, and Stafford-Smith, 2020) and the evaluation should assess how these have been utilized in the program. Did TC training/education incorporate case studies, role-playing exercises (Guerra, et al., 2018, p. 1679), and draw on the other recommended approaches and methods identified in Chapters 5 and 6? Was the training program infused with experiential challenges set in transnational contexts? Did TC training include relevant field or distance-learning experiences under mentors from multiple (including resource-poor) countries and professional backgrounds? To what extent did instructor assessments of student TC development address transnational mobility insights and contributions?

Evaluating the content of training programs also is important. Did transdisciplinary interaction and integration occur (ibid., p. 1678)? Did assigned resources, instruction, and mentoring emphasize upstream influences and social determinants? Did training include preparation for peace-through-health advocacy work? Did training aim to provide social justice skills at the micro and macro levels?

The crux of transnational competency evaluation in displaced contexts is based on outcomes and impacts. Both responder-centered and affected person-centered training (see Jogerst, et al., 2015, p. 242) require review. For responders, evaluators distinguish levels of skill attainment: learn, practice, and demonstrate (Desha and Hargroves, 2014, p. 143). Eliciting the perceptions of targeted trainees should be incorporated as a core component of practitioner TC competency evaluations. Multisource feedback, especially from stakeholders, promotes comprehensive-skill assessment and enables the prepared professional trainee to grasp "both his or her personal strengths and areas in need of development" (Shuman, Besterfield-Sacre, and McGourty, 2005, p. 50).

Training outcome evaluations are concerned with individual human capabilities; they explore the presence or absence of growth across all five TC dimensions (see Koehn and Uitto, 2017, pp. 139–143). The outcome emphasis is on evidence of "behavioral additionality" (Ravetz, 2007, p. 83) and regarding which TC components prove to be more or less valuable.

Competencies developed or diminished after graduation or completion of a specific training program should be documented over the long term through follow-up studies. A 360-degree evaluation approach "is widely recognized as a quality improvement method … able to assess multiple aspects of competence" (Maki, et al., 2008).

Individual learning outcomes also can be measured usefully in relation to asset-building as reflected in "health, family life and social capital" (Schuller, Hammond, and Preston, 2004, p. 12). How did TC education and experiential learning impact the life trajectory of humanitarian-aid workers and persons affected by climate and conflict displacement (Sykes, 2014, p. e44)?

Impact evaluations center on demonstrated trainee contributions. Graduates are expected to demonstrate individual and transdisciplinary team achievements across all five transnational-competency domains, and when confronted by varying migration circumstances.[5] Evaluators are interested in whether practitioners working in transnational displacement contexts serve as change agents; i.e., "actually do exercise their professional capabilities in ways that further social transformation" (Walker, et al., 2009, p. 568; also Frenk, et al., 2010, p. 1952) rather than perpetuate or exacerbate inequities (Schuller and Desjardins, 2007, pp. 59, 114). Have individual learning assets been used to generate "social outcomes that benefit others and future generations" (McMahon, 2009, p. 5, 38)? Have TC-prepared professionals and aid receivers demonstrated sound ethical reasoning and responsibility (Cole, et al., 2013, p. 156)? Did TC eLearning contribute to the beneficial impact of humanitarian practice (Teitelbaum, 2019)? What impact shortfalls can be identified?

To facilitate meaningful impact evaluation, evaluators establish observable and measurable standards of activity and task performance that are representative of the desired transnational competencies along with explicit criteria for measuring the extent to which objectives have been attained. Bearing in mind that trainees are the experts in judging and identifying how TC training has affected their lives, evaluators can secure revealing participant reflections on the personal and professional impact of TC training through application of the "most significant change" technique (see Davies and Dart, 2005).[6] Collecting "most significant change stories" (Brundiers, et al., 2014, pp. 220–221) and critical incident debriefings (Cole, et al., 2013, p. 157) can offer particularly revealing means of identifying impacts. Identifying learning impacts "requires not just the assessment of the learner, but a holistic approach that attempts to assess the various actors and entities in the ecosystem in which the learned is situated" (Teitelbaum, 2019).

Another methodology to determine the impact of an activity is contribution analysis, a theory-based approach to assess causality and attribution in the real-world context. According to contribution analysis, a reasonable contribution story can be claimed through: (1) providing a well-articulated presentation of the context, aims, and strategies of the intervention; (2) presenting a plausible theory of change leading to the articulated aims; (3) describing the activities and outputs produced; (4) indicating the association between the intervention actions and results through contribution analysis; and (5) pointing out that alternative explanations for the outcomes have been ruled out or have limited influence (Mayne, 2001, pp. 21–22).[7]

For Amartya Sen (e.g., Sen, 1999), life improvements are about expanding a person's functionings and capabilities – things they are able to "do" and "be" – and their set of available options. In what ways did TC preparation enhance individual and community functioning? Is there evidence that TC training/education contributed to advances or setbacks in human well-being? Did work with displaced migrants and other affected persons relieve distress, demoralization, and stigma (Becker, et al., 2013, p. 242)?

Impact evaluations aim to generate insights regarding ways to reduce vulnerability among men, women, and children on the move due to climate change and conflict displacement (McMichael, Barnett, and McMichael, 2012, p. 652). Individual well-being and social impacts – including the creation of employment opportunities (Tarabini, 2010, p. 209), the reduction of poverty and inequality (Singh, 2007, p. 76; Bailey, 2010, p. 44), and contributions to the strengthening of civil society (Schuller and Desjardins, 2007, pp. 68, 88; McMahon, 2009, p. 34) – should be addressed. Impact evaluations often are best served by targeting specific aspects of well-being, belonging, and sustainable development that are perceived to qualify as successful and unsuccessful on a small and local, national, or transnational scale and, then, identifying "why" (Smith, 2000, p. 217). In addition, evaluators should allow for serendipity of outcomes and catalytic impacts and be alert to unexpected impacts and spin-offs, both positive and negative. To what extent were any shortcomings identified and reported by evaluators rectified by participants?

Another key question pertains to the sustainability of impact. Evidence from the field shows a number of key factors that influence post-completion sustainability, including broad stakeholder buy-in, political support, and continued availability of needed financing (Negi and Watts-Sohn, 2022, pp. 51–53). Have stakeholders permanently adopted TC training innovations? Do project benefits (intended and unintended, tangible and intangible, wanted and unwanted) continue to outweigh the costs and difficulties of interacting and coordinating for participants? Have local participants taken over responsibility for making key project decisions, adapting, and innovating (Bates, et al., 2011)? Is there evidence of community-based ownership that has increased the likelihood of self-generated stakeholder initiatives and replications? Are additional players (NGOs, governments, for-profit firms, community members) committed to maintaining key TC training activities? Has long-term funding for core TC development been secured (ibid.)?

Framework for Practical Evaluations Encompassing TC Development

Focusing on a limited number of agreed-upon pre-identified core criteria and adoption of a pre-analysis plan enables time-constrained evaluators to complete a meaningful assessment with modest resources and to avoid selective data mining. TC evaluators understand that context matters and that flexibility will be necessary. The contextual nature of TC development evaluations requires that trainers/educators, other stakeholders, and participants identify their most critical shared process, outcome, and impact objectives (Gibson, 2005, p. 84). To promote rough consistency in approach, internal and external evaluators choose and adapt relevant questions from those provided in the generic evaluation framework provided here, identify issues for in-depth attention, and concentrate on progress or setbacks. Applying contextually based core questions will facilitate a series of partial cross-context parameter comparisons (Razak, et al., 2013, p. 153) and generate insights and supplemental guidance for reaching compromises, determining tradeoffs (Gibson, 2005, pp. 93, 177–178), and identifying promising pathways to TC development that can be more widely adapted in situations where conditions and challenges are similar.

The illustrative schema presented here can be used as guidelines or as a checklist when conducting an evaluation. The questions require probing responses and detailed behavioral descriptions rather than simple "yes or no" answers (Darla Deardorf, cited in Colvin and Edwards, 2018, p. 18). At times, evaluators will encounter incomplete information and be unable to determine positive or negative effects (see Gibson, 2005, p. 119). Evaluators are encouraged to focus on initiatives or combinations of undertakings that trainers designate as most important and that scoping suggests involve the greatest potential for major gains or serious losses in individual, social, and environmental well-being (ibid., pp. 146, 152–154). Actual applications might engage different core questions, further narrow inquiries found in the menu presented here, and tailor evaluation probes and methods to fit unique contextual conditions. In common, however, will be focus on a short list of key questions regarding process, outcome, capacity, impact, and evaluation along with care and rigor in executing integrated evaluations that can still encompass new and expanded objectives and criteria (ibid., pp. 93, 115).

Process Questions: Design and Implementation of Training/Education Interventions

The process dimension of the suggested evaluation framework is concerned with the conduct of training interventions. In TC development evaluations, evaluators focus on determining how process is linked to competency outcomes and impact additionalities. Process evaluations should encompass the three life-course phases of training undertakings: planning, implementing, and sustaining. Key questions in this connection are contained in Box 7.2.

Box 7.2 Illustrative Core Questions for Evaluating TC Development Processes

- Did collaborating actors and key stakeholders conduct a needs assessment that included identifying participant vulnerabilities, assets, and resilience and linking stakeholder objectives with specific evaluation criteria?
- Did training implementers utilize theory-of-change methodology from the start?
- To what extent did community members, stakeholders, practitioners, and policy makers participate in defining and refining the principal evaluation questions and initiating and designing the research process? Did periodic multi-stakeholder meetings occur where participants clarified roles and contributions and agreed on interventions and revisions? Did training beneficiaries participate in the planning, implementation, and maintenance, and capability-building phases (Oakley, 1991, pp. 253–254) of the TC evaluation?
- How broad and diverse was the configuration of stakeholder participation in the selected TC development challenge? To what extent were stakeholders involved in all stages of the TC development undertaking? How deep was the actual level of each stakeholder's involvement in goal setting and in curriculum, training methods, and outreach activities? Did stakeholders report that they "had been appropriately included in the process, adequately informed, and prepared for decision making" (Brundiers and Wiek, 2011, p. 116)?
- To what extent were budgets equitably distributed among trainers, stakeholders, and transnational partners according to agreed-upon responsibilities?
- Were trainers at the "prepare," "explore," "test and pilot," and/or "integrate and implement learning pathways" stage?
- Did trainers do "all the things that are necessary and feasible to maximize the likelihood" that the intended outcomes would be realized; i.e., performance appraisal (Norgbey and Spilsbury, 2014, pp. 142–143; also Oakley, 1991, p. 264)?
- Were all five components of TC preparation adequately addressed during the training/education and evaluation processes?
- To what extent were the teaching content, training methods, and community engagement components integrated?
- Was the TC curriculum transformative (aimed to change participants' long-term behavior) rather than only transmissive (knowledge-imparting) (Trad, 2019, p. 289; Ssosse, Wagner, and Hopper, 2021, p. 13)?
- To what extent were TC development interventions primarily outcome- and impact-driven rather than activity- or output-driven?
- To what extent have training program participants collaborated with stakeholders in addressing sustainable development challenges?

- Were positive/negative and unintended/unanticipated consequences plausibly connected to the TC development initiatives included in stakeholder evaluations?
- Did evaluators explore differences in impacts and trajectories plausibly associated with those exposed to TC training and those initially similar who did not receive any TC training; i.e., engage in pre- and post-test "counterfactual analysis" (see Ssosse, Wagner, and Hopper, 2021, pp. 7, 9–11)?
- Did a guiding coalition of TC transformation advocates "ensure that direction and momentum were sustained" (de la Harpe and Thomas, 2009, p. 82)?
- Did project directors resist imposing burdensome administrative procedures so that all participants were able to focus on the principal objectives of the TC development initiative?
- Did the humanitarian responders provide training support to local public agencies, NGOs, community groups, and private firms?
- To what extent have disseminated research findings been utilized by stakeholders to refine TC training for displaced populations and enhance sustainable development?
- Did the process result in continuing "experimentation for learning and adjustment" (Gibson, 2005, p. 84)?

Outcome Questions

We now turn to a practical set of questions that facilitate assessment of TC operationalization outcomes. Box 7.3 presents an illustrative list of queries that lend themselves to meaningful and manageable TC development contribution analysis and learning outcome evaluations.

Box 7.3 Illustrative Core Questions for Evaluating the Outcomes of TC Capability-building Contributions

- To what extent did the TC training components convey glocal connectivity among social, economic, and environmental drivers and barriers (Martin, et al., 2021, pp. 145–146; Uitto, 2021, pp. 447–448)?
- To what extent did trainers and encountered support personnel (on the latter, see Chen, 2011) develop transnationally useful analytic, emotional, creative, communicative, and functional competencies (refer to Chapter 5)? Each TC learning dimension can be explored through participant inter-subjective interviewing (see Koehn, 2006, especially pp. 139–140), including self-evaluations (Rishko-Porcescu, 2018, p. 311), and scored using a Likert scale (Pechak, Howe, Padilla, and Frietze,

2020, p. e133) or according to the following rating scheme (Todd and Craig, 2014, pp. 67–68): 0 (not achieved); 1 (poorly achieved); 2 (partially achieved); 4 (fully achieved).[8]

- To what extent did trainees develop transnationally useful analytic, emotional, creative, communicative, and functional competencies (refer to Chapter 6)? Each TC dimension can be explored through participant inter-subjective interviewing (see Koehn, 2005), including self-evaluations (Rishko-Porcescu, 2018, p. 311), and scored according to the following rating scheme (Todd and Craig, 2014, pp. 67–68): 0 (not achieved); 1 (poorly achieved); 2 (partially achieved); 4 (fully achieved).
- Did trainers and trainees develop life-long and life-wide learning capability (Trad, 2019, p. 294)?
- To what extent did trainees develop competency in sustainable development?
- What behavioral demonstrations of each domain of transnational competence can be identified? Which TC skills are associated with desired impacts in which contexts? In such assessments, use collaboratively developed and cross-culturally reviewed measures of transnational performance (Murdoch-Eaton, Redmond, and Bax, 2011, p. 566).
- Did enhanced local capabilities include Indigenous knowledge and insights?
- Did capability strengthening emphasize "in-depth understanding of the local context" and linkage with domestic and transnational priorities?
- What evidence is there that the TC training initiative enhanced innovative capabilities?
- Did TC training build on and strengthen local capabilities in ways that were linked to national, regional, and local development policy priorities?
- Did the TC training intervention enable trainees to become "agents of change capable of dealing with systemic, ambiguous, uncertain, changing problems" and to become transition managers and leaders (Ssosse, Wagner, and Hopper, 2021, p. 13)?
- How do trainees/graduates rate the capability-strengthening contributions of the TC training/education program?
- Have trainers and involved stakeholders built capabilities to respond to emerging displacement situations?
- Is there evidence of improvement in the training methods employed?
- How often are TC-prepared humanitarian responders called upon by external agencies and displaced communities for training programs?

Impact Questions

Box 7.4 presents an illustrative list of common queries that lend themselves to meaningful and manageable evaluations of the impact of the contribution of TC. These core questions address both immediate and long-term contributions and "making a difference" impacts (Uitto, 2021, p. 446). Additional in-depth and ongoing longitudinal impact inquiries attend to complex issues, especially converging, cumulative, mutually reinforcing, and synergizing (Norgbey and Spilsbury, 2014, p. 145) effects and compounding factors, *with a dose of humility* (Gibson, 2005, pp. 16, 32–33; Ssosse, Wagner, and Hopper, 2021, p. 21).

Box 7.4 Illustrative Core Questions for Evaluating the Impacts of TC Capability-building Contributions

- How have program graduates and trainees exercised (or not exercised) professional capabilities and transnational competence in ways that further well-being, social capital expansion (Wells, et al., 2018, p. 11), adaptation and belonging, and sustainable development in economic, psychosocial, and/or ecological[9] arenas among populations affected by climate and conflict displacement?
- Have program graduates and trainees exercised (or not exercised) professional capabilities and transnational competence in ways that restore, maintain, or improve living conditions and avoid exclusion for relocated persons and hosts (White House, 2021, p. 24)?
- Were the action contributions of TC-prepared graduates and trainees enhanced over time by the multiplier effect?
- To what extent did the TC training initiative enhance sustainable development practice at one or more of the following levels of activity: improved individual-practitioner decision making when confronted by practical and contextual challenges; improved group-level collaboration on a shared challenge; improved community-level response to a specific small-scale economic, social, or ecological challenge; improved national and/or transnational response to a sustainable development challenge with cross-boundary effects?
- Is there evidence of increases in sustainable social, economic, and ecological innovations that can plausibly be attributed to the TC training/education initiative?
- Is there evidence that the TC training/education initiative plausibly contributed to reductions or increases in local social and economic inequality?
- Is there evidence that the TC training/education initiative plausibly contributed to advances or setbacks in human well-being?
- Is there evidence that the TC training/education initiative plausibly contributed to participant resilience?
- Is there evidence that the TC training/education initiative plausibly contributed to improved relations among displaced groups and between displaced populations and host communities?

- How did exogenous pressures, opportunities, and facilitating and constraining factors influence local impacts (Gibson, 2005, p. 85)?
- What tradeoffs did the TC training/education initiative catalyze among economic, ecological, and social aspirations, between immediate and long-term benefits, and among beneficiaries (ibid., p. 85)?
- What intended and unintended impact contributions are revealed by the chain of impact?
- What evidence is there that policy makers have recognized the social and economic contributions and well-being benefits of the TC training/education initiative and resulting outreach activities?
- Is there evidence of scaling up the TC training initiation to reach more dislocated and other affected populations and through replication?
- Did individual and community well-being, sustainable development, and belonging impacts continue beyond the termination of external involvement by humanitarian responders?
- Are other stakeholders (NGOs, governments, for-profit firms, community members) committed to maintaining key project activities?
- Is there evidence that community-based ownership has increased the likelihood of stakeholder self-generated initiatives and replications?

Evaluation Questions

The often-overlooked capability to monitor and evaluate the evaluation process itself (Stevens, 2012, p. 62) and ensure its validity and reliability constitutes the final component of a comprehensive TC evaluation framework. Training in meta-evaluation, that is, how to conduct "an evaluation of an evaluation, as a critical assessment of the strengths and weaknesses of an evaluation" (Ramos and Pires, 2013, p. 87) is vital in this connection and should be included in trainer TC preparation. Early training in data processing and analytic support (Poister, Aristigueta, and Hall, 2015, p. 420) also will be needed in some situations.

Frequently, a multiplicity of donors, partners, and stakeholders with diverse evaluation mandates and evaluation capacities will be involved. Evaluators need to be adept at multiple and multidisciplinary methodologies so that they will be able to select and apply the approaches and methods that are most suitable for the evaluation questions that require answering (Uitto, 2021, pp. 446–447).[10]

Stakeholders in TC evaluations include community members in areas where TC training programs operate – both the intended beneficiaries of such programs as well as people otherwise affected because of their physical location or their position in society. Although stakeholder skills form an important aspect of capacity to conduct an impact evaluation, they can by no means be taken as given. Indeed, skill deficiencies constitute one of the principal constraints on stakeholder involvement in participatory monitoring and evaluation (M&E). It is particularly important, therefore, that training and education programs incorporate the development by program participants (as well as affected non-participants) of capabilities to evaluate how the TC intervention is affecting their lives and well-being. Following the principle of learning by doing, engaging in the practice of participatory TC evaluation offers "an indirect approach to evaluation capacity building" (Chouinard and Cousins, 2013, pp. 67, 72–73; also Anderson and Woodrow, 1998, p. 94). When trainees and other persons affected by displacement by conflict and climate change are active in evaluating outcomes and impacts, the "process, itself, becomes developmental" (Anderson and Woodrow, 1998, p. 93). Thus, the overall capability-building question to ask is: did the project leaders train stakeholders in collaborative and participatory evaluation practices and, if not, why not?

Here, we offer a further set of illustrative core questions concerning the evaluation process that lend themselves to practical application. Box 7.5 sets forth these questions.

Box 7.5 Illustrative Core Questions for Assessing Evaluation Processes

- Did evaluators utilize appropriate methods to validate TC learning outcomes/non-outcomes and to assess TC behavioral performance/non-performance (Karam, Monaghan, and Yoder, 2017, pp. 455–456; Wells, et al., 2018, pp. 10–11)?
- Did the evaluation explore "competing options for positive action" (Gibson, 2005, p. 84)?
- Did the evaluation consider alternative futures (ibid., p. 84)?
- Did evaluators explore mutually reinforcing contributions as well as "avoidance or mitigation of negative effects" (ibid., p. 146)?
- Did the project leaders train stakeholders in collaborative-evaluation practices?
- Did project leaders involve young and emerging multinational evaluators and provide supportive mentoring, webinars, and on-line capability-building workshops (Rishko-Porcescu, 2018, pp. 308–311)?
- Did the evaluation process emphasize "open discussion and participative engagement of local residents" (Gibson, 2005, p. 84)?
- How did evaluators overcome the "lack of data on all dimensions of sustainability" that prevails in refugee camps (Karl and Karl, 2022, p. 395)?
- Did external evaluators possess the ability to understand local conditions and to link them to the bigger context?
- Did training participants join in the analysis of evaluation data, deciding how results will be used, and reporting and presenting findings (Oakley, 1991, p. 266)?

- What internal and independent external evaluation processes have been put in place that utilize multiple-assessment methods to probe the sustainable capacity of educators, trainers, trainees, and communities to develop themselves?
- Were findings reported in a timely and concise manner of strategic value to decision makers at all levels?
- Are procedures in place that ensure that evaluation findings and recommendations reach intended users?

The ability to utilize evaluation results is critically important (Brundiers, et al., 2014, p. 203). Too many evaluation reports gather dust in archives or on bookshelves without having made an outcome or impact contribution. Attention needs to be devoted to secure storage arrangements, notification of report availability, and procedures that ensure ready access. Even if reports reach their target audiences, it is not a given that they will be perused, understood, and acted upon. Thus, there is a need to provide time and training on how to interpret and utilize (performance) evaluation data (Newcomer, El Baradei, and Garcia, 2013, p. 74). In terms of capacity for use, commissioning/management, and conduct of evaluations, field situations call for coordination and harmonization of expectations from a diverse range of external and internal evaluations. Frequently, there also is a need to work on how to counter inertia and resistance to change so that participants in TC development initiatives understand how evaluations catalyze opportunities to improve the performance and impact of the evaluand (i.e., the object of the evaluation). There also is a need to sensitize evaluation users – including funders, evaluation commissioners, and decision makers – regarding the need for evaluations to be open to side effects and unintended consequences that were not identified in the intervention theory of change and design.

Concluding Observations

In this chapter, we have made a case for enhanced evaluation capabilities and usage across the board for TC development evaluations; our recommendations range from generating demand for evaluation, to employing and managing evaluations, to enhanced TC evaluation utilization. Humanitarian organizations often employ independent evaluation systems either by hiring private consulting firms or by using their own internal independent evaluation units (where such exist). Such independent evaluations typically emphasize accountability for the proper (cost-benefit) use of funds, efficiency, and the effectiveness of the intervention, with some concern for learning lessons for the future. We draw attention to participatory evaluation that emphasizes downward accountability to the intended beneficiaries and affected people. The commissioners of independent evaluations should understand that accountability, effectiveness, and efficiency must be seen in the context of whether the TC training initiatives benefit vulnerable people and lead to desired behavioral changes[11] rather than only attempting to analyze how much activity was generated or output was produced per dollar invested. In short, TC evaluations can be "made accountable to project participants without 'sacrificing' reasonable reporting to donors, governments, and the general public" (Anderson and Woodrow, 1998, p. 93).

Evaluation can contribute to transformational change by identifying promising approaches and successful initiatives as well as by shedding light on any needed tradeoffs (Uitto, 2021, p. 445). Wide adoption of the principal components of TC training and education elaborated in this book depends upon collaborative and credible evaluations of outcomes and impacts. In order that critical lessons regarding migration and displacement are learned from and improved upon, quality outcome and impact evaluations should be "universally included" in training/education, partnership, and project activities (Sykes, 2014, pp. e45–e46). The comprehensive guidelines for evaluating illustrated in this chapter offer a practical foundation to build upon in the interest of conducting meaningful evaluations in circumstances of conflict and climate change dislocation that focus on training initiatives and move beyond outputs.

Notes

1 www.alnap.org
2 https://www.environmentalpeacebuilding.org/
3 Most of these questions are adapted from Todd and Craig (2014, pp. 66, 84).
4 Outputs relate to the extent (amount, volume) of completion of the goals that actors set for themselves (Poister, Aristigueta, and Hall, 2015, p. 58). Outputs are the type of results over which program and project managers can exert the most influence. However, the generation of outputs provides "no guarantee that outcomes will result" (ibid., p. 58) and exclusive reliance on output evaluations, the "default approach," "precludes the ability to measure efficacy of interventions performed" (Sykes, 2014, p. e44).
5 On specific demonstrations of "operational" global health transnational competencies, see Jogerst, et al. (2015, pp. 243–245).
6 Also see https://www.te.columbia.edu/refugeeeducation/projects/teachers-for-teachers/training/
7 Further elaborating on the approach, Mayne (2011, pp. 62–87) outlines seven steps for conducting a contribution analysis.
8 Decisions regarding the most insightful methods of inquiry, "such as analysis of programme records or use of a questionnaire, will also be influenced by the capabilities of the people involved, and by how much time and how many resources are available for evaluation" (Oakley, 1991, p. 265).
9 The CARE International and UNHCR Framework for Assessing, Monitoring, and Evaluating the Environment in Refugee-related Operations (FRAME) (Karl and Karl, 2022, p. 389) can be a useful tool for assessing, monitoring, and evaluating the local impact of humanitarian-responder TC training. Indigenous evaluation (Mustonen and Feodoroff, 2018, pp. 112, 115–116) also can be incorporated in certain situations.

10 Situations where choice of evaluation approach is influenced by the familiarity of a specific methodology by the evaluators – or by a perception by the evaluation commissioner of what is a reliable or "scientific" method – should be avoided as inappropriate methods may skew the results. In general, there is no single approach or method that is superior in evaluation; a mix of both qualitative and quantitative methods can be used to explore different aspects of the evaluand.

11 That is, "what works and in what circumstances" (Uitto, 2014, p. 4).

References

Anderson, Mary B.; and Woodrow, Peter J. 1998. *Rising from the Ashes: Development Strategies in Times of Disaster*. Boulder, CO: Lynne Rienner.

Baarnhielm, Sofie; Laban, Kees; Schouler-Ocak, Meryam; Rousseau, Cecile; and Kirmayer, Laurence J. 2017. "Mental Health for Refugees, Asylum Seekers and Displaced Persons: A Call for a Humanitarian Agenda." *Transcultural Psychiatry* 54 (5–6): 565–574.

Bailey, Tracy. 2010. "The Research-Policy Nexus: Mapping the Terrain of the Literature." Paper prepared for the Higher Education Research and Advocacy Network in Africa (HERANA). Wynberg, UK: Centre for Higher Education Transformation.

Bates, Imelda; Taegtmeyer, Miriam; Squire, S. Bertel; Ansong, Daniel; Nhlema-Simwaka, Bertha; Baba, Amuda; and Theobald, Sally. 2011. "Indicators of Sustainable Capacity Building for Health Research: Analysis of Four African Case Studies." *Health Research Policy and Systems* 9: 14.

Becker, Anne; Motgi, Anjali; Weigel, Jonathan; Raviola, Giuseppe; Keshavjee, Salmaan; and Kleinman, Arthur. 2013. "The Unique Challenges of Mental Health and MDRTB." In *Reimagining Global Health: An Introduction*, edited by Paul Farmer; Jim Yong Kim; Arthur Kleinman; and Matthew Basilico. Berkeley, CA: University of California Press, pp. 212–244.

Brookings Institution, Georgetown University's School of Foreign Service, and UNHCR. 2015. *Guidance on Protecting People from Disasters and Environmental Change through Planned Relocation*. Washington, D.C.: Brookings Institution.

Brundiers, Katja; Savage, Emma; Mannell, Steven; Lang, Daniel J.; and Wiek, Arnim. 2014. "Educating Sustainability Change Agents by Design: Appraisals of the Transformative Role of Higher Education." In *Sustainable Development and Quality Assurance in Higher Education: Transformation of Learning and Society*, edited by Zinaida Fadeeva; Laima Galkute; Clemens Mader; and Geoff Scott. New York: Palgrave Macmillan, pp. 196–229.

Brundiers, Katja; and Wiek, Arnim. 2011. "Educating Students in Real-world Sustainability Research: Vision and Implementation." *Innovative Higher Education* 36: 107–124.

Chambers, Robert. 1994. "The Origins and Practice of Participatory Rural Appraisal." *World Development* 22 (7): 953–969.

Chen, Pauline W. 2011. "Doctor and Patient: Unsung Heroes at the Front Lines of Patient Care." *New York Times*, July 5, p. D5.

Chouinard, Jill A.; and Cousins, J. Bradley. 2013. "Participatory Evaluation for Development: Examining Research-Based Knowledge from Within the African Context." *African Evaluation Journal* 1 (1): 66–74.

Cole, Donald C.; Hanson, Lori; Rouleau, Katherine D.; Pottie, Kevin; and Arya, Neil. 2013. "Teaching Global Ethics." In *An Introduction to Global Health Ethics*, edited by Andrew D. Pinto and Ross E.G. Upshur. London: Routledge, pp. 148–158.

Colvin, Richard L.; and Edwards, Virginia. 2018. *Teaching for Global Competence in a Rapidly Changing World*. Paris: OECD. New York: Asia Society.

da Silva, AnnorJr; Martins-Silva, Priscilla; Vasconcelos, Katia; da Silva, Vitor; de Melo, Mariana; and Dumer, Miguel. 2018. "Sustainability Indicators for the Management of Brazilian Higher Education Institutions." *Brazilian Administration Review* 15 (3): 1–20.

Davies, Rick. 2013. "Planning Evaluability Assessments: A Synthesis of the Literature with Recommendations." Working Paper No. 40. London: Department for International Development.

Davies, Rick; and Dart, Jess. 2005. "The 'Most Significant Change' (MSC) Technique: A Guide to Its Use." London: Care International. Available at: http://www.mande.co.uk/docs/MSCGuide.pdf

de la Harpe, Barbara; and Thomas, Ian. 2009. "Curriculum Change in Universities: Conditions that Facilitate Education for Sustainable Development ." *Journal of Education for Sustainable Development* 3 (1): 75–85.

Desha, Cheryl; and Hargroves, Karlson C. 2014. *Higher Education and Sustainable Development: A Model for Curriculum Renewal*. London: Routledge.

Frenk, Julio; Chen, Lincoln; Bhutta, Zulfiqar A.; Cohen, Jordan; Crisp, Nigel; Evans, Timothy; Fineberg, Harvey; Garcia, Patricia; Ke, Yang; Kelley, Patrick; … and Zurayk, Huda. 2010. "Health Professionals for a New Century: Transforming Education to Strengthen Health Systems in an Interdependent World." *Lancet* 376 (December 4): 1923–1958.

Gibson, Robert B. 2005. *Sustainability Assessment: Criteria and Processes*. London: Earthscan.

Gruppen, Larry D.; Mangrulkar, Rajesh; and Kolars, Joseph C. 2012. "The Promise of Competence-based Education in the Health Professions for Improving Global Health." *Human Resources for Health* 10: 43–48.

Guerra, Jose B; Garcia, Jessica; Lima, Maurico; Barbosa, Samuel B; Heerdt, Mauri L; and Berchin, Issa I. 2018. "A Proposal of a Balanced Scorecard for an Environmental Education Program at Universities." *Journal of Cleaner Production* 172: 1674–1690.

Hammick, Marilyn; and Anderson, Elizabeth. 2009. "Sustaining Interprofessional Education in Professional Award Programmes." In *Interprofessional Education: Making It Happen*, edited by Patricia Bluteau and Ann Jackson. New York: Palgrave Macmillan, pp. 202–226.

Hollenbeck, George P.; McCall, Morgan W. Jr.; and Silzer, Robert F. 2006. "Leadership Competency Models." *Leadership Quarterly* 17: 398–413.

Jogerst, Kristen; Callender, Brian; Adams, Virginia; Evert, Jessica; Fields, Elise; Hall, Thomas; Olsen, Jody; Rowthorn, Virginia; Rudy, Sharon; Shen, Jiabin; … and Wilson, Lynda L. 2015. "Identifying Interprofessional Global Health Competencies for 21st-Century Health Professionals." *Annals of Global Health* 81 (2): 239–248.

Karam, Fares J.; Monaghan, Christine; and Yoder, Paul J. 2017. "'The Students Do Not Know Why They Are Here': Education Decision-Making for Syrian Refugees." *Globalisation, Societies and Education* 15 (4): 448–463.

Karl, Alexandre A.; and Karl, Julia S. 2022. "Human Rights for Refugees: Enhancing Sustainable Supply Chain to Guarantee a Health Environment in Refugee Settlements." *Journal of Humanitarian Logistics and Supply Chain Management* 12 (3): 382–403.

Koehn, Peter H. 2005. "Medical Encounters in Finnish Reception Centres: Asylum-Seeker and Clinician Perspectives." *Journal of Refugee Studies* 18 (1): 47–75.

Koehn, Peter H. 2006. "Health-Care Outcomes in Ethnoculturally Discordant Medical Encounters: The Role of Physician Transnational Competence in Consultations with Asylum Seekers." *Journal of Immigrant and Minority Health* 8 (2): 137–147.

Koehn, Peter H.; and Uitto, Juha I. 2017. *Universities and the Sustainable Development Future: Evaluating Higher-Education Contributions to the 2030 Agenda.* London: Routledge.

Maki, Jesse; Qualls, Munirih; White, Benjamin; Kleefield, Sharon; and Crone, Robert. 2008. "Health Impact Assessment and Short-Term Medical Missions: A Methods Study to Evaluate Quality of Care." *BMC Health Services Research* 8 (2).

Martin, Susan F.; Bergmann, Jonas; Rigaud, Kanta; and Yameogo, Nadege D. 2021. "Climate Change, Human Mobility, and Development." *Migration Studies* 9 (1): 142–149.

Mayne, John. 2001. "Addressing Attribution through Contribution Analysis: Using Performance Measures Sensibly." *Canadian Journal of Program Evaluation* 16 (1): 1–24.

Mayne, John. 2011. "Contribution Analysis: Addressing Cause and Effect." In *Evaluating the Complex: Attribution, Contribution, and Beyond,* edited by Kim Forss; Mita Marra; and Robert Schwartz. New Brunswick, NJ: Transaction Publishers, pp. 53–95.

McMahon, Walter W. 2009. *Higher Learning, Greater Good: The Private and Social Benefits of Higher Education.* Baltimore, MD: Johns Hopkins University Press.

McMichael, Anthony J. 2013. "Globalization, Climate Change, and Human Health." *New England Journal of Medicine* 368: 1335–1343.

McMichael, Celia; Barnett, Jon; and McMichael, Anthony J. 2012. "An Ill Wind? Climate Change, Migration, and Health." *Environmental Health Perspectives* 120 (5): 646–654.

Metternicht, Graciela; Carr, Edward R.; and Stafford-Smith, Mark. 2020. *Why Behavioral Change Matters to the GEF and What to Do About It?* Washington, D.C.: Scientific and Technical Advisory Panel of the Global Environment Facility.

Morra-Imas, Linda G.; and Rist, Ray C. 2009. *The Road to Results: Designing and Conducting Effective Development Evaluations.* Washington, D.C.: The World Bank.

Murdoch-Eaton, Deborah; Redmond, Anthony; and Bax, Nigel. 2011. "Training Healthcare Professionals for the Future: Internationalism and Effective Inclusion of Global Health Training." *Medical Teacher* 33: 562–569.

Mustonen, Tero; and Feodoroff, Pauliina. 2018. "Skolt Sami and Atlantic Salmon Collaborative Management of Naatamo Watershed, Finland as a Case of Indigenous Evaluation and Knowledge in the Eurasian Artic." In *Indigenous Evaluation: New Directions for Evaluation, 159,* edited by F. Cram; K.A. Tibbets; and J. LaFrance. Wiley Online Library.

Negi, Neeraj K.; and Watts-Sohn, Molly. 2022. "Sustainability after Project Completion: Evidence from the GEF." In *Transformational Change for People and the Planet: Evaluating Environment and Development,* edited by Juha I. Uitto and Geeta Batra. Cham, Switzerland: Springer, pp. 43–57.

Newcomer, Kathryn; El Baradei, Laila; and Garcia, Sandra. 2013. "Expectations and Capacity of Performance Measurement in NGOs in the Development Context." *Public Administration and Development* 33: 62–79.

Norgbey, Segbedzi; and Spilsbury, Michael. 2014. "A Programme Theory Approach to Evaluating Normative Environmental Interventions." In *Evaluating Environment in International Development,* edited by Juha I. Uitto. London: Routledge, pp. 123–147.

Oakley, Peter. 1991. *Projects with People: The Practice of Participation in Rural Development*. Geneva: International Labour Office.

OECD. 2021. *Applying Evaluation Criteria Thoughtfully*. Paris: OECD.

Patton, Michael Q. 2002. *Qualitative Research and Evaluation Methods*, 3rd edition. Thousand Oaks, CA: Sage.

Patton, Michael Q. 2008. *Utilization-Focused Evaluation*, 4th edition. Thousand Oaks, CA: Sage.

Pechak, Celia; Howe, Vicki; Padilla, Margie; and Frietze, Gabriel A. 2020. "Preparing Students to Serve a Refugee Population through a Health-Focused Interprofessional Education Experience ." *Journal of Applied Health* 49 (3): e131–e138.

Poister, Theodore H.; Aristigueta, Maria P.; and Hall, Jeremy L. 2015. *Managing and Measuring Performance in Public and Nonprofit Organizations: An Integrated Approach*, 2nd edition. San Francisco, CA: Jossey-Bass.

Ramos, Tomas; and Pires, Sara M. 2013. "Sustainability Assessment: The Role of Indicators." In *Sustainability Assessment Tools in Higher Education Institutions: Mapping Trends and Good Practices Around the World*, edited by Sandra Caeiro; Walter L. Filho; Charbel Jabbour; and Ulisses M. Azeiteiro. Cham, Switzerland: Springer International Publishing, pp. 81–99.

Ravetz, Joe. 2007. "The Role of Evaluation in Regional Sustainable Development." In *Impact Assessment and Sustainable Development: European Practice and Experience*, edited by Clive George and Colin Kirkpatrick. Cheltenham: Edward Elgar, pp. 65–89.

Razak, Dzulkifli A.; Sanusi, Zainal A.; Jegatesen, Govindran; and Khelghat-Doost, Hamoon. 2013. "Alternative University Appraisal (AUA): Reconstructing Universities' Ranking and Rating toward a Sustainable Future." In *Sustainability Assessment Tools in Higher Education Institutions: Mapping Trends and Good Practices Around the World*, edited by Sandra Caeiro; Walter L. Filho; Charbel Jabbour; and Ulisses M. Azeiteiro. Cham, Switzerland: Springer International Publishing, pp. 139–154.

Rishko-Porcescu, Antonina. 2018. "Building Evaluation Capacities for Evaluation of the SDGs: The Role of Young and Emerging Evaluators." In *People, Planet and Progress in the SDG Era; Proceedings from the National Evaluation Capacities Conference 2017*. New York: Independent Evaluation Office, United Nations Development Programme, pp. 307–312.

Schuller, Tom; and Desjardins, Richard. 2007. *Understanding the Social Outcomes of Learning*. Paris: OECD.

Schuller, Tom; Hammond, Cathie; and Preston, John. 2004. "Reappraising Benefits." In *The Benefits of Learning: The Impact of Education on Health, Family Life and Social Capital*, edited by Tom Schuller; John Preston; Cathie Hammond; Angela Brassett-Grundy; and John Bynner. London: RoutledgeFalmer, pp. 179–193.

Sen, Amartya. 1999. *Development as Freedom*. New York: Anchor Books.

Shuman, Larry J.; Besterfield-Sacre, Mary; and McGourty, Jack. 2005. "The ABET 'Professional Skills' – Can They Be Taught? Can They Be Assessed?" *Journal of Engineering Education* 94 (1): 41–53.

Singh, Mala. 2007. "Universities and Society: Whose Terms of Engagement?" In *Knowledge Society vs. Knowledge Economy: Knowledge, Power, and Politics*, edited by Sverker Sorlin and Hebe Vessuri. Basingstoke: Palgrave Macmillan, pp. 53–78.

Smith, Harvey. 2000. "Transforming Education through Donor-Funded Projects: How Do We Measure Success?" In *Globalisation, Educational Transformation and Societies in Transition*, edited by Teame Mebrahtu; Michael Crossley; and David Johnson. Oxford: Symposium Books, pp. 207–218.

Ssosse, Quentin; Wagner, Johanna; and Hopper, Carina. 2021. "Assessing the Impact of ESD: Methods, Challenges, Results." *Sustainability* 13 (2854): 1–26. doi:10.3390/su13052854.

Stevens, Candice. 2012. "A Basic Roadmap for Sustainability Assessments: The SIMPLE Methodology." In *Sustainable Development, Evaluation and Policy-Making: Theory, Practise and Quality Assurance*, edited by Anneke von Raggamby and Frieder Rubik. Cheltenham: Edward Elgar, pp. 57–72.

Sykes, Kevin J. 2014. "Short-Term Medical Trips: A Systematic Review of the Evidence." *Systematic Review* 104 (7): e38–e48.

Tarabini, Aina. 2010. "Education and Poverty in the Global Development Agenda: Emergence, Evolution and Consolidation." *International Journal of Education and Development* 30 (2): 204–212.

Taylor, Peter. 2008. "Higher Education Curricula for Human and Social Development." In *Higher Education in the World 3: New Challenges and Emerging Roles for Human and Social Development*. London: Palgrave Macmillan, pp. 89–101.

Teitelbaum, Pamela. 2019. *Pilot Evaluation to Assess the Impact of eLearning on Humanitarian Aid Work: Final Report*. Geneva: Medair, Humanitarian Leadership Academy.

Thomas, Vinod; and Tominaga, Jiro. 2013. "Development Evaluation in an Age of Turbulence." In *Evaluation and Turbulent Times: Reflections on a Discipline in Disarray*, edited by Jan-Eric Furubo; Ray C. Rist; and Sandra Speer. New Brunswick, NJ: Transaction Publishers, pp. 57–70.

Todd, David; and Craig, Rob. 2014. "Assessing Progress towards Impacts in Environmental Programmes Using the Field Review of Outcomes to Impacts Methodology." In *Evaluating Environment in International Development*, edited by Juha I. Uitto. London: Routledge, pp. 62–86.

Trad, Sloan P. 2019. "A Framework for Mapping Sustainability Within Tertiary Curriculum." *International Journal of Sustainability in Higher Education* 20 (2): 288–308.

Uitto, Juha I. 2014. "Evaluating Environment in International Development." In *Evaluating Environment in International Development*, edited by Juha I. Uitto. London: Routledge, pp. 3–16.

Uitto, Juha I. 2016. "Evaluating the Environment as a Global Public Good." *Evaluation* 22 (1): 108–115.

Uitto, Juha I. 2021. "Surviving the Anthropocene: How Evaluation Can Contribute to Knowledge and Better Policymaking." *Evaluation* 27 (4): 436–452.

Walker, Melanie; McLean, Monica; Dison, Arona; and Peppin-Vaughn, Rosie. 2009. "South African Universities and Human Development: Towards a Theorisation and Operationalisation of Professional Capabilities for Poverty Reduction." *International Journal of Educational Development* 29: 565–572.

Wells, Ruth; Lawsin, Catalina; Hunt, Caroline; Youssef, Omar Said; Abujado, Fayzeh; and Steel, Zachary. 2018. "An Ecological Model of Adaptation to Displacement: Individual, Cultural and Community Factors Affecting Psychological Adjustment among Syrian Refugees in Jordan." *Global Mental Health* 5: 1–13. doi:10.1017/gmh.2018.30.

White House. 2021. *Report on the Impact of Climate Change on Migration*. Washington, D.C.: The White House.

Zint, Michaela. 2011. "Evaluating Education for Sustainable Development Programs." In *World Trends in Education for Sustainable Development*, edited by Walter L. Filho. Frankfurt: Peter Lang, pp. 329–347.

8 Ways TC Development Can Improve Resettlement Outcomes and Impacts

The prevailing state of global politics and policy making forecasts continued internal and transnational displacement and health crises generated by armed conflicts, climate disruptions, and pandemics. In the time we have been working on this book alone, the number of forcibly displaced persons world-wide has grown from 82 million (see Introduction) to at least 103 million (Turkewitz, 2022, p. A1) and continues to increase.

In *Migrant Health and Resilience: Transnational Competence in Conflict and Climate Displacement Situations*, we envision a brighter future for those displaced and other affected persons based on anticipatory and responsive individual and collective actions guided by transnational competency on the part of current and future stakeholders (also see, for instance, Murdoch-Eaton, Redmond, and Bax, 2011, p. 564). The health, resilience, and welfare of dislocated people will depend on carefully planned and properly supported approaches to just resettlement or repatriation that feature transnational competence (TC) training/education and devote particular attention to outcomes and impacts. The outcomes for human capability and the social, economic, political, and environmental impacts of TC preparation are what ultimately matter. Proactive policy and partnering initiatives need to engage the drivers of transnational human mobility, the resulting conditions, and the coordinated, TC-informed adaptive approaches suited for humanitarian responders, for physical and mental health-care providers, for hosts, for community volunteers, and for the displaced themselves.

In addressing the paramount challenges that concern stakeholders involved in conflict- and climate-displacement situations, we have highlighted several recurring themes of current and future importance to those engaged in education and training. First and foremost, the five dimensions of TC need to be at the forefront of humanitarian responses. TC learning provides an indispensable gateway to addressing the daunting challenges to be faced. TC also is useful for displaced people so that they can enjoy well-being and health, build resilience, facilitate social integration and belonging, and contribute to sustainable development locally and transnationally. TC is important for host communities so that their members help and support the displaced through constructive and mutually beneficial inter-group relations. TC is useful for

DOI: 10.4324/9781003330493-9

social-justice workers of all backgrounds who strive to tackle migration challenges through proactive policy and partnering initiatives at the local, global, and glocal levels and to mitigate the drivers of transnational human dislocations. In sum, humanitarian responders, physical and mental health-care providers, host-community members, local service agents and volunteers, and the displaced themselves should all be TC-prepared.

Intended TC development *outcomes* are: (1) to equip humanitarian responders with TC skill sets relevant for assisting dislocated persons who possess diverse nationality and ethnic backgrounds; (2) to equip dislocated persons with TC skill sets relevant for advancing personal/family integration[1] and health promotion in a new location and for contributing to local adaptation and sustainable development; (3) to equip hosts and other affected persons with TC skill sets relevant for contributing to local adaptation and sustainable development; and (4) to ensure that initiated TC training programs incorporate lessons learned and become self-sustaining. Specifically, we would expect TC trainers, displaced persons, and hosts to develop contextually valuable analytic, emotional, creative, communicative, and functional competence.

Intended TC development *impacts* are: (1) dislocated individuals/families use their new transnational competencies to enhance resiliency, health, and well-being, and achieve integration and belonging, in a new location; (2) dislocated individuals/families and hosts use their new transnational competencies to contribute to health promotion, adaptation, and sustainable development; (3) humanitarian responders employ their new transnational competencies to advocate successfully for policies and approaches that enhance resilience, health, and well-being, and achieve integration and belonging, among dislocated populations; and (4) humanitarian responders use their new transnational competencies to advocate successfully for policy changes that mitigate persecution, conflict-induced migration, or climate-generated dislocations. Individual and societal benefits and conditions supporting sustainable development for all are most likely to be realized fully when every participant is transnationally competent.

TC for Humanitarian Responders

Humanitarian-aid providers shoulder professional and ethical responsibility for acquiring competencies and undertaking many non-technical functions. Tomorrow's humanitarian responders will be expected to serve and equip persons uprooted by dislocation in diverse and often unanticipated displacement settings over the course of their careers. They cannot assume that their skill strengths are universally transferable from one transboundary context and dislocation challenge to another. Therefore, it is important to undertake TC preparation during the windows of opportunity that precede engagement and as an ongoing training resource. In addition, supervisors and debriefers who scaffold field workers' well-being and performance need

TC preparation in order to employ trauma-informed and transnationally responsive approaches in their mentoring and consultation. For care providers and beneficiaries alike, aspirations to become transnationally competent require commitment to life-long learning.

Going forward, humanitarian responders will require abilities to access and process accurate current information and knowledge, to sustain their service commitment and resilience, to employ on-site and immediate creativity and persuasive communication, and to engage in transnational collaboration with other providers, migrants, and host communities. We believe that students and trainees who embark on careers in humanitarian service will find applications of transnational competence more powerful and rewarding than applications of intercultural competence are when challenged in the field by such practical, multidimensional, transboundary interfaces. The TC framework is particularly relevant and inclusive in that it addresses conditions brought about by population movement, multiple identities, porous boundaries, socio-economic divides, and health crises. And, TC education is distinguished by its emphases on transforming the social and environmental determinants of inequality, health, and dispossession and on advocacy in addressing driving institutional and policy inequities rooted in local, national, and international conditions.

TC for Displaced Populations

Forced displacement is triggered by a wide range of factors, including climate disturbances and degradation of the natural resource base, armed violence, oppressive policies, and persecution. Whether the specific context is a camp, an informal rural or urban settlement, a detention center, or a climate-induced resettlement site, the humanitarian challenges faced by dislocated migrants, other affected persons, and care responders are complex and manifold. The overarching aims embedded in stakeholder TC preparation are to enable the development and implementation of education and training programs that will bolster participants' holistic wellness, resilience, and ability to negotiate encountered transnational challenges while promoting sustainable development and collaboration among dislocated and host communities.

Reframing complex humanitarian emergencies as opportunities for sustainable development and resilience-building, for both the displaced and their hosts, offers promise as a unifying long-term strategic response. Along with opportunities to access resources and acquire skills tailored to available employment and volunteer opportunities, TC preparation promises to facilitate adaptation to proactive and reactive climate-generated migration. Concomitantly, gaining TC capabilities will facilitate psychosocial belonging and enable dislocated individuals, hosts, and other affected persons to contribute to sustainable development in multiple contexts. Among young refugees, TC education offers a particularly empowering source of resilience and is a facilitator of enhanced living and upward mobility. Ideally, TC education also should be available for the benefit of affected host communities.

TC for Host Communities

Host-community members drawn from civil society, including "social or religious organizations, grassroots initiatives, civil society networks ... [along with] individual helpers" and educators can be mobilized for humanitarian assistance when dislocated persons arrive (Raithelhuber, 2018, p. 251). The kinds of local help they can offer include accessing social services and support and transitioning to social and economic integration. Host-community members who dedicate themselves to improving life conditions for vulnerable and marginalized displaced individuals are especially likely to benefit from TC training.

TC-prepared helping professionals and volunteers also "confront injustices that, increasingly, are locally and globally interconnected." Thus, they "need to take this action commitment to a new level where borders are removed from their thinking about social action and policy" and strive to "empower diverse individuals and groups for full societal inclusion and participation, enjoyment of their legal and human rights" (Koehn and Rosenau, 2010, p. 82). At the macro level, host civil-society actors who want to help need to advocate for "transforming the inequities and injustices that burden individuals, communities, societies and the world through reflective, proactive practice and through advocacy for the people with whom they work", they need to challenge "negative discrimination and unjust policies and practices particularly when such ... perpetuate global economic and environmental inequities" that often are the root causes of migration (ibid., p. 82).

TC Training and Development

Chapters 5 and 6 offered detailed suggestions for TC development across the analytic, emotional, creative, communicative, and functional domains. These guidelines can inform continuous university-led education, pre-departure and on-site training, and training of trainers. A range of training methods and approaches are available for building and enhancing the transnational competence of the displaced and others affected by climate and conflict dislocation, the humanitarian-aid workers, and host-community members. In this book, we offered suggestions and guidelines for educators and trainers that relate to one or more of the five domains of TC.

For acquiring analytic competence, case studies, simulations, experiential learning, cultural-discourse analysis, and inquiry-based learning are useful. Critical Digital Pedagogy allows for developing the analytic competence required to identify specific underlying ideologies within the digital environment and to recognize disinformation. Regarding emotional competence, we offered guidance in applying the strengths-based training approach, intercultural sensitivity development, group training, and intergroup training. For both displaced persons and their hosts, inter-group sensitivity development is crucial for emotional competence. In terms of developing transnational creative/innovative competence, exposure to diversity provides one key. Useful TC training for creative competence should provide space for a diverse set of participants to converse about their backgrounds and countries of origin, share migration experiences and lessons, and explore common ground as well as differences.

The suggested communicative competence training approach focuses on helping trainees connect language learning to their transnational-communication encounters in the humanitarian-assistance context. Local language learning, coupled with intercultural communication training, can serve as a pathway to integration and as a vehicle promoting resilience. Special TC training on how to work collaboratively with multi-sector interpreters is a particularly valuable communicative competence preparation for humanitarian responders in displacement contexts. For TC functional competence development, incorporating contextualized inter-personal training approaches that focus on trust-building and peer support is likely to be essential. Training approaches useful for negotiation, problem solving, teamwork, and alliance building include case studies that provide concrete situations that engage participants through the exploration of possible solutions, simulations that involve experiential learning, role plays that provide a mechanism for generating feedback on possible applications, and group activities (games, discussions, structured learning exercises) that can engage migrants and members of host communities face-to-face with guidance and feedback from trained facilitators. Attention to approaches that enable self-care and burnout prevention also are critical for humanitarian-aid providers.

In TC training efforts, transnational learning networks and platforms increasingly will be called upon for internet-supplemented and continuous TC learning. In low-resource settings, e-learning has advantages in supporting the delivery of outcome-based TC education/training programs. Initial in-person training sessions for the displaced and other affected persons can be continuously reinforced and augmented by proximate and/or remote supervised simulation-based and experiential learning and by mobile mentoring. Technological methods like using web-based or mobile phones, e-conferencing, WhatsApp messages, and emailing also can be explored for imparting professional health-care skills, technology skills, business skills, social work skills, sustainable development administration skills, etc., among displaced populations and local volunteers.

TC Evaluations

Attention to initiative evaluations is essential at all stages of, and with regard to all participants in, TC learning. Evaluation not only provides accountability for the results achieved; it is particularly useful for learning lessons for future program improvement. Evaluation should be planned from the outset and based on a systematic monitoring of activities, outcomes, and impacts.

The TC approach emphasizes resilience enhancement and community-facilitated support. For this reason, we devoted recurring attention to the role of evaluation in the TC training initiatives to be introduced by institutions and organizations involved in the initiatives and by humanitarian responders. The theory-of-change approach featured in this connection helps understand the outcome to impact pathways. Once specific training outcomes and impacts are identified, the theory-of-change approach articulates plausible causal hypotheses with explicit assumptions, baselines, and key indicators. It also is important to be vigilant regarding unintended or unanticipated consequences, which may be either positive (thus providing further opportunities) or negative (to be corrected for and avoided in the future).

Chapter 7 set forth detailed recommendations for conducting TC preparation evaluations. The chapter provided an adaptable TC assessment scheme centered on process, outcomes, and impacts at individual and grassroots levels, along with for evaluation process recommendations for conducting tailored TC development and TC e-learning outcome and impact evaluations.

Looking ahead, wide adoption of the principal components of TC training and education depends upon collaborative and credible evaluations of outcomes and impacts. Evaluation also can contribute to transformational change by identifying promising approaches and successful initiatives.

Future Opportunities

Sustainable development for all in the wake of continued conflict-induced and climate-induced dislocations constitutes the long-term TC-impact objective. The TC framework embodies a set of transferable skills and training approaches that can be applied to inter-personal and inter-group dynamics as well as to intra-group needs (e.g., supporting migrants who also identify as gender minorities). In the context of growing health and education disparities among marginalized groups, transnational competence can be used as a tool that enhances the ability of humanitarian responders to self-reflect and pursue social justice efforts.

The surge of displaced persons world-wide calls for international efforts to recruit responders who are available to deliver aid promptly. Given present staffing shortages, especially in the field of MHPSS, it is critical that TC-informed training programs are established and initiated among volunteers, activists, and non-specialists who might be the primary source of assistance for newly displaced populations. Since practice-informed migrant aid frameworks are scarce, this book can serve as a useful and practical guide that is rooted in interdisciplinary research and collaboration as well as insights drawn from humanitarian-aid fieldwork. Future efforts also can involve digitalizing TC-informed resources to equip aiders in remote areas who possess limited ability to access specialized training programs.

In the interests of ethical responsibility and social justice, we also call upon foundations, NGOs, and universities to step up in a forward-looking manner to the ongoing displacement crisis. While limited, there are some promising signs in this connection.

The Global Forum on Migration and Development

Unsurprisingly, transnational and within-borders collaboration among development actors and humanitarian responders operating through an explicit sustainable-development lens is "indispensable for approaching climate change and human mobility" (Martin, Bergmann, Rigaud, and Yameogo, 2021, p. 147). Fortuitously, the linkage of climate change, migration, TC, and sustainable development fits within the mandate of the Global Forum on Migration and Development (GFMD). The GFMD, established in 2007, engages North and South in informal and non-binding processes that bring governments and civil-society actors together around multi-stakeholder challenges of migration and development (Micinski, 2021, p. 139). Specifically, the GFMD "analyzes and discusses sensitive issues, creates consensus, poses innovative solutions, and shares policy and practices."[2] Coincidently, the GFMD Chairmanship has chosen "the impact of climate change on human mobility" as the Forum's main topic for discussion in 2022–2023.[3] Partnering with TC training and education offers a ground-breaking complement to the GFMD's agenda.

Participation by Universities in North and South

As repositories of unmatched knowledge infrastructure, including research findings on migrant health and development beyond the reach of fully occupied practitioners, universities are positioned to play a central role in the preparation of transnationally competent humanitarian responders. One promising advance on the training approach elaborated in this book could be the multi-institutional establishment of resourced higher-education TC programs modeled on the BSc degree in Community Health Education at Moi University in Kenya. Such advanced TC-centered higher-educational programs would be offered online and via Zoom to previously TC-prepared humanitarian-aid workers, refugees and other displaced persons, and their hosts (see Pilkington and Mbai, 2016, pp. 12–13).

Education and training curricula and approaches need to be designed in ways that equip humanitarian responders, collaborating specialists, affected persons, and hosts with transnational competencies for conflict- and climate-induced displacements. Chapters 5 and 6 provided detailed suggestions for TC development across the analytic, emotional, creative, communicative, and functional domains that should be integrated into higher-education curricula. In addition to facilitating pre-departure and on-site trainings, these guides can inform and enhance continuous university-led education.

Individual and Organizational Commitments

TC development enables humanitarian responders and social justice workers to act collaboratively with the displaced to address needs that emerge during migration and (re)settlement and on behalf of other affected persons within a framework of sustainable development for all. Ultimately, the spread of TC education and training initiatives rests on the commitment of individuals, governments, non-governmental organizations, foundations, and universities that recognize its promise in responding to climate-displaced and conflict-displaced challenges and are able to convince donors to support and expand the interventions, evaluated by outcome and impact, outlined in *Migrant Health and Resilience: Transnational Competence in Conflict and Climate Displacement Situations* (also see Teitelbaum, 2019).

Notes

1 Including political participation (Eckenwiler and Wild, 2021, pp. 243–244).
2 https://www.gfmd.org/
3 https://www.gfmd.org/meetings/france-senegal-gfmd-2022-2023/overview (accessed October 10, 2022).

References

Eckenwiler, Lisa; and Wild, Verina. 2021. "Refugees and Others Enduring Displacement: Structural Injustice, Health, and Ethical Placemaking." *Journal of Social Philosophy* 52: 234–250.

Koehn, Peter H.; and Rosenau, James N. 2010. *Transnational Competence: Empowering Professional Curricula for Horizon-Rising Challenges*. Boulder, CO: Paradigm Publishers.

Martin, Susan F.; Bergmann, Jonas; Rigaud, Kanta; and Yameogo, Nadege D. 2021. "Climate Change, Human Mobility, and Development." *Migration Studies* 9 (1): 142–149.

Micinski, Nicholas R. 2021. "Migration and Development in the UN Global Compacts." In *Routledge Handbook on the UN and Development*, edited by Stephen Browne and Thomas G. Weiss. London: Routledge, pp. 135–147.

Murdoch-Eaton, Deborah; Redmond, Anthony; and Bax, Nigel. 2011. "Training Healthcare Professionals for the Future: Internationalism and Effective Inclusion of Global Health Training." *Medical Teacher* 33: 562–569.

Pilkington, F. Beryl; and Mbai, Isabella. 2016. "Researching the Gap between the Existing and Potential Community Health Worker Education and Training in the Refugee Context: An Intersectoral Approach." *Final Interim Report to IDRC.* Toronto: York University, July 31.

Raithelhuber, Eberhard. 2018. "How 'Godparents' Are Made for 'Unaccompanied Refugee Minors': An Ethnographic View into the Training of Future Youth Mentors." *Child & Youth Services* 39 (4): 250–283.

Teitelbaum, Pamela. 2019. *Pilot Evaluation to Assess the Impact of eLearning on Humanitarian Aid Work: Final Report.* Geneva: Medair3, Humanitarian Leadership Academy.

Turkewitz, Julie. 2022. "Climbing the 'Hill of Death' Without Her Mother." *New York Times*, November 12, pp. A1, A6–A7.

Index